Characters

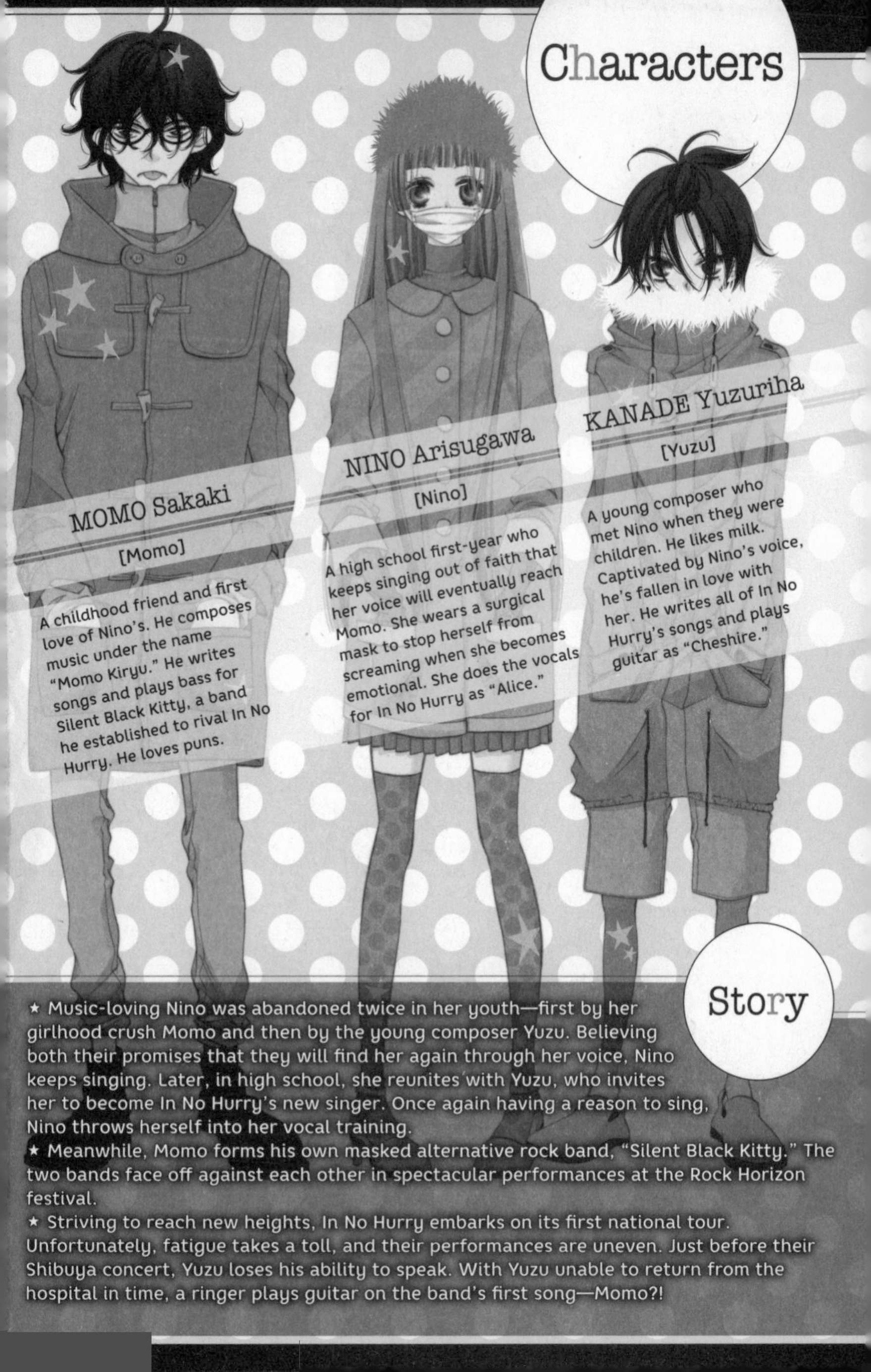

MOMO Sakaki

[Momo]

A childhood friend and first love of Nino's. He composes music under the name "Momo Kiryu." He writes songs and plays bass for Silent Black Kitty, a band he established to rival In No Hurry. He loves puns.

NINO Arisugawa

[Nino]

A high school first-year who keeps singing out of faith that her voice will eventually reach Momo. She wears a surgical mask to stop herself from screaming when she becomes emotional. She does the vocals for In No Hurry as "Alice."

KANADE Yuzuriha

[Yuzu]

A young composer who met Nino when they were children. He likes milk. Captivated by Nino's voice, he's fallen in love with her. He writes all of In No Hurry's songs and plays guitar as "Cheshire."

Story

★ Music-loving Nino was abandoned twice in her youth—first by her girlhood crush Momo and then by the young composer Yuzu. Believing both their promises that they will find her again through her voice, Nino keeps singing. Later, in high school, she reunites with Yuzu, who invites her to become In No Hurry's new singer. Once again having a reason to sing, Nino throws herself into her vocal training.

★ Meanwhile, Momo forms his own masked alternative rock band, "Silent Black Kitty." The two bands face off against each other in spectacular performances at the Rock Horizon festival.

★ Striving to reach new heights, In No Hurry embarks on its first national tour. Unfortunately, fatigue takes a toll, and their performances are uneven. Just before their Shibuya concert, Yuzu loses his ability to speak. With Yuzu unable to return from the hospital in time, a ringer plays guitar on the band's first song—Momo?!

Shojo Beat

ANONYMOUS NOISE

Ryoko Fukuyama

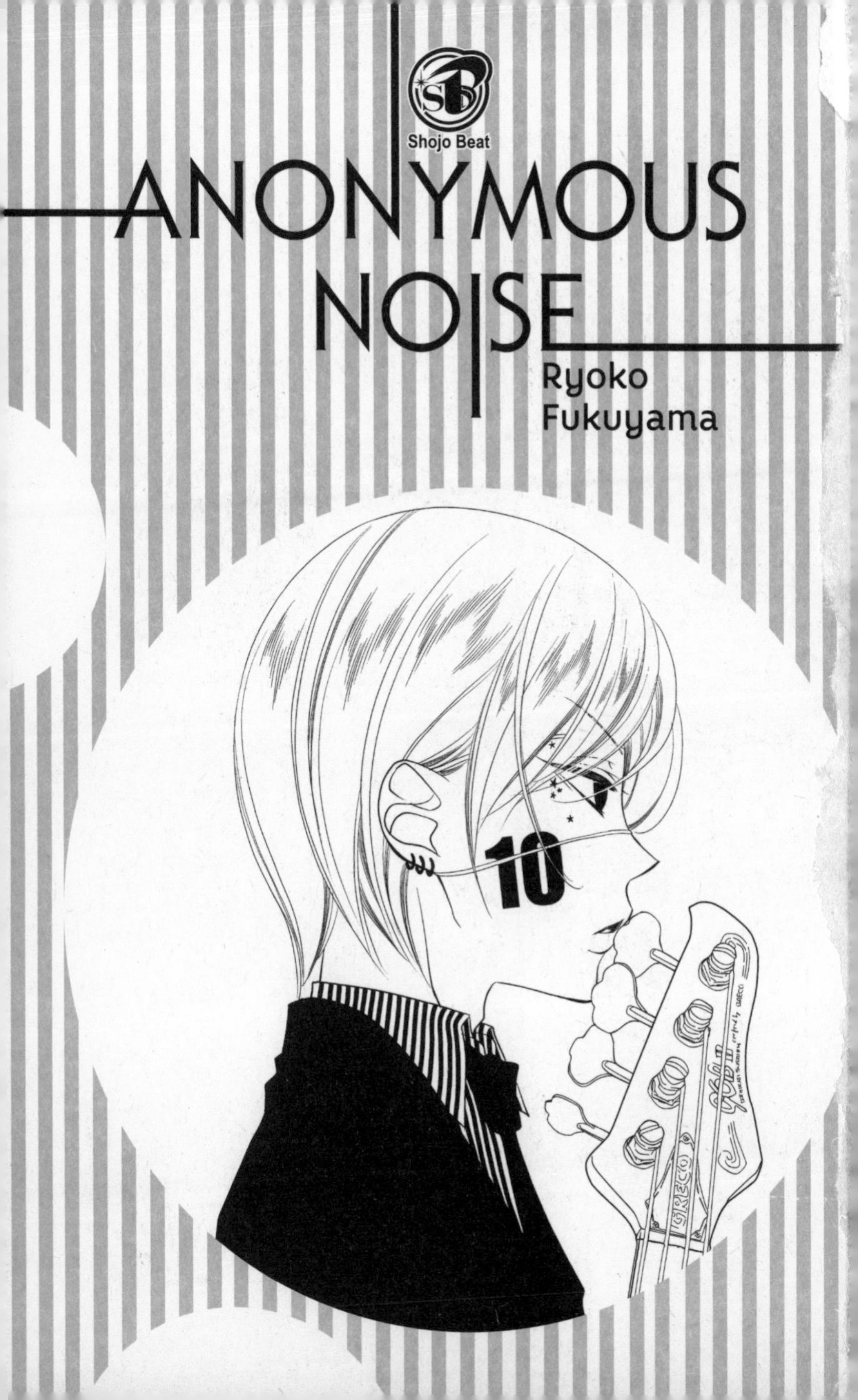
10

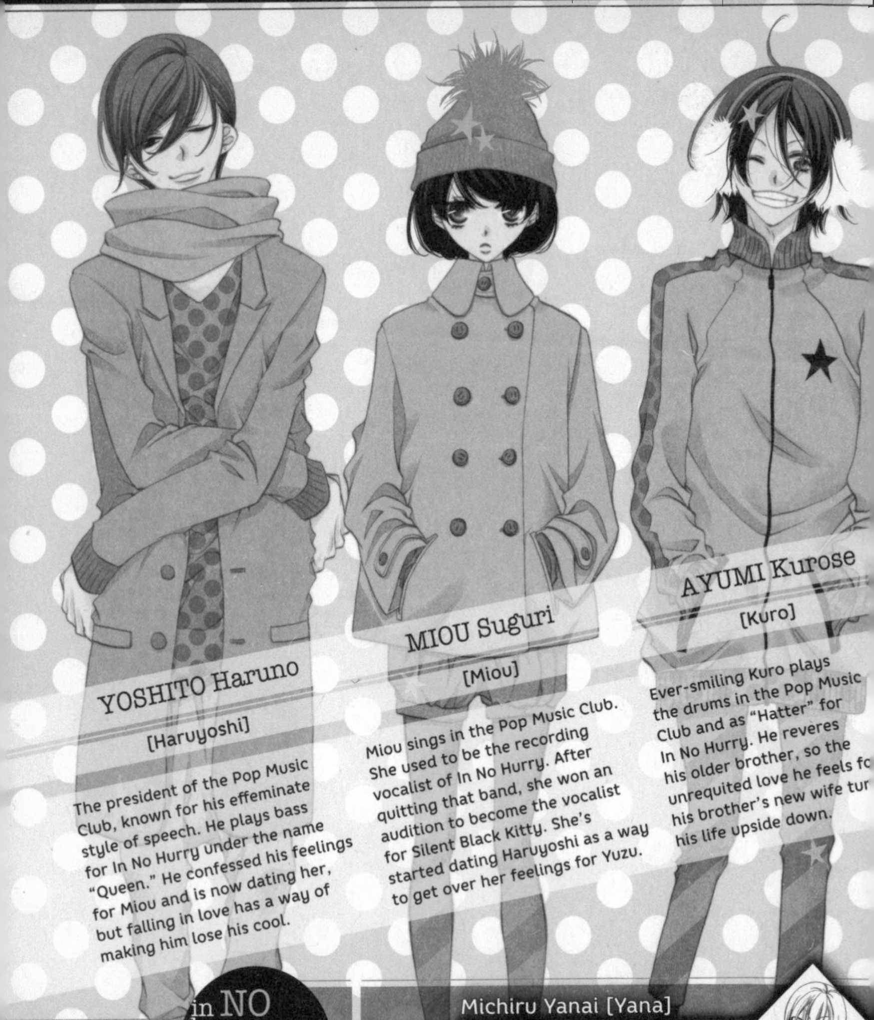
YOSHITO Haruno
[Haruyoshi]
The president of the Pop Music Club, known for his effeminate style of speech. He plays bass for In No Hurry under the name "Queen." He confessed his feelings for Miou and is now dating her, but falling in love has a way of making him lose his cool.
MIOU Suguri
[Miou]
Miou sings in the Pop Music Club. She used to be the recording vocalist of In No Hurry. After quitting that band, she won an audition to become the vocalist for Silent Black Kitty. She's started dating Haruyoshi as a way to get over her feelings for Yuzu.
AYUMI Kurose
[Kuro]
Ever-smiling Kuro plays the drums in the Pop Music Club and as "Hatter" for In No Hurry. He reveres his older brother, so the unrequited love he feels fo his brother's new wife tur his life upside down.

in NO hurry to shout;

In No Hurry to Shout

A popular rock band whose members hide their identities with masks and eye patches.
Vocals: Alice
Guitar: Cheshire
Bass: Queen
Drums: Hatter

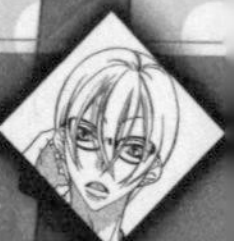

Michiru Yanai [Yana]

In No Hurry's business manager.
A heavy smoker.

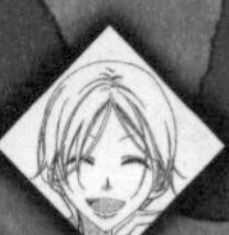

Tsukika Kuze

Momo's manager who acts as something of a foster mother to him.

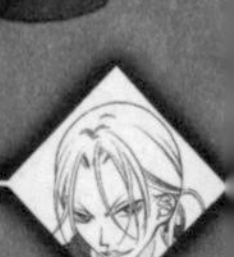

Ayame Hojo

Silent Black Kitty's drummer.

Anonymous
Noise
Volume 10

CONTENTS

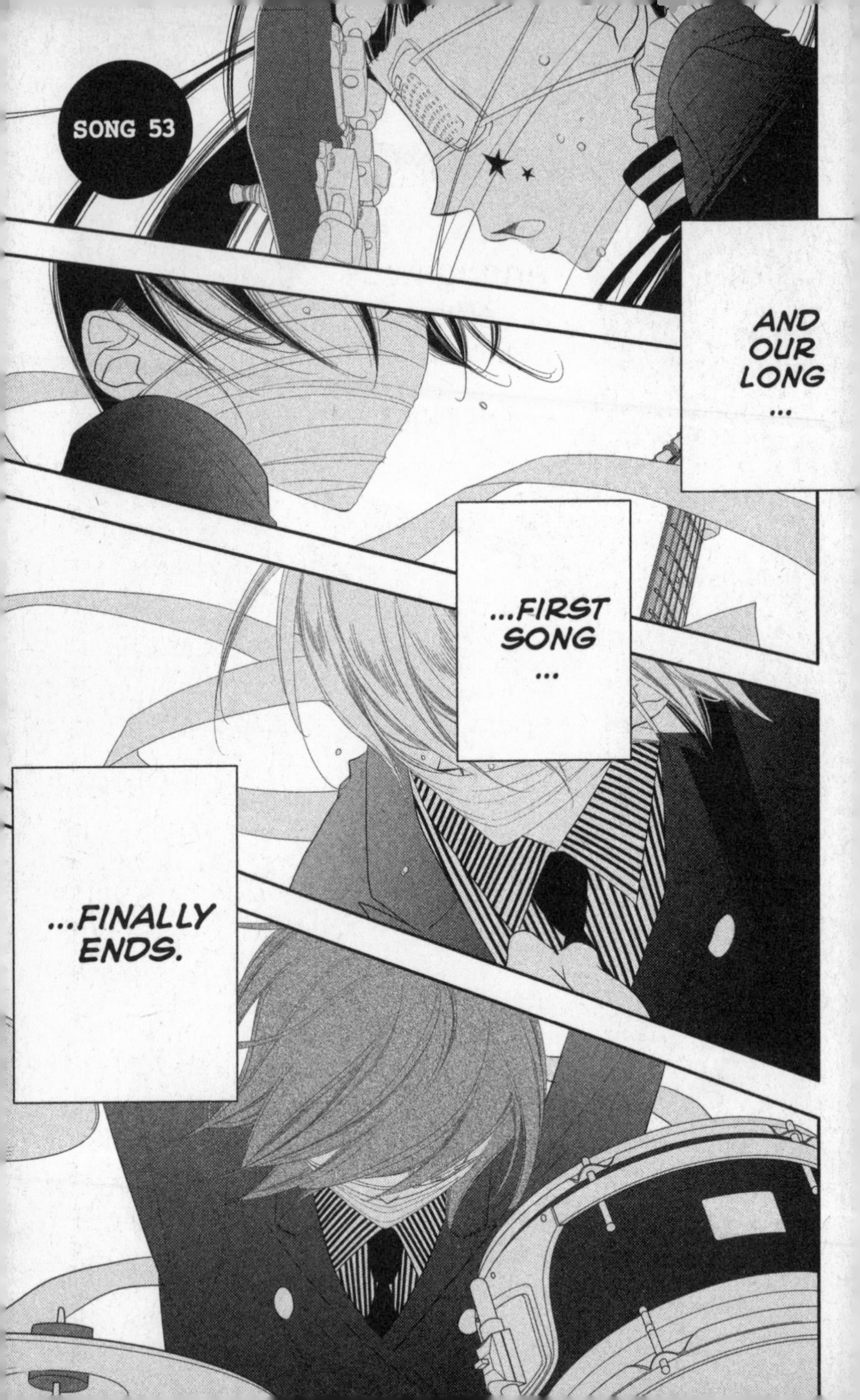
SONG 53
AND OUR LONG ...
...FIRST SONG ...
...FINALLY ENDS.

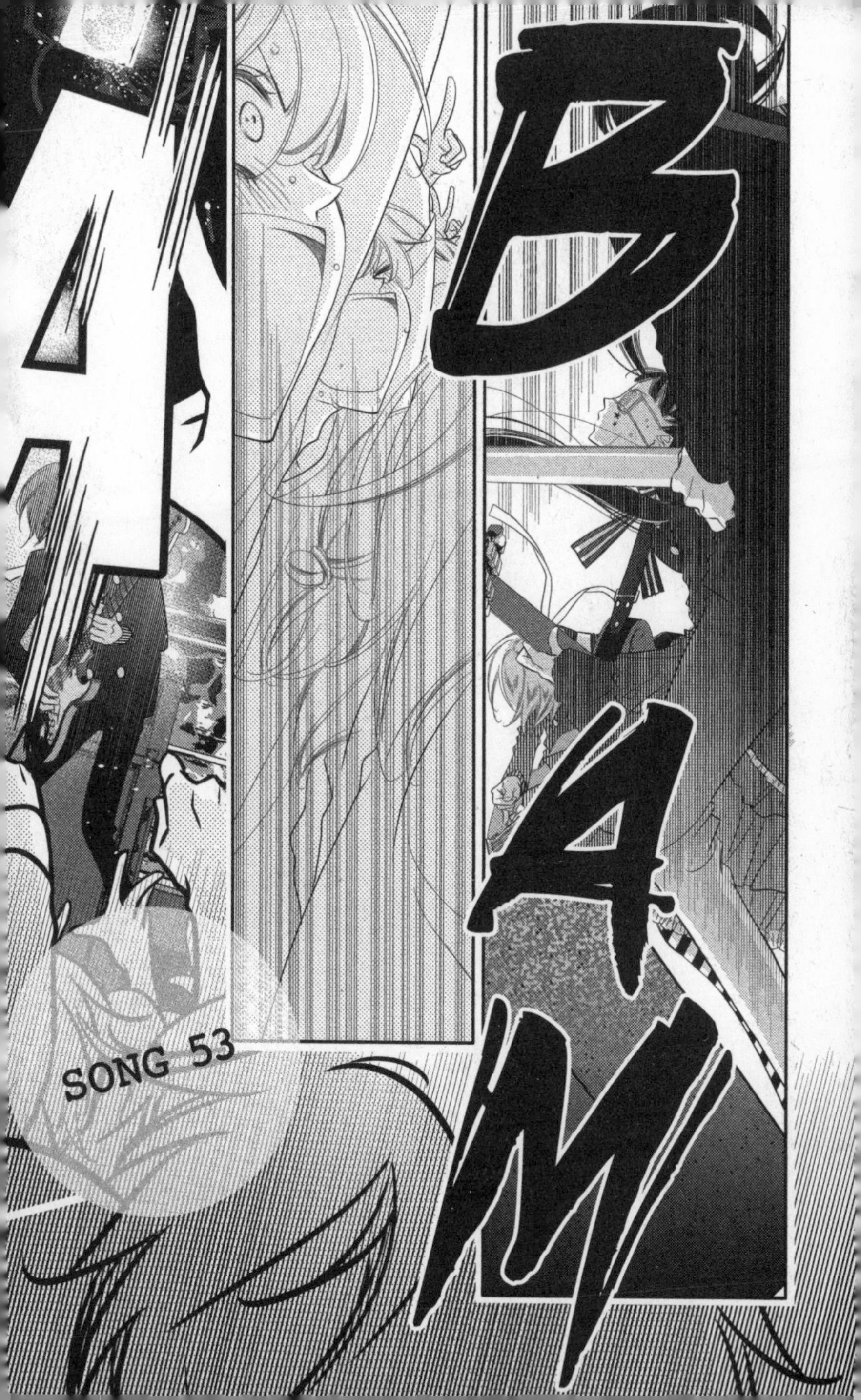
BAM
SONG 53

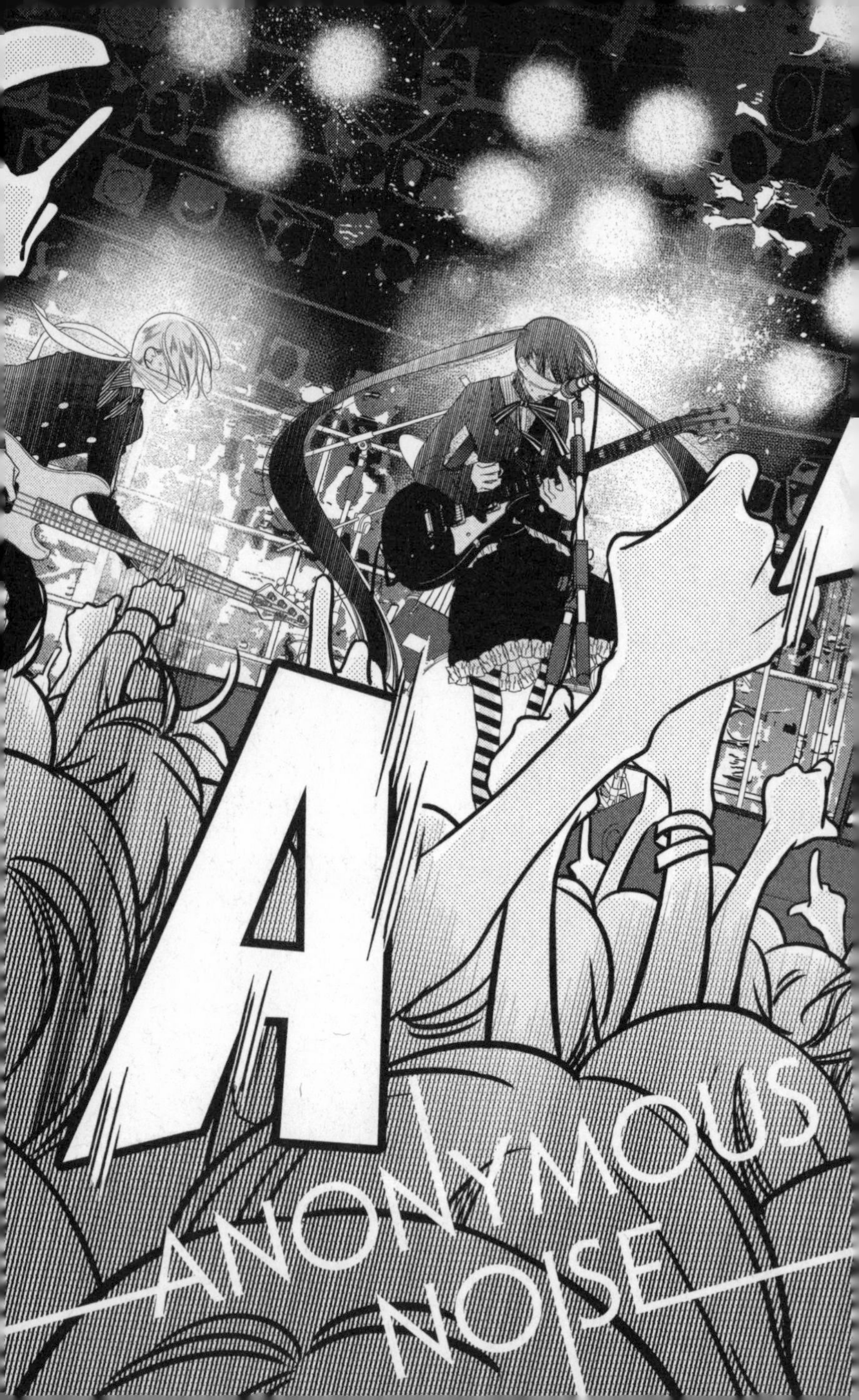
A
ANONYMOUS
NOISE

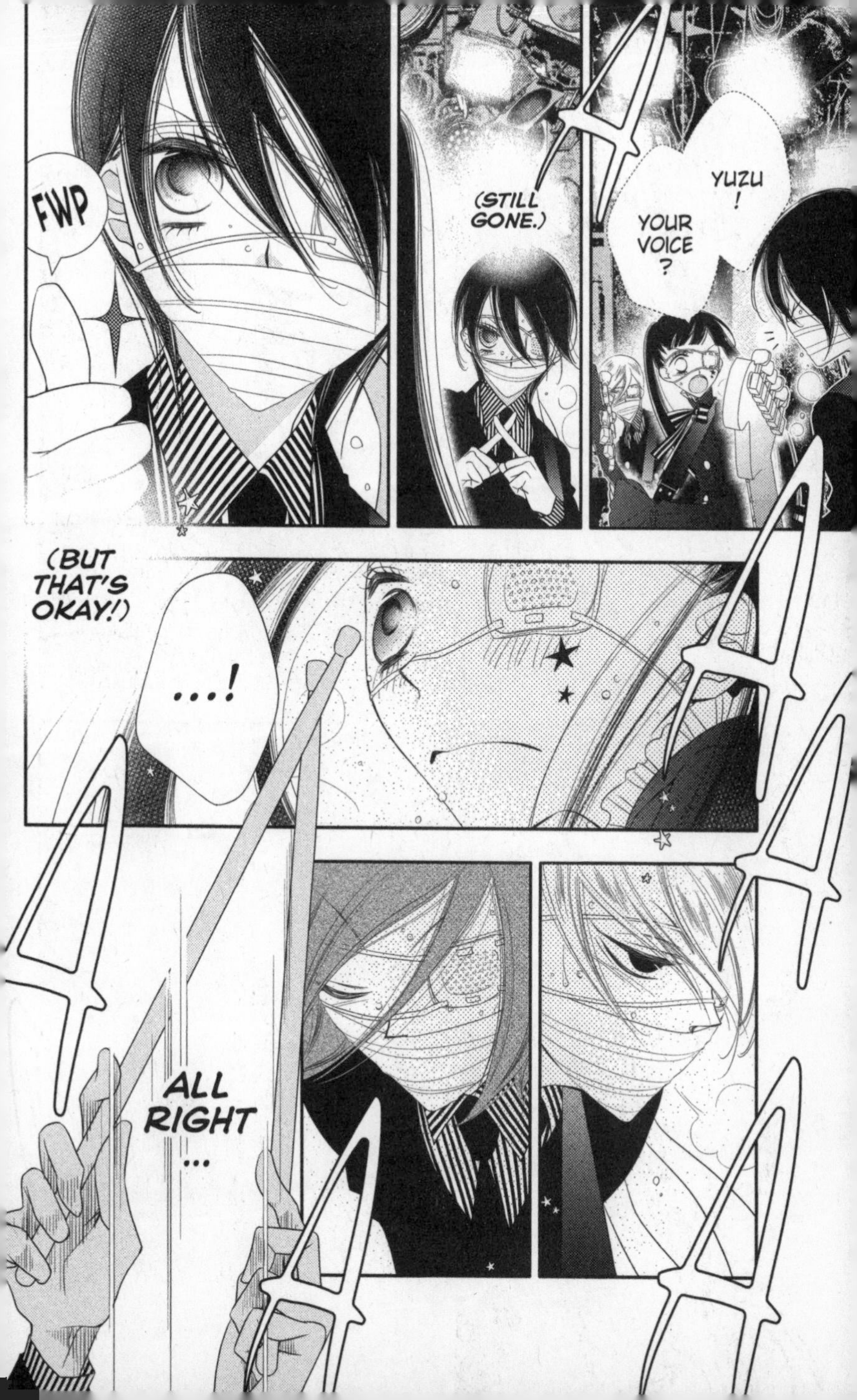
YUZU! YOUR VOICE?
(STILL GONE.)
FWP
(BUT THAT'S OKAY!)
...!
ALL RIGHT ...

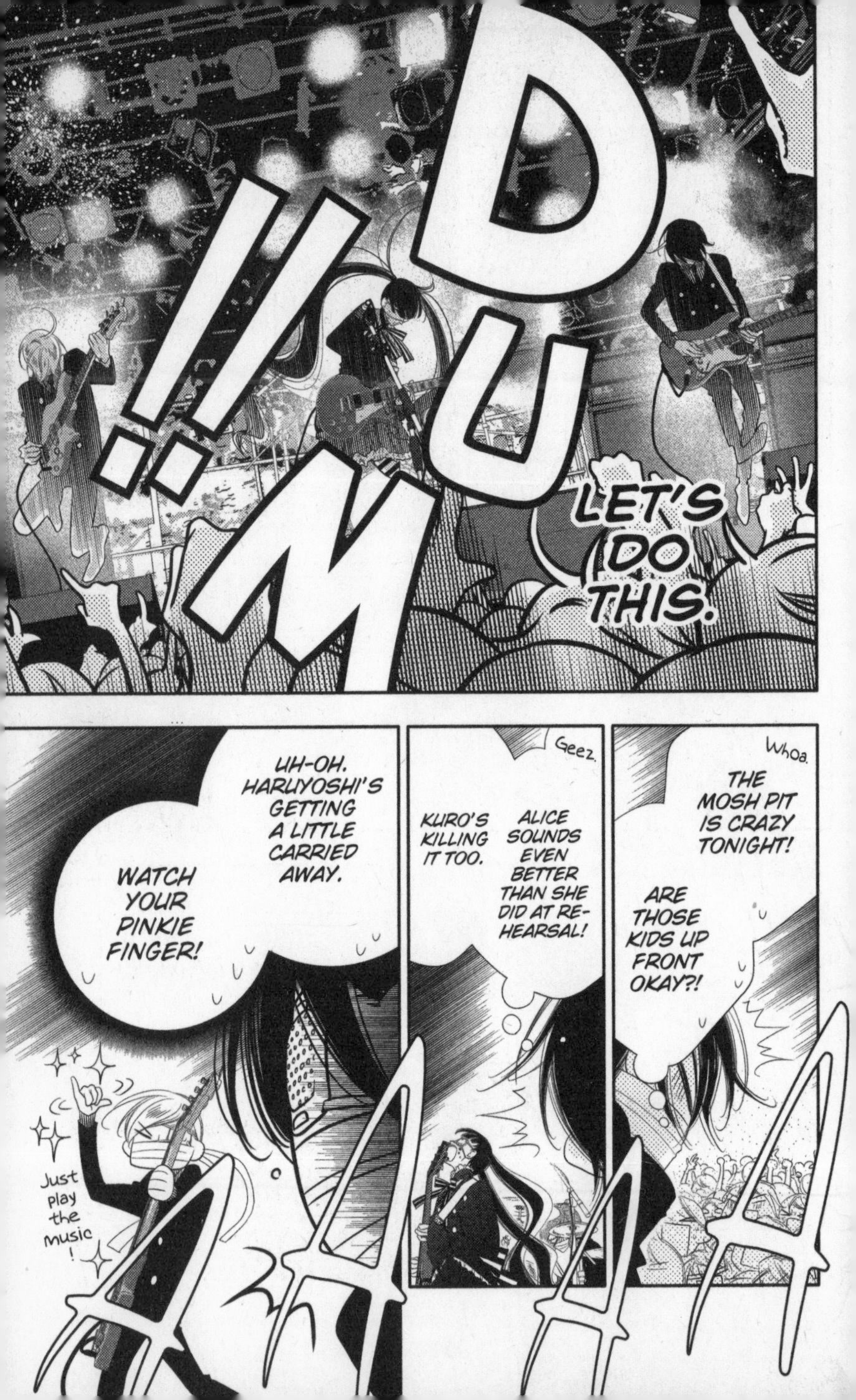
DUM!!
LET'S DO THIS.
Whoa.
THE MOSH PIT IS CRAZY TONIGHT!
ARE THOSE KIDS UP FRONT OKAY?!
Geez.
ALICE SOUNDS EVEN BETTER THAN SHE DID AT RE-HEARSAL!
KURO'S KILLING IT TOO.
UH-OH. HARUYOSHI'S GETTING A LITTLE CARRIED AWAY.
WATCH YOUR PINKIE FINGER!
Just play the music!

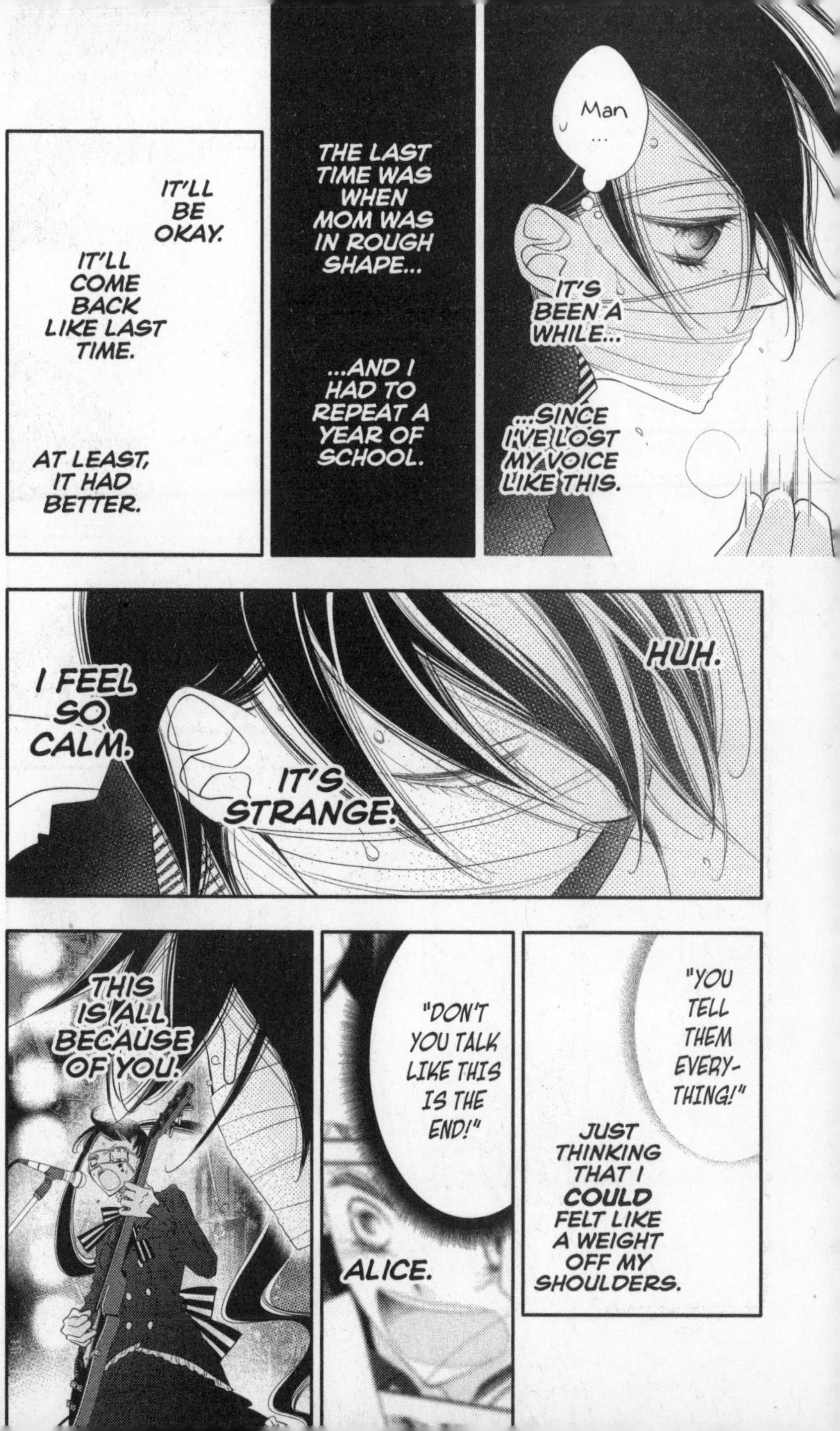
Man...
IT'S BEEN A WHILE...
...SINCE I'VE LOST MY VOICE LIKE THIS.
THE LAST TIME WAS WHEN MOM WAS IN ROUGH SHAPE...
...AND I HAD TO REPEAT A YEAR OF SCHOOL.
IT'LL BE OKAY.
IT'LL COME BACK LIKE LAST TIME.
AT LEAST, IT HAD BETTER.
HUH.
I FEEL SO CALM.
IT'S STRANGE.
"YOU TELL THEM EVERY-THING!"
JUST THINKING THAT I COULD FELT LIKE A WEIGHT OFF MY SHOULDERS.
"DON'T YOU TALK LIKE THIS IS THE END!"
ALICE.
THIS IS ALL BECAUSE OF YOU.

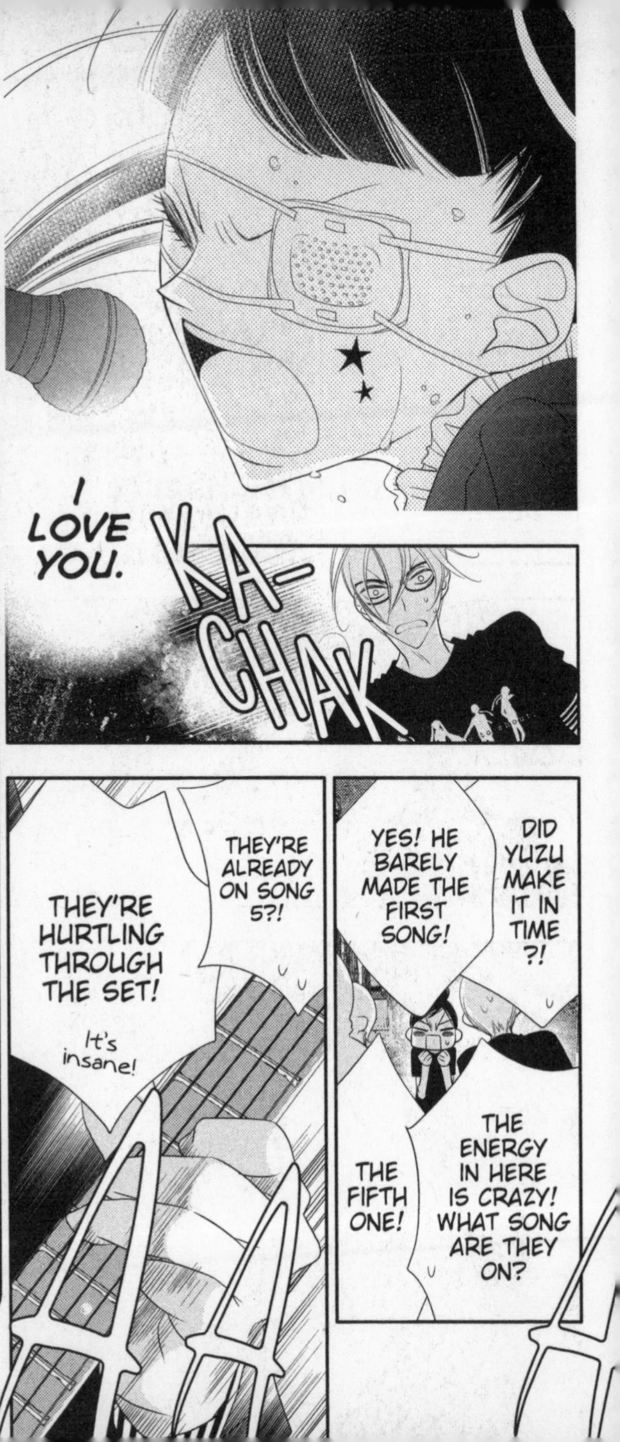
I LOVE YOU.
KA-CHAK
DID YUZU MAKE IT IN TIME?!
YES! HE BARELY MADE THE FIRST SONG!
THE ENERGY IN HERE IS CRAZY! WHAT SONG ARE THEY ON?
THE FIFTH ONE!
THEY'RE ALREADY ON SONG 5?!
THEY'RE HURTLING THROUGH THE SET!
It's insane!

1

Hello, I'm Ryoko Fukuyama. It's good to see you!

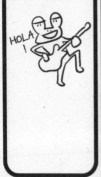

YAY!

Thank you so much for picking up volume 10 of Anonymous Noise. Whoa, double digits already! I can't believe how time flies.

This issue's cover has Haruyoshi. He's so easy to draw that it saved me a lot of time. Thanks, Haruyoshi! Anyway, I really hope you enjoy Anonymous Noise volume 10!

HOLA!

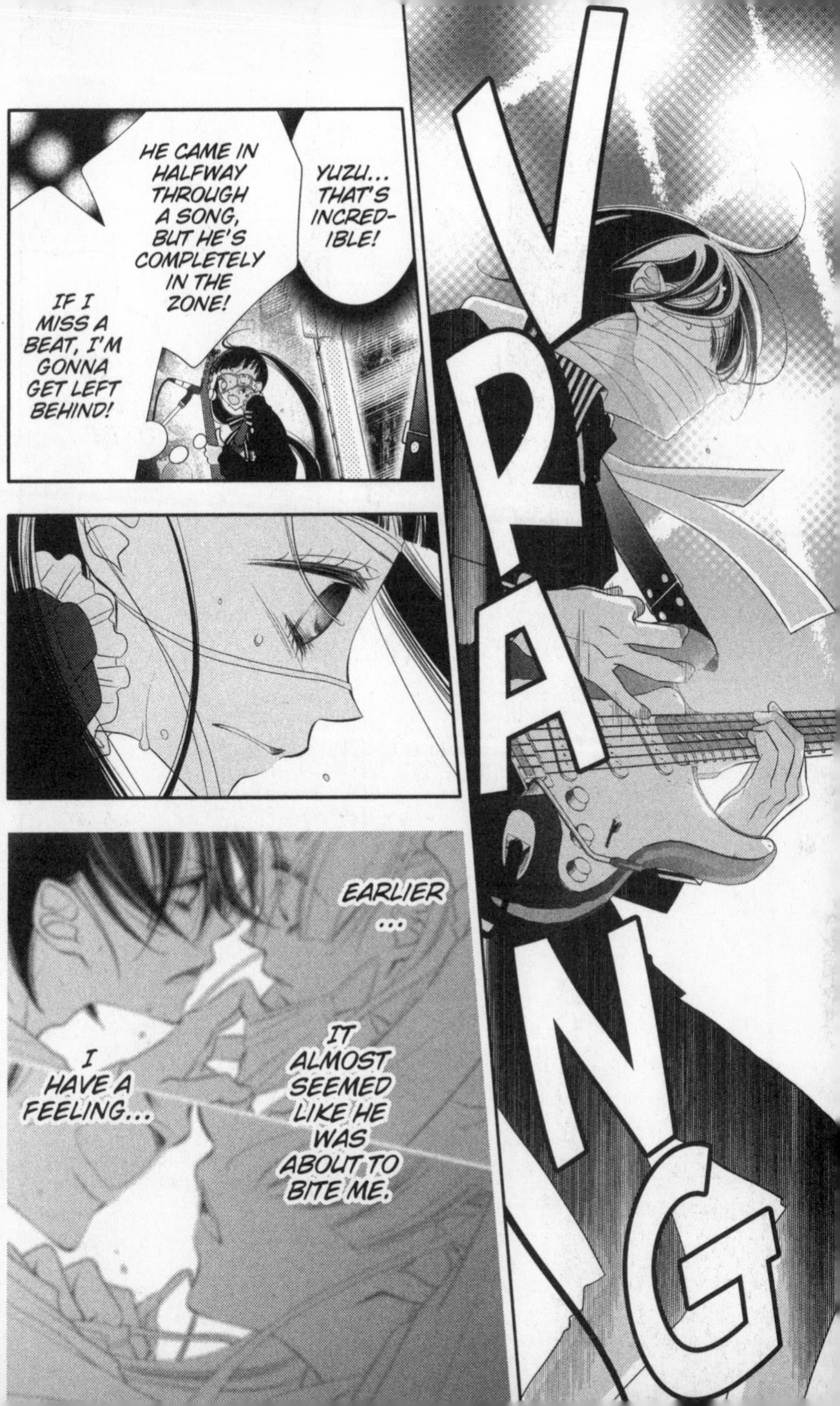
VRANG
YUZU... THAT'S INCRED-IBLE!
HE CAME IN HALFWAY THROUGH A SONG, BUT HE'S COMPLETELY IN THE ZONE!
IF I MISS A BEAT, I'M GONNA GET LEFT BEHIND!
EARLIER...
IT ALMOST SEEMED LIKE HE WAS ABOUT TO BITE ME.
I HAVE A FEELING...

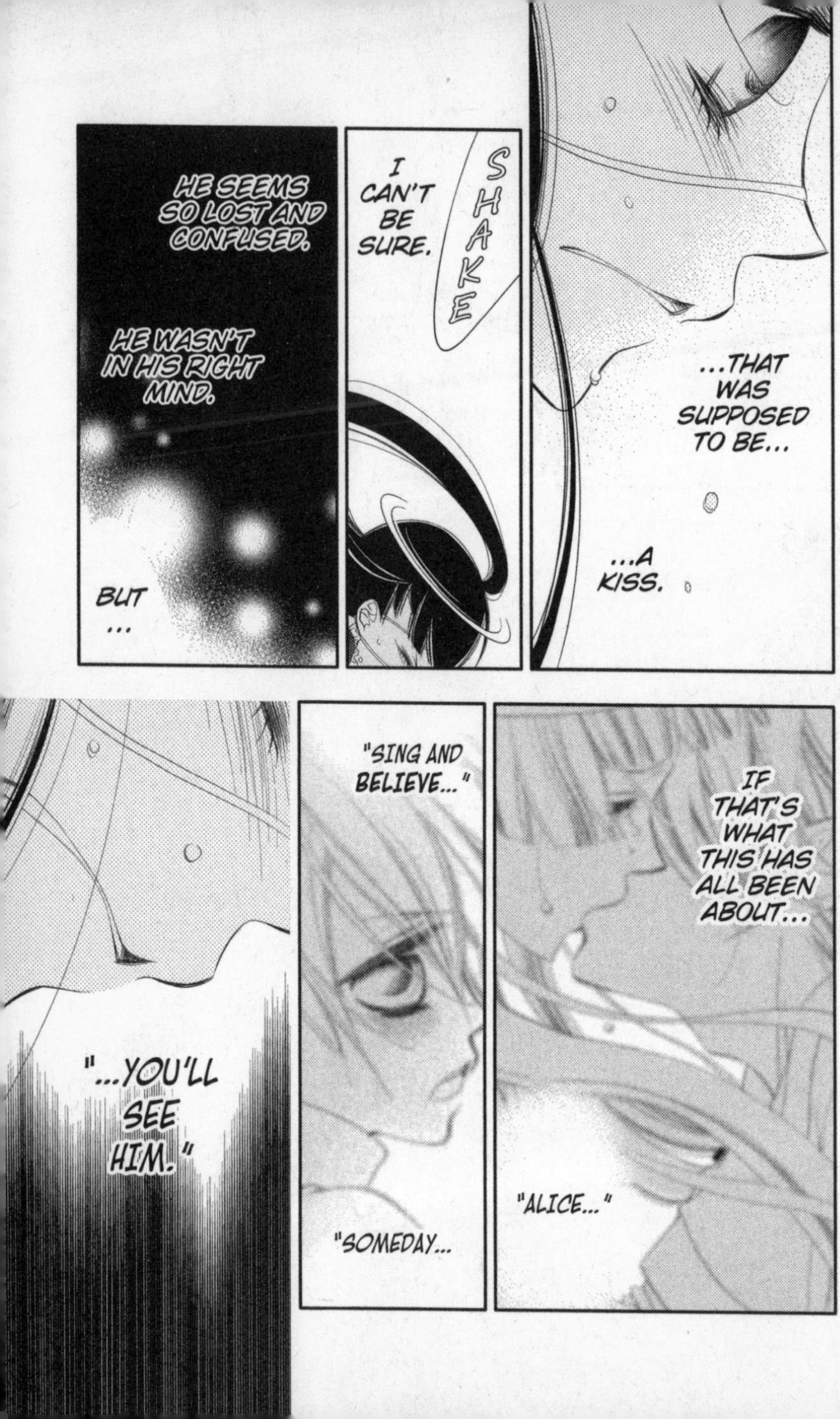
...THAT WAS SUPPOSED TO BE...
...A KISS.
SHAKE
I CAN'T BE SURE.
HE SEEMS SO LOST AND CONFUSED.
HE WASN'T IN HIS RIGHT MIND.
BUT ...
IF THAT'S WHAT THIS HAS ALL BEEN ABOUT...
"ALICE..."
"SING AND BELIEVE..."
"SOMEDAY...
"...YOU'LL SEE HIM."

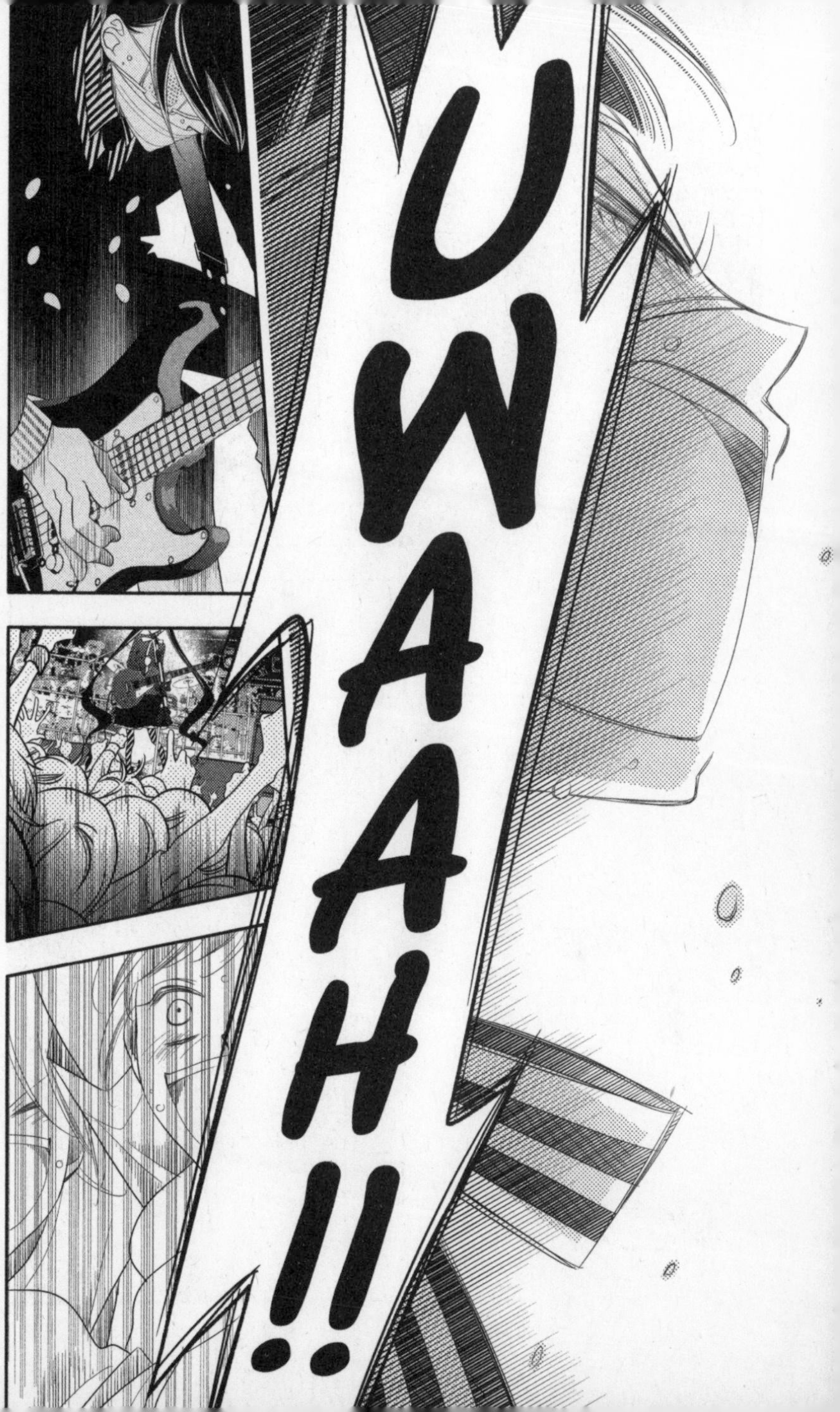
UWAAAH!!

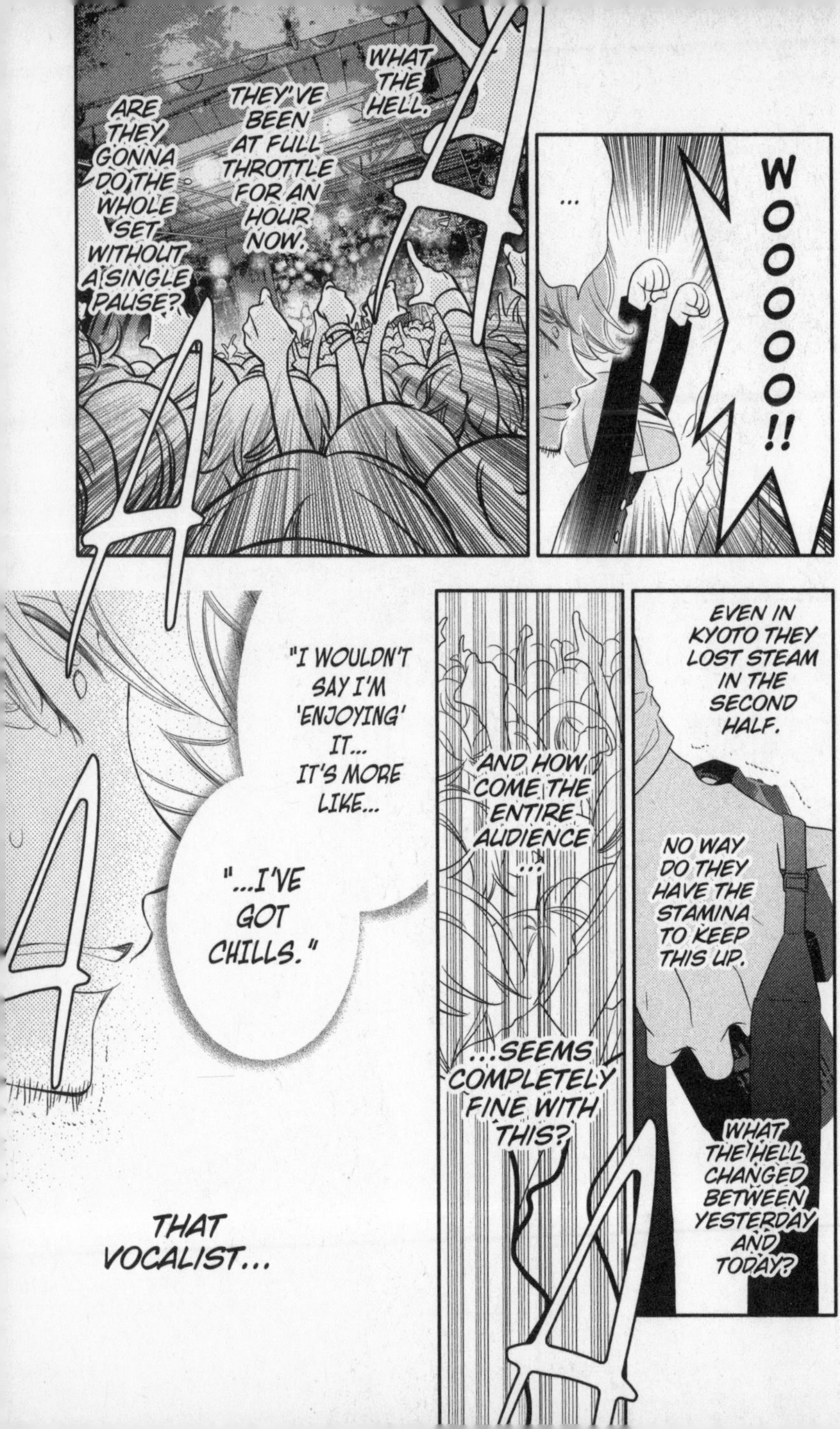
WOOOOOO!!
...
WHAT THE HELL.
THEY'VE BEEN AT FULL THROTTLE FOR AN HOUR NOW.
ARE THEY GONNA DO THE WHOLE SET WITHOUT A SINGLE PAUSE?
EVEN IN KYOTO THEY LOST STEAM IN THE SECOND HALF.
NO WAY DO THEY HAVE THE STAMINA TO KEEP THIS UP.
WHAT THE HELL CHANGED BETWEEN YESTERDAY AND TODAY?
AND HOW COME THE ENTIRE AUDIENCE ...
...SEEMS COMPLETELY FINE WITH THIS?
"I WOULDN'T SAY I'M 'ENJOYING' IT... IT'S MORE LIKE...
"...I'VE GOT CHILLS."
THAT VOCALIST...

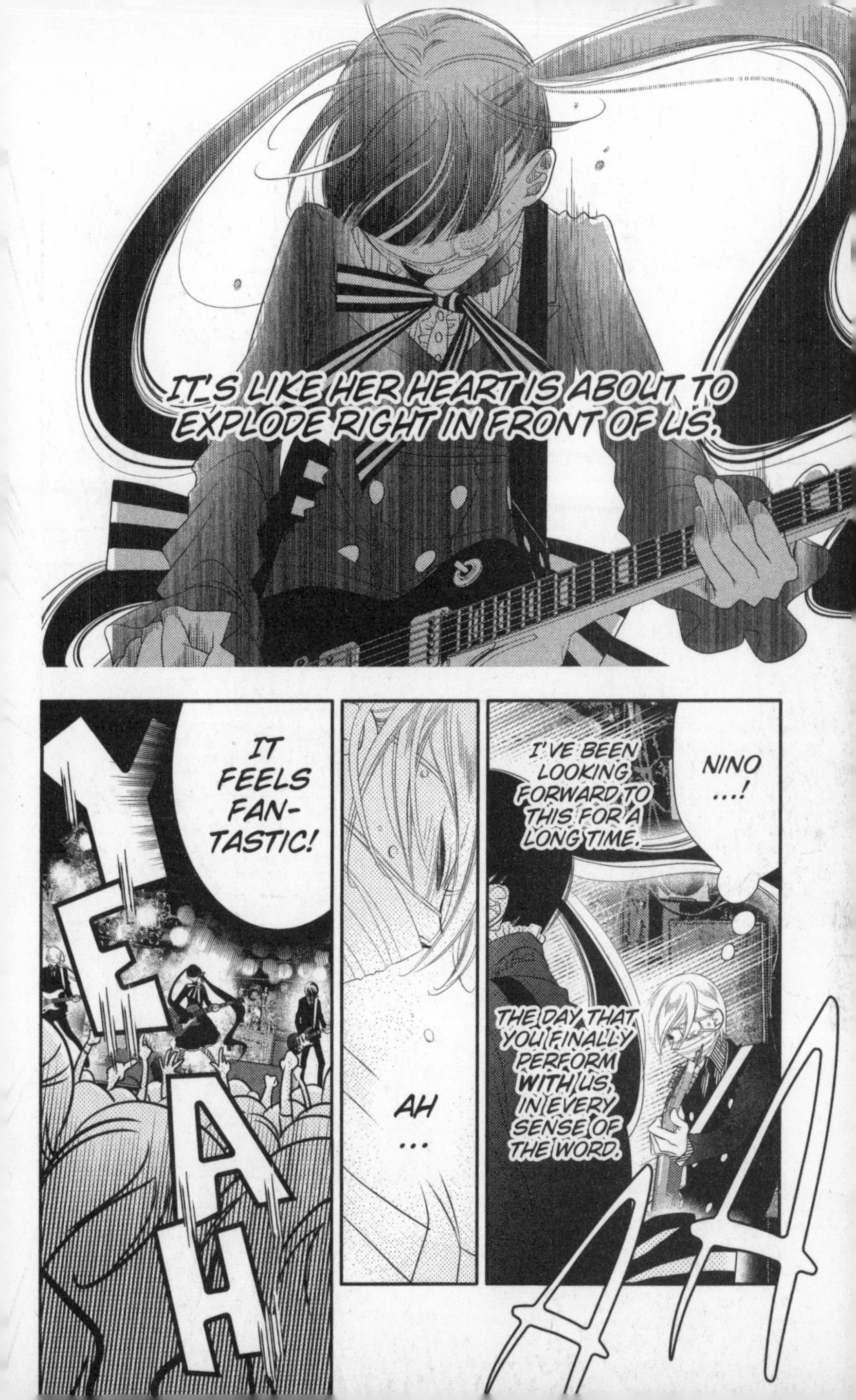
IT'S LIKE HER HEART IS ABOUT TO EXPLODE RIGHT IN FRONT OF US.
NINO ...!
I'VE BEEN LOOKING FORWARD TO THIS FOR A LONG TIME.
THE DAY THAT YOU FINALLY PERFORM WITH US, IN EVERY SENSE OF THE WORD.
AH ...
IT FEELS FAN-TASTIC!
YEAH

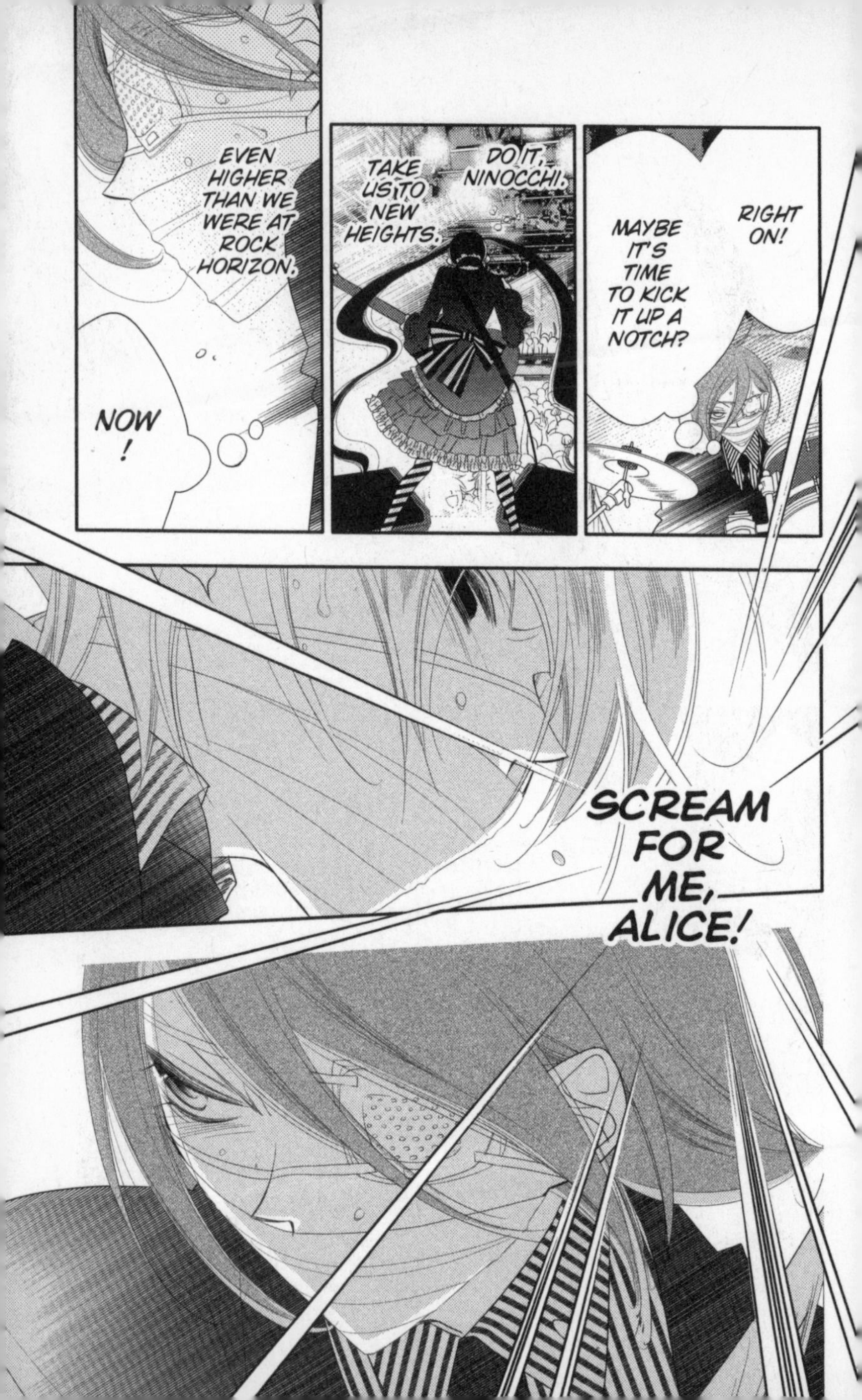
RIGHT ON!
MAYBE IT'S TIME TO KICK IT UP A NOTCH?
DO IT, NINOCCHI.
TAKE US TO NEW HEIGHTS.
EVEN HIGHER THAN WE WERE AT ROCK HORIZON.
NOW!
SCREAM FOR ME, ALICE!

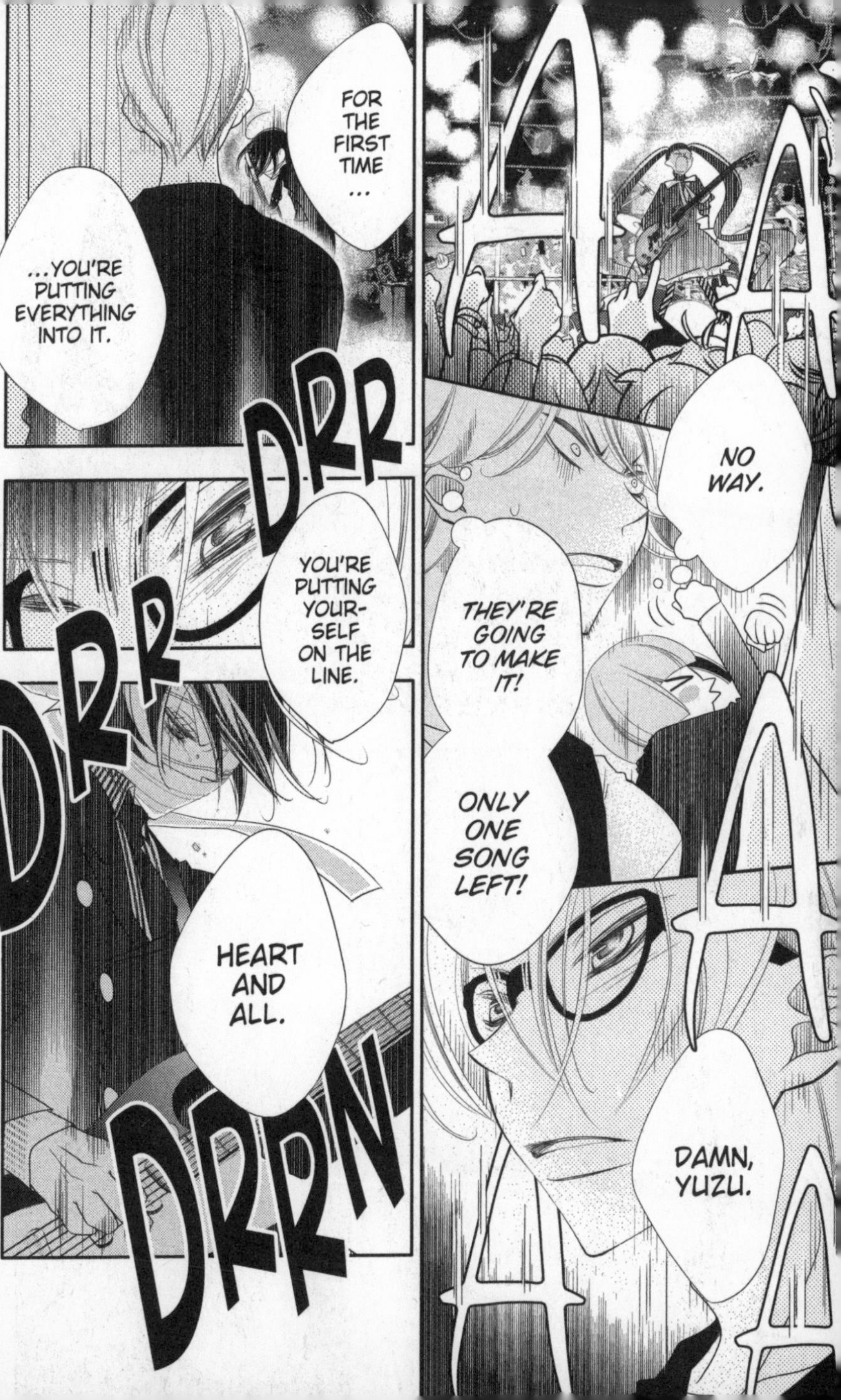
NO WAY.
THEY'RE GOING TO MAKE IT!
ONLY ONE SONG LEFT!
DAMN, YUZU.
FOR THE FIRST TIME...
...YOU'RE PUTTING EVERYTHING INTO IT.
DRR
DRR
YOU'RE PUTTING YOUR-SELF ON THE LINE.
HEART AND ALL.
DRRN

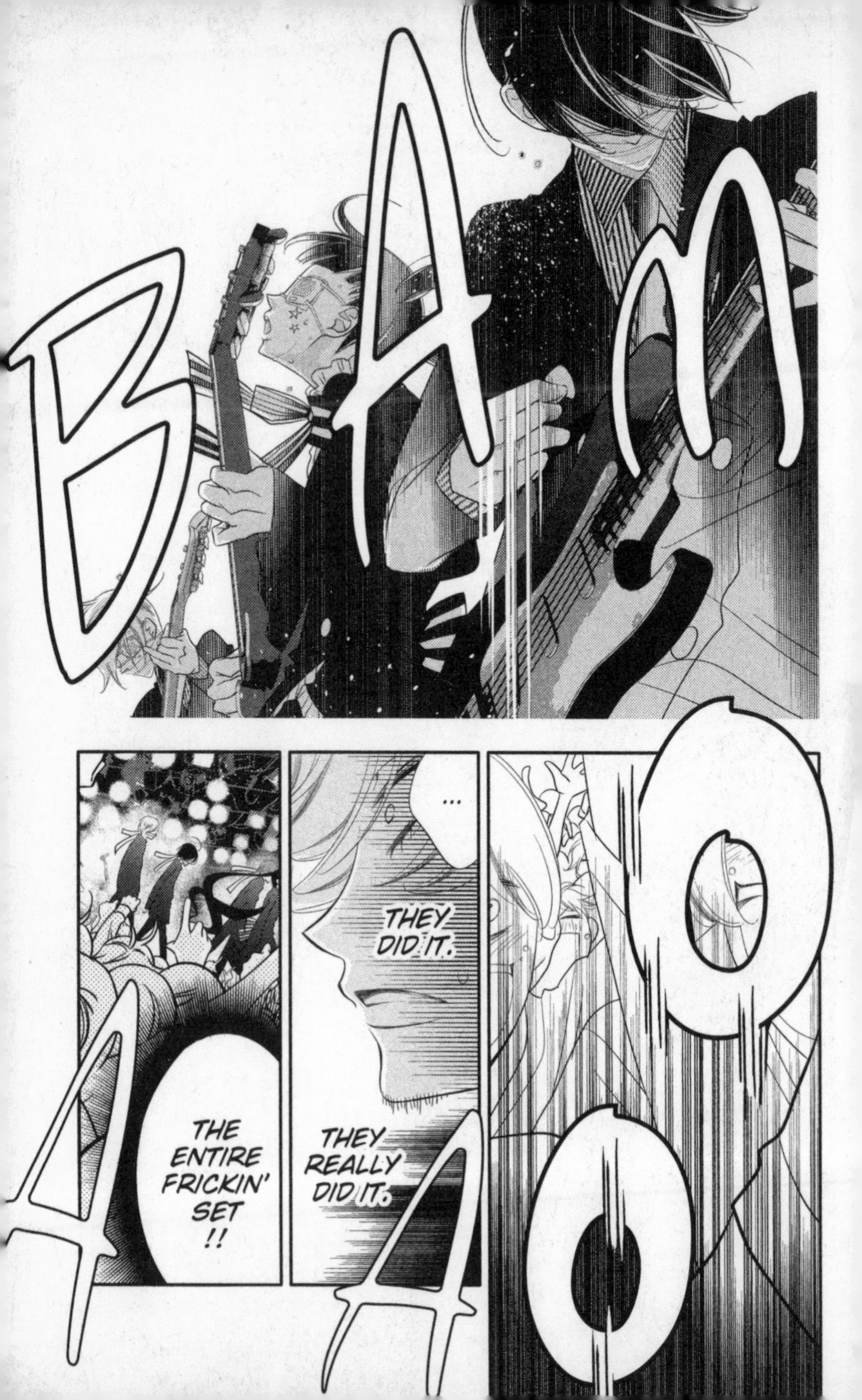
BAM
...
THEY DID IT.
THEY REALLY DID IT.
THE ENTIRE FRICKIN' SET !!
AAOO

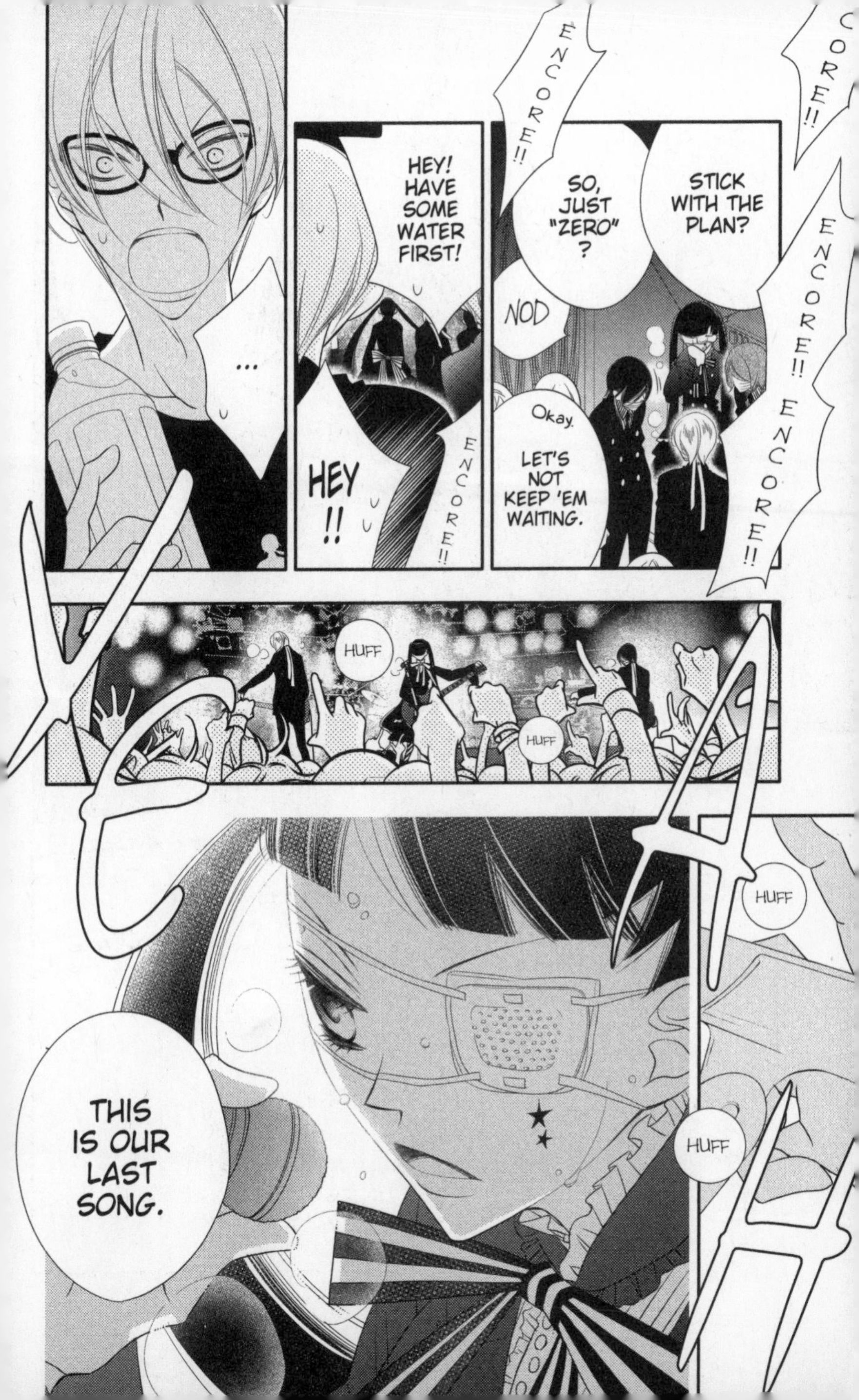
CORE!!
ENCORE!!
STICK WITH THE PLAN?
SO, JUST "ZERO"?
ENCORE!!
NOD
ENCORE!!
Okay.
LET'S NOT KEEP 'EM WAITING.
HEY! HAVE SOME WATER FIRST!
ENCORE!!
HEY!!
...
HUFF
HUFF
HUFF
HUFF
THIS IS OUR LAST SONG.

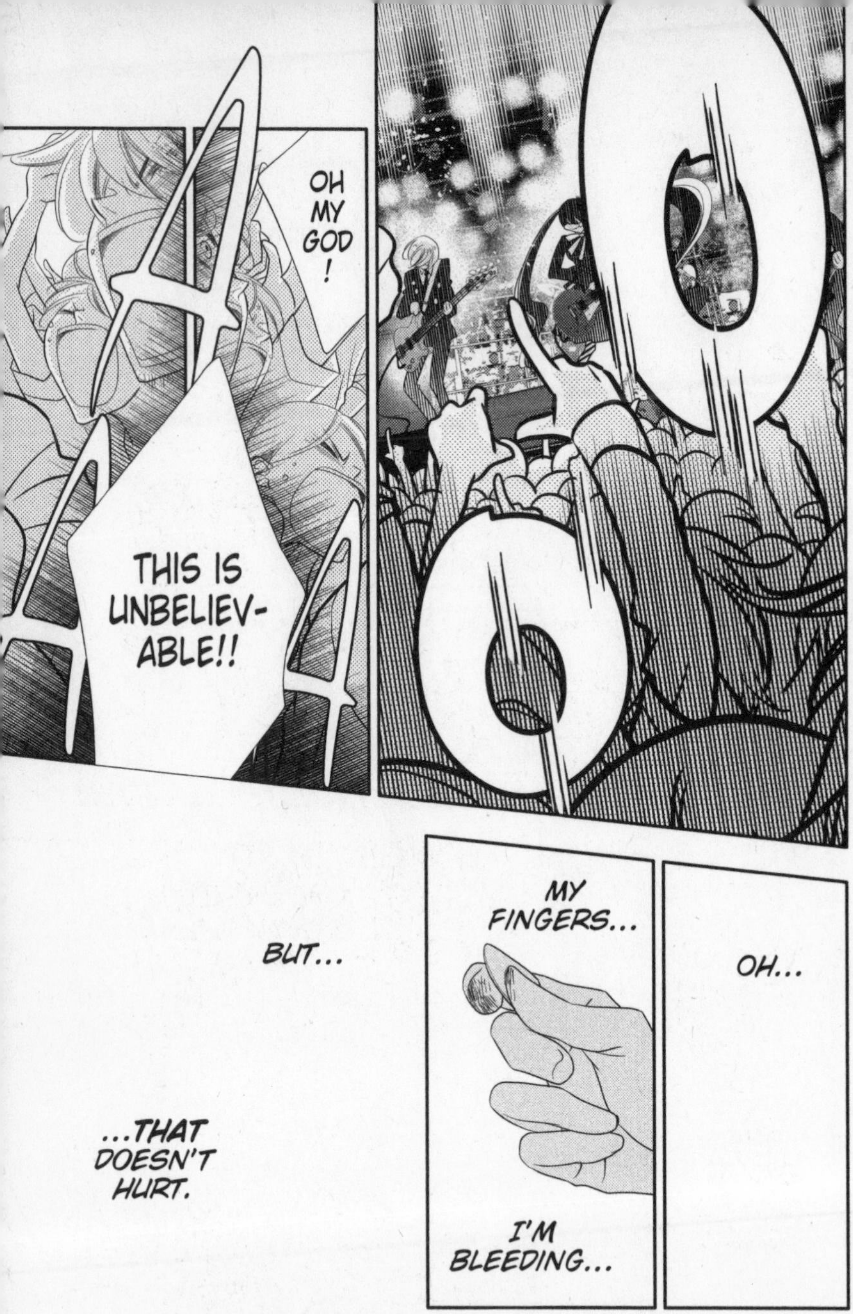
OH MY GOD!
THIS IS UNBELIEV-ABLE!!
OH...
MY FINGERS...
I'M BLEEDING...
BUT...
...THAT DOESN'T HURT.

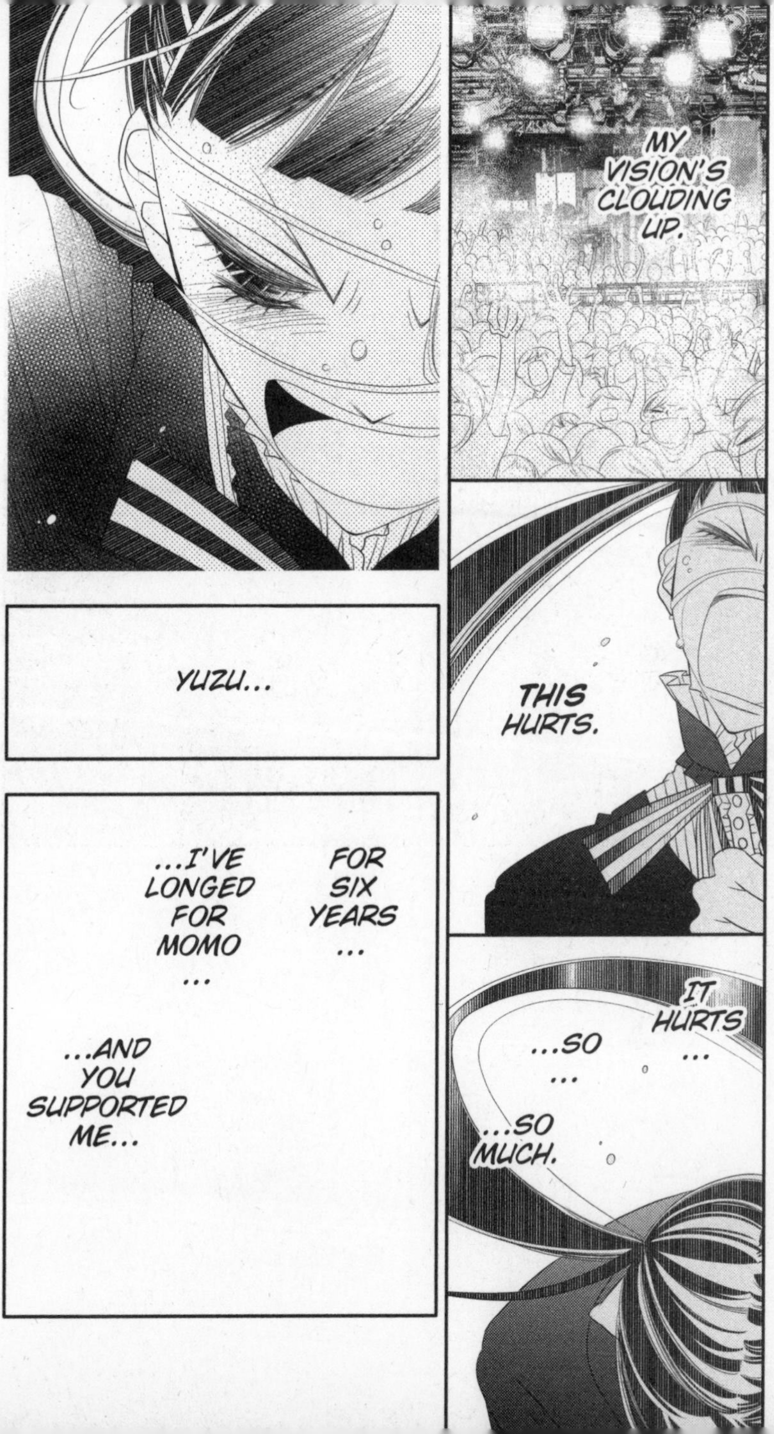
MY VISION'S CLOUDING UP.
THIS HURTS.
IT HURTS...
...SO...
...SO MUCH.
YUZU...
FOR SIX YEARS...
...I'VE LONGED FOR MOMO...
...AND YOU SUPPORTED ME...

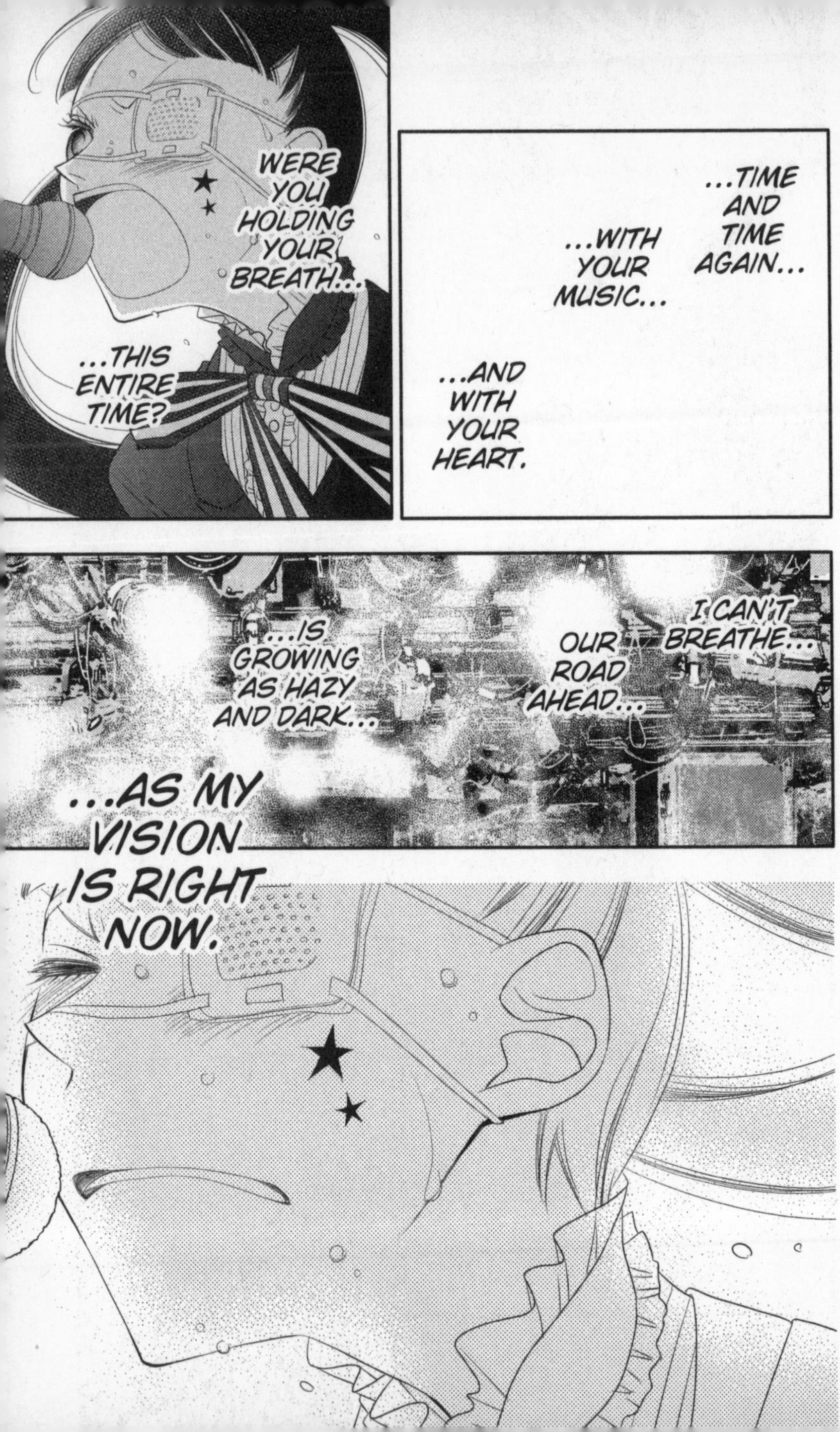
...TIME AND TIME AGAIN...
...WITH YOUR MUSIC...
...AND WITH YOUR HEART.
WERE YOU HOLDING YOUR BREATH...
...THIS ENTIRE TIME?
I CAN'T BREATHE...
OUR ROAD AHEAD...
...IS GROWING AS HAZY AND DARK...
...AS MY VISION IS RIGHT NOW.

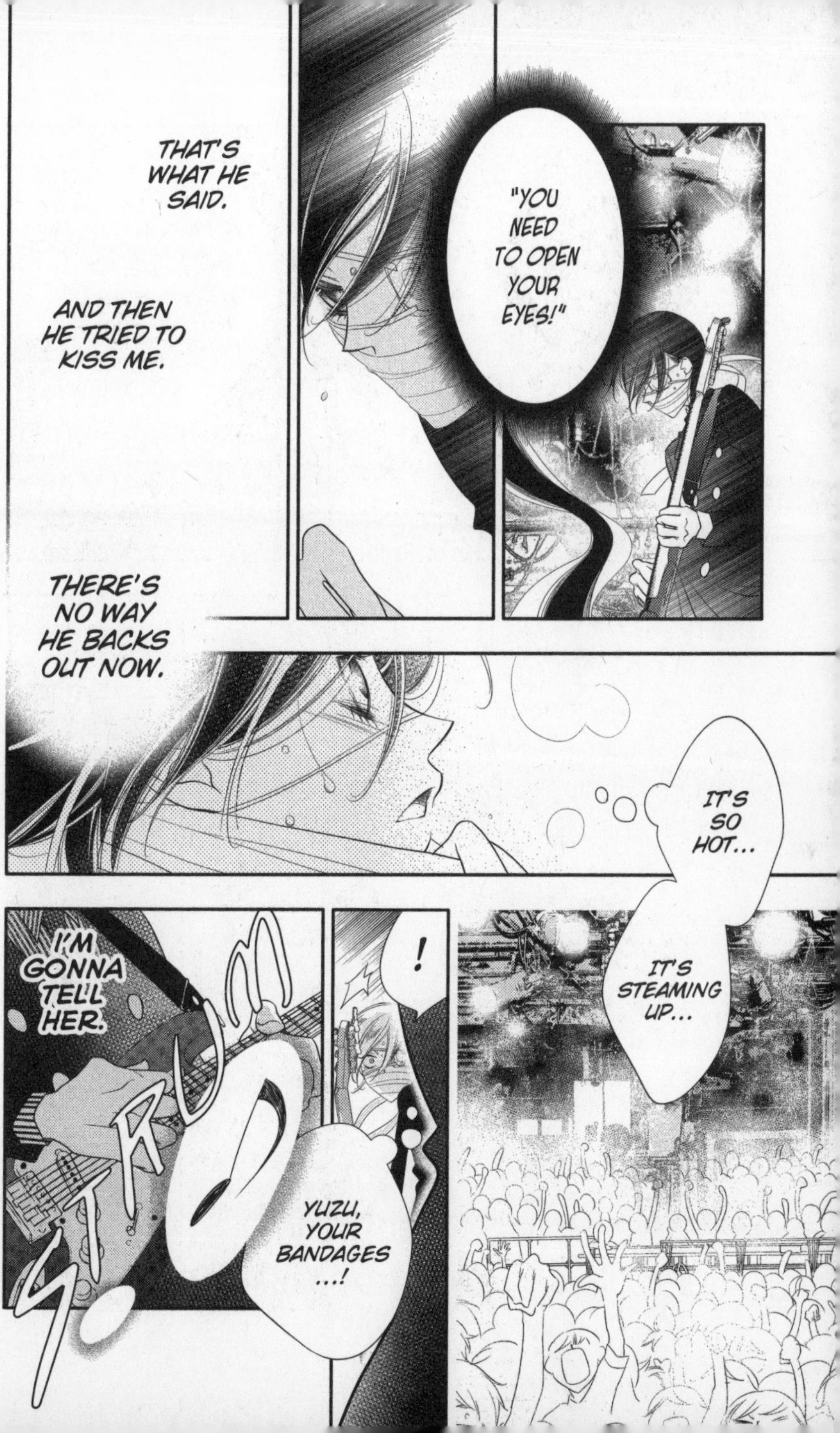
"YOU NEED TO OPEN YOUR EYES!"
THAT'S WHAT HE SAID.
AND THEN HE TRIED TO KISS ME.
THERE'S NO WAY HE BACKS OUT NOW.
IT'S SO HOT...
IT'S STEAMING UP...
!
YUZU, YOUR BANDAGES...!
I'M GONNA TELL HER.
STRUM

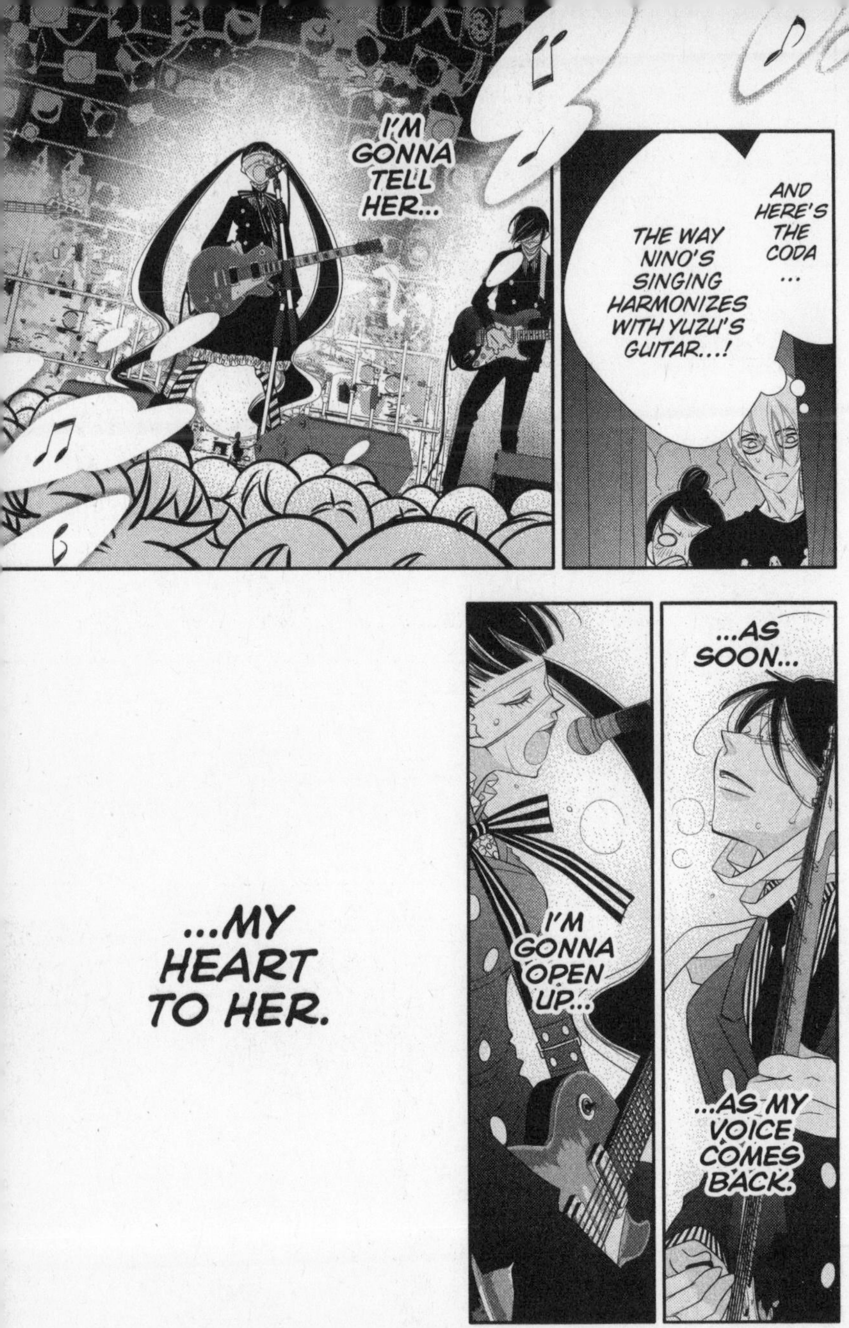
AND HERE'S THE CODA ...
THE WAY NINO'S SINGING HARMONIZES WITH YUZU'S GUITAR...!
I'M GONNA TELL HER...
...AS SOON...
...AS MY VOICE COMES BACK.
I'M GONNA OPEN UP...
...MY HEART TO HER.

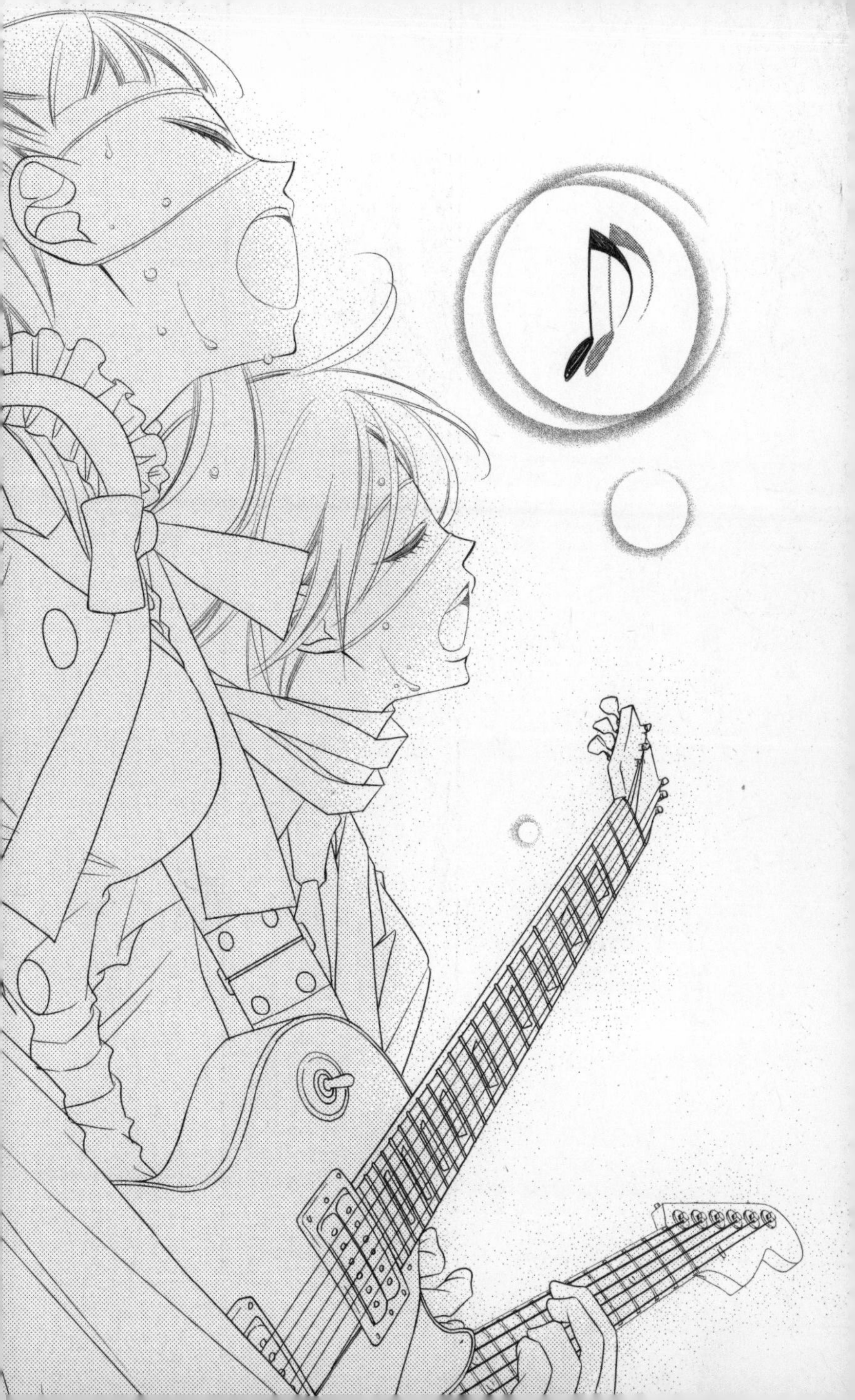

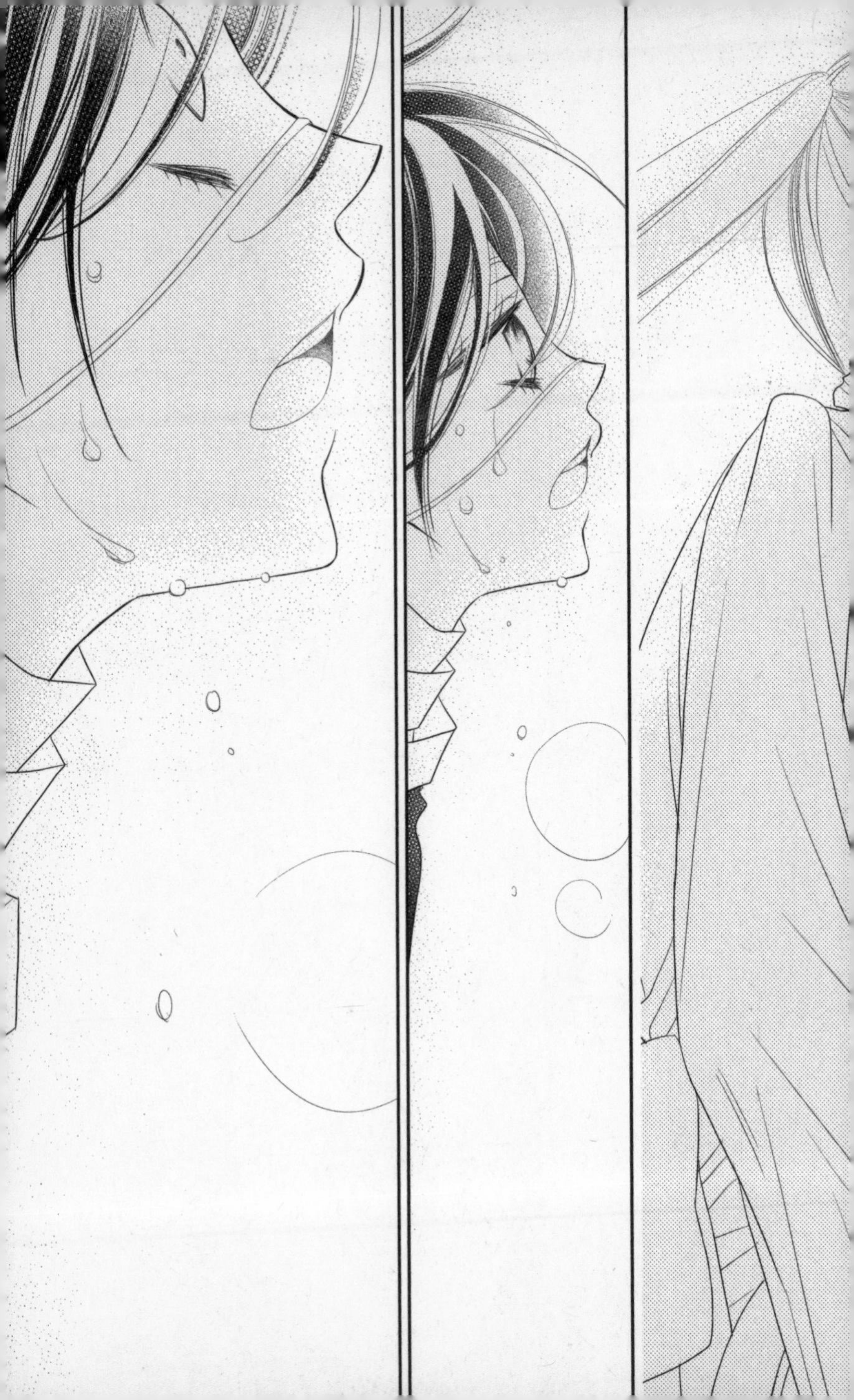

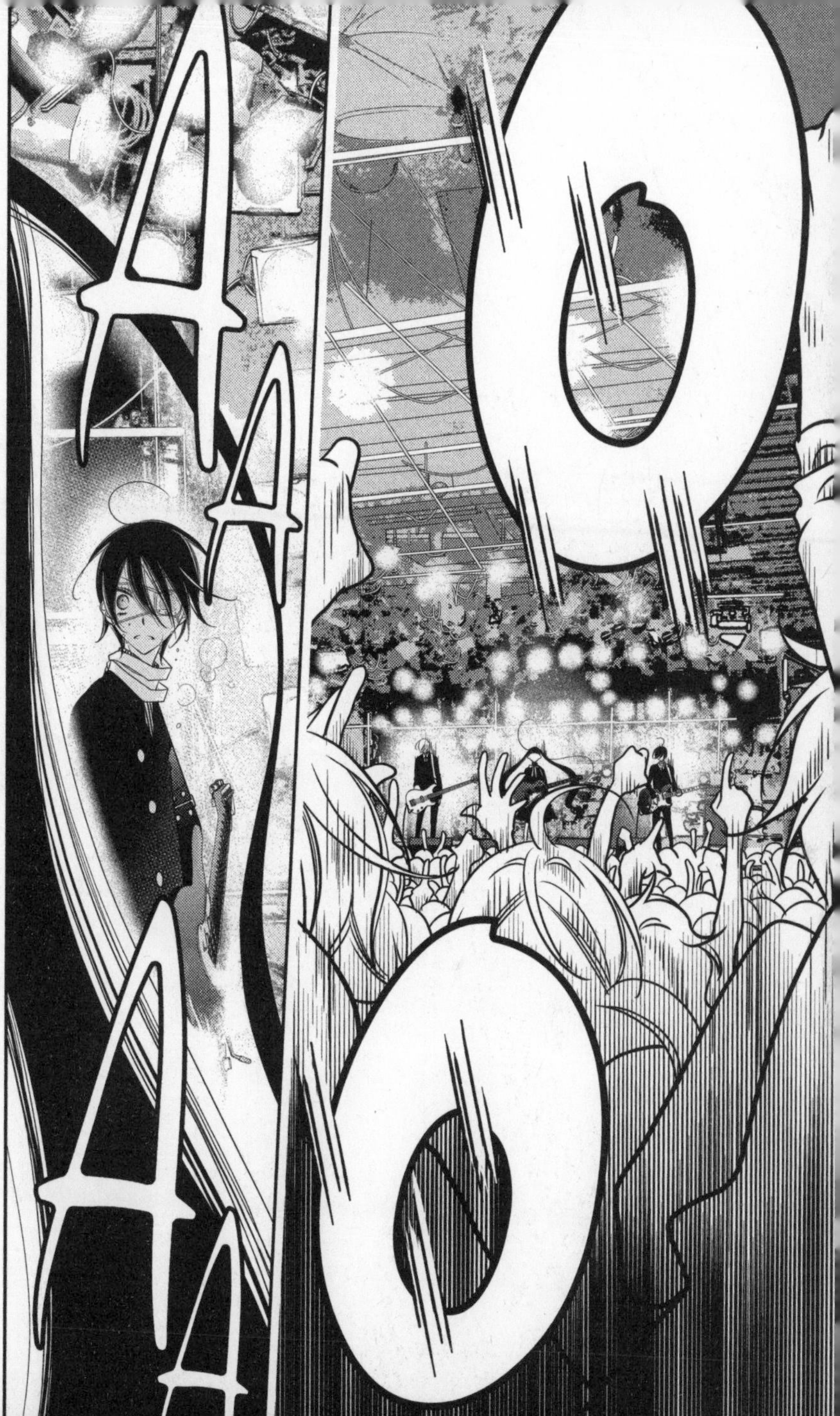
OO
AAAA

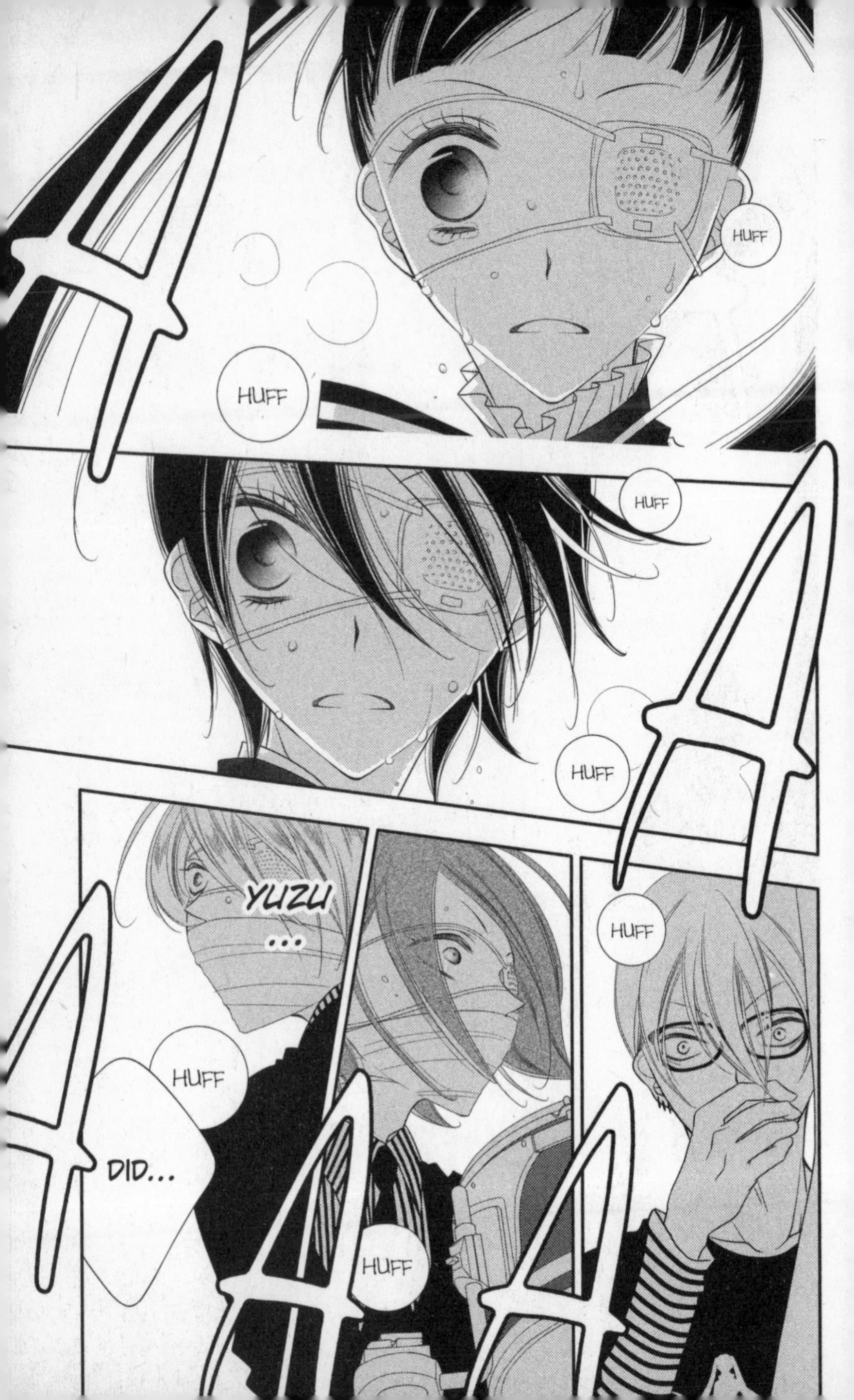
HUFF
HUFF
HUFF
HUFF
HUFF
HUFF
YUZU ...
HUFF
DID...

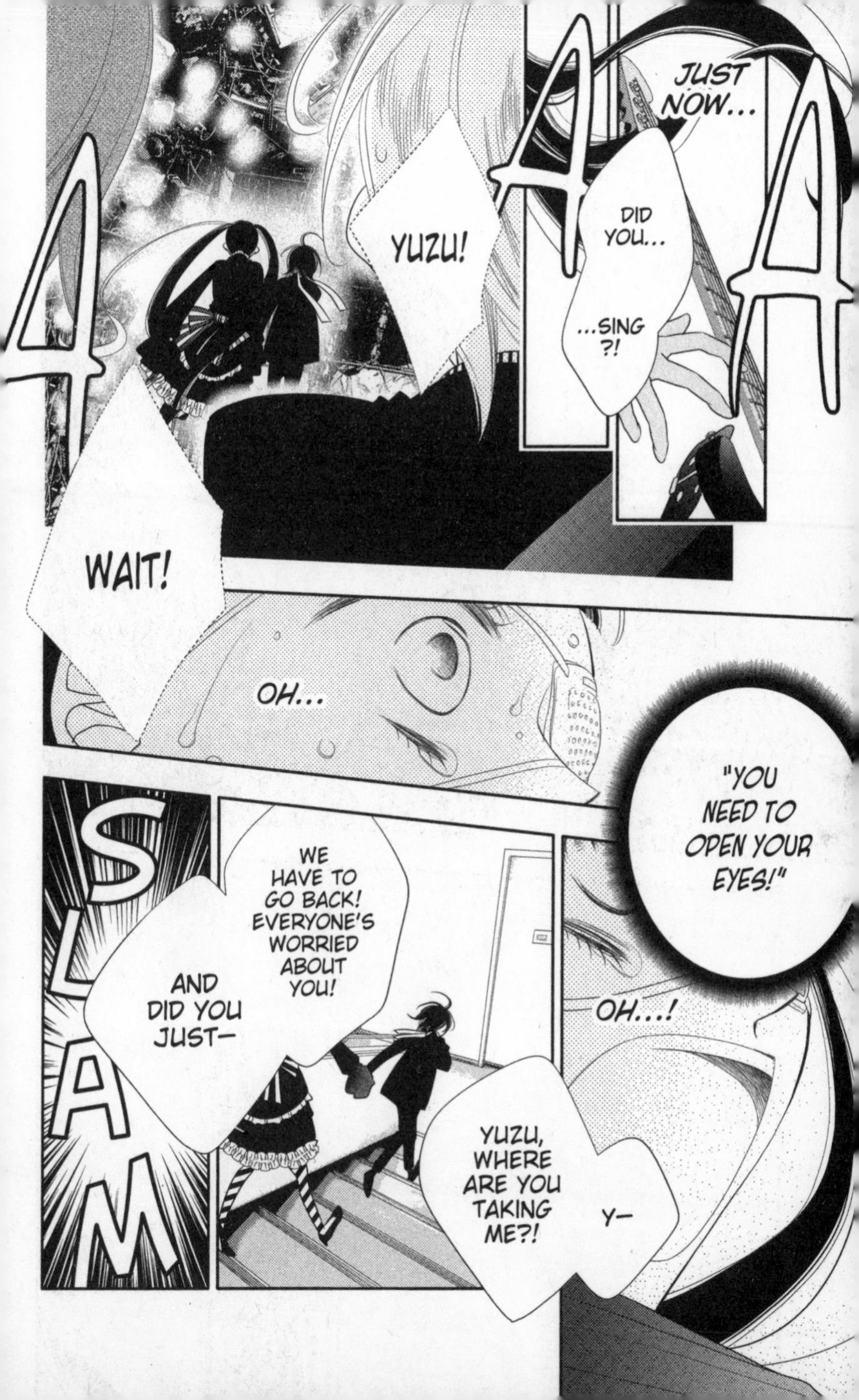
JUST NOW...
DID YOU...
...SING ?!
AAA
YUZU!
WAIT!
OH...
"YOU NEED TO OPEN YOUR EYES!"
OH...!
Y—
YUZU, WHERE ARE YOU TAKING ME?!
WE HAVE TO GO BACK! EVERYONE'S WORRIED ABOUT YOU!
AND DID YOU JUST—
SLAM

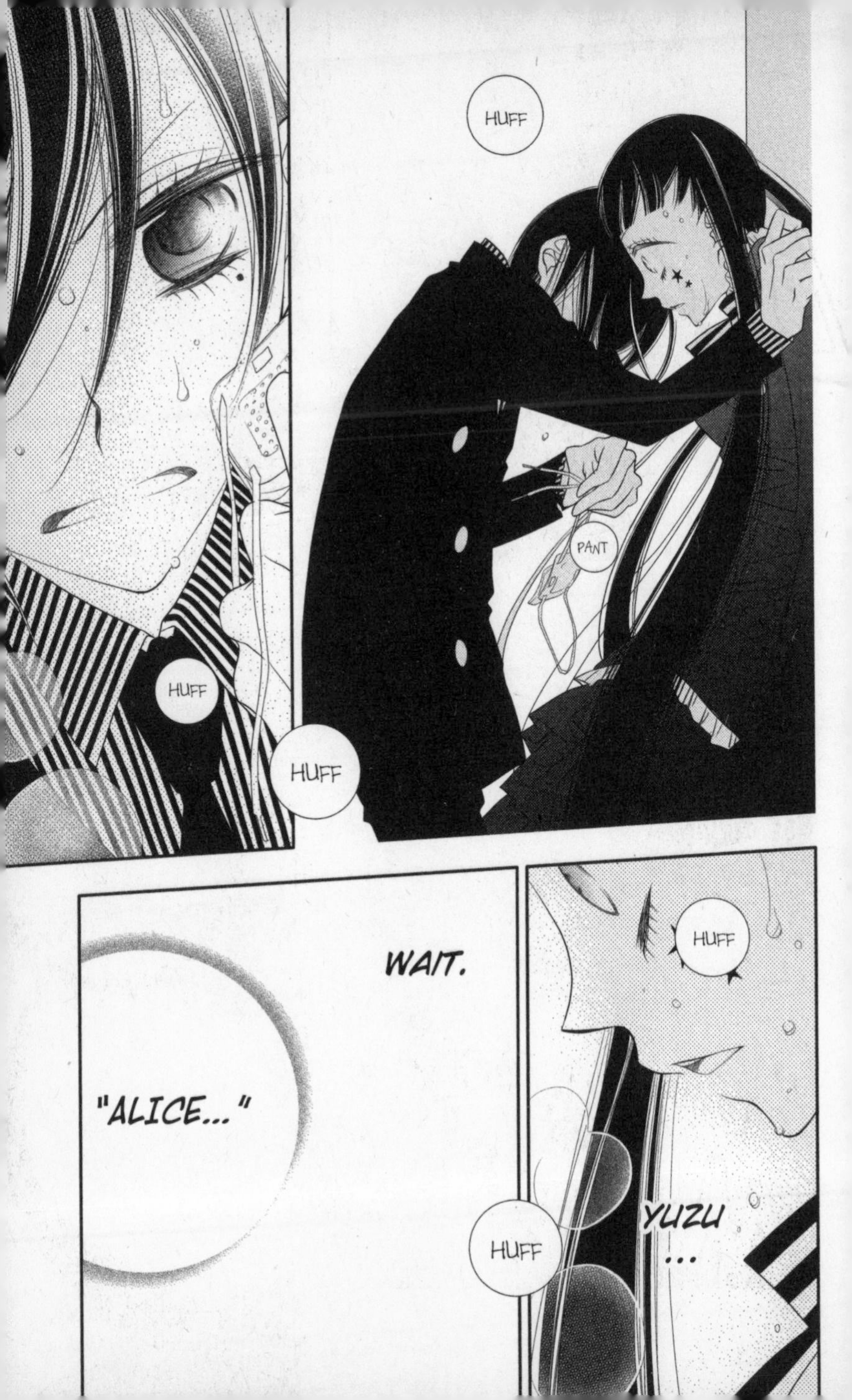
HUFF
PANT
HUFF
HUFF
HUFF
YUZU ...
HUFF
WAIT.
"ALICE..."

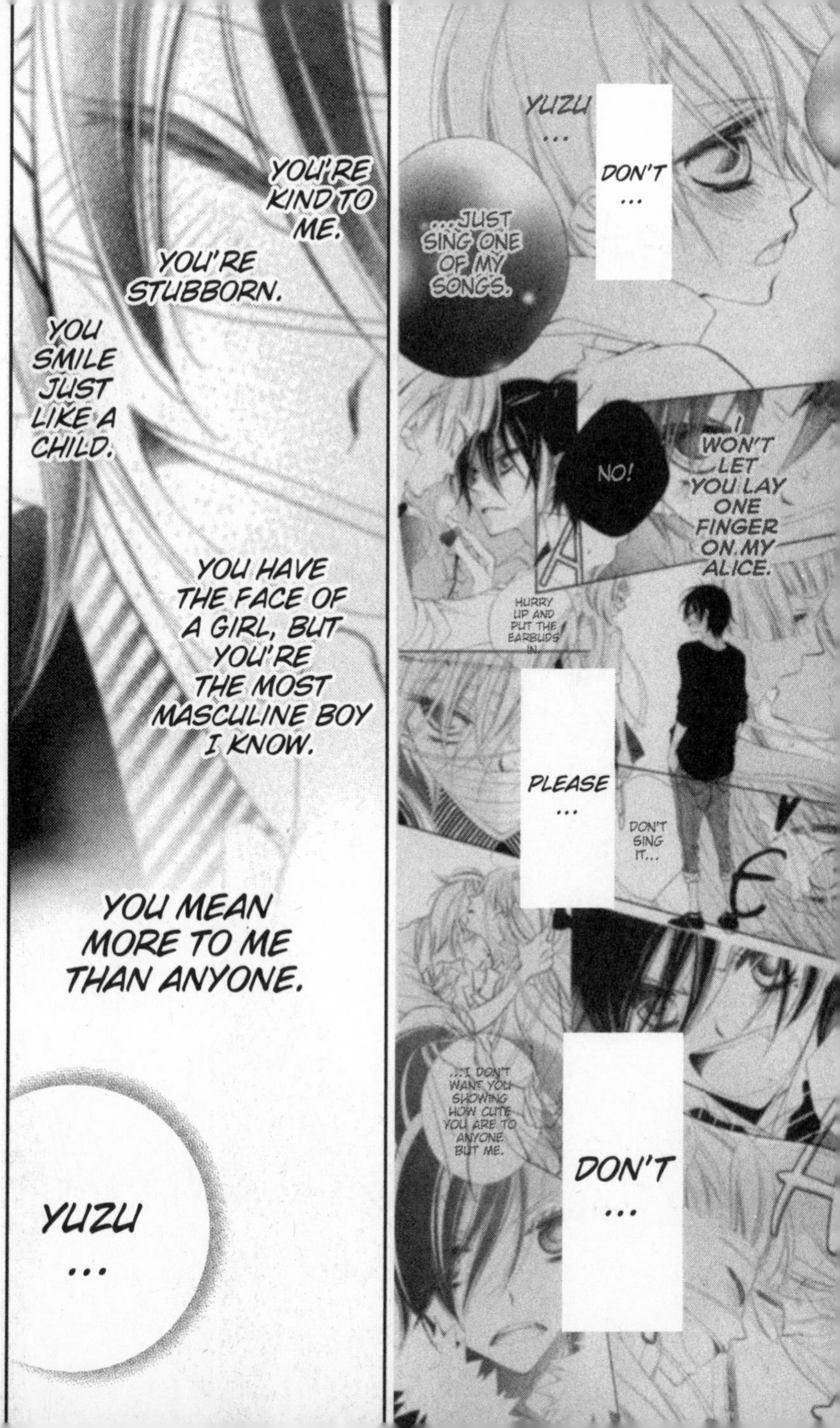
DON'T ...
YUZU ...
...JUST SING ONE OF MY SONGS.
I WON'T LET YOU LAY ONE FINGER ON MY ALICE.
NO!
HURRY UP AND PUT THE EARBUDS IN.
DON'T SING IT...
PLEASE ...
DON'T ...
...I DON'T WANT YOU SHOWING HOW CUTE YOU ARE TO ANYONE BUT ME.
YOU'RE KIND TO ME.
YOU'RE STUBBORN.
YOU SMILE JUST LIKE A CHILD.
YOU HAVE THE FACE OF A GIRL, BUT YOU'RE THE MOST MASCULINE BOY I KNOW.
YOU MEAN MORE TO ME THAN ANYONE.
YUZU ...

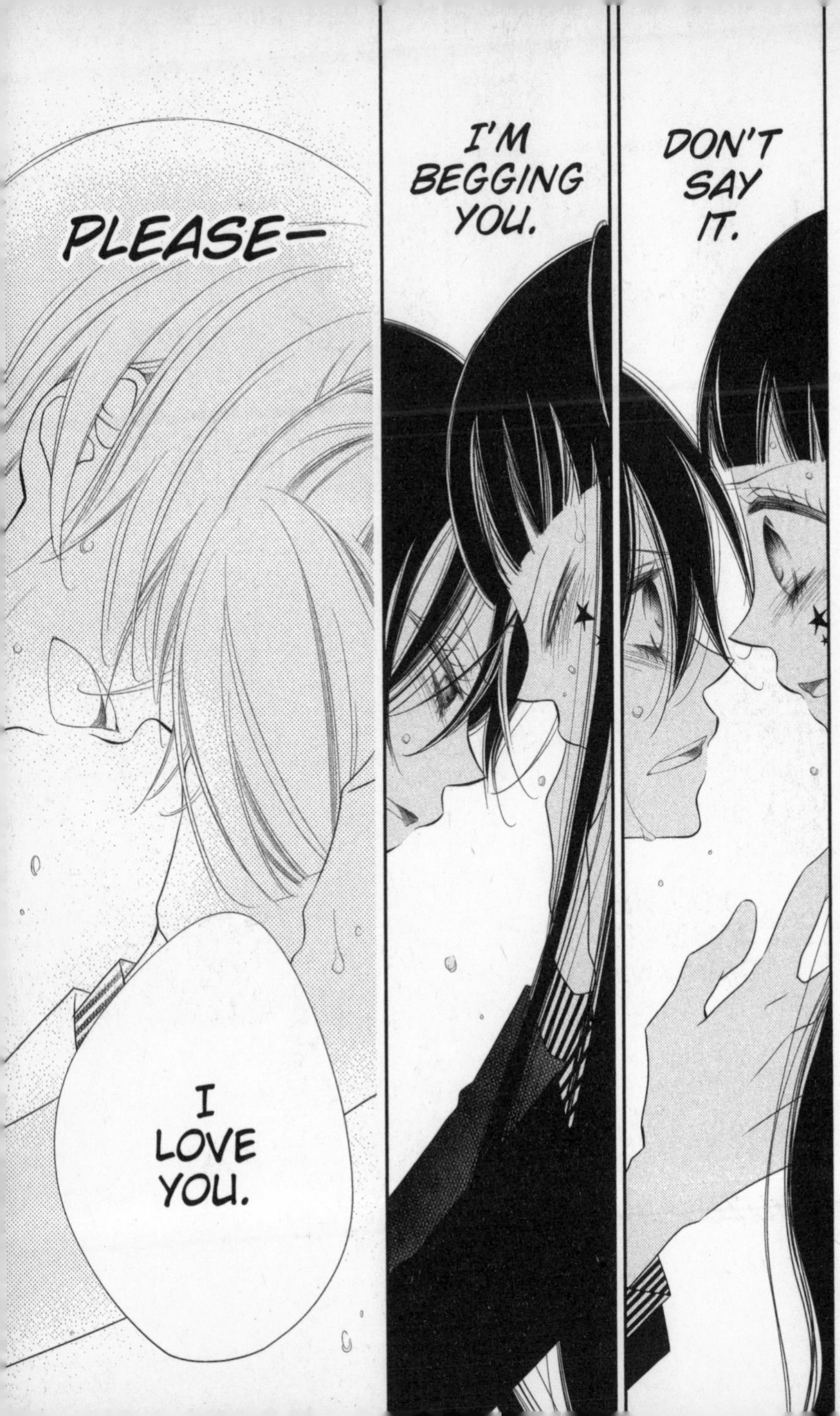
DON'T SAY IT.
I'M BEGGING YOU.
PLEASE—
I LOVE YOU.

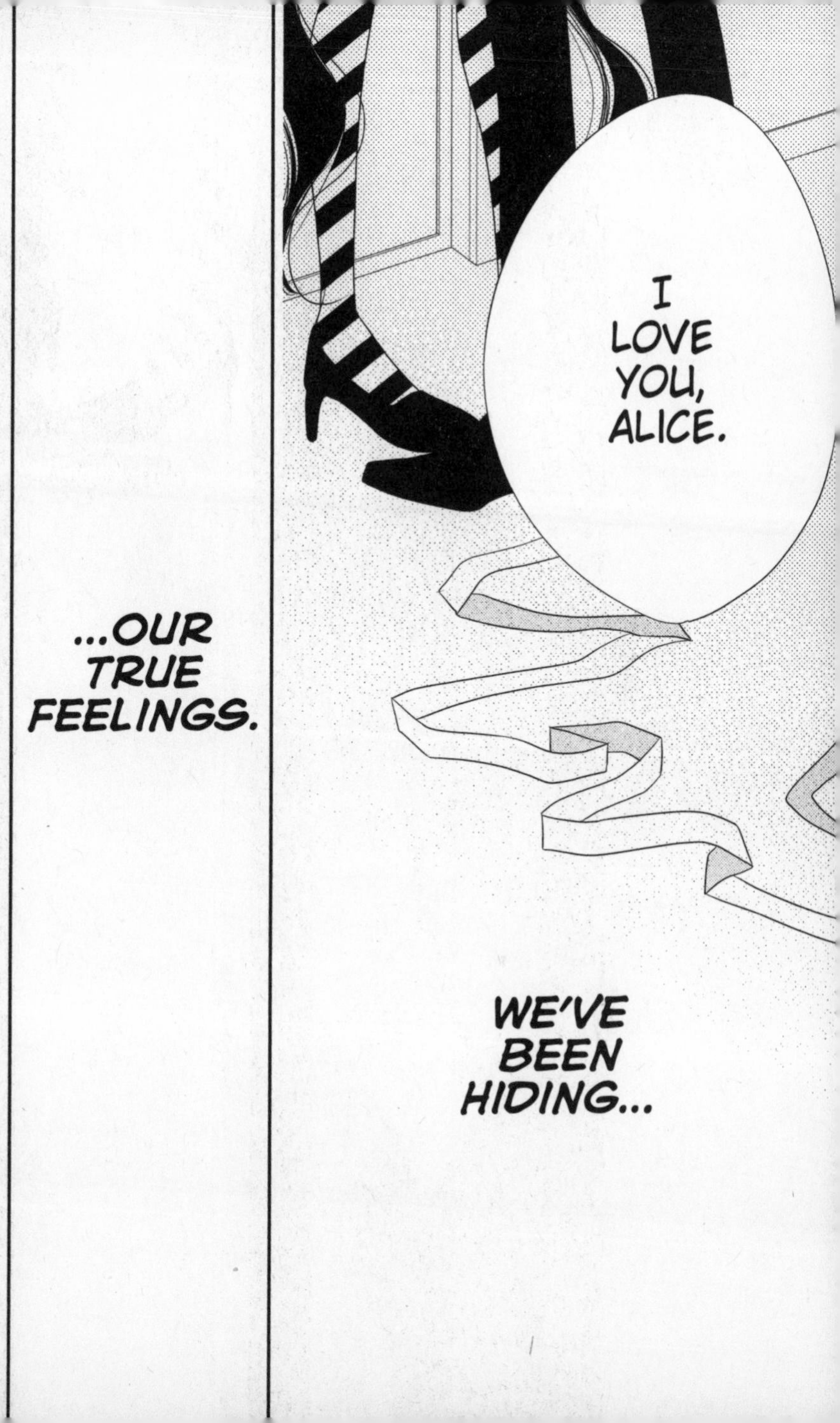
I LOVE YOU, ALICE.
WE'VE BEEN HIDING...
...OUR TRUE FEELINGS.

SONG 54

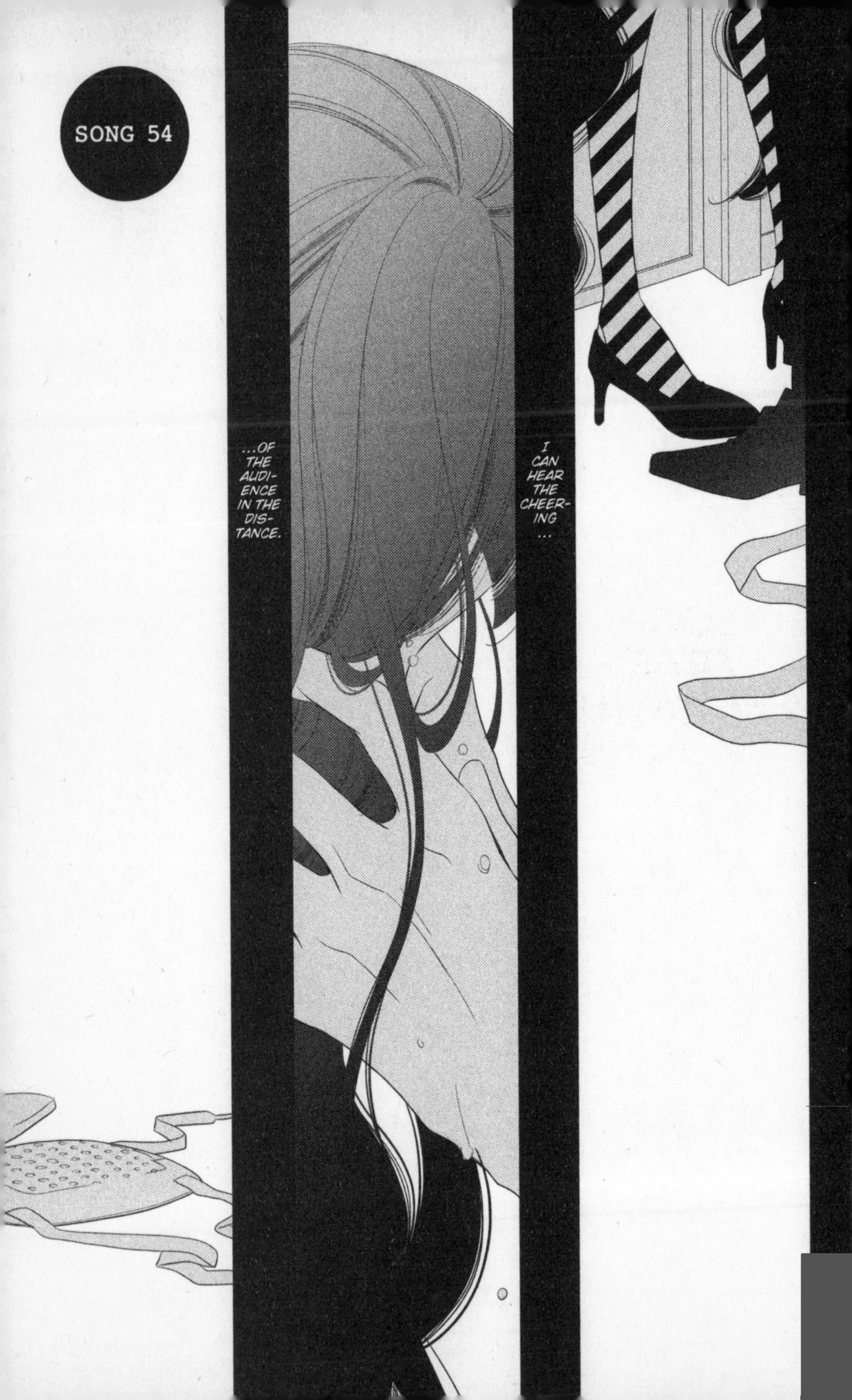
I CAN HEAR THE CHEER-ING...
...OF THE AUDI-ENCE IN THE DIS-TANCE.

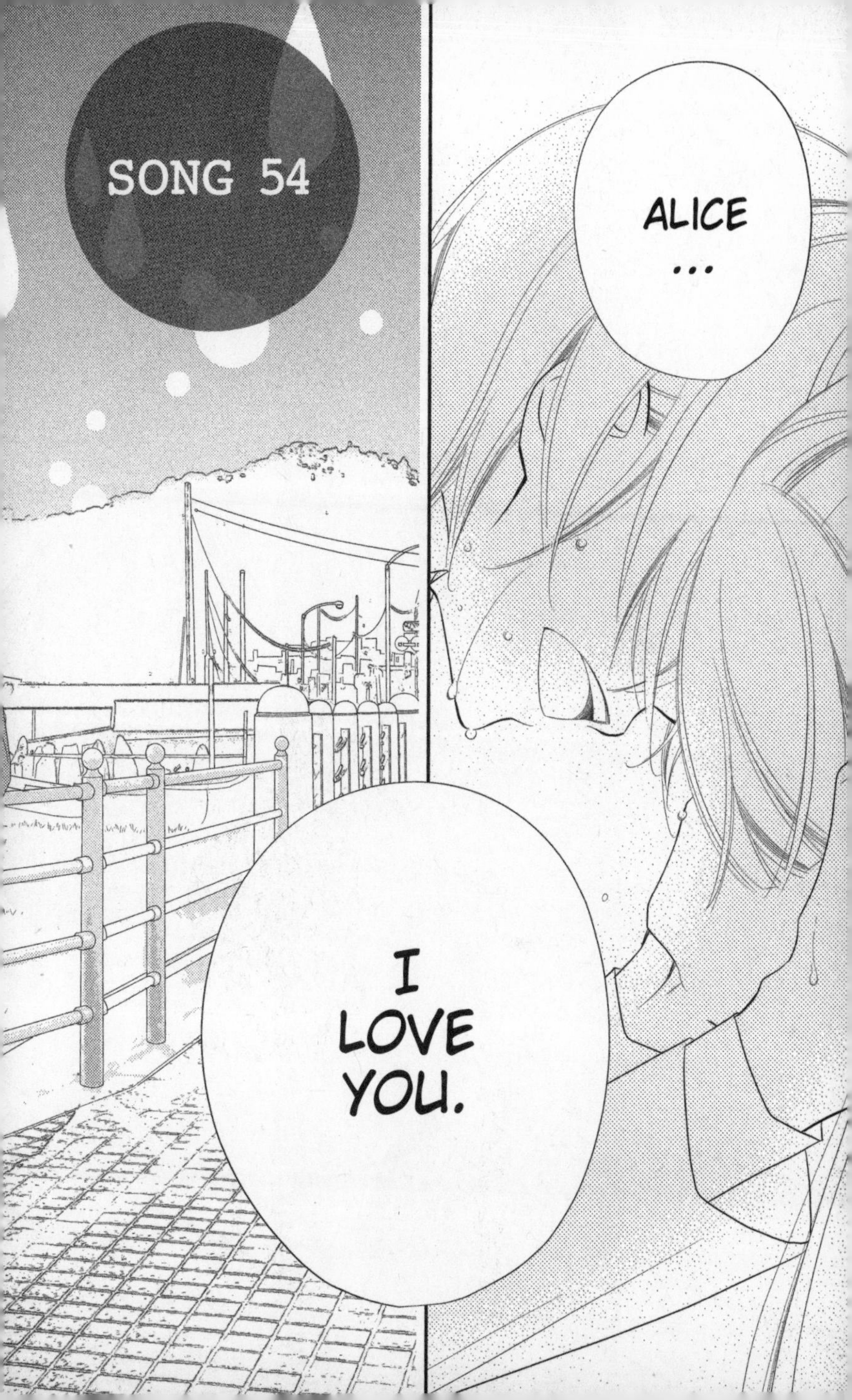
ALICE ...
I LOVE YOU.
SONG 54

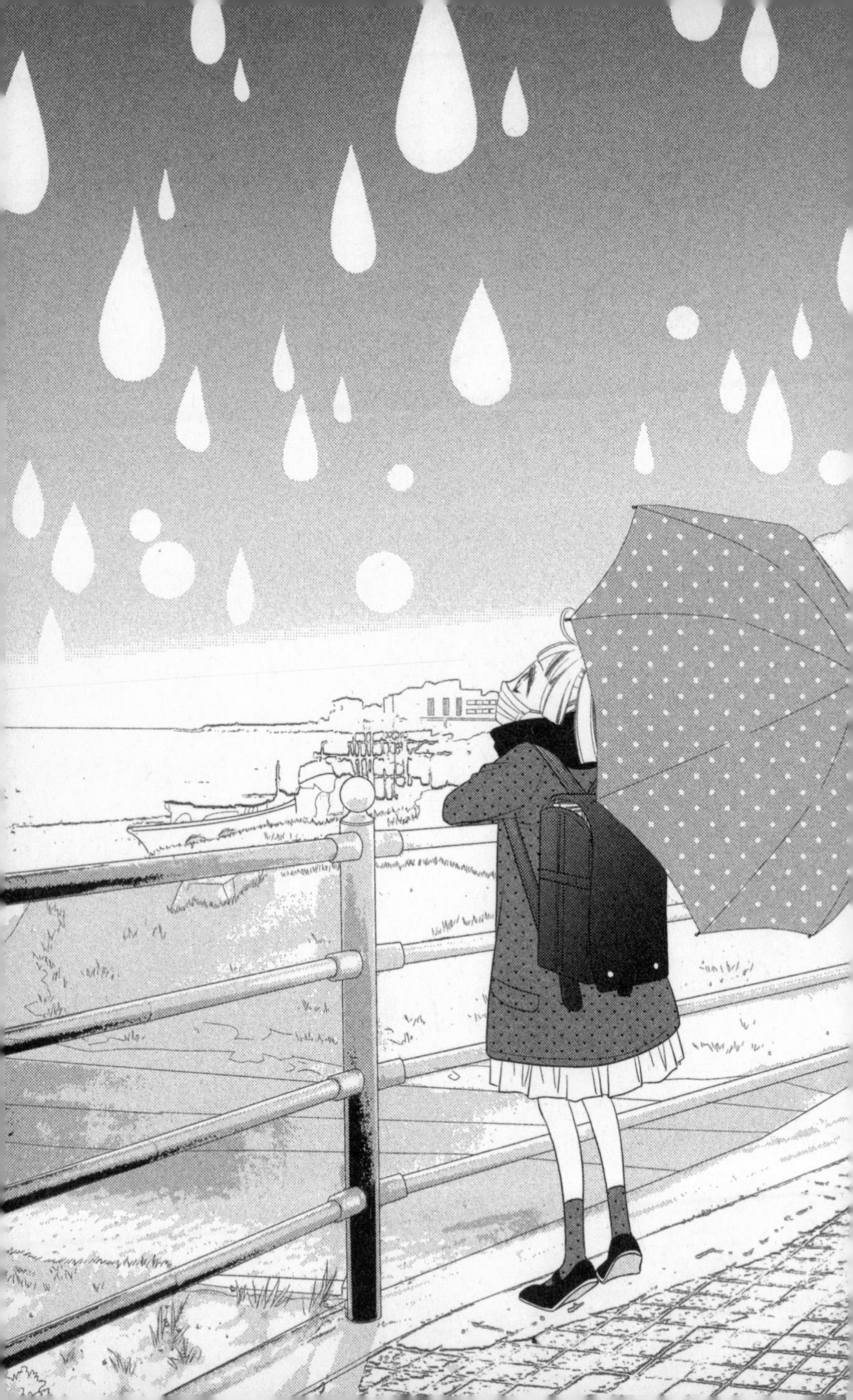

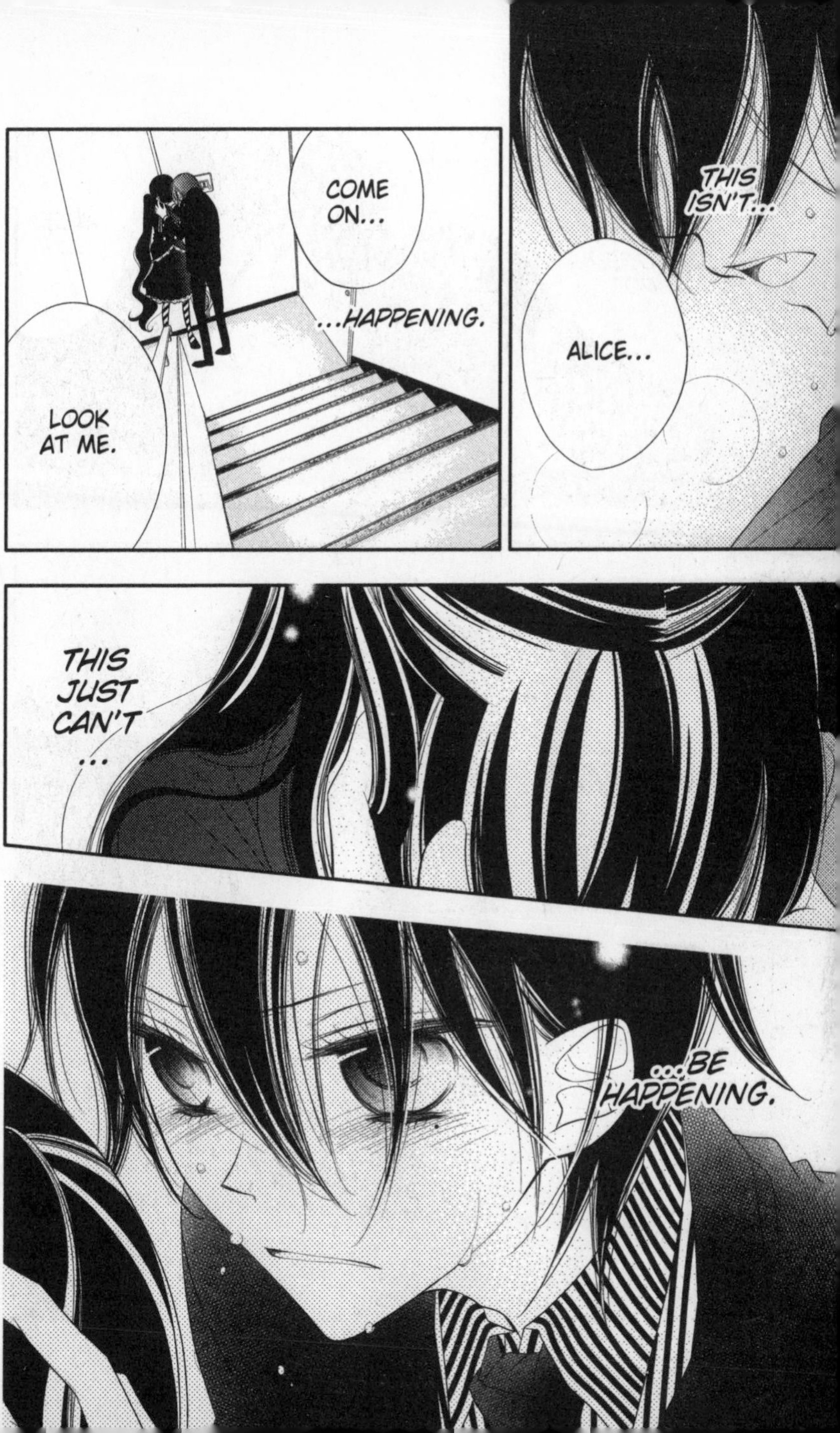
THIS ISN'T...
ALICE...
COME ON...
...HAPPENING.
LOOK AT ME.
THIS JUST CAN'T ...
...BE HAPPENING.

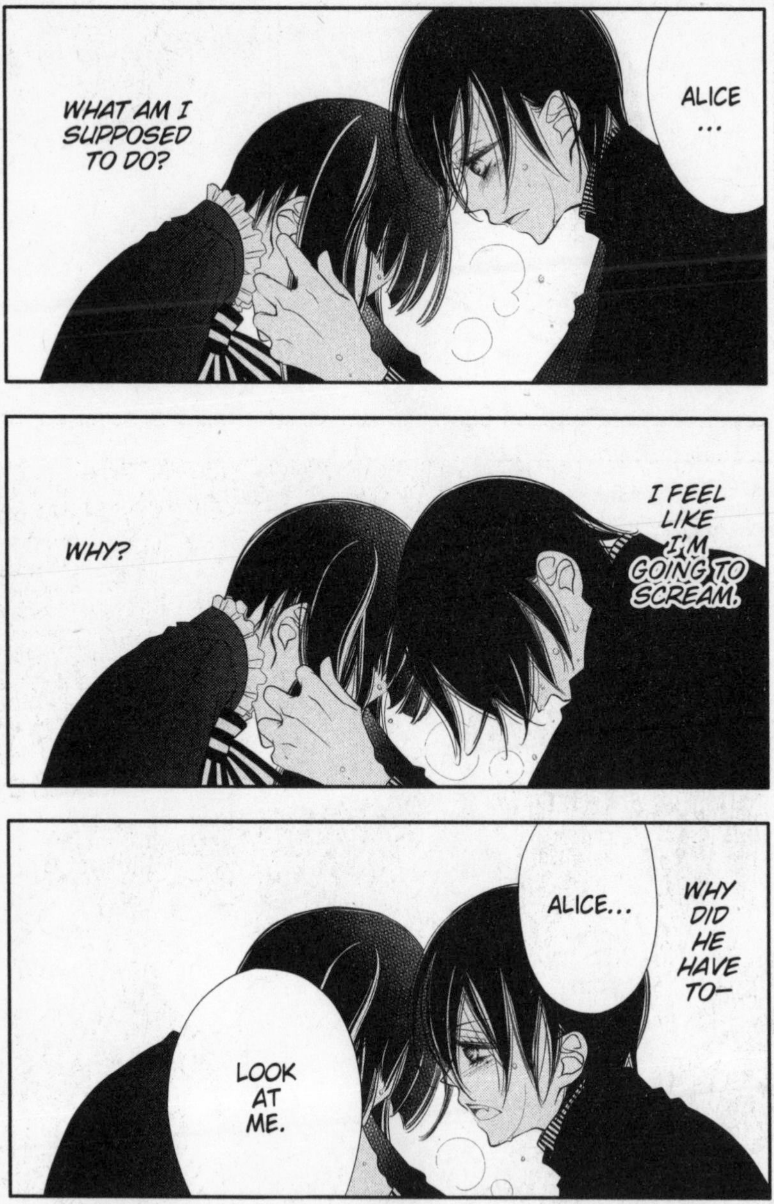
ALICE...
WHAT AM I SUPPOSED TO DO?
I FEEL LIKE I'M GOING TO SCREAM.
WHY?
WHY DID HE HAVE TO—
ALICE...
LOOK AT ME.

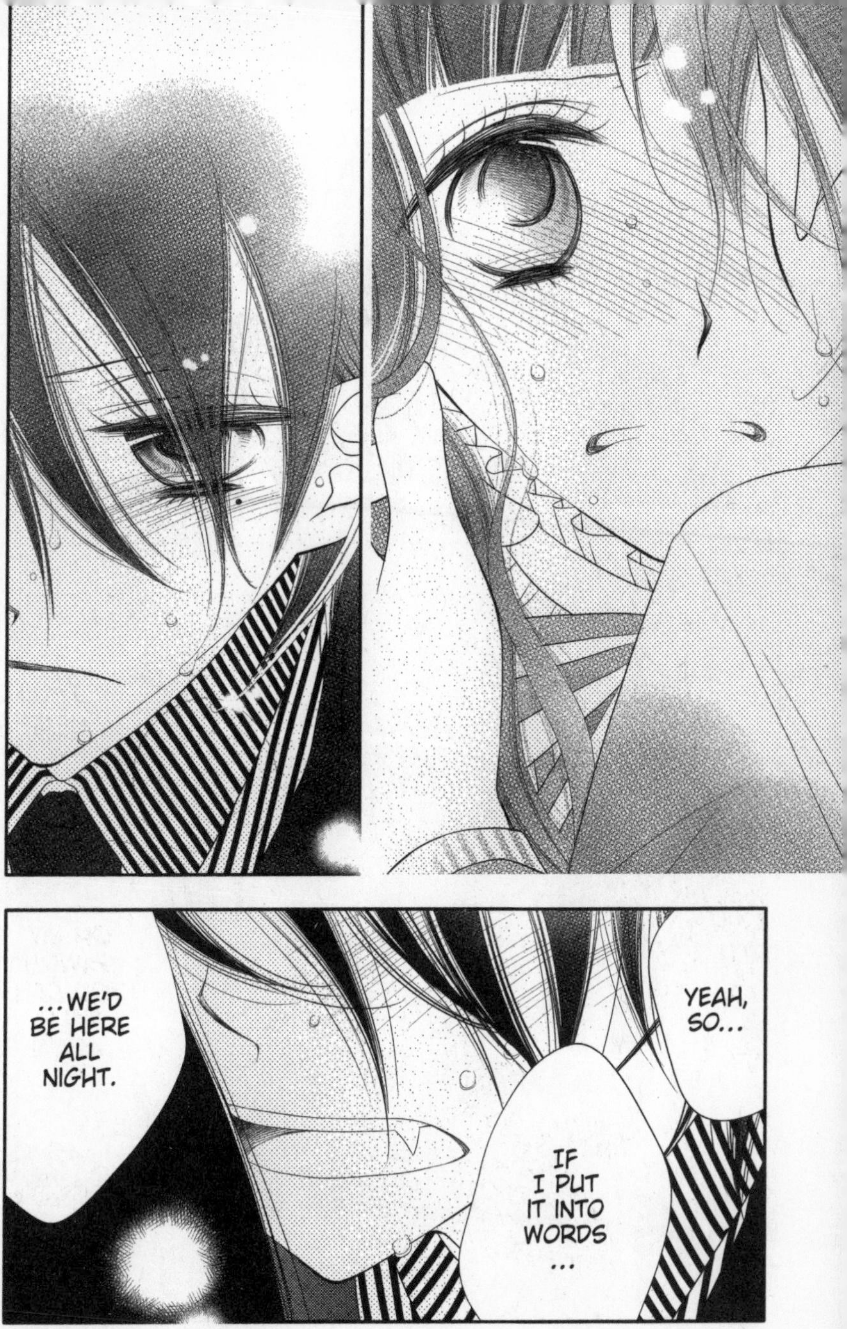
YEAH, SO...
IF I PUT IT INTO WORDS...
...WE'D BE HERE ALL NIGHT.

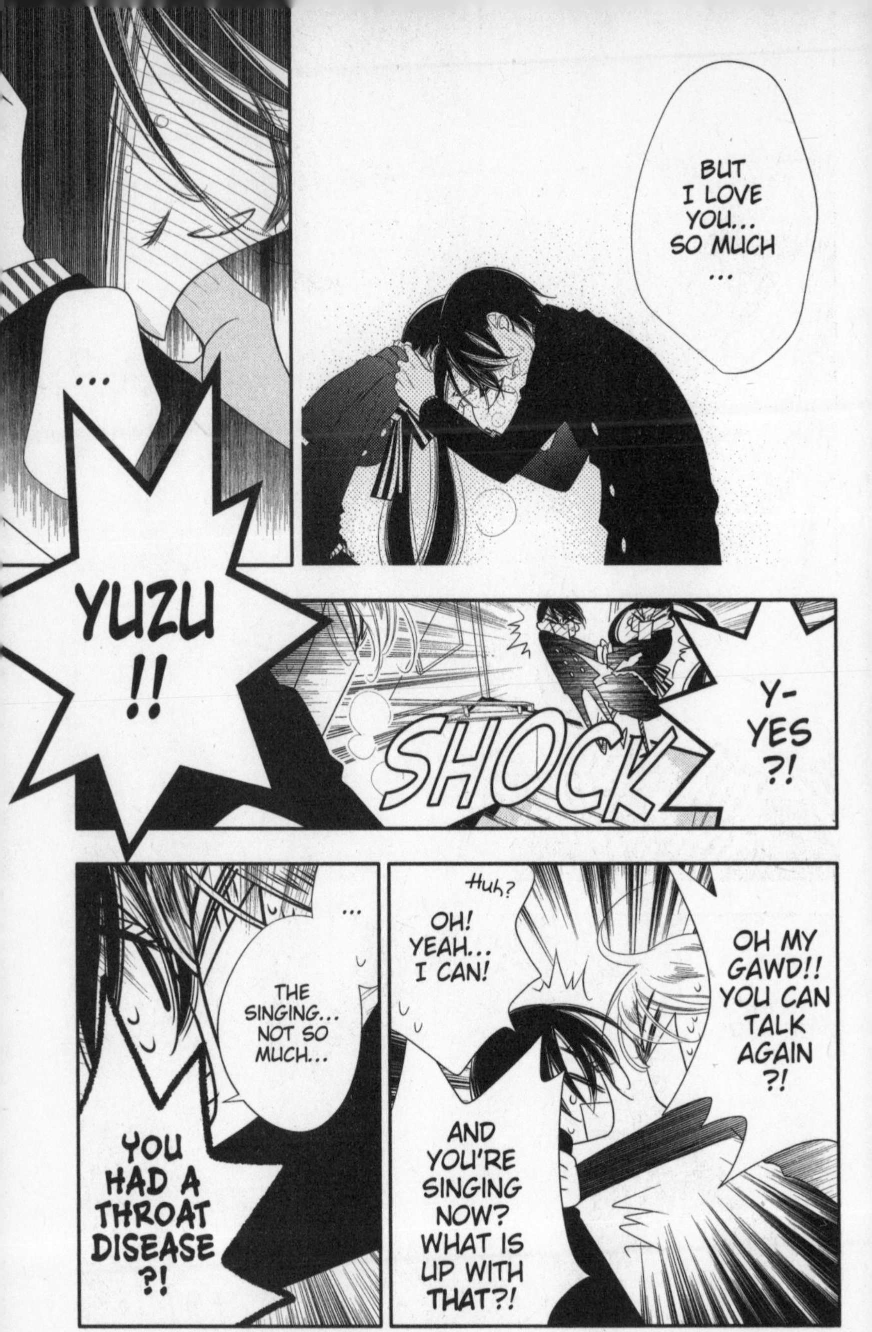

BUT I LOVE YOU... SO MUCH ...
...
YUZU !!
Y- YES ?!
SHOCK
OH MY GAWD!! YOU CAN TALK AGAIN ?!
Huh?
OH! YEAH... I CAN!
AND YOU'RE SINGING NOW? WHAT IS UP WITH THAT?!
...
THE SINGING... NOT SO MUCH...
YOU HAD A THROAT DISEASE ?!

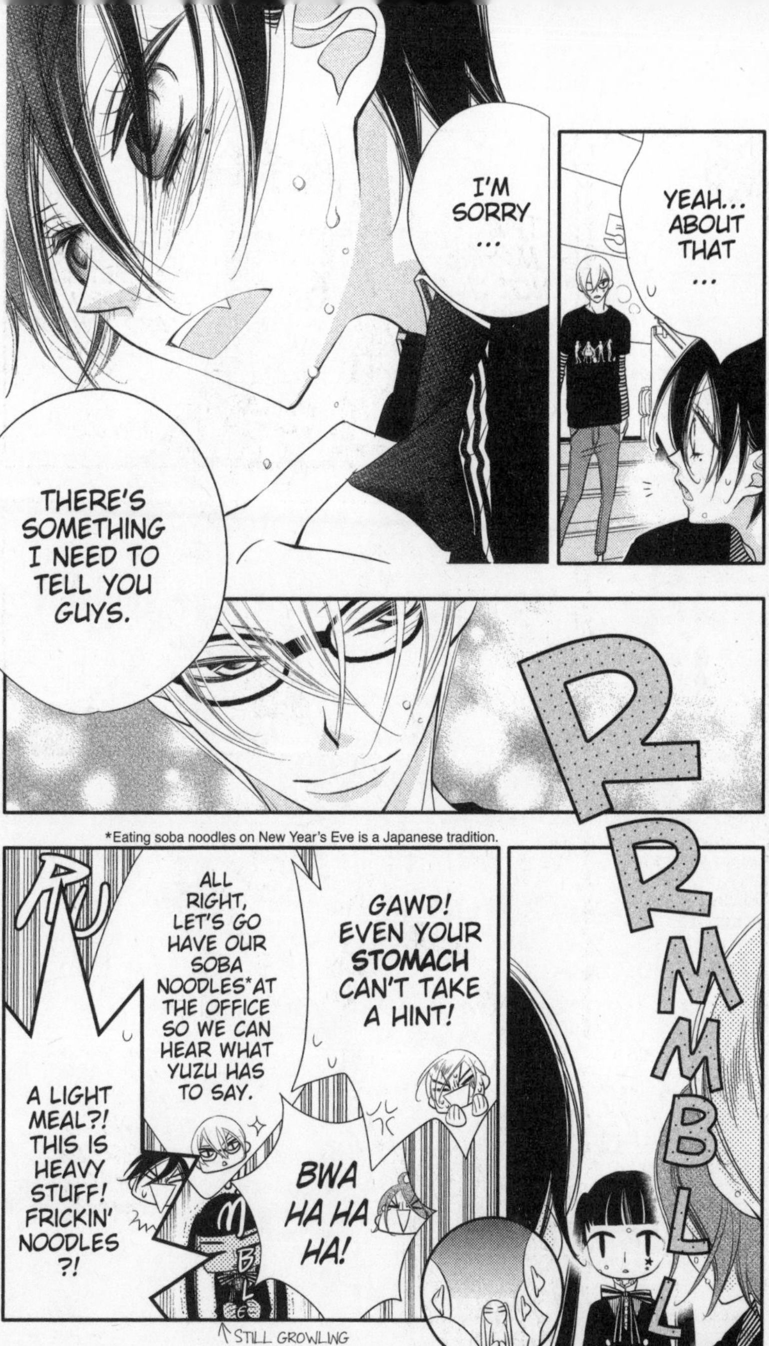
YEAH... ABOUT THAT...
I'M SORRY...
THERE'S SOMETHING I NEED TO TELL YOU GUYS.
RRRMMMBLL
GAWD! EVEN YOUR STOMACH CAN'T TAKE A HINT!
ALL RIGHT, LET'S GO HAVE OUR SOBA NOODLES* AT THE OFFICE SO WE CAN HEAR WHAT YUZU HAS TO SAY.
BWA HA HA HA!
RU
A LIGHT MEAL?! THIS IS HEAVY STUFF! FRICKIN' NOODLES?!
MBLE
↑STILL GROWLING
*Eating soba noodles on New Year's Eve is a Japanese tradition.

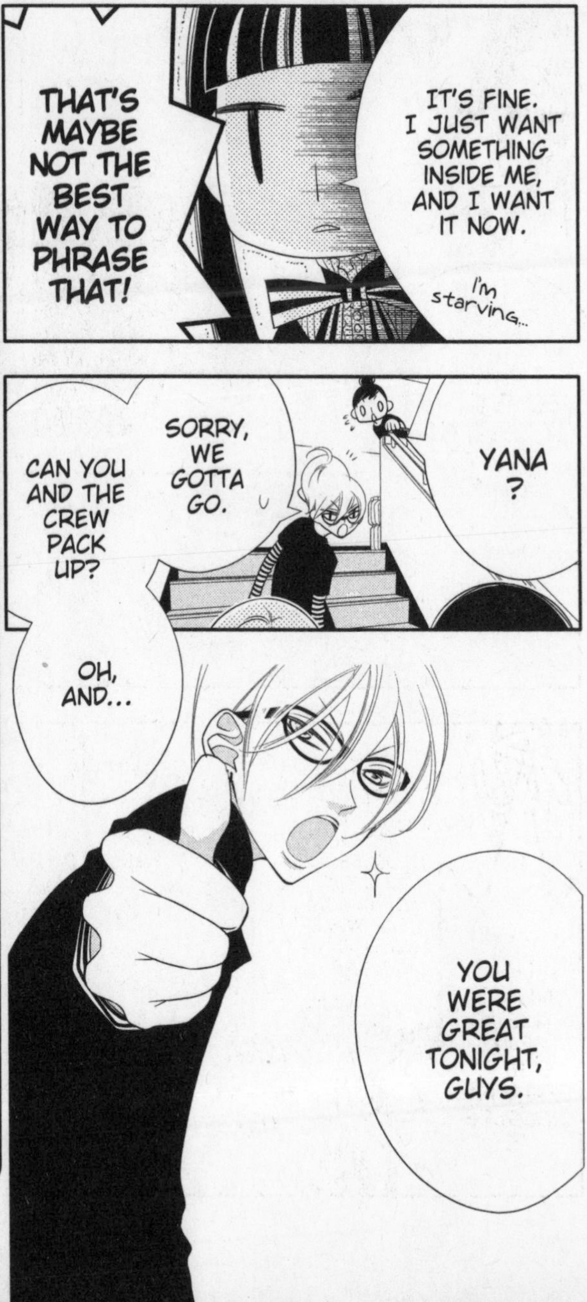
IT'S FINE. I JUST WANT SOMETHING INSIDE ME, AND I WANT IT NOW.
I'm starving...
THAT'S MAYBE NOT THE BEST WAY TO PHRASE THAT!
YANA?
SORRY, WE GOTTA GO.
CAN YOU AND THE CREW PACK UP?
OH, AND...
YOU WERE GREAT TONIGHT, GUYS.

2

Lately I've had a cough that I just can't shake, so I went to see a specialist. They had me take an allergy test, just in case, and it revealed that I do have an allergy—to cats!

WHAAAT?!

Okay, it's true that when I'm at home my sinuses drive me crazy and then they clear up as soon as I leave the house, so the thought had crossed my mind, but I was still completely shocked to hear it.

(To be continued)

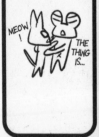

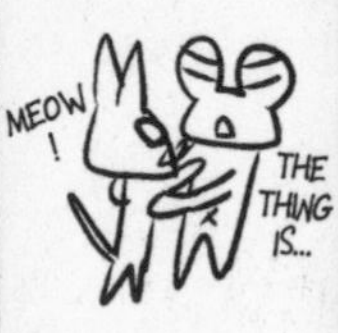
MEOW!
THE THING IS...

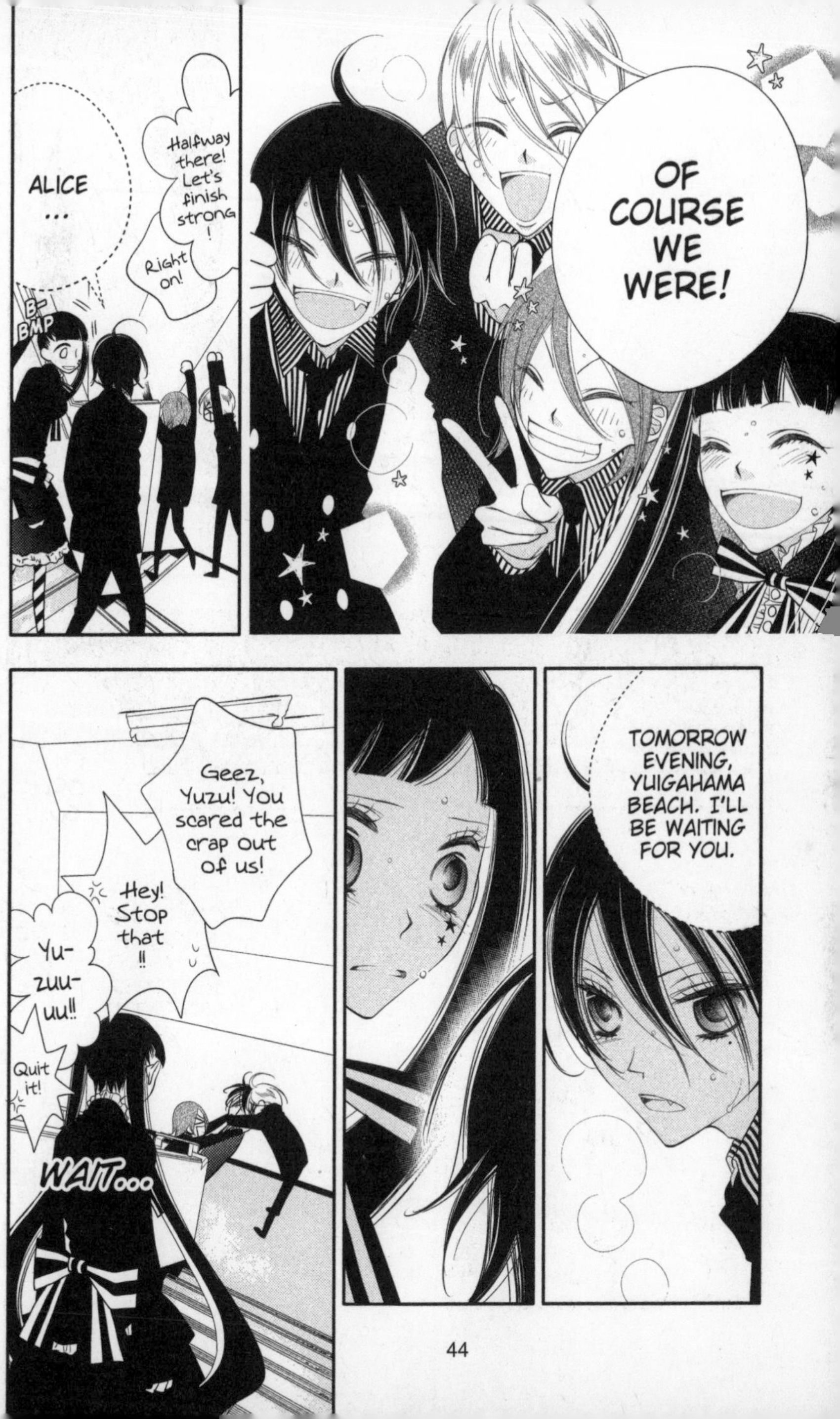
OF COURSE WE WERE!
Halfway there! Let's finish strong!
ALICE ...
Right on!
B-BMP
TOMORROW EVENING, YUIGAHAMA BEACH. I'LL BE WAITING FOR YOU.
Geez, Yuzu! You scared the crap out of us!
Hey! Stop that!!
Yu-zuu-uu!!
Quit it!
WAIT...

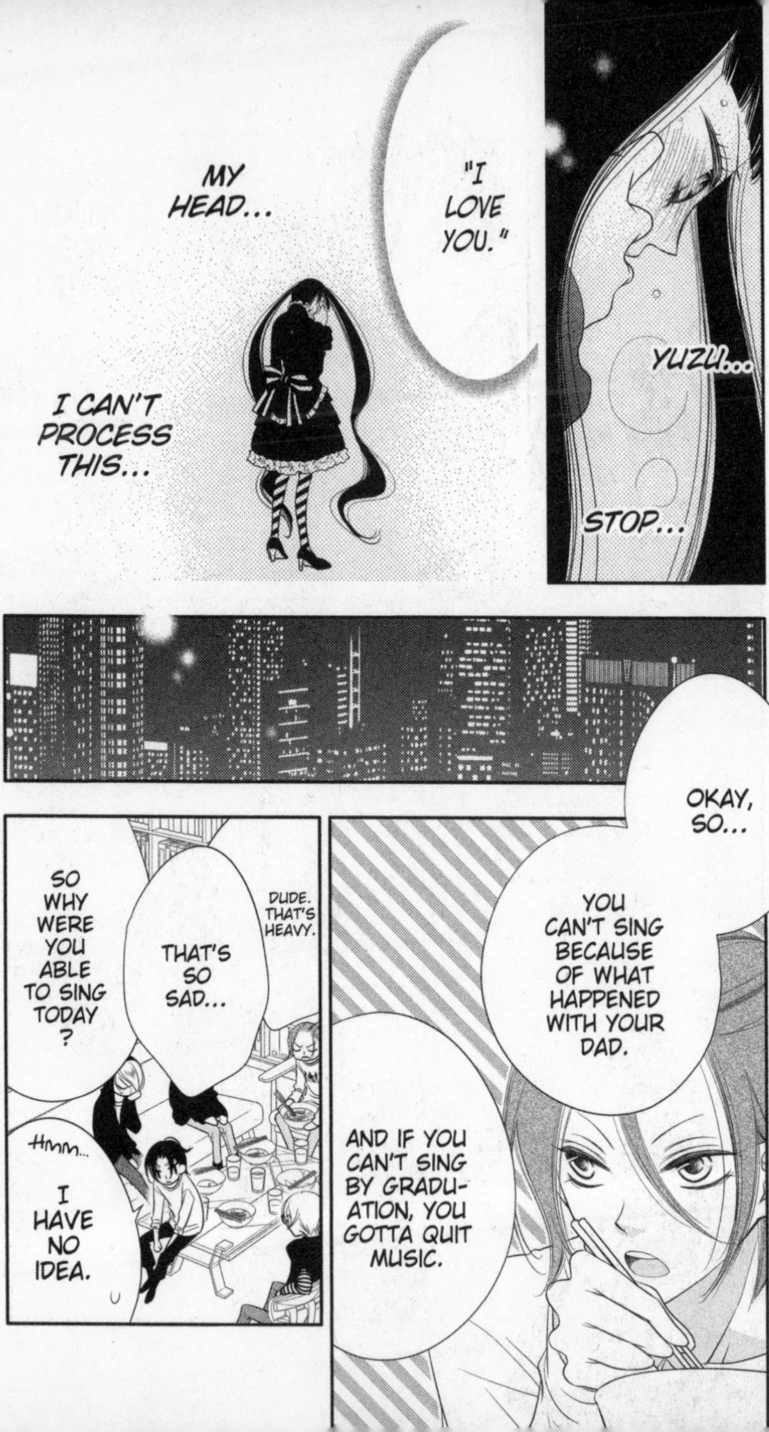
YUZU...
STOP...
"I LOVE YOU."
MY HEAD...
I CAN'T PROCESS THIS...
OKAY, SO...
YOU CAN'T SING BECAUSE OF WHAT HAPPENED WITH YOUR DAD.
AND IF YOU CAN'T SING BY GRADUATION, YOU GOTTA QUIT MUSIC.
DUDE. THAT'S HEAVY.
THAT'S SO SAD...
SO WHY WERE YOU ABLE TO SING TODAY?
Hmm...
I HAVE NO IDEA.

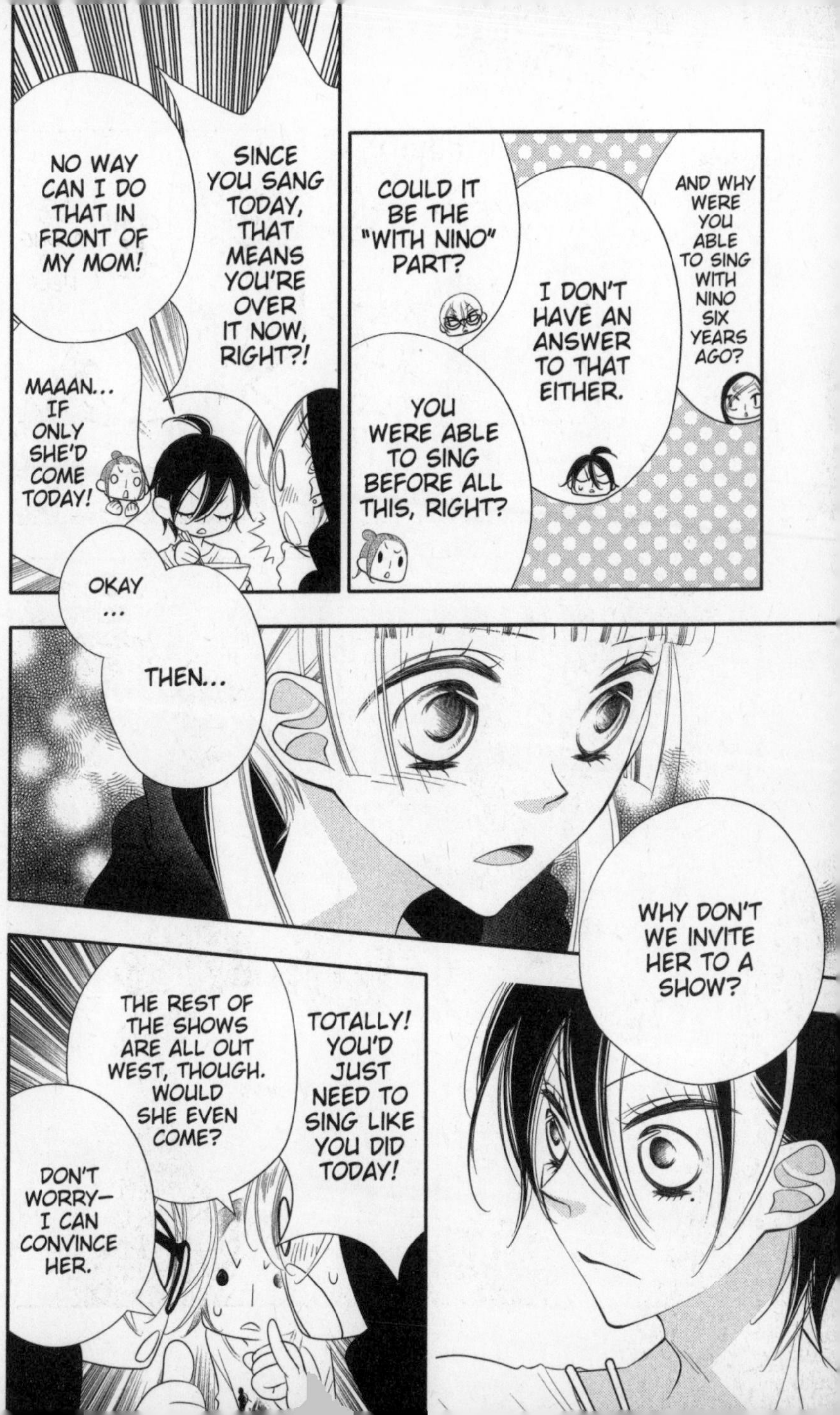
AND WHY WERE YOU ABLE TO SING WITH NINO SIX YEARS AGO?
I DON'T HAVE AN ANSWER TO THAT EITHER.
COULD IT BE THE "WITH NINO" PART?
YOU WERE ABLE TO SING BEFORE ALL THIS, RIGHT?
SINCE YOU SANG TODAY, THAT MEANS YOU'RE OVER IT NOW, RIGHT?!
NO WAY CAN I DO THAT IN FRONT OF MY MOM!
MAAAN... IF ONLY SHE'D COME TODAY!
OKAY ...
THEN...
WHY DON'T WE INVITE HER TO A SHOW?
TOTALLY! YOU'D JUST NEED TO SING LIKE YOU DID TODAY!
THE REST OF THE SHOWS ARE ALL OUT WEST, THOUGH. WOULD SHE EVEN COME?
DON'T WORRY— I CAN CONVINCE HER.

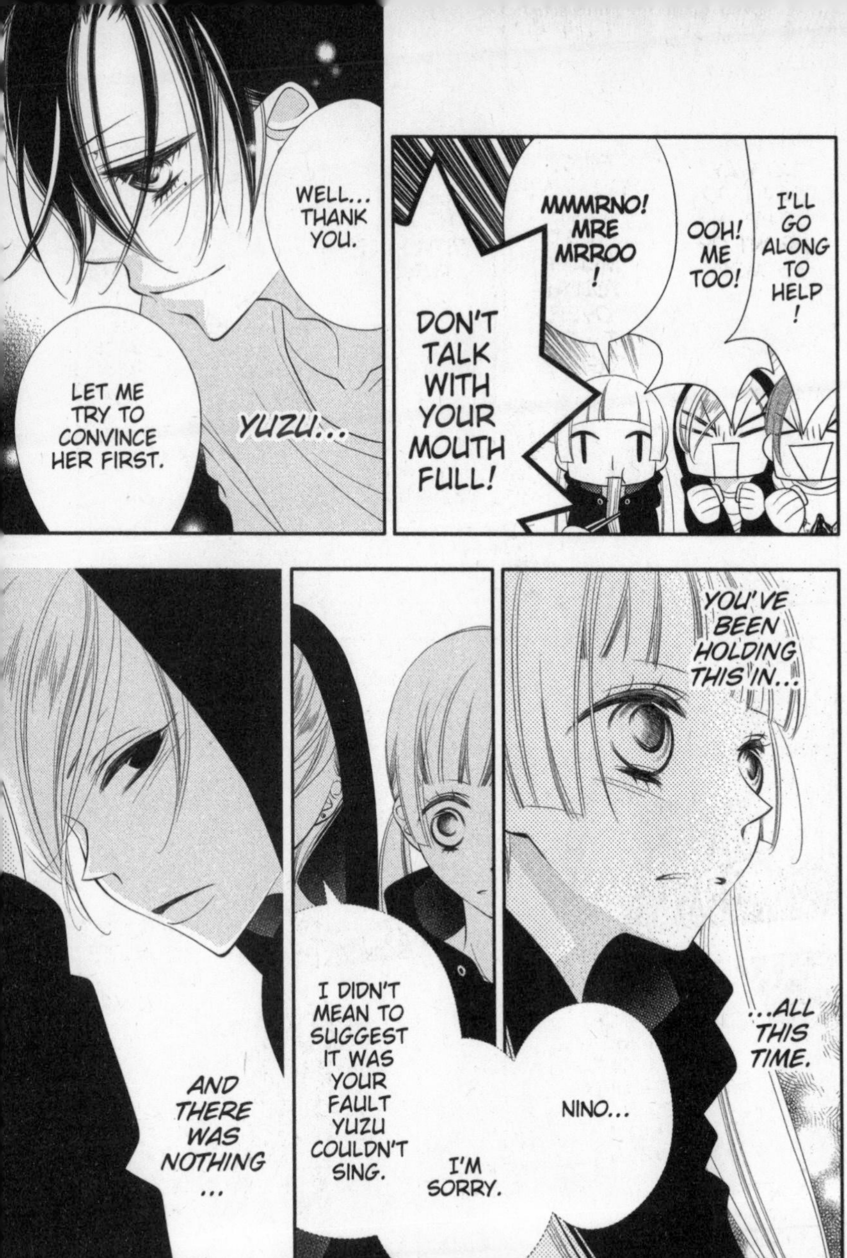
I'LL GO ALONG TO HELP!
OOH! ME TOO!
MMMRNO! MRE MRROO!
DON'T TALK WITH YOUR MOUTH FULL!
WELL... THANK YOU.
YUZU...
LET ME TRY TO CONVINCE HER FIRST.
YOU'VE BEEN HOLDING THIS IN...
...ALL THIS TIME.
NINO...
I'M SORRY.
I DIDN'T MEAN TO SUGGEST IT WAS YOUR FAULT YUZU COULDN'T SING.
AND THERE WAS NOTHING...

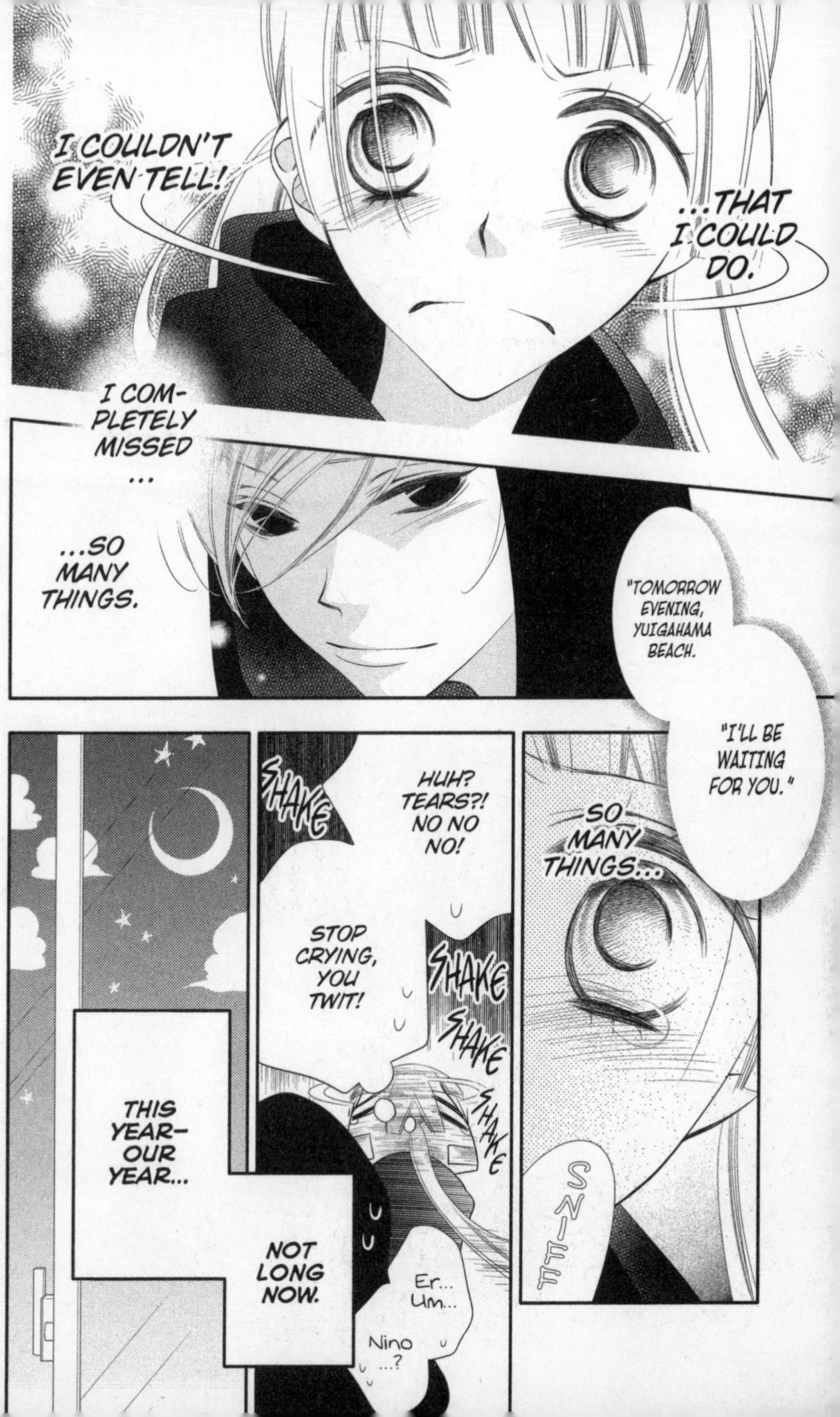
I COULDN'T EVEN TELL!
...THAT I COULD DO.
I COM-PLETELY MISSED ...
...SO MANY THINGS.
"TOMORROW EVENING, YUIGAHAMA BEACH.
"I'LL BE WAITING FOR YOU."
SO MANY THINGS...
SNIFF
SHAKE
HUH? TEARS?! NO NO NO!
STOP CRYING, YOU TWIT!
SHAKE
SHAKE
SHAKE
Er... Um...
Nino ...?
THIS YEAR— OUR YEAR...
NOT LONG NOW.

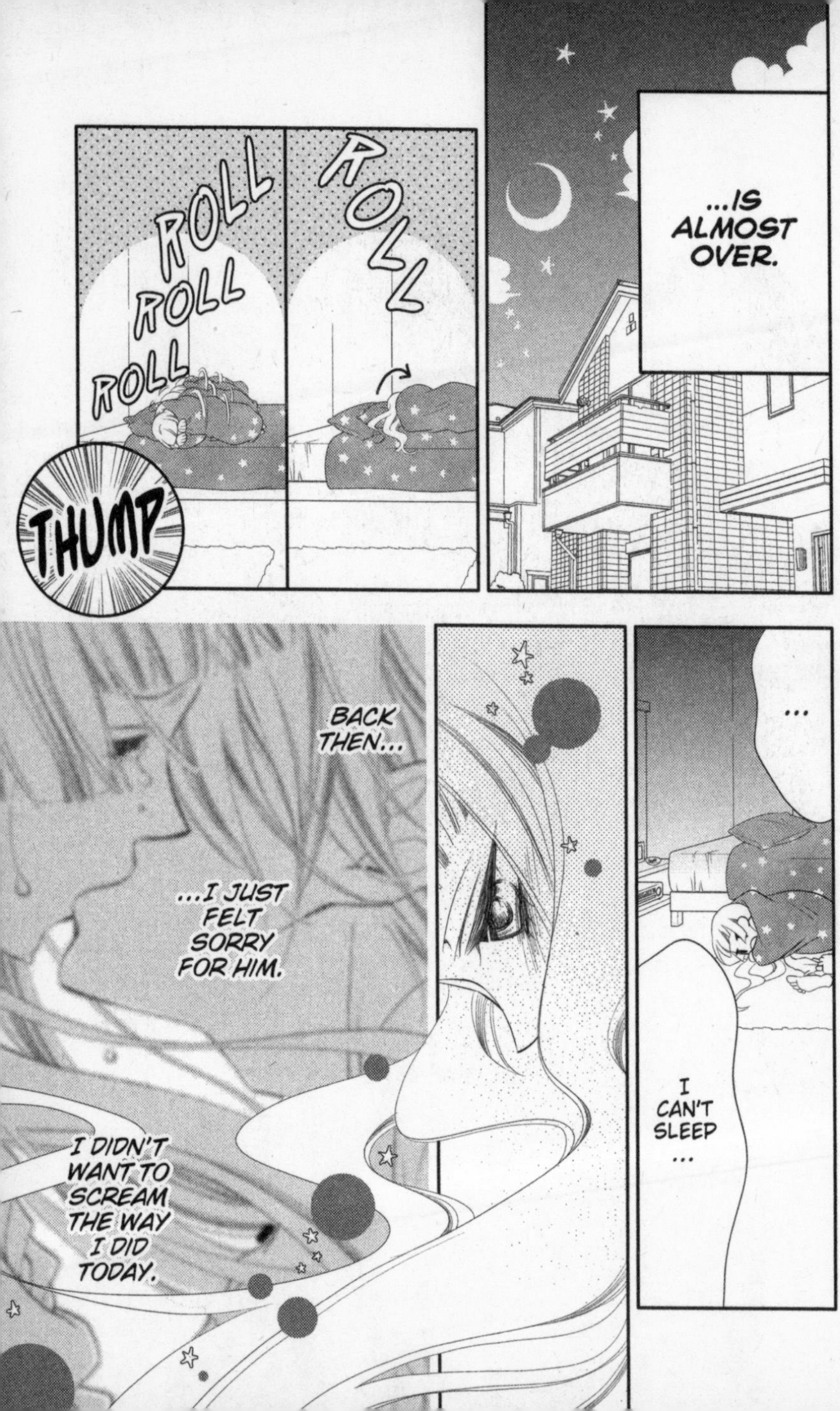
...IS ALMOST OVER.
ROLL
ROLL ROLL ROLL
THUMP
...
I CAN'T SLEEP ...
BACK THEN...
...I JUST FELT SORRY FOR HIM.
I DIDN'T WANT TO SCREAM THE WAY I DID TODAY.

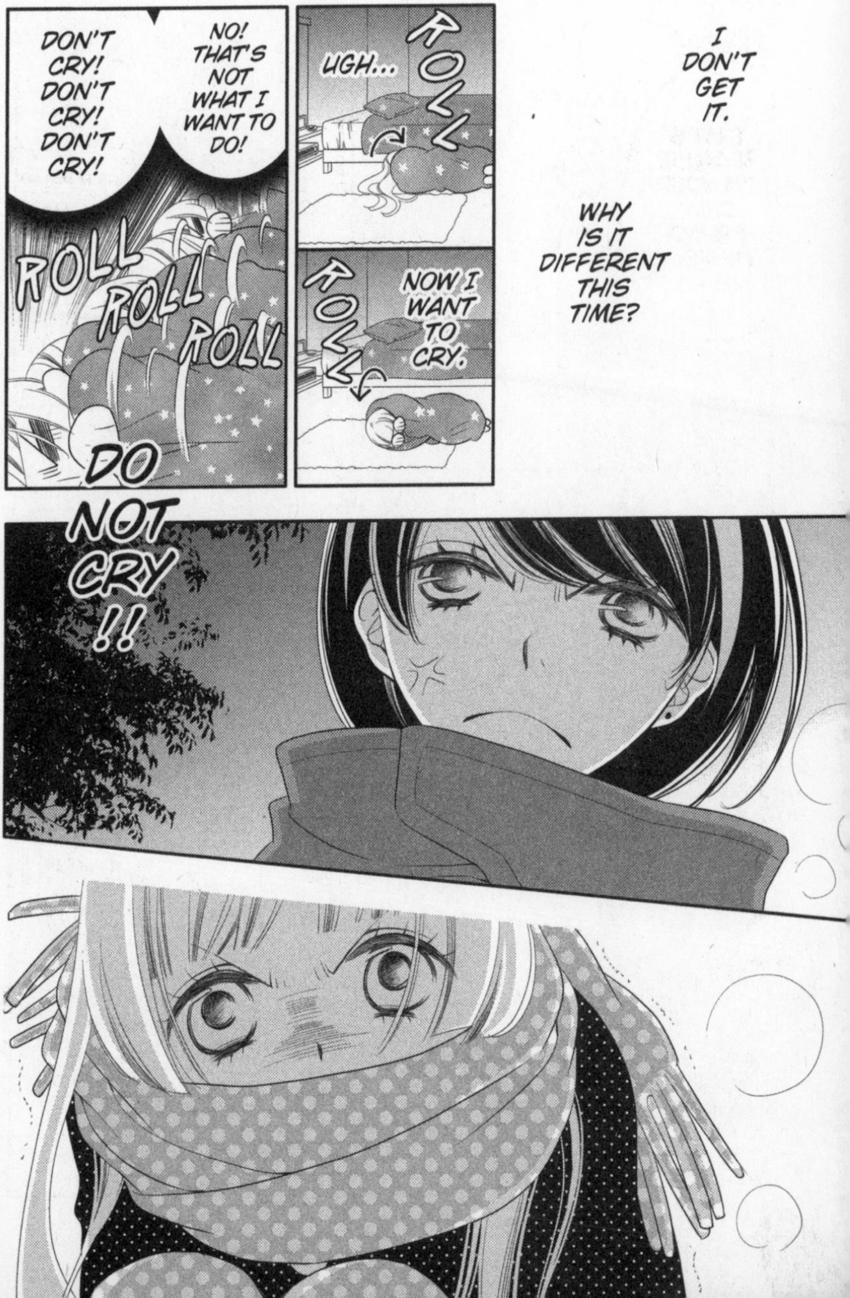
I DON'T GET IT.
WHY IS IT DIFFERENT THIS TIME?
UGH...
ROLL
NOW I WANT TO CRY.
ROLL
NO! THAT'S NOT WHAT I WANT TO DO!
DON'T CRY! DON'T CRY! DON'T CRY!
ROLL ROLL ROLL
DO NOT CRY!!

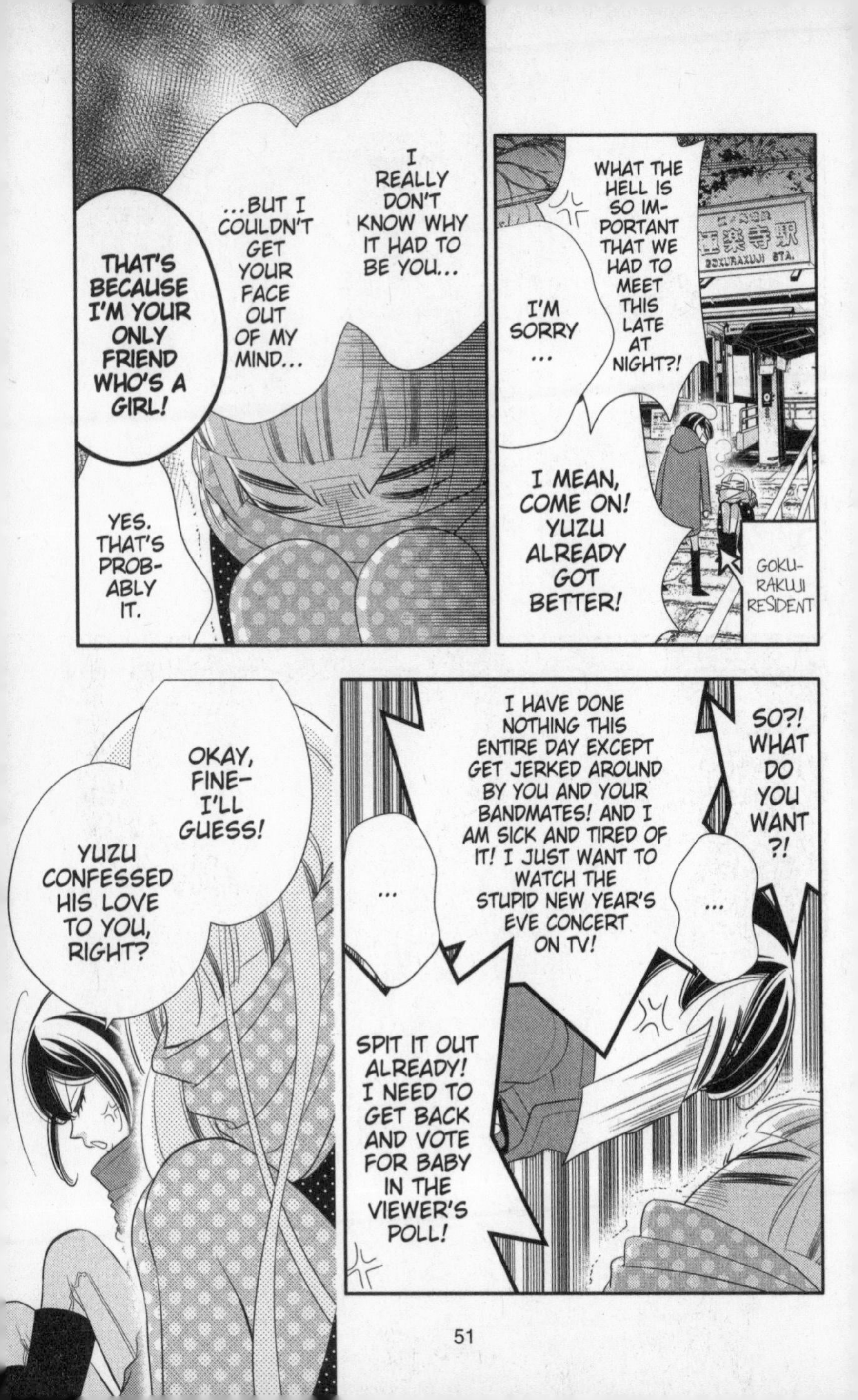
WHAT THE HELL IS SO IMPORTANT THAT WE HAD TO MEET THIS LATE AT NIGHT?!
I'M SORRY...
I MEAN, COME ON! YUZU ALREADY GOT BETTER!
GOKU-RAKUJI RESIDENT
I REALLY DON'T KNOW WHY IT HAD TO BE YOU...
...BUT I COULDN'T GET YOUR FACE OUT OF MY MIND...
THAT'S BECAUSE I'M YOUR ONLY FRIEND WHO'S A GIRL!
YES. THAT'S PROBABLY IT.
SO?! WHAT DO YOU WANT?!
...
I HAVE DONE NOTHING THIS ENTIRE DAY EXCEPT GET JERKED AROUND BY YOU AND YOUR BANDMATES! AND I AM SICK AND TIRED OF IT! I JUST WANT TO WATCH THE STUPID NEW YEAR'S EVE CONCERT ON TV!
...
SPIT IT OUT ALREADY! I NEED TO GET BACK AND VOTE FOR BABY IN THE VIEWER'S POLL!
OKAY, FINE— I'LL GUESS!
YUZU CONFESSED HIS LOVE TO YOU, RIGHT?

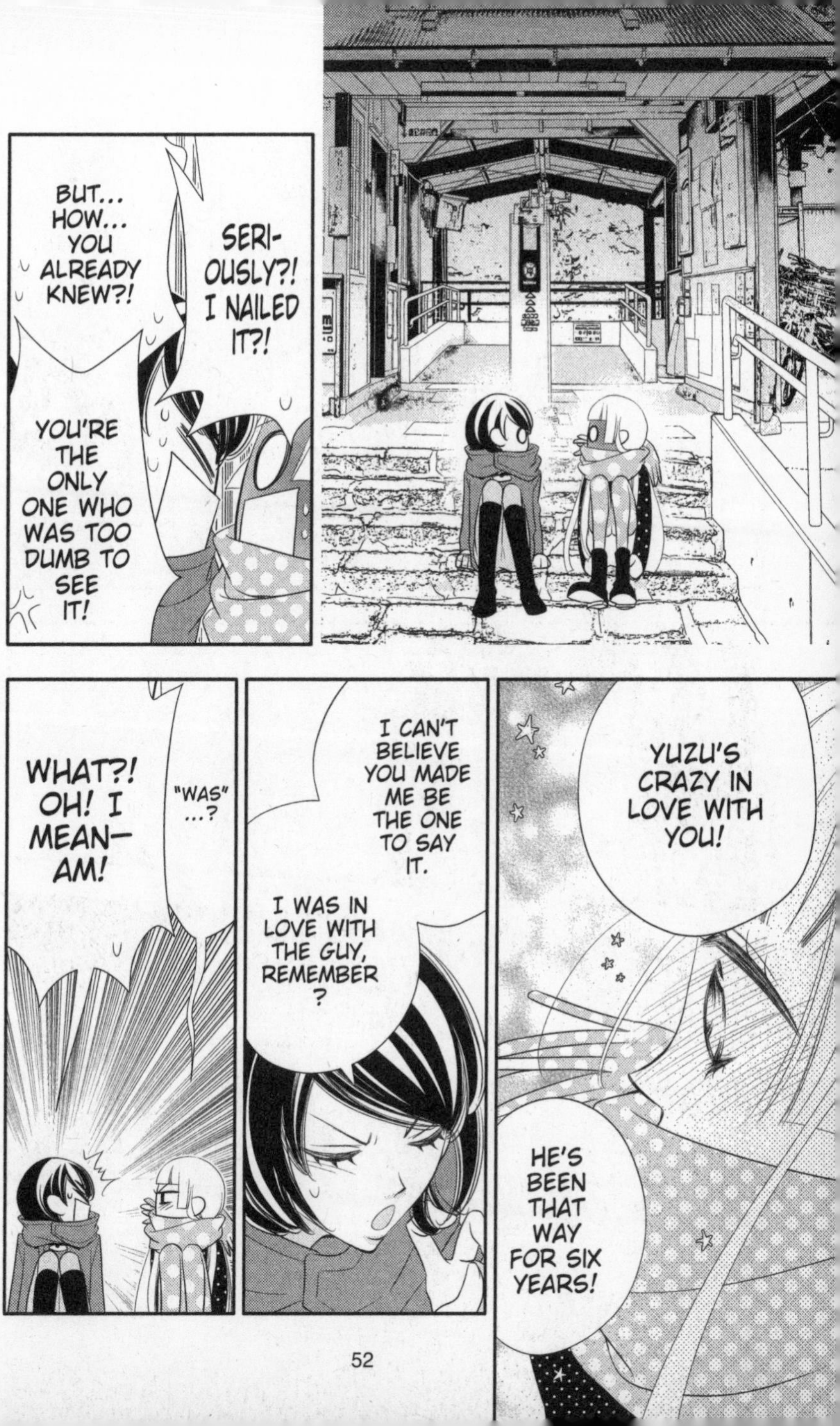
SERI-OUSLY?! I NAILED IT?!
BUT... HOW... YOU ALREADY KNEW?!
YOU'RE THE ONLY ONE WHO WAS TOO DUMB TO SEE IT!
YUZU'S CRAZY IN LOVE WITH YOU!
HE'S BEEN THAT WAY FOR SIX YEARS!
I CAN'T BELIEVE YOU MADE ME BE THE ONE TO SAY IT.
I WAS IN LOVE WITH THE GUY, REMEMBER?
"WAS" ...?
WHAT?! OH! I MEAN—AM!

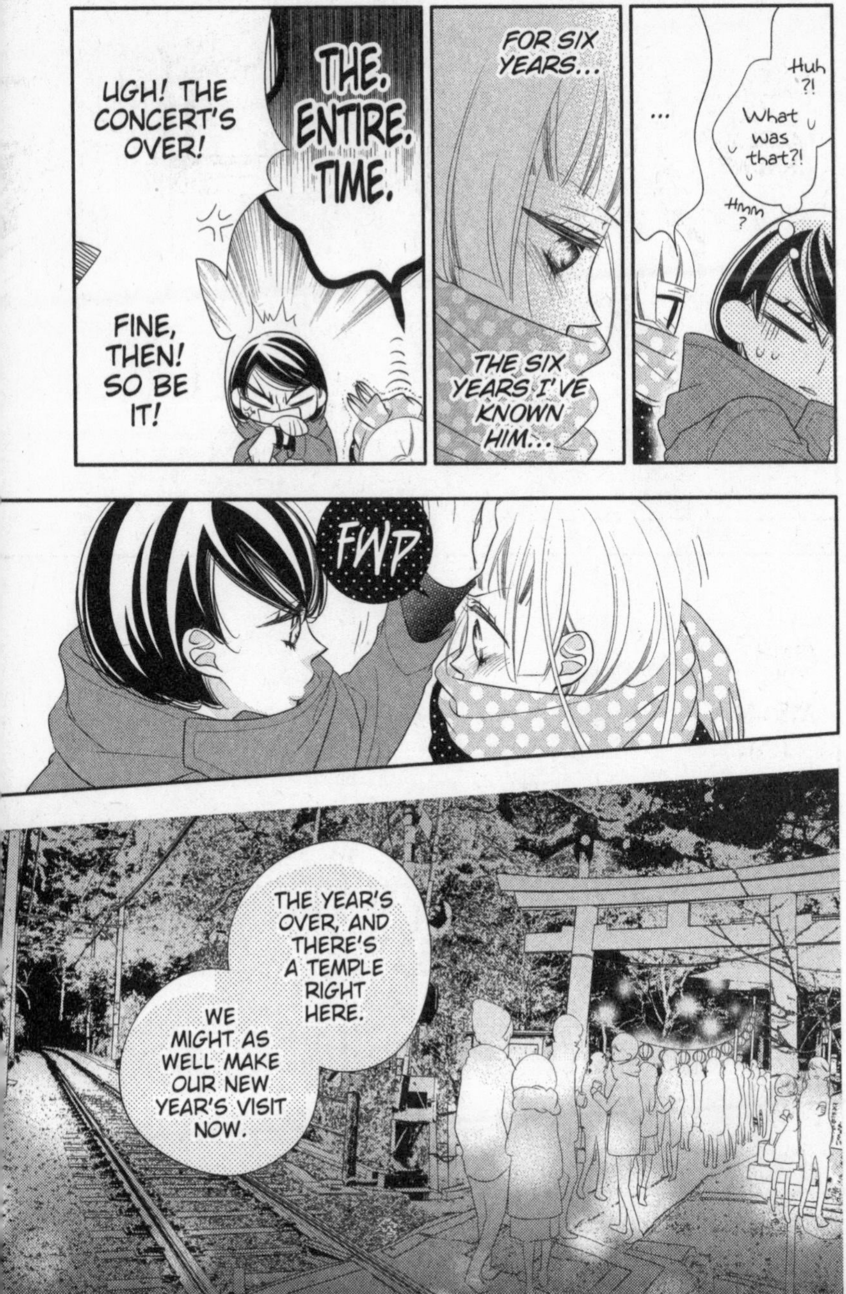
Huh?!
What was that?!
...
Hmm?
FOR SIX YEARS...
THE SIX YEARS I'VE KNOWN HIM...
THE. ENTIRE. TIME.
UGH! THE CONCERT'S OVER!
FINE, THEN! SO BE IT!
FWP
THE YEAR'S OVER, AND THERE'S A TEMPLE RIGHT HERE.
WE MIGHT AS WELL MAKE OUR NEW YEAR'S VISIT NOW.

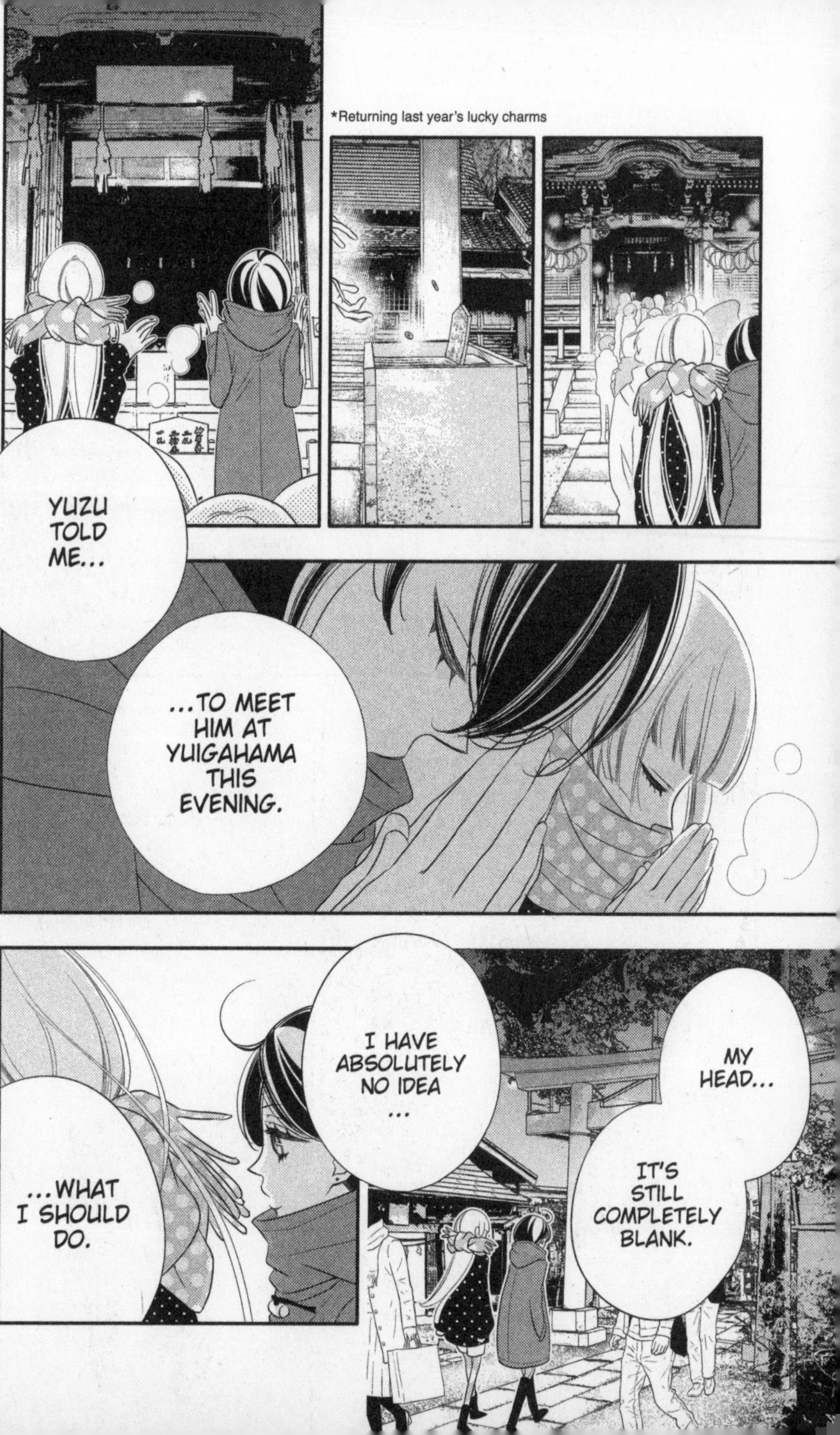
*Returning last year's lucky charms
YUZU TOLD ME...
...TO MEET HIM AT YUIGAHAMA THIS EVENING.
MY HEAD...
IT'S STILL COMPLETELY BLANK.
I HAVE ABSOLUTELY NO IDEA ...
...WHAT I SHOULD DO.

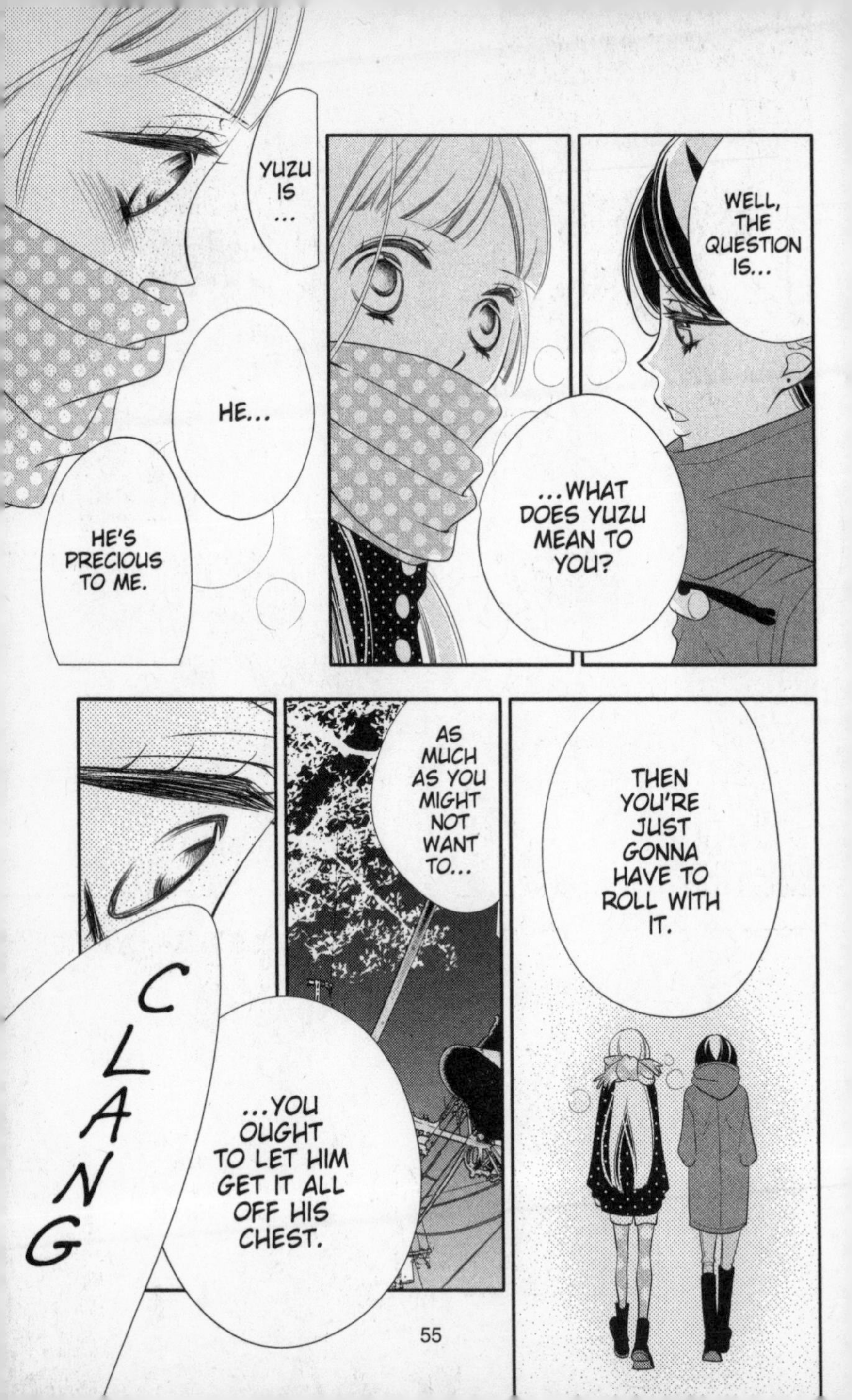
WELL, THE QUESTION IS...
...WHAT DOES YUZU MEAN TO YOU?
YUZU IS ...
HE...
HE'S PRECIOUS TO ME.
THEN YOU'RE JUST GONNA HAVE TO ROLL WITH IT.
AS MUCH AS YOU MIGHT NOT WANT TO...
...YOU OUGHT TO LET HIM GET IT ALL OFF HIS CHEST.
CLANG

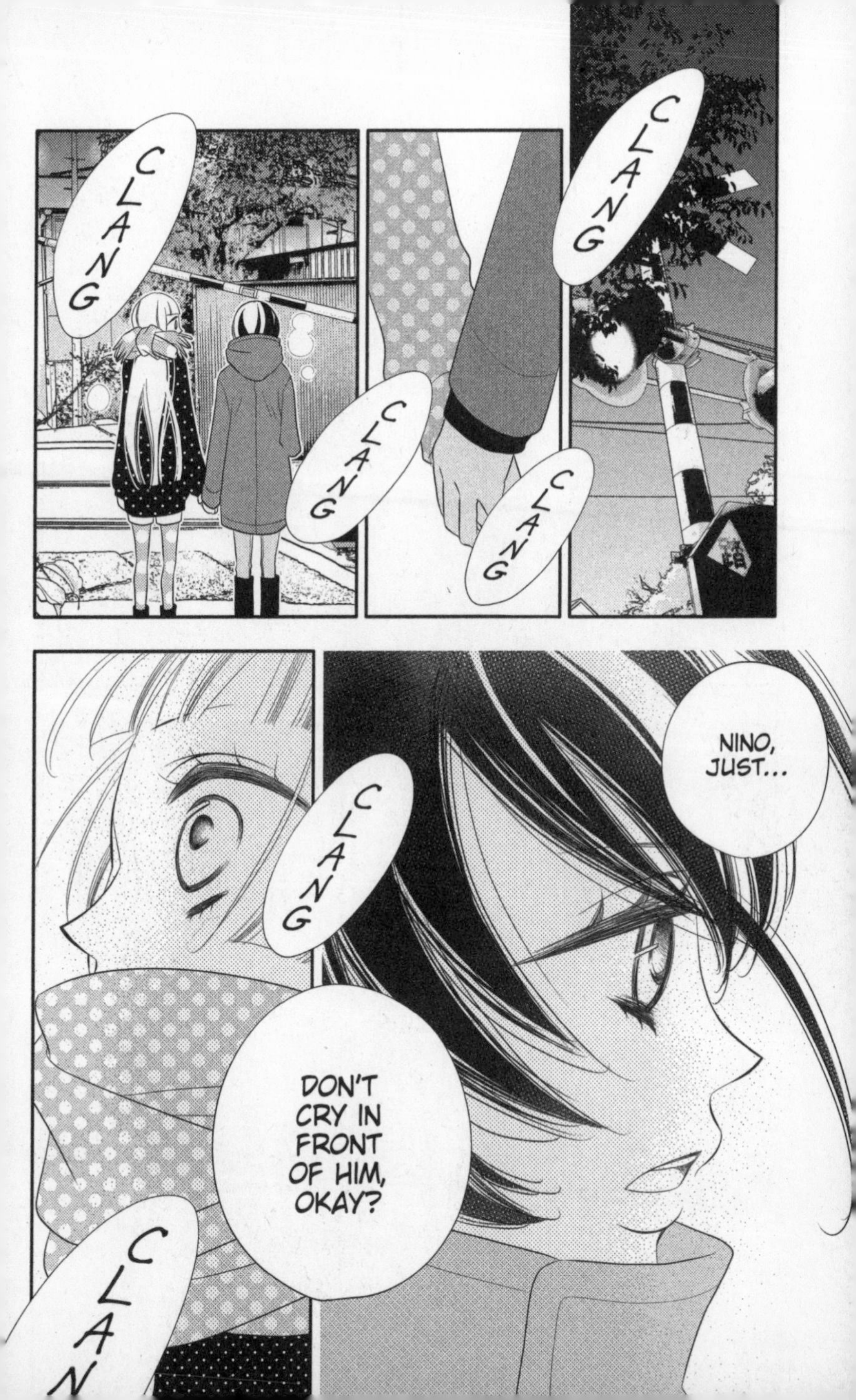
CLANG
CLANG
CLANG
CLANG
NINO, JUST...
DON'T CRY IN FRONT OF HIM, OKAY?
CLANG
CLAN

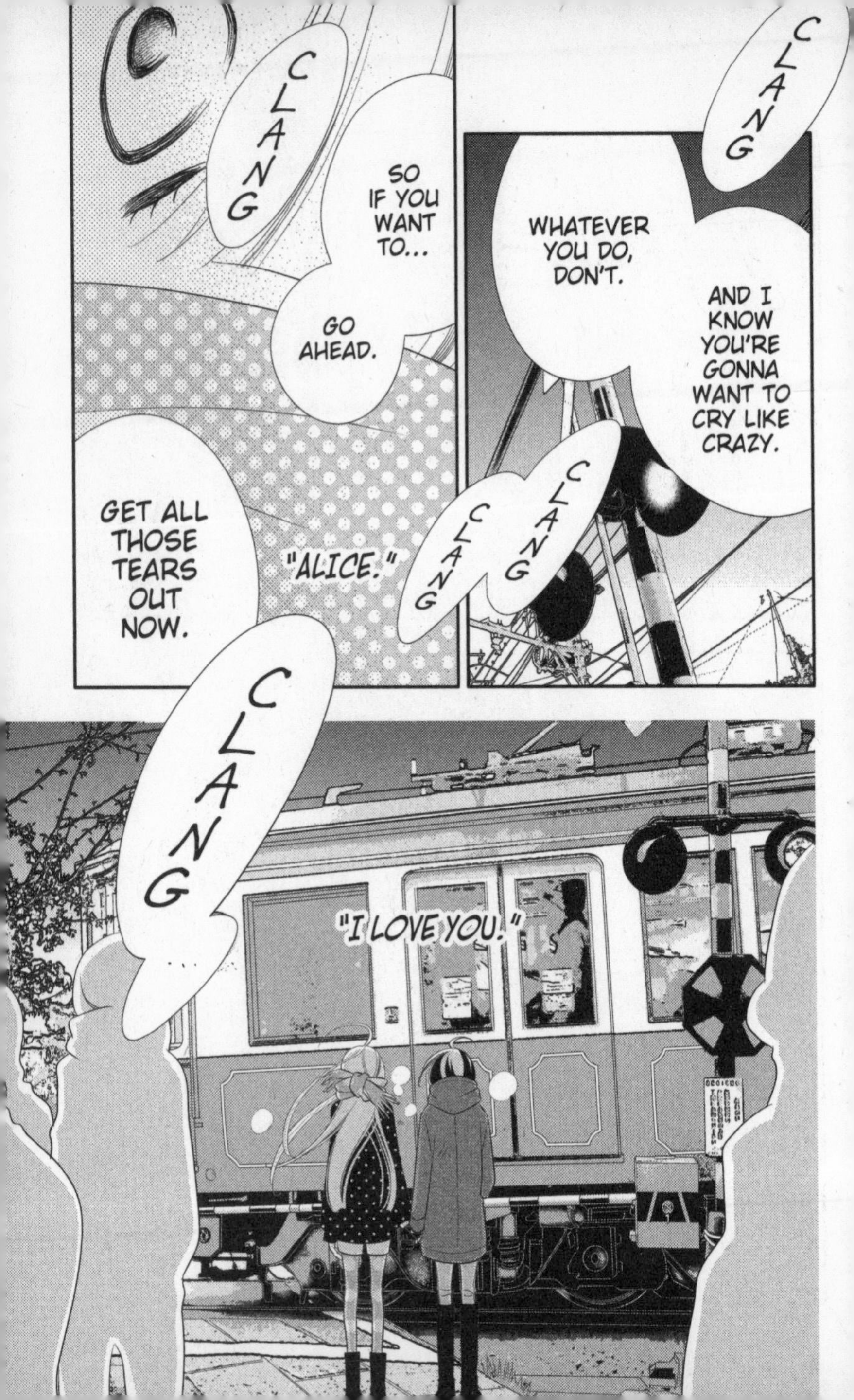
CLANG
WHATEVER YOU DO, DON'T.
AND I KNOW YOU'RE GONNA WANT TO CRY LIKE CRAZY.
CLANG
CLANG
CLANG
SO IF YOU WANT TO...
GO AHEAD.
"ALICE."
GET ALL THOSE TEARS OUT NOW.
CLANG
"I LOVE YOU."

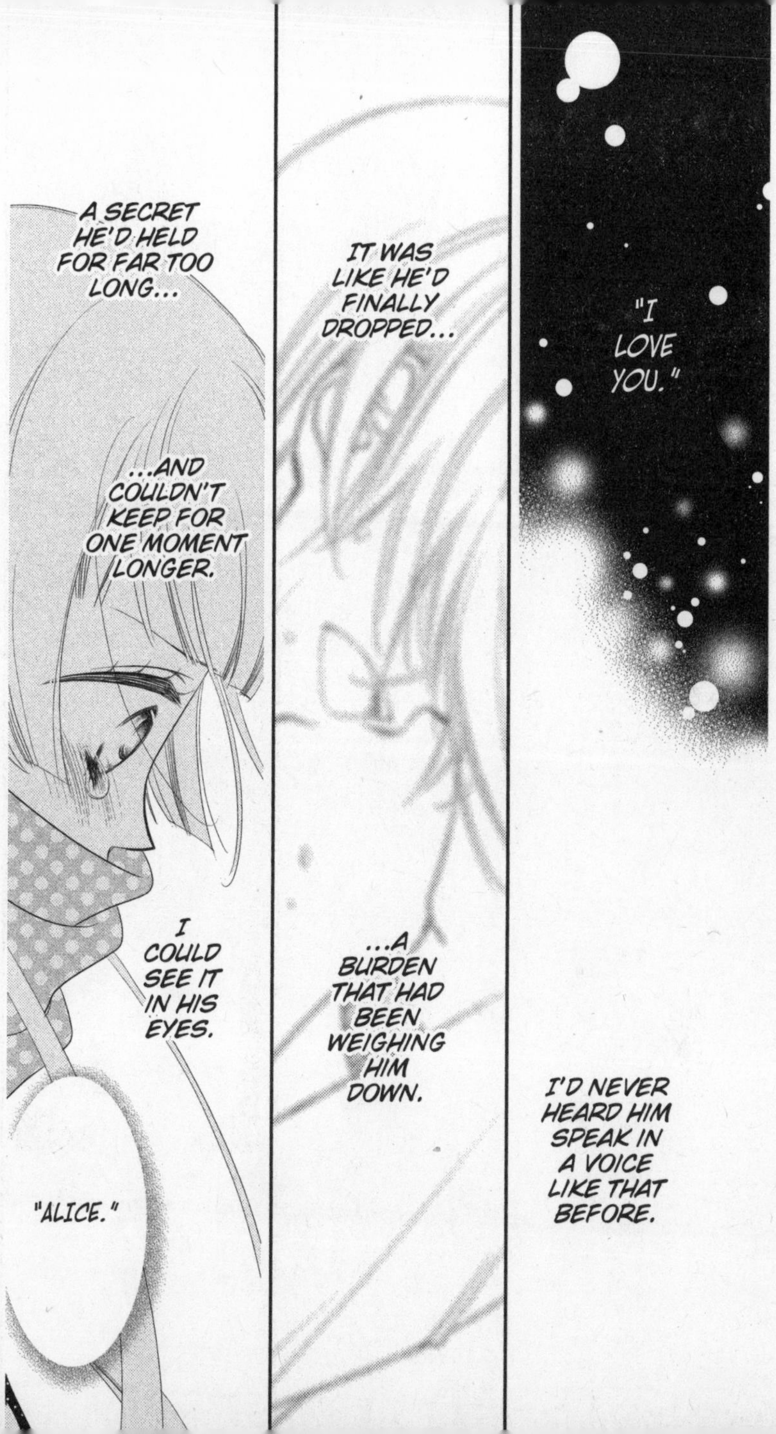
"I LOVE YOU."
I'D NEVER HEARD HIM SPEAK IN A VOICE LIKE THAT BEFORE.
IT WAS LIKE HE'D FINALLY DROPPED...
...A BURDEN THAT HAD BEEN WEIGHING HIM DOWN.
A SECRET HE'D HELD FOR FAR TOO LONG...
...AND COULDN'T KEEP FOR ONE MOMENT LONGER.
I COULD SEE IT IN HIS EYES.
"ALICE."

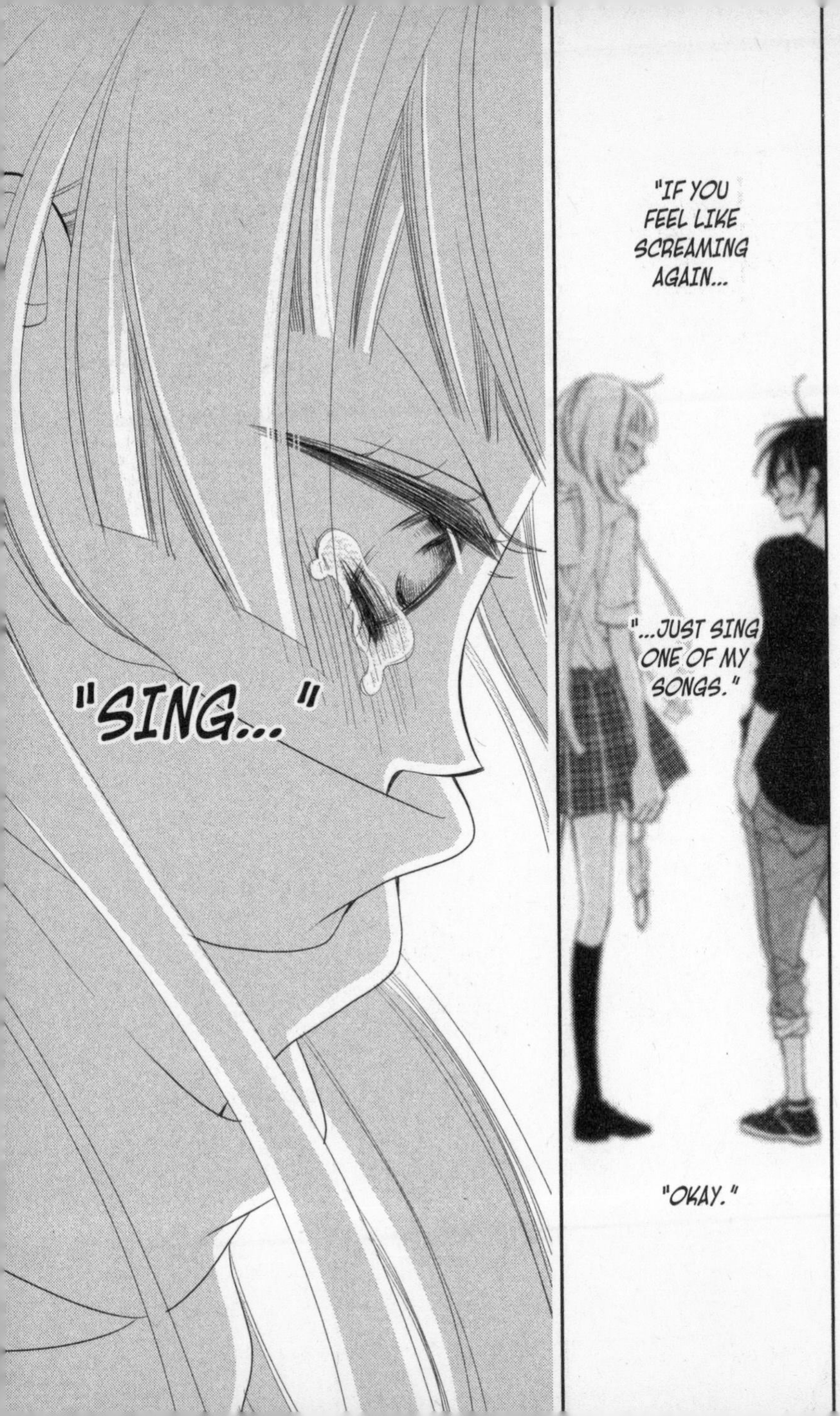
"IF YOU FEEL LIKE SCREAMING AGAIN...
"...JUST SING ONE OF MY SONGS."
"OKAY."
"SING..."

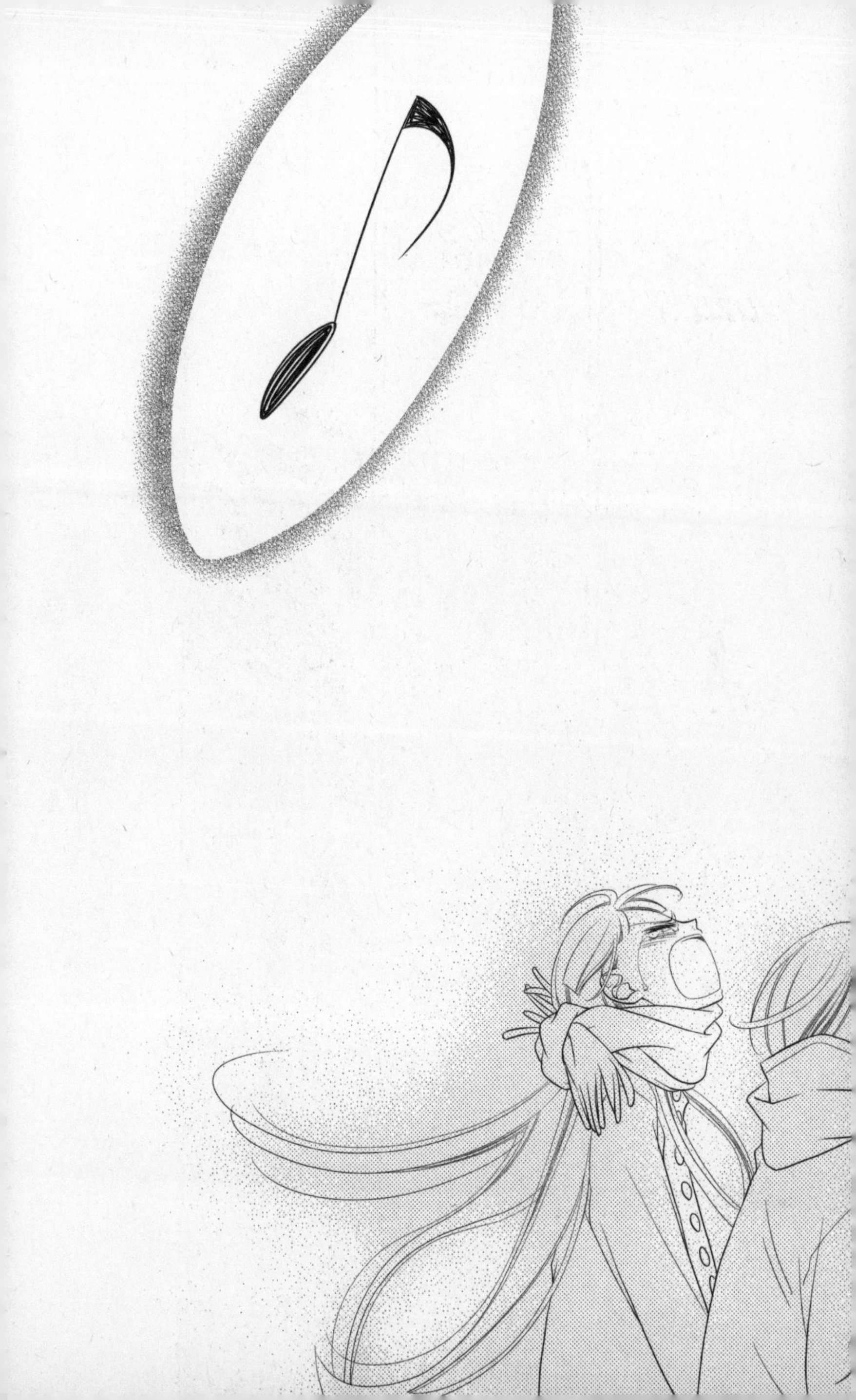

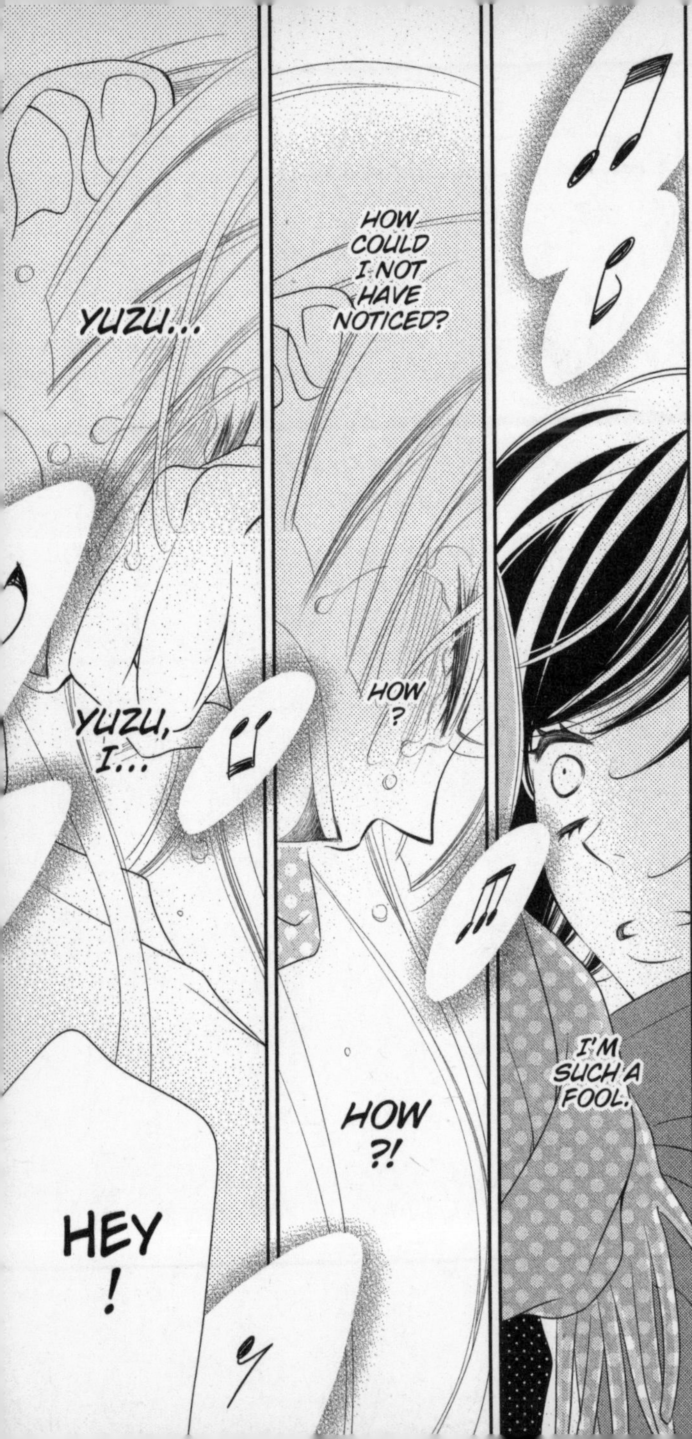
I'M SUCH A FOOL.
HOW COULD I NOT HAVE NOTICED?
HOW?
HOW?!
YUZU...
YUZU, I...
HEY!

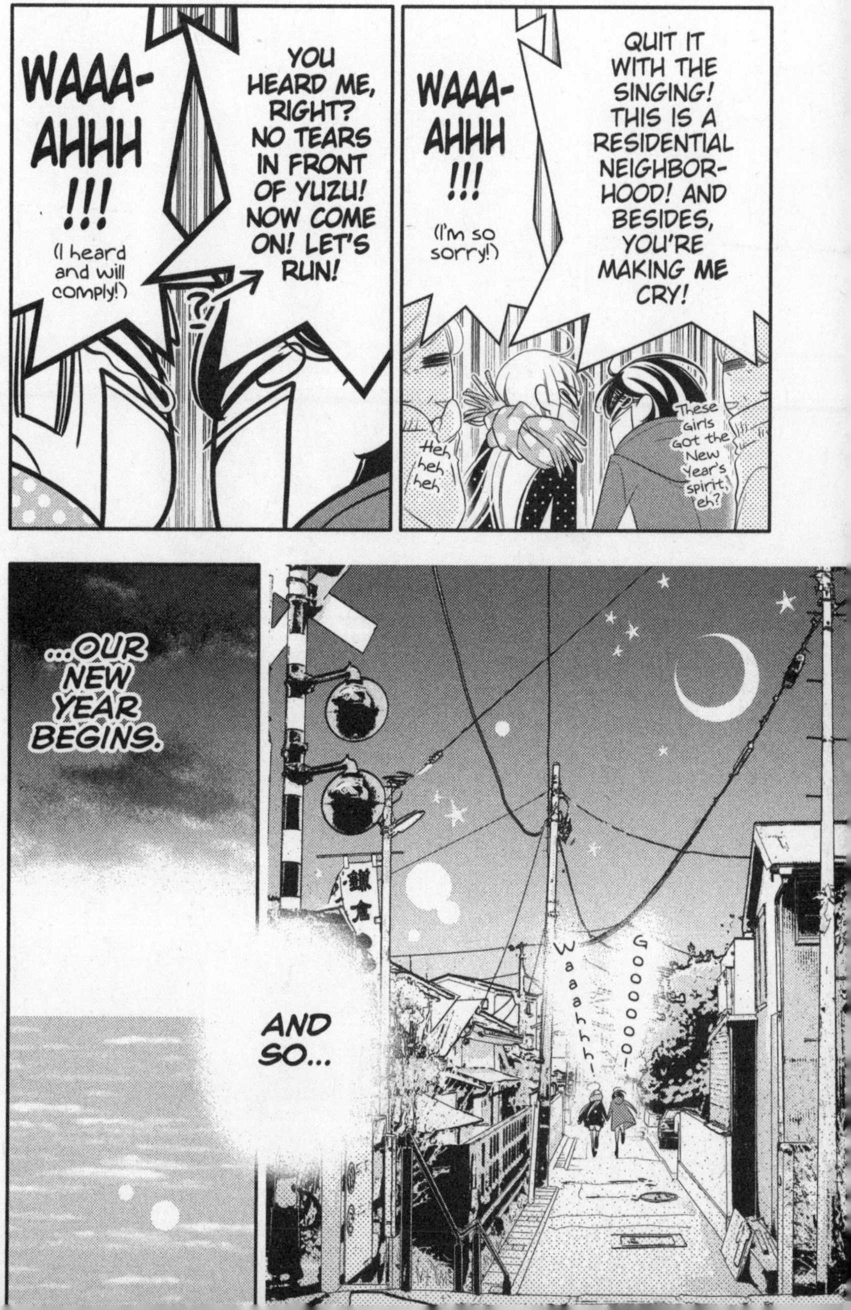
QUIT IT WITH THE SINGING! THIS IS A RESIDENTIAL NEIGHBOR-HOOD! AND BESIDES, YOU'RE MAKING ME CRY!
WAAA-AHHH!!!
(I'm so sorry!)
These girls got the New Year's spirit, eh?
Heh heh heh
YOU HEARD ME, RIGHT? NO TEARS IN FRONT OF YUZU! NOW COME ON! LET'S RUN!
WAAA-AHHH!!!
(I heard and will comply!)
?
Gooooooo!
Waaahhh!
鎌倉
AND SO...
...OUR NEW YEAR BEGINS.

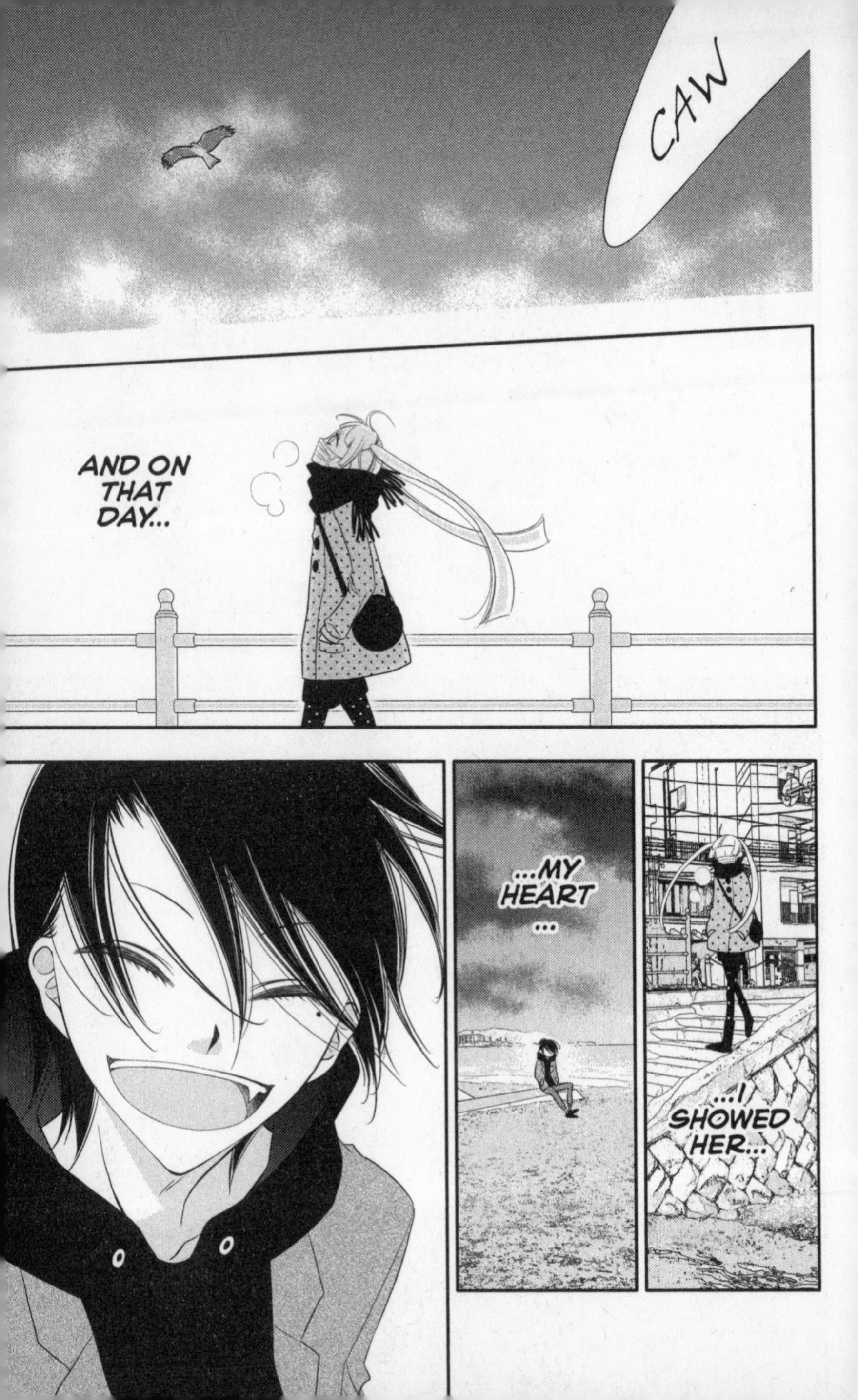
CAW
AND ON THAT DAY...
...I SHOWED HER...
...MY HEART ...

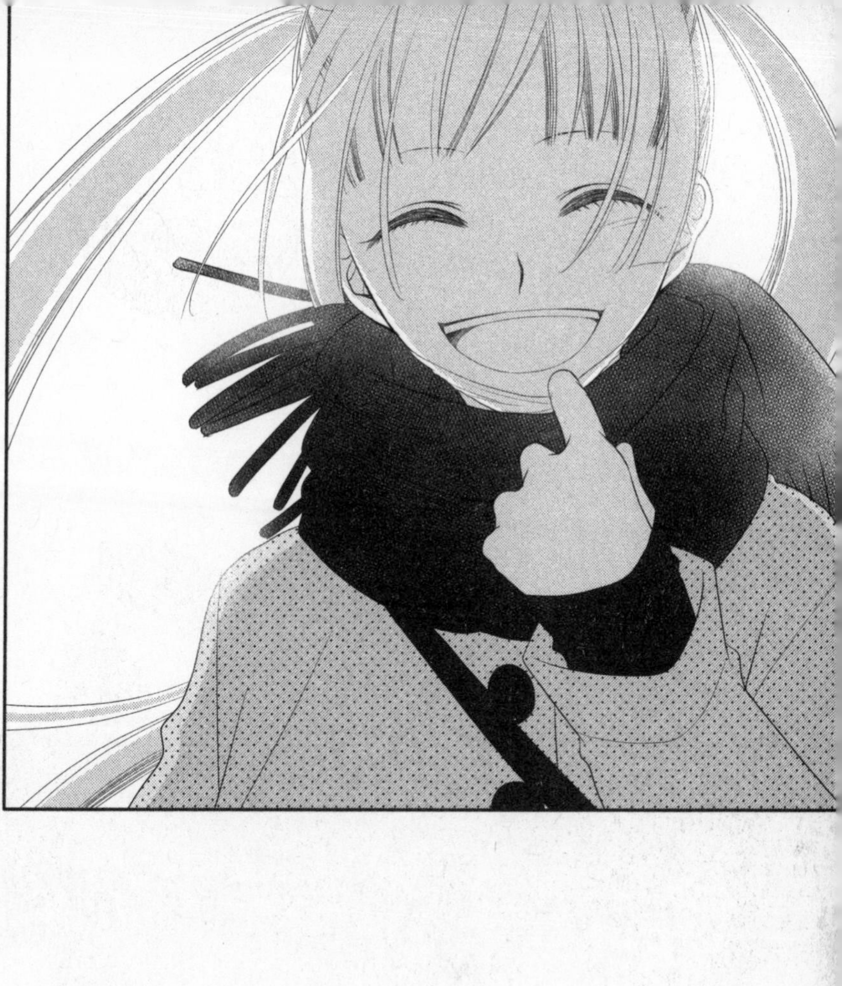

SCABS AND ALL.

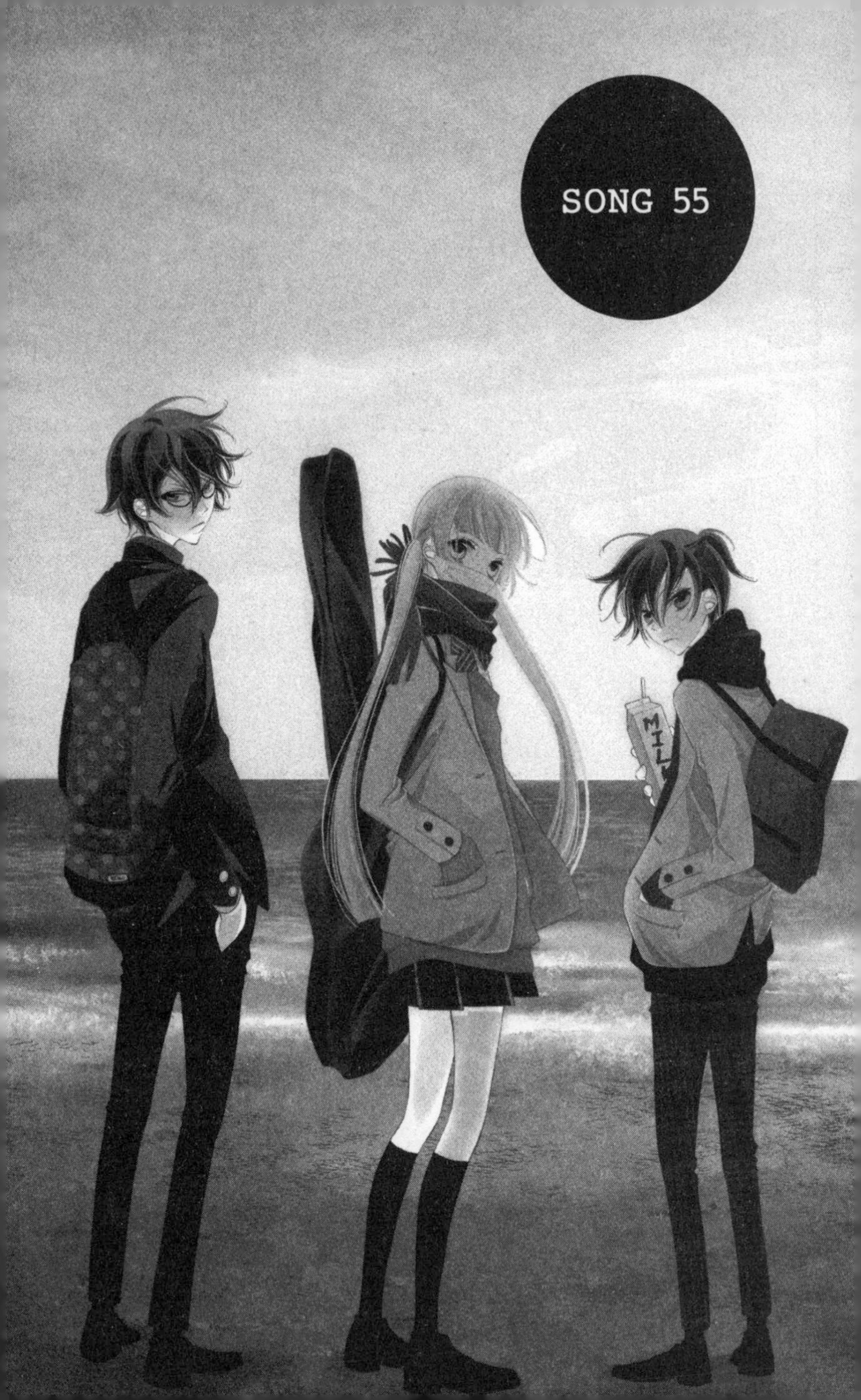
SONG 55

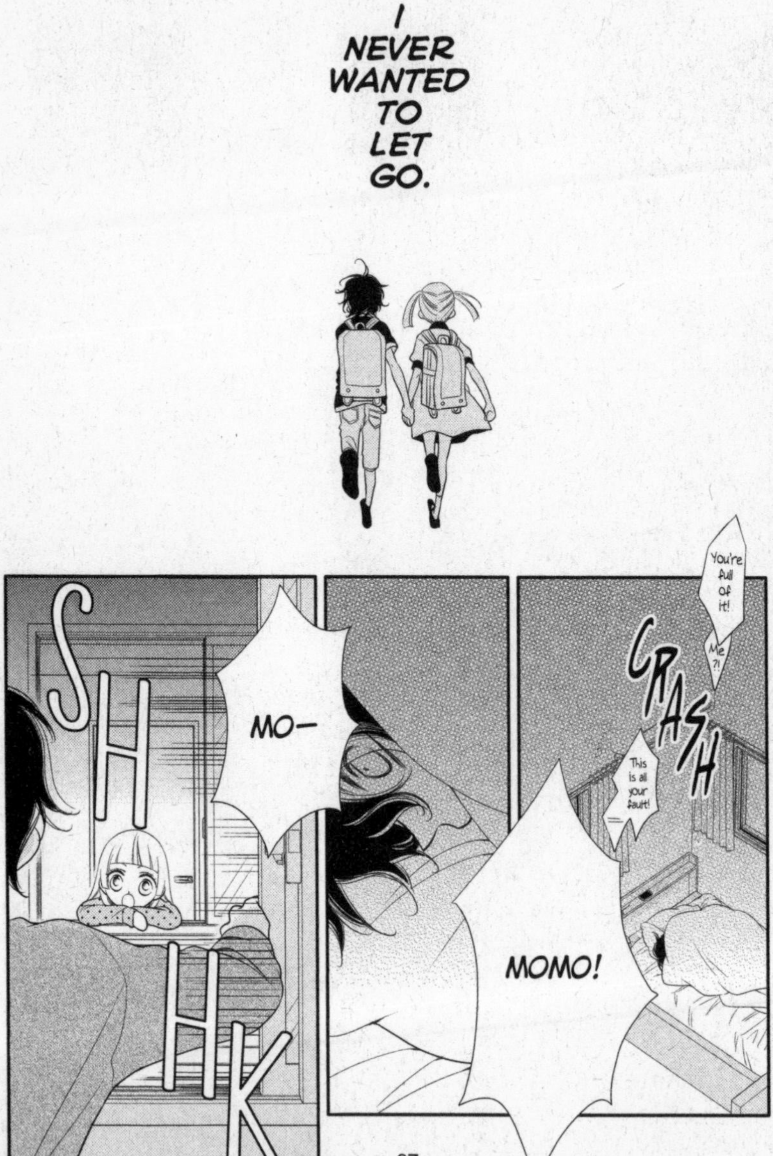
I NEVER WANTED TO LET GO.
You're full of it!
Me ?!
CRASH
This is all your fault!
MOMO!
MO—
SHHK

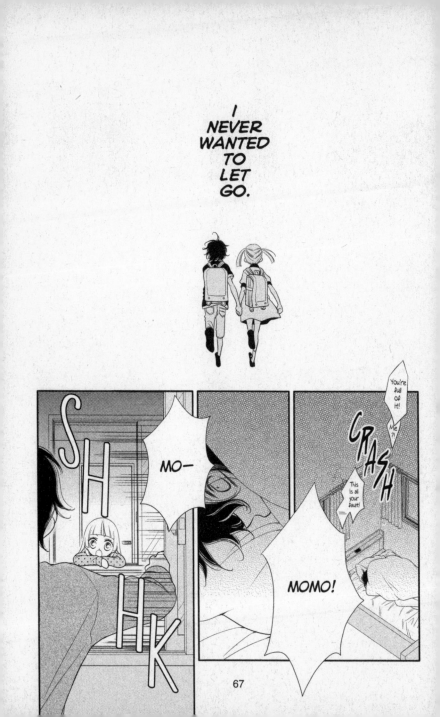

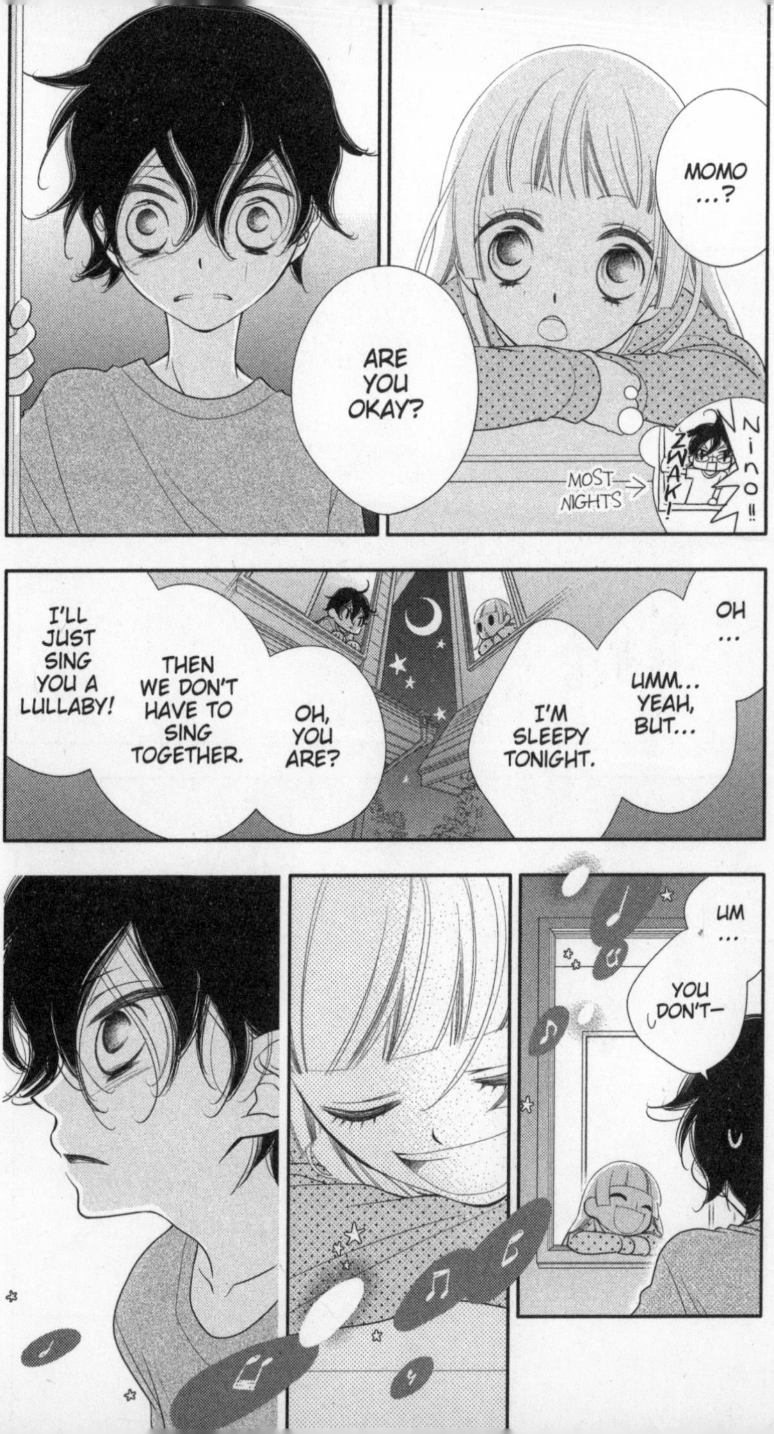
MOMO ...?
ARE YOU OKAY?
Nino!!
ZWAK!
MOST NIGHTS
OH ...
UMM... YEAH, BUT...
I'M SLEEPY TONIGHT.
OH, YOU ARE?
THEN WE DON'T HAVE TO SING TOGETHER.
I'LL JUST SING YOU A LULLABY!
UM ...
YOU DON'T—

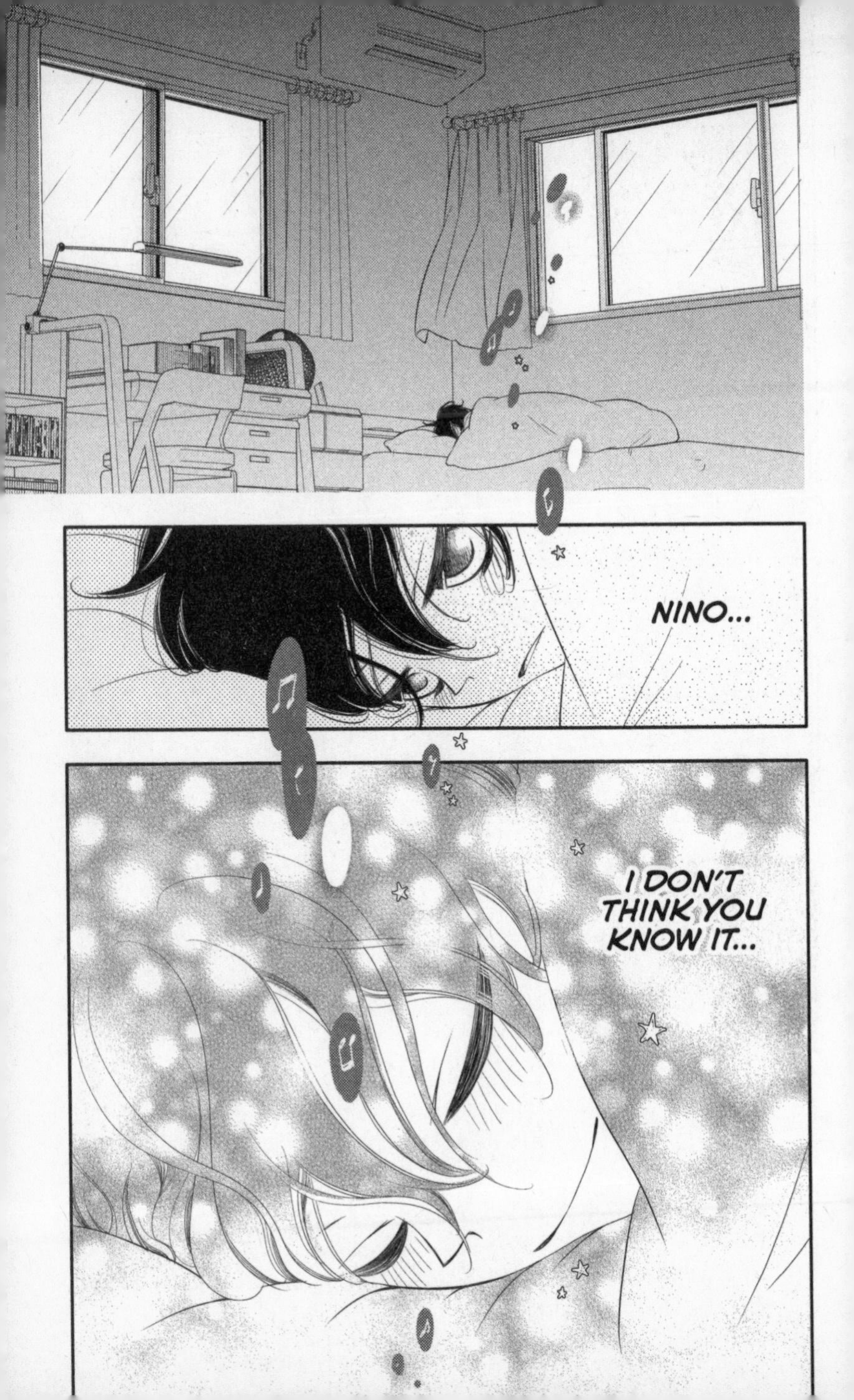
NINO...
I DON'T THINK YOU KNOW IT...

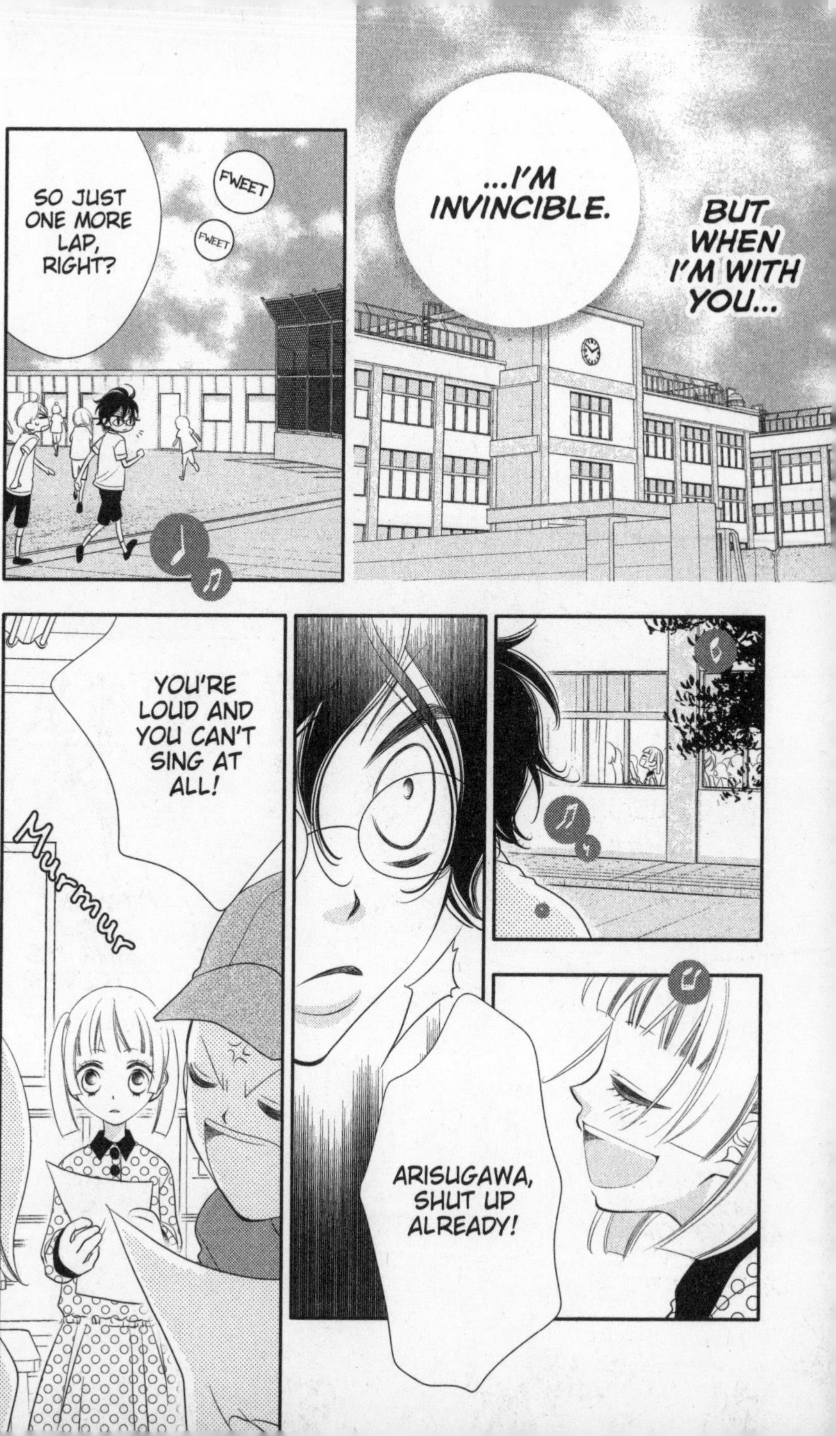
BUT WHEN I'M WITH YOU...
...I'M INVINCIBLE.
FWEET
FWEET
SO JUST ONE MORE LAP, RIGHT?
ARISUGAWA, SHUT UP ALREADY!
YOU'RE LOUD AND YOU CAN'T SING AT ALL!
Murmur

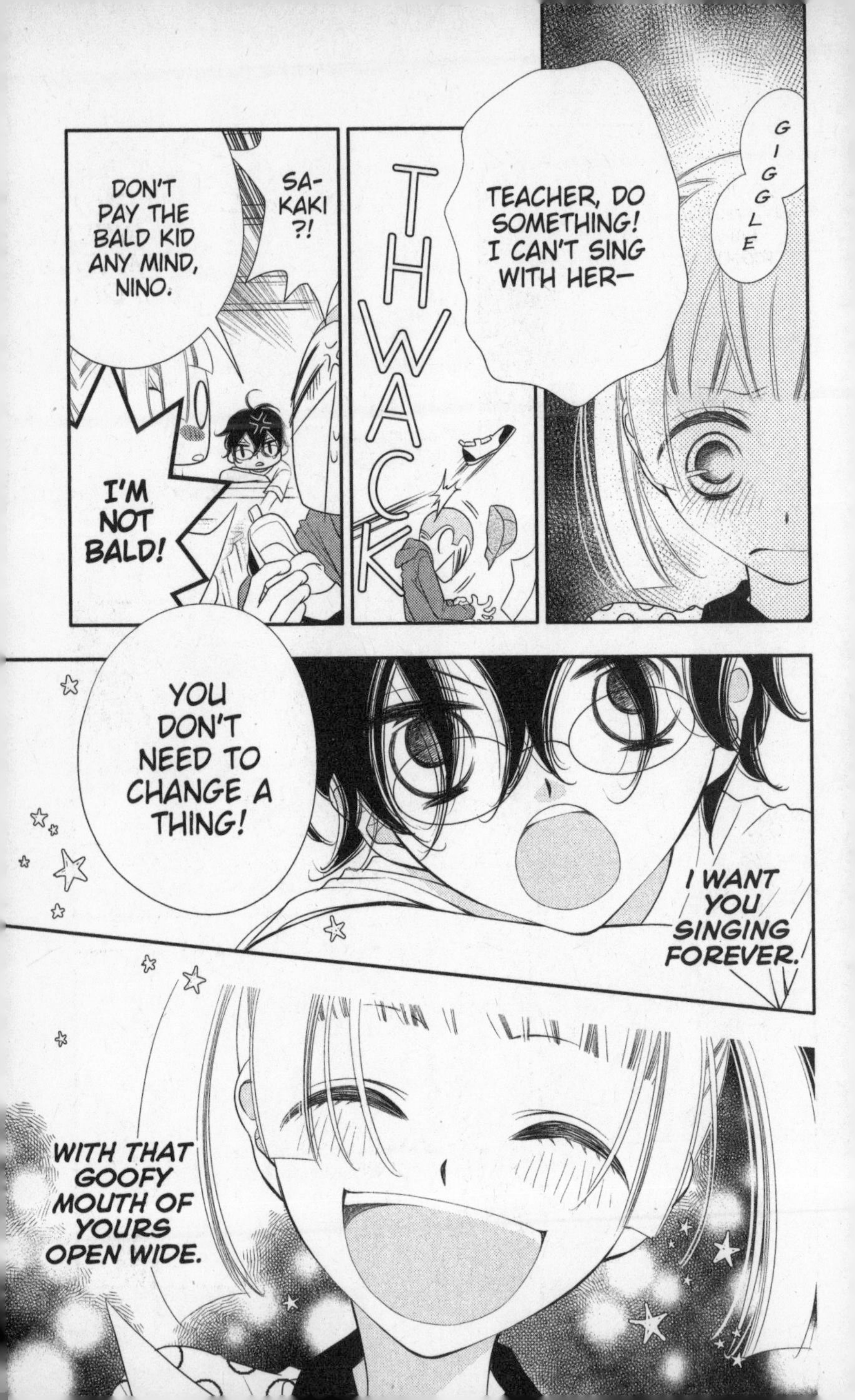
GIGGLE
TEACHER, DO SOMETHING! I CAN'T SING WITH HER—
THWACK
SA-KAKI?!
DON'T PAY THE BALD KID ANY MIND, NINO.
I'M NOT BALD!
YOU DON'T NEED TO CHANGE A THING!
I WANT YOU SINGING FOREVER.
WITH THAT GOOFY MOUTH OF YOURS OPEN WIDE.

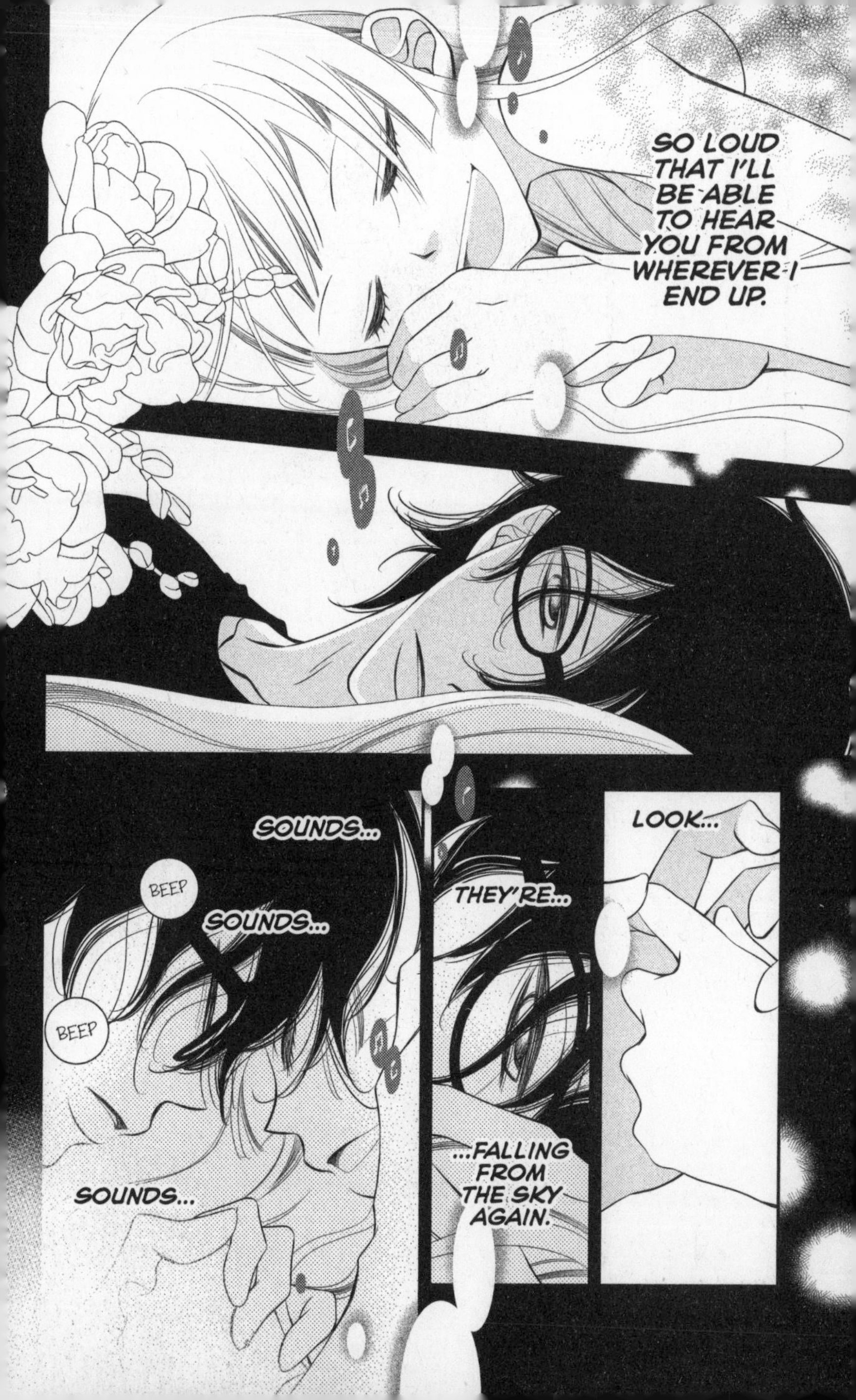
SO LOUD THAT I'LL BE ABLE TO HEAR YOU FROM WHEREVER I END UP.
LOOK...
THEY'RE...
...FALLING FROM THE SKY AGAIN.
SOUNDS...
BEEP
SOUNDS...
BEEP
SOUNDS...

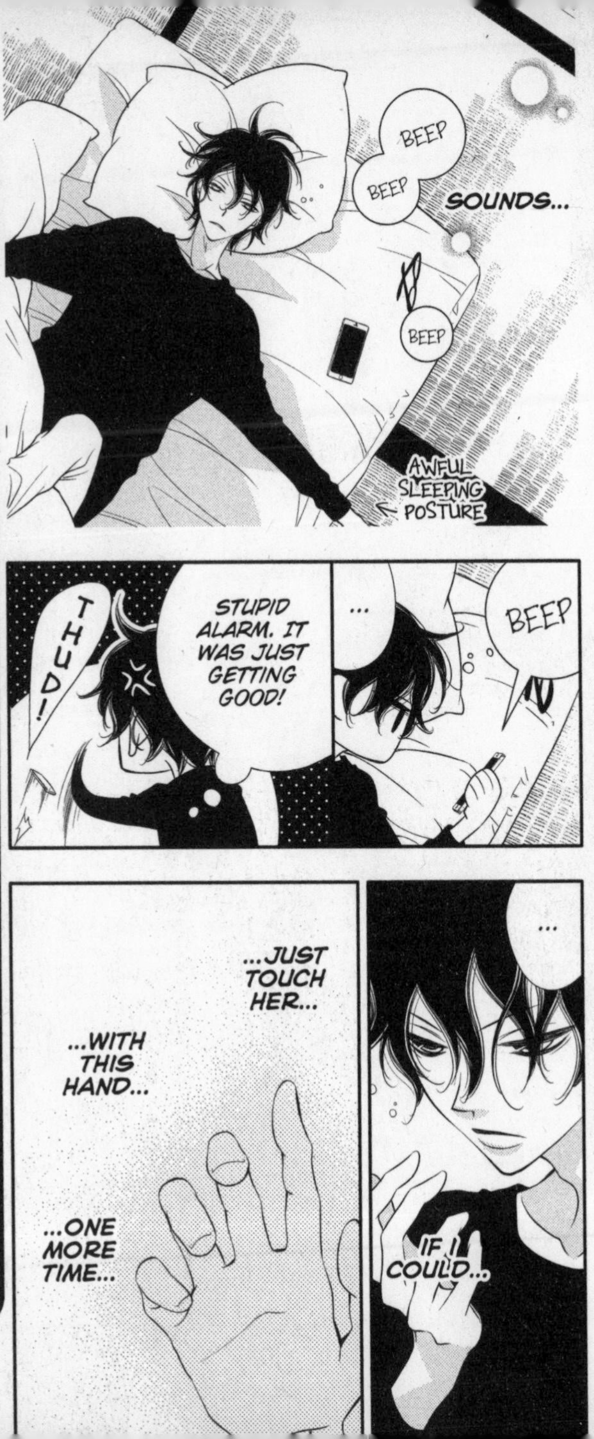
BEEP
BEEP
SOUNDS...
BEEP
AWFUL SLEEPING POSTURE
BEEP
...
STUPID ALARM. IT WAS JUST GETTING GOOD!
THUD!
...
IF I COULD...
...JUST TOUCH HER...
...WITH THIS HAND...
...ONE MORE TIME...

3

Fortunately, my allergy wasn't a strong one, so I decided to focus my energy on keeping my room immaculately clean.

My Roomba was busted, so I bought a new one, along with a Braava that mops floors.

I named the new Roomba "Ikura" and the Braava "Engawa." I've assigned them to clean my room on alternating shifts, pretty much every day.

I also make sure to turn on my air purifier every day. And with that...

(Continued yet again!)

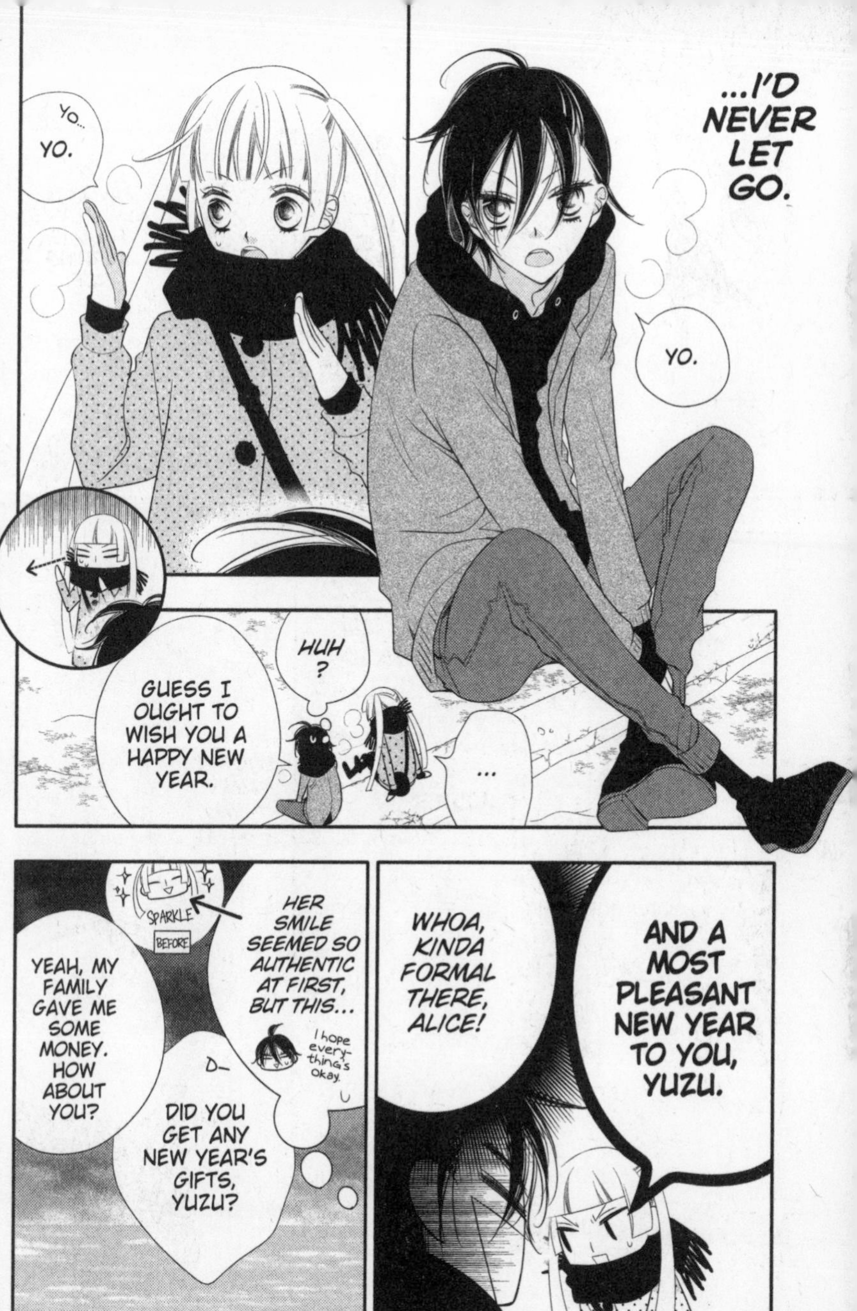
...I'D NEVER LET GO.
YO.
YO... YO.
HUH?
...
GUESS I OUGHT TO WISH YOU A HAPPY NEW YEAR.
AND A MOST PLEASANT NEW YEAR TO YOU, YUZU.
WHOA, KINDA FORMAL THERE, ALICE!
SPARKLE
BEFORE
HER SMILE SEEMED SO AUTHENTIC AT FIRST, BUT THIS...
I hope every-thing's okay.
D—
DID YOU GET ANY NEW YEAR'S GIFTS, YUZU?
YEAH, MY FAMILY GAVE ME SOME MONEY. HOW ABOUT YOU?

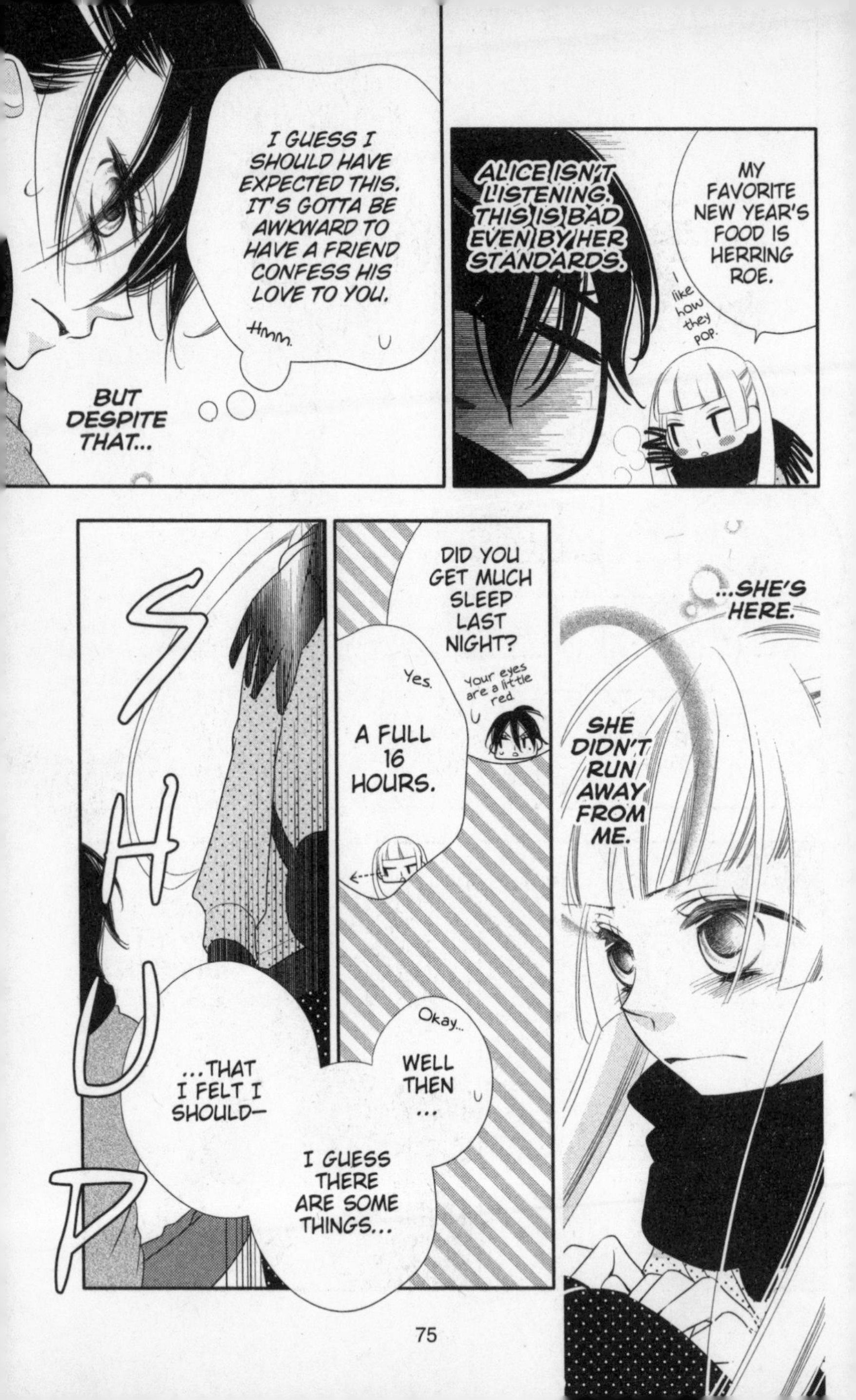
MY FAVORITE NEW YEAR'S FOOD IS HERRING ROE.
I like how they pop.
ALICE ISN'T LISTENING. THIS IS BAD EVEN BY HER STANDARDS.
I GUESS I SHOULD HAVE EXPECTED THIS. IT'S GOTTA BE AWKWARD TO HAVE A FRIEND CONFESS HIS LOVE TO YOU.
Hmm.
BUT DESPITE THAT...
...SHE'S HERE.
SHE DIDN'T RUN AWAY FROM ME.
DID YOU GET MUCH SLEEP LAST NIGHT?
Yes.
Your eyes are a little red.
A FULL 16 HOURS.
SHUP
Okay...
WELL THEN...
I GUESS THERE ARE SOME THINGS...
...THAT I FELT I SHOULD—

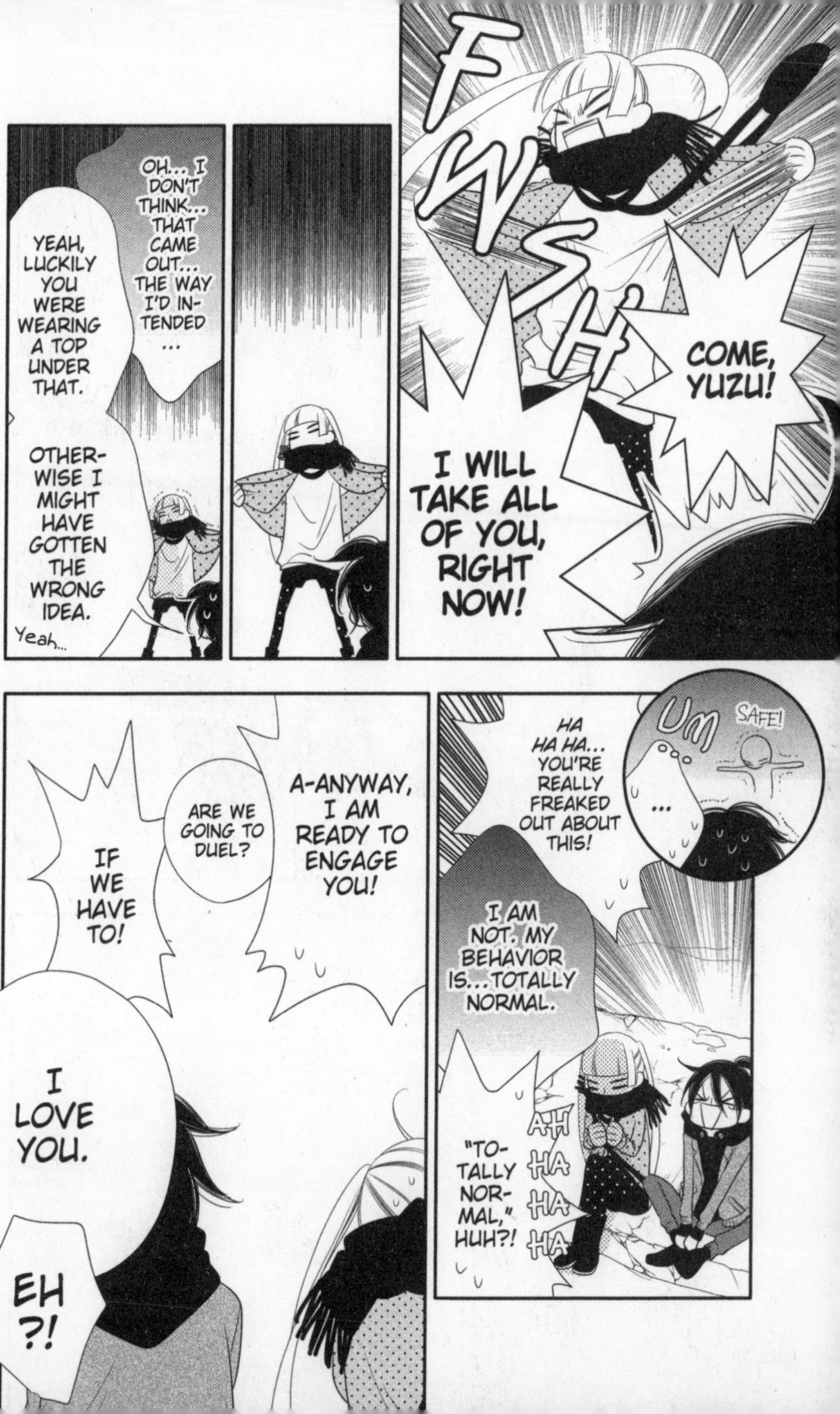
FWSH
COME, YUZU!
I WILL TAKE ALL OF YOU, RIGHT NOW!
OH... I DON'T THINK... THAT CAME OUT... THE WAY I'D INTENDED...
YEAH, LUCKILY YOU WERE WEARING A TOP UNDER THAT.
OTHERWISE I MIGHT HAVE GOTTEN THE WRONG IDEA.
Yeah...
SAFE!
Um
...
HA HA HA... YOU'RE REALLY FREAKED OUT ABOUT THIS!
I AM NOT. MY BEHAVIOR IS... TOTALLY NORMAL.
AH HA HA HA HA
"TOTALLY NORMAL," HUH?!
A-ANYWAY, I AM READY TO ENGAGE YOU!
ARE WE GOING TO DUEL?
IF WE HAVE TO!
I LOVE YOU.
EH?!

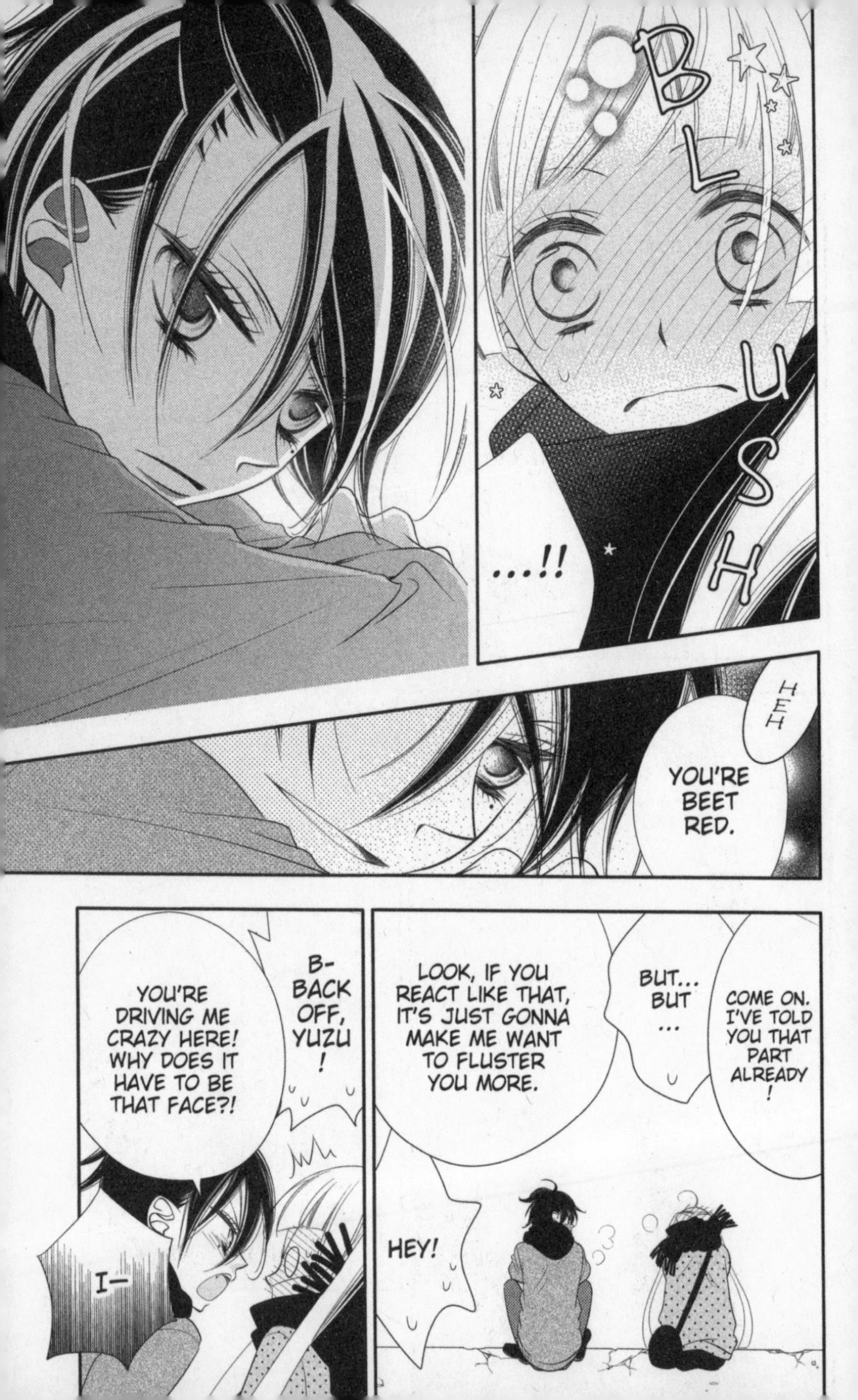
BLUSH
...!!
HEH
YOU'RE BEET RED.
COME ON. I'VE TOLD YOU THAT PART ALREADY!
BUT... BUT...
LOOK, IF YOU REACT LIKE THAT, IT'S JUST GONNA MAKE ME WANT TO FLUSTER YOU MORE.
HEY!
B-BACK OFF, YUZU!
YOU'RE DRIVING ME CRAZY HERE! WHY DOES IT HAVE TO BE THAT FACE?!
I—

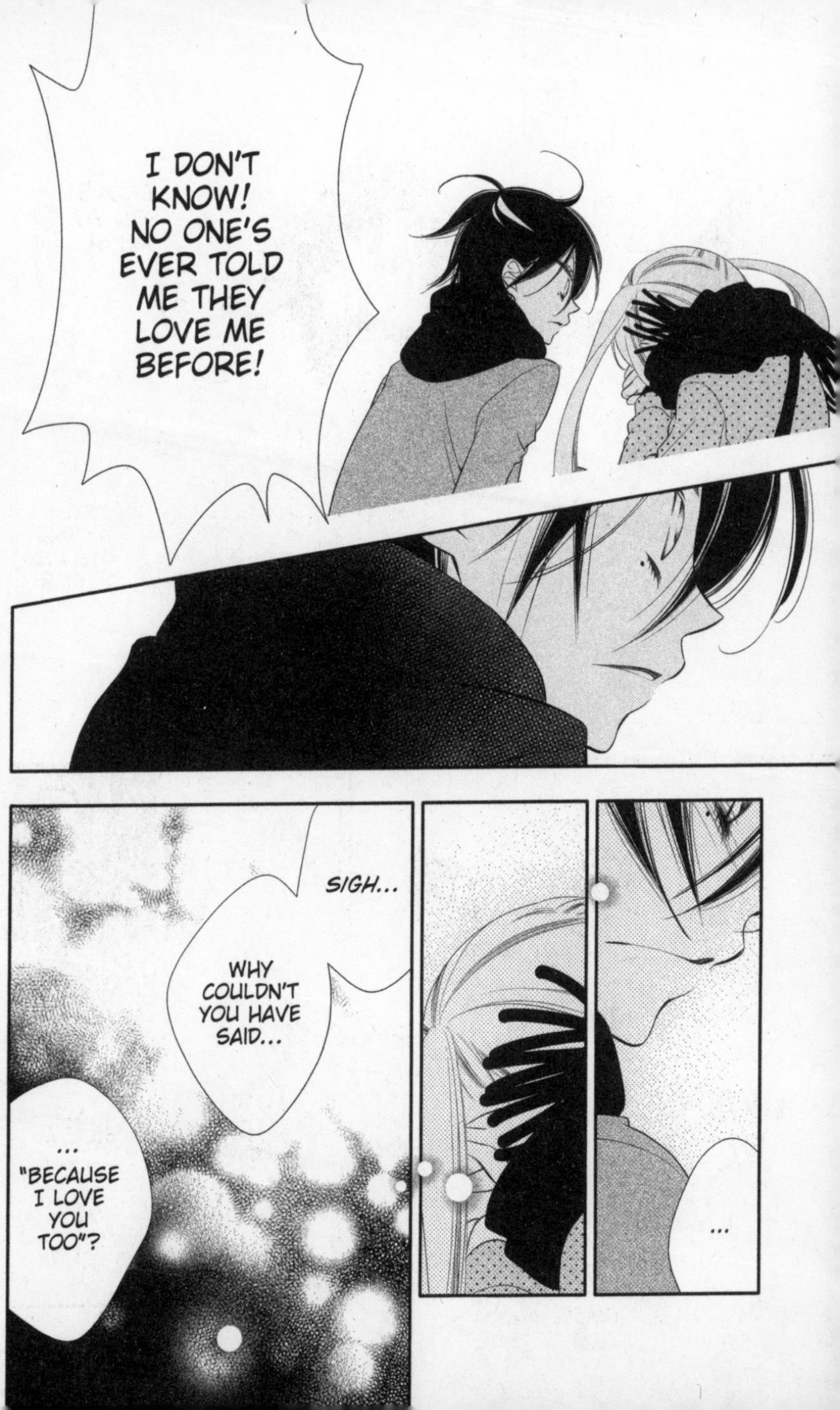
I DON'T KNOW! NO ONE'S EVER TOLD ME THEY LOVE ME BEFORE!
...
SIGH...
WHY COULDN'T YOU HAVE SAID...
... "BECAUSE I LOVE YOU TOO"?

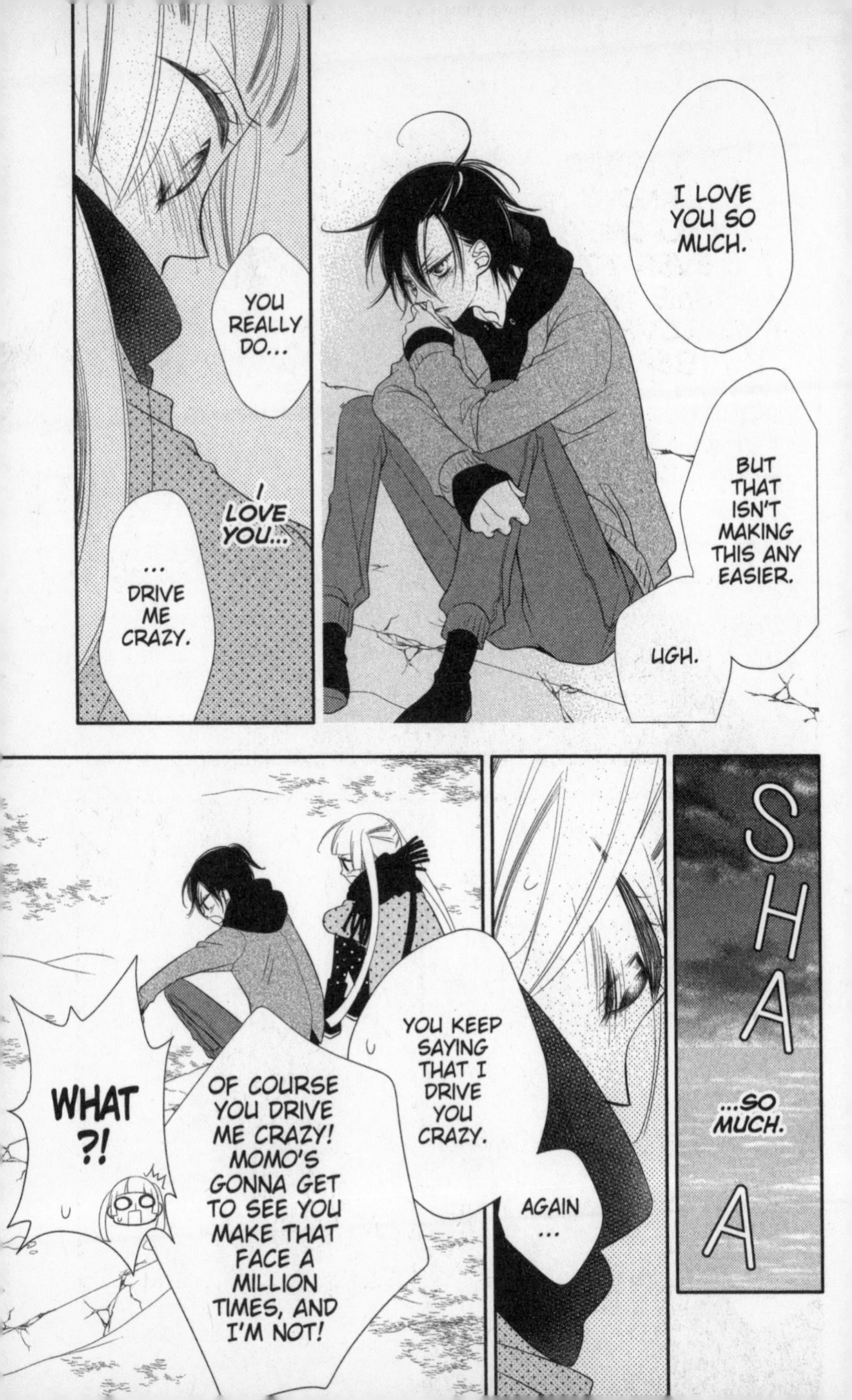
I LOVE YOU SO MUCH.
BUT THAT ISN'T MAKING THIS ANY EASIER.
UGH.
YOU REALLY DO...
I LOVE YOU...
...DRIVE ME CRAZY.
SHAA
...SO MUCH.
YOU KEEP SAYING THAT I DRIVE YOU CRAZY.
AGAIN...
OF COURSE YOU DRIVE ME CRAZY! MOMO'S GONNA GET TO SEE YOU MAKE THAT FACE A MILLION TIMES, AND I'M NOT!
WHAT?!

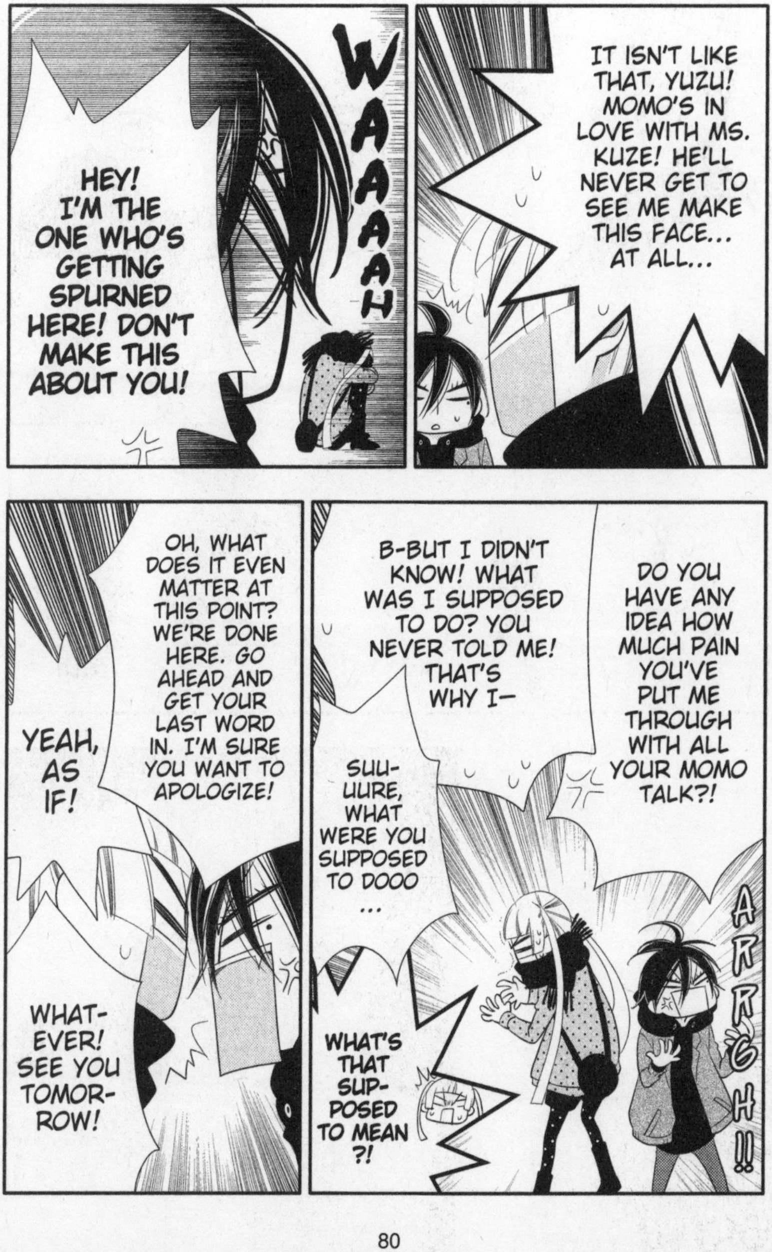
IT ISN'T LIKE THAT, YUZU! MOMO'S IN LOVE WITH MS. KUZE! HE'LL NEVER GET TO SEE ME MAKE THIS FACE... AT ALL...
WAAAAAH
HEY! I'M THE ONE WHO'S GETTING SPURNED HERE! DON'T MAKE THIS ABOUT YOU!
DO YOU HAVE ANY IDEA HOW MUCH PAIN YOU'VE PUT ME THROUGH WITH ALL YOUR MOMO TALK?!
B-BUT I DIDN'T KNOW! WHAT WAS I SUPPOSED TO DO? YOU NEVER TOLD ME! THAT'S WHY I—
SUUU-UURE, WHAT WERE YOU SUPPOSED TO DOOO...
ARRGH!!
WHAT'S THAT SUPPOSED TO MEAN?!
OH, WHAT DOES IT EVEN MATTER AT THIS POINT? WE'RE DONE HERE. GO AHEAD AND GET YOUR LAST WORD IN. I'M SURE YOU WANT TO APOLOGIZE!
YEAH, AS IF!
WHAT-EVER! SEE YOU TOMOR-ROW!

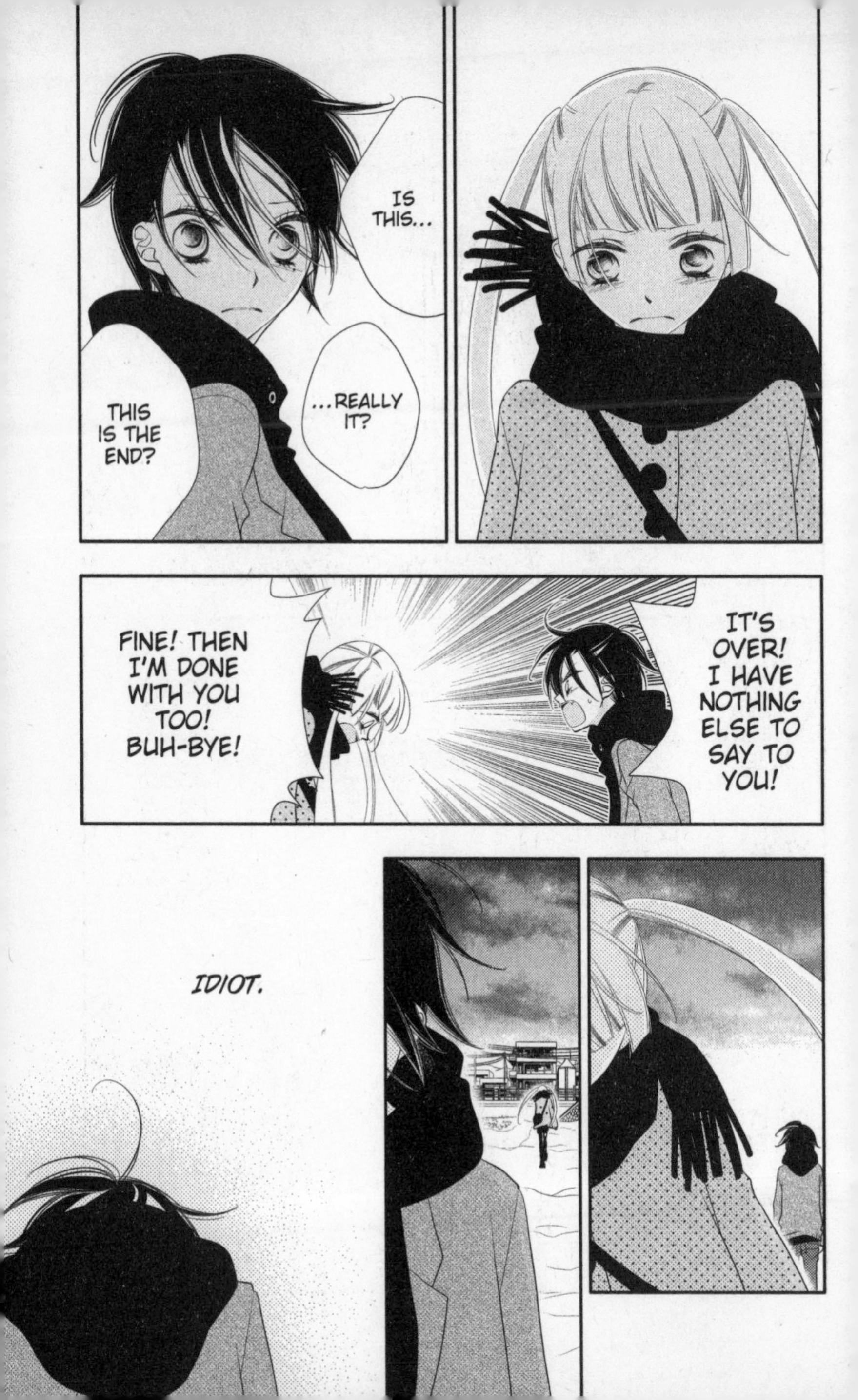
IS THIS...
...REALLY IT?
THIS IS THE END?
IT'S OVER! I HAVE NOTHING ELSE TO SAY TO YOU!
FINE! THEN I'M DONE WITH YOU TOO! BUH-BYE!
IDIOT.

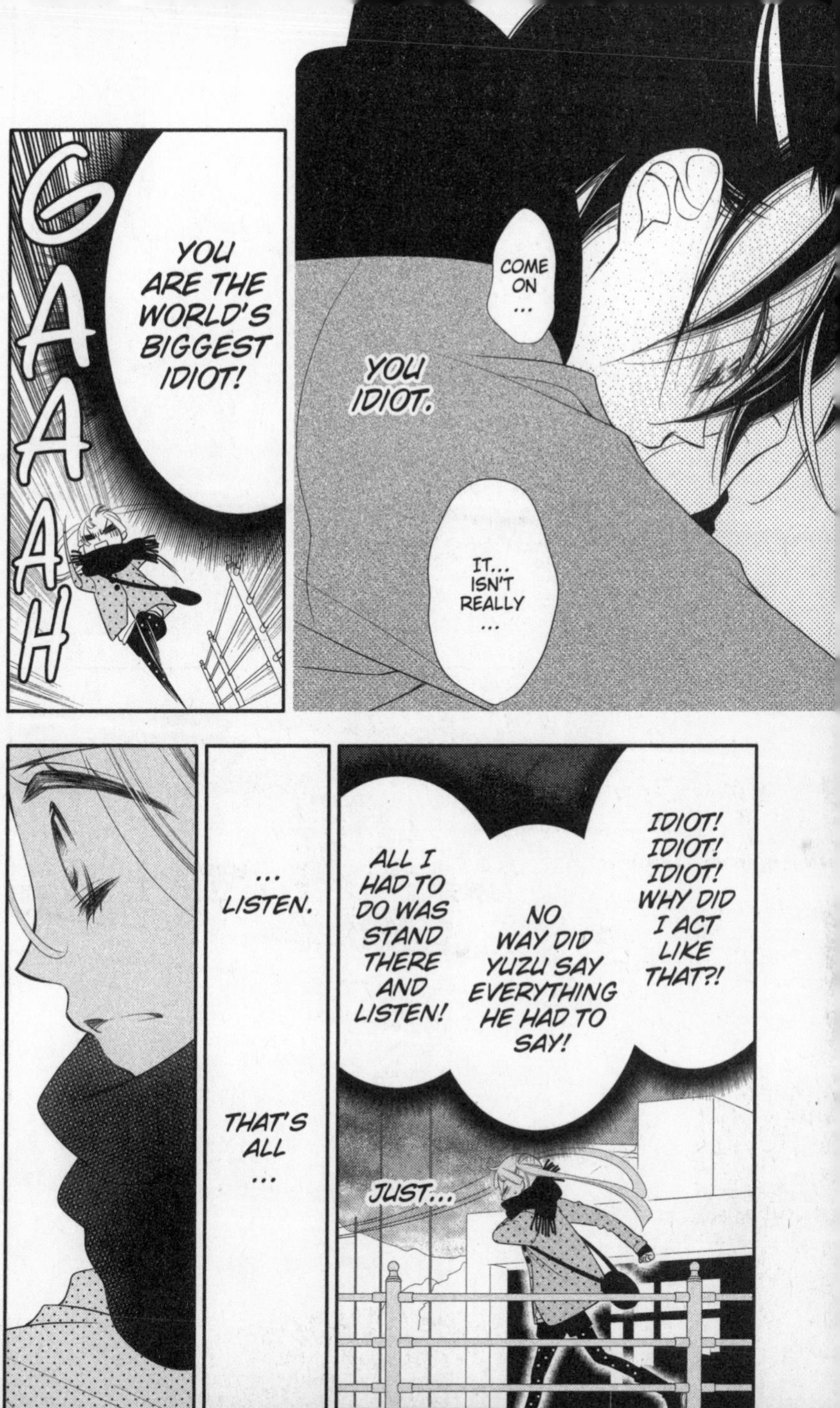
COME ON ...
YOU IDIOT.
IT... ISN'T REALLY ...
YOU ARE THE WORLD'S BIGGEST IDIOT!
GAAAH
IDIOT! IDIOT! IDIOT! WHY DID I ACT LIKE THAT?!
NO WAY DID YUZU SAY EVERYTHING HE HAD TO SAY!
ALL I HAD TO DO WAS STAND THERE AND LISTEN!
JUST...
... LISTEN.
THAT'S ALL ...

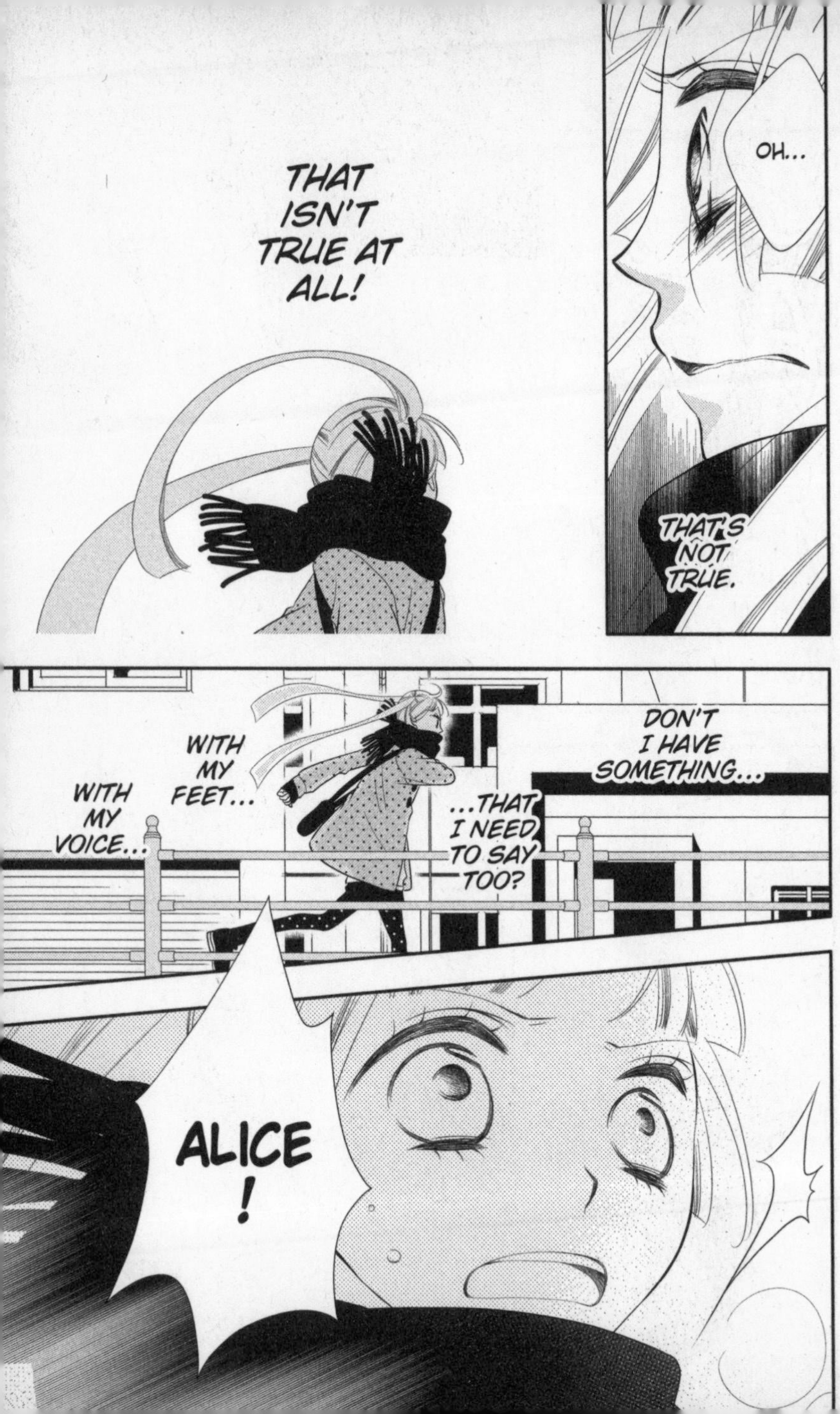
OH...
THAT'S NOT TRUE.
THAT ISN'T TRUE AT ALL!
DON'T I HAVE SOMETHING...
...THAT I NEED TO SAY TOO?
WITH MY FEET...
WITH MY VOICE...
ALICE!

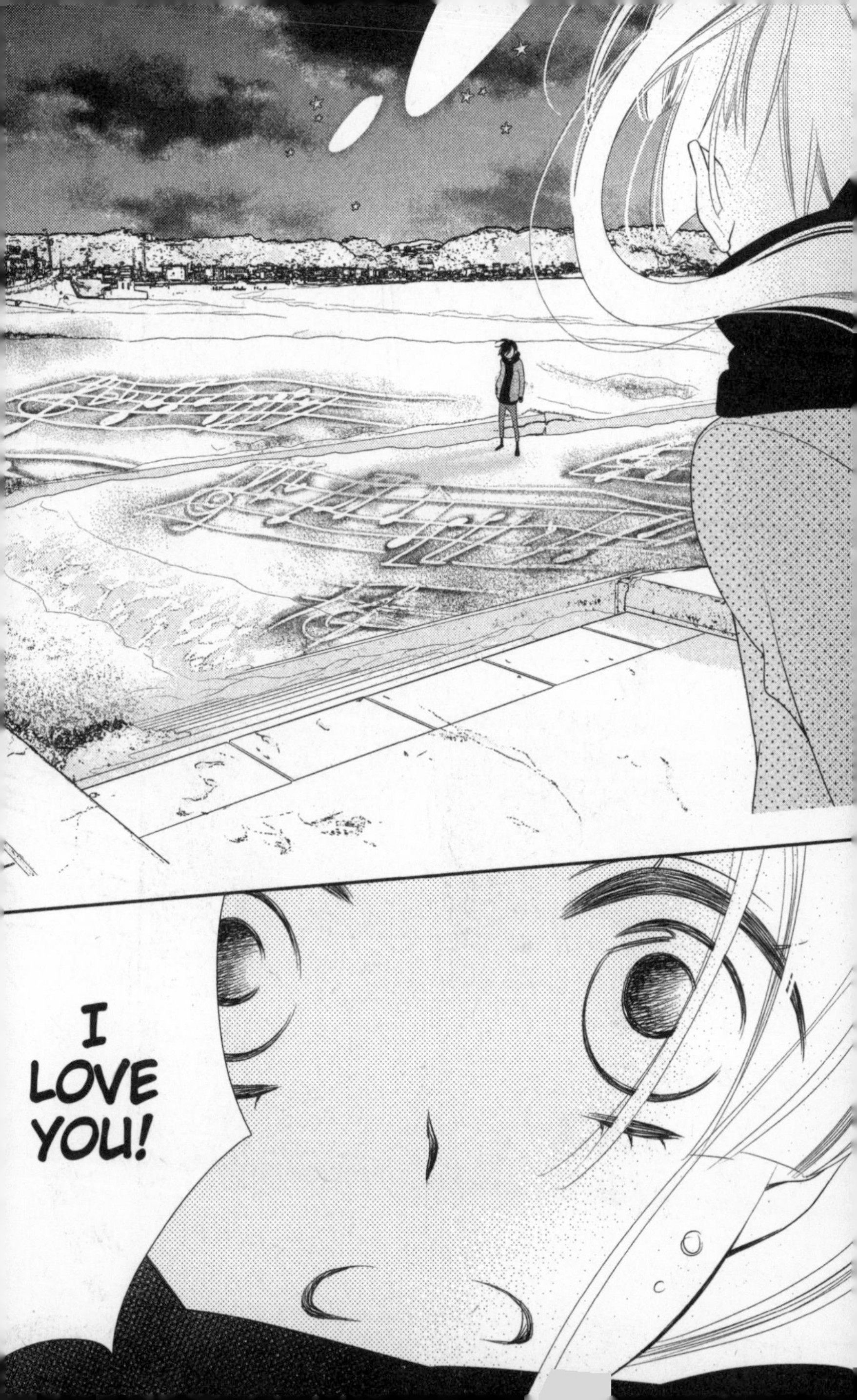
I LOVE YOU!

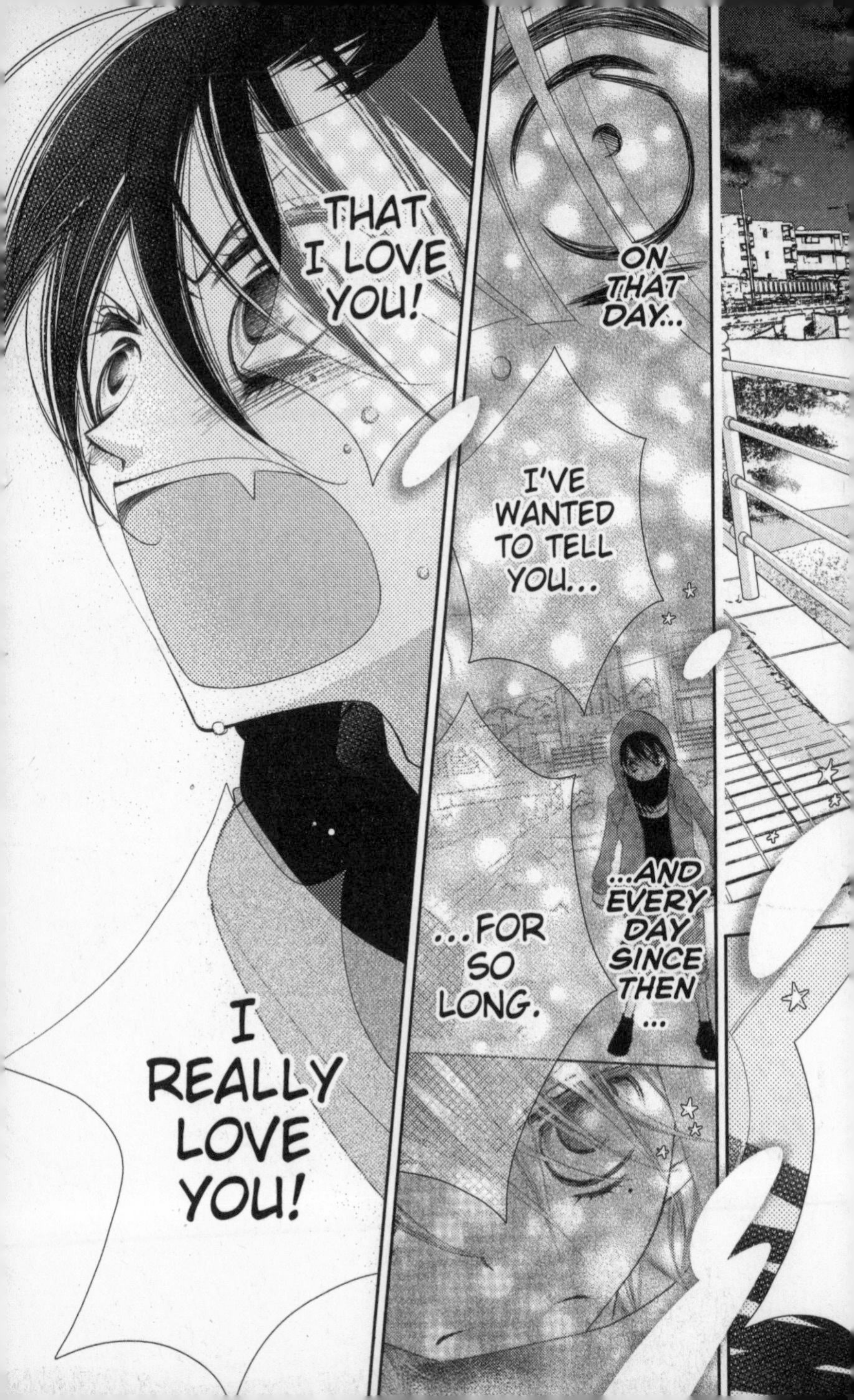
ON THAT DAY...
I'VE WANTED TO TELL YOU...
...AND EVERY DAY SINCE THEN...
...FOR SO LONG.
THAT I LOVE YOU!
I REALLY LOVE YOU!

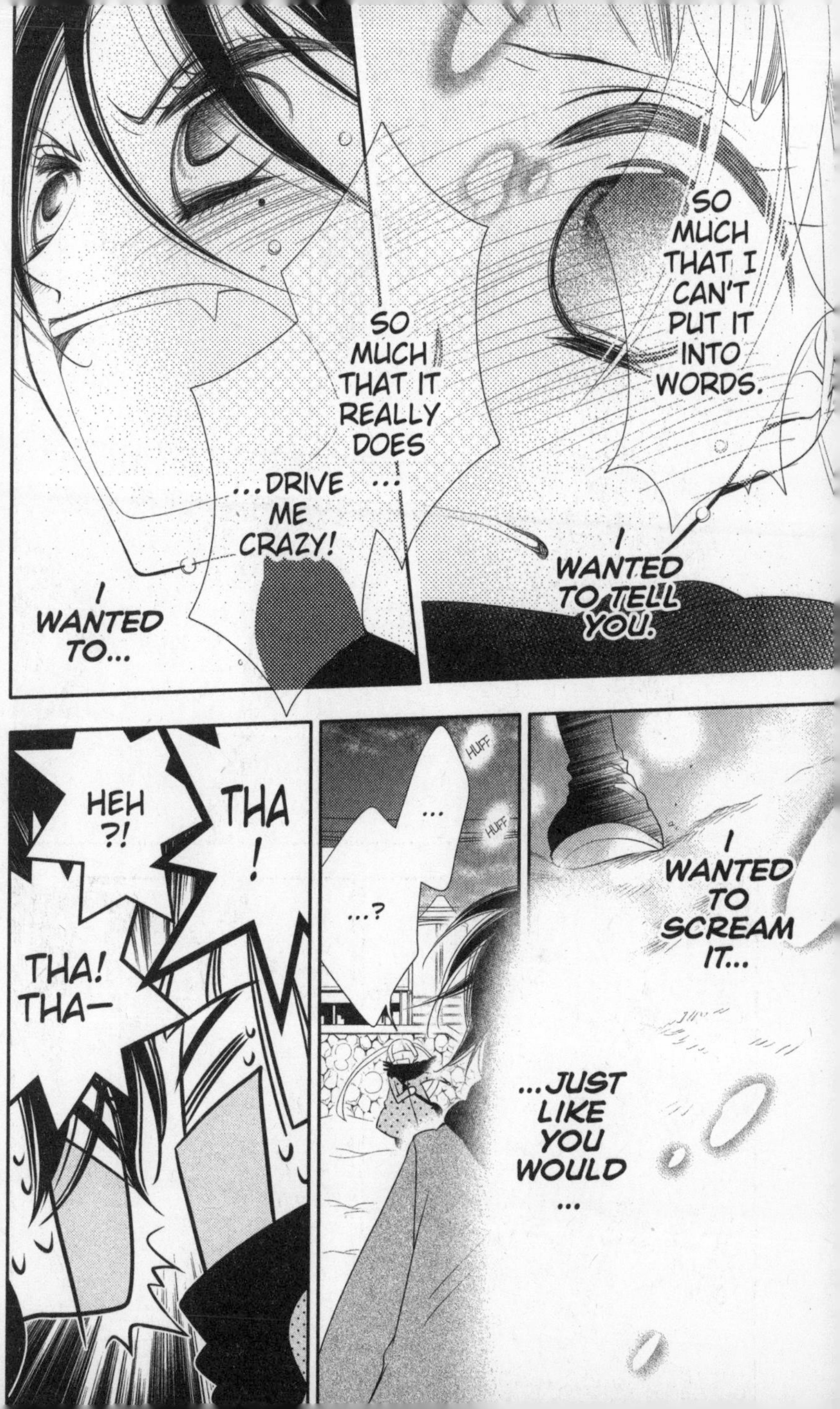
SO MUCH THAT I CAN'T PUT IT INTO WORDS.
I WANTED TO TELL YOU.
SO MUCH THAT IT REALLY DOES ...
...DRIVE ME CRAZY!
I WANTED TO...
I WANTED TO SCREAM IT...
...JUST LIKE YOU WOULD ...
HUFF
HUFF
...
...?
THA!
HEH?!
THA! THA-

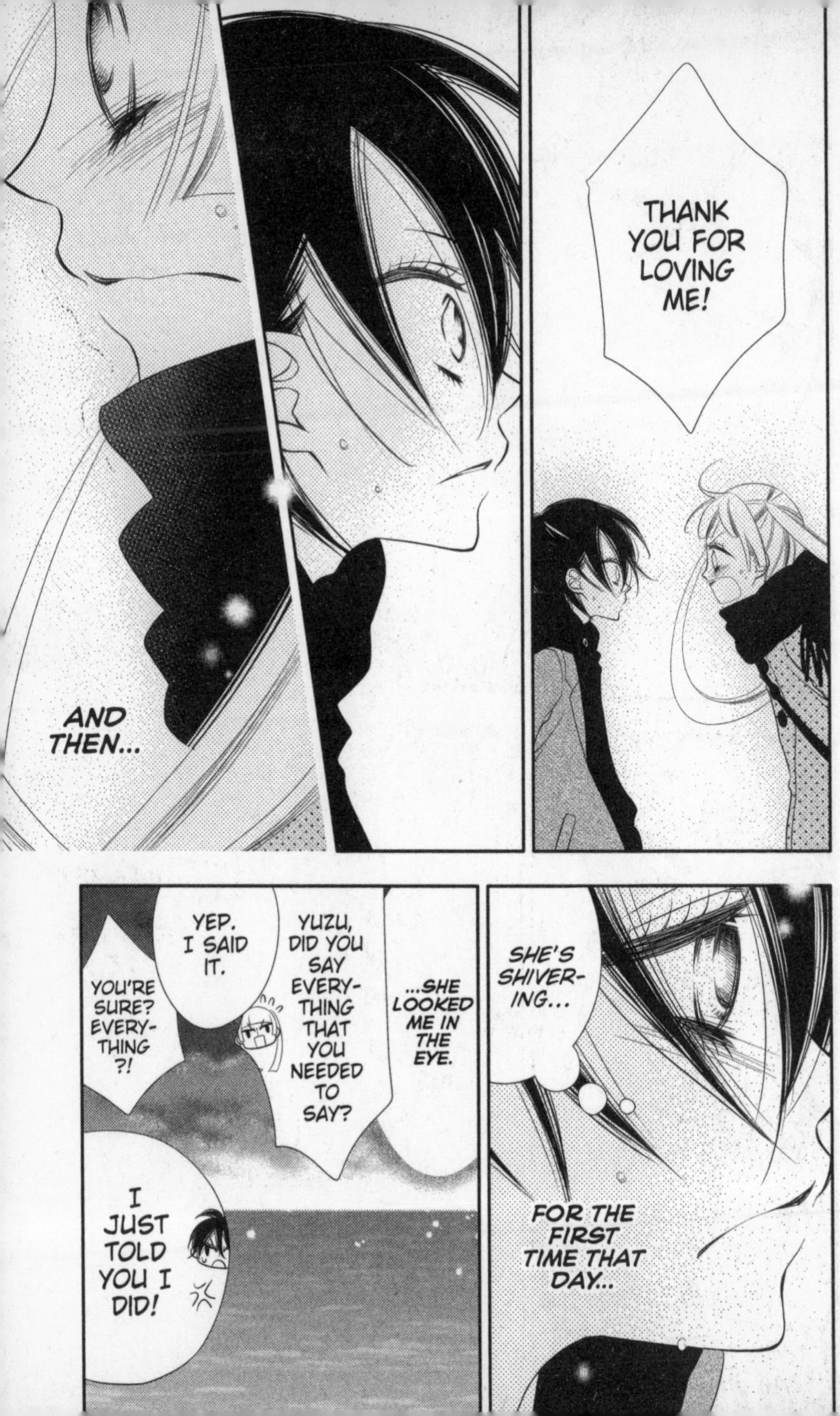
THANK YOU FOR LOVING ME!
AND THEN...
SHE'S SHIVERING...
FOR THE FIRST TIME THAT DAY...
...SHE LOOKED ME IN THE EYE.
YUZU, DID YOU SAY EVERYTHING THAT YOU NEEDED TO SAY?
YEP. I SAID IT.
YOU'RE SURE? EVERYTHING?!
I JUST TOLD YOU I DID!

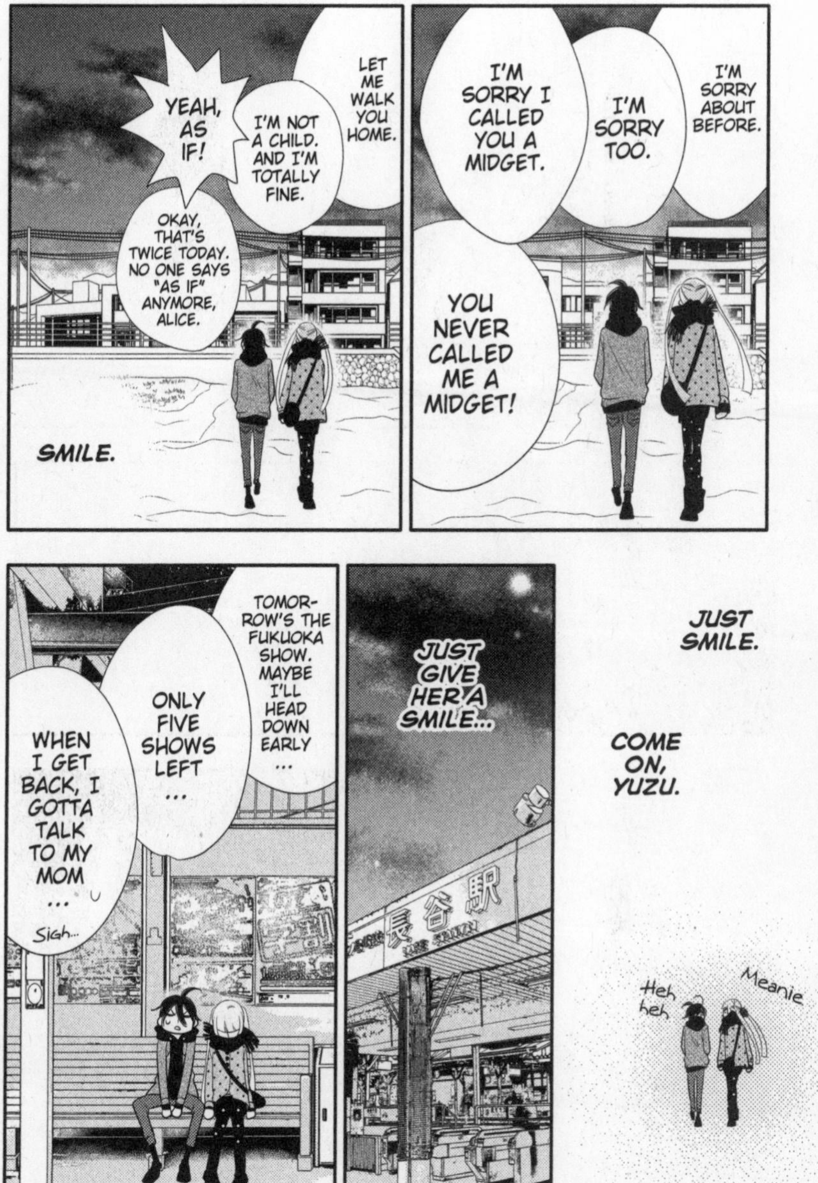
I'M SORRY ABOUT BEFORE.
I'M SORRY TOO.
I'M SORRY I CALLED YOU A MIDGET.
YOU NEVER CALLED ME A MIDGET!
LET ME WALK YOU HOME.
I'M NOT A CHILD. AND I'M TOTALLY FINE.
YEAH, AS IF!
OKAY, THAT'S TWICE TODAY. NO ONE SAYS "AS IF" ANYMORE, ALICE.
SMILE.
JUST SMILE.
COME ON, YUZU.
Meanie
Heh heh
JUST GIVE HER A SMILE...
長谷駅
TOMORROW'S THE FUKUOKA SHOW. MAYBE I'LL HEAD DOWN EARLY...
ONLY FIVE SHOWS LEFT...
WHEN I GET BACK, I GOTTA TALK TO MY MOM...
Sigh...

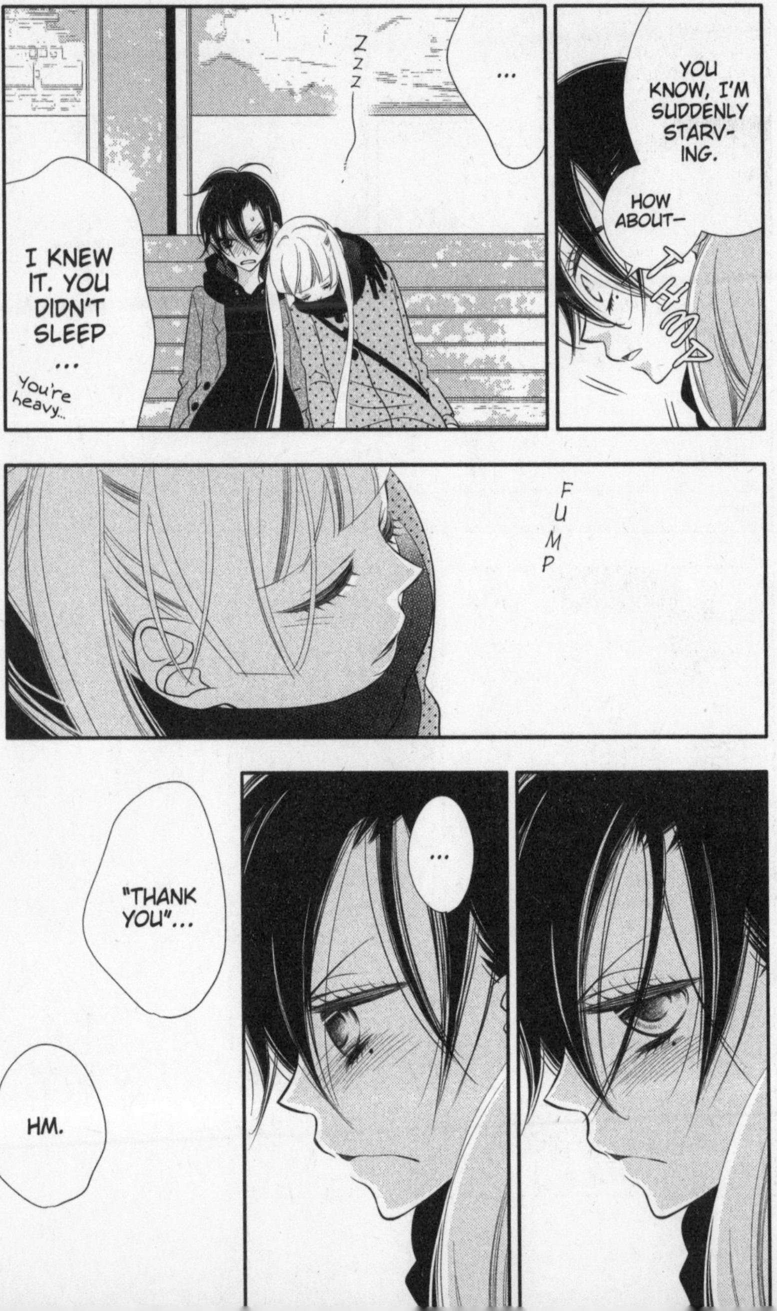
YOU KNOW, I'M SUDDENLY STARV-ING.
HOW ABOUT—
THMP
...
ZZZ
I KNEW IT. YOU DIDN'T SLEEP ...
You're heavy...
FUMP
...
"THANK YOU"...
HM.

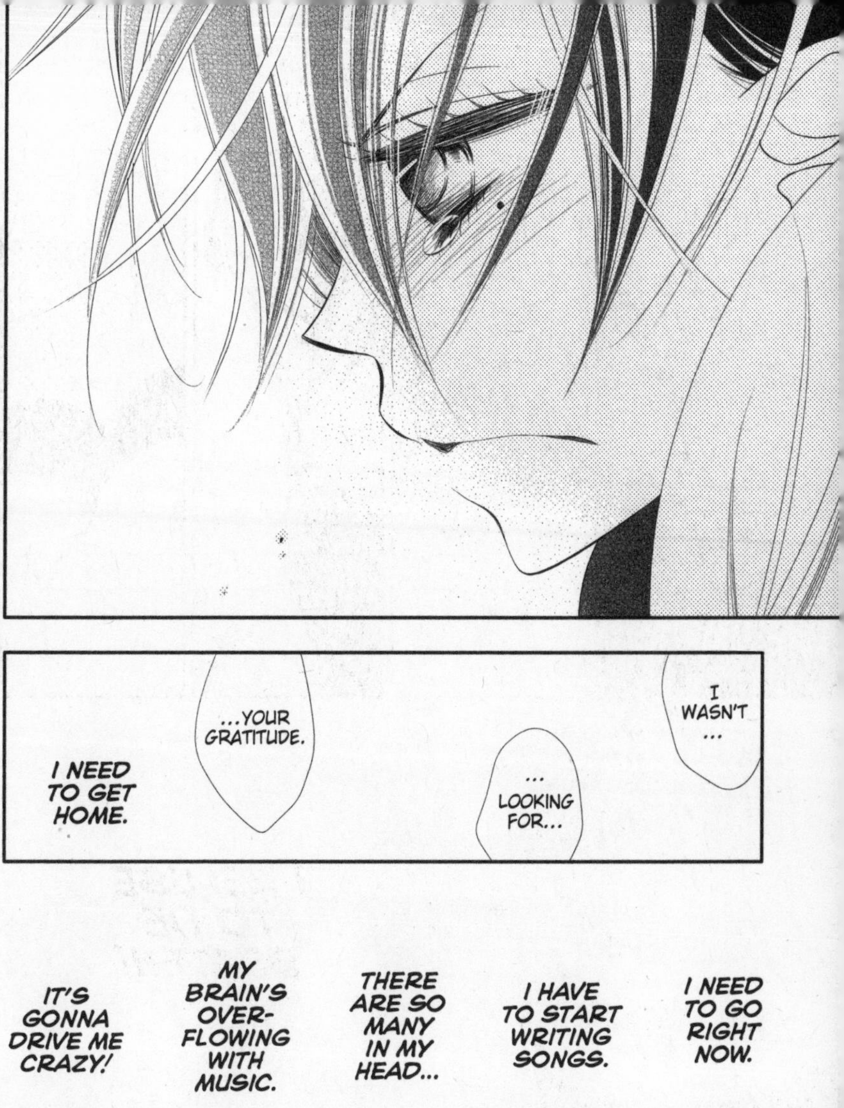
I WASN'T ...
... LOOKING FOR...
...YOUR GRATITUDE.
I NEED TO GET HOME.
I NEED TO GO RIGHT NOW.
I HAVE TO START WRITING SONGS.
THERE ARE SO MANY IN MY HEAD...
MY BRAIN'S OVER-FLOWING WITH MUSIC.
IT'S GONNA DRIVE ME CRAZY!

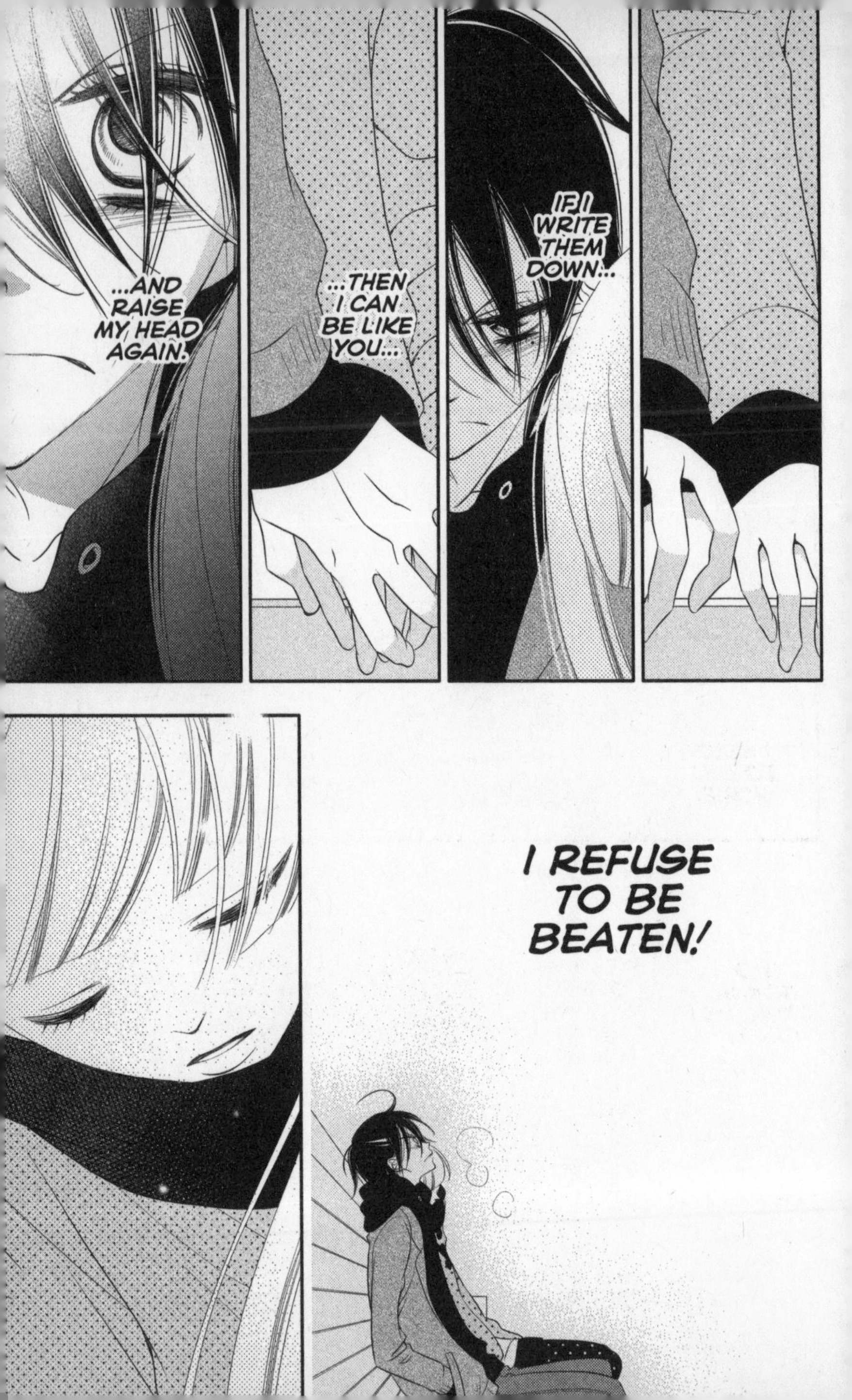
IF I WRITE THEM DOWN...
...THEN I CAN BE LIKE YOU...
...AND RAISE MY HEAD AGAIN.
I REFUSE TO BE BEATEN!

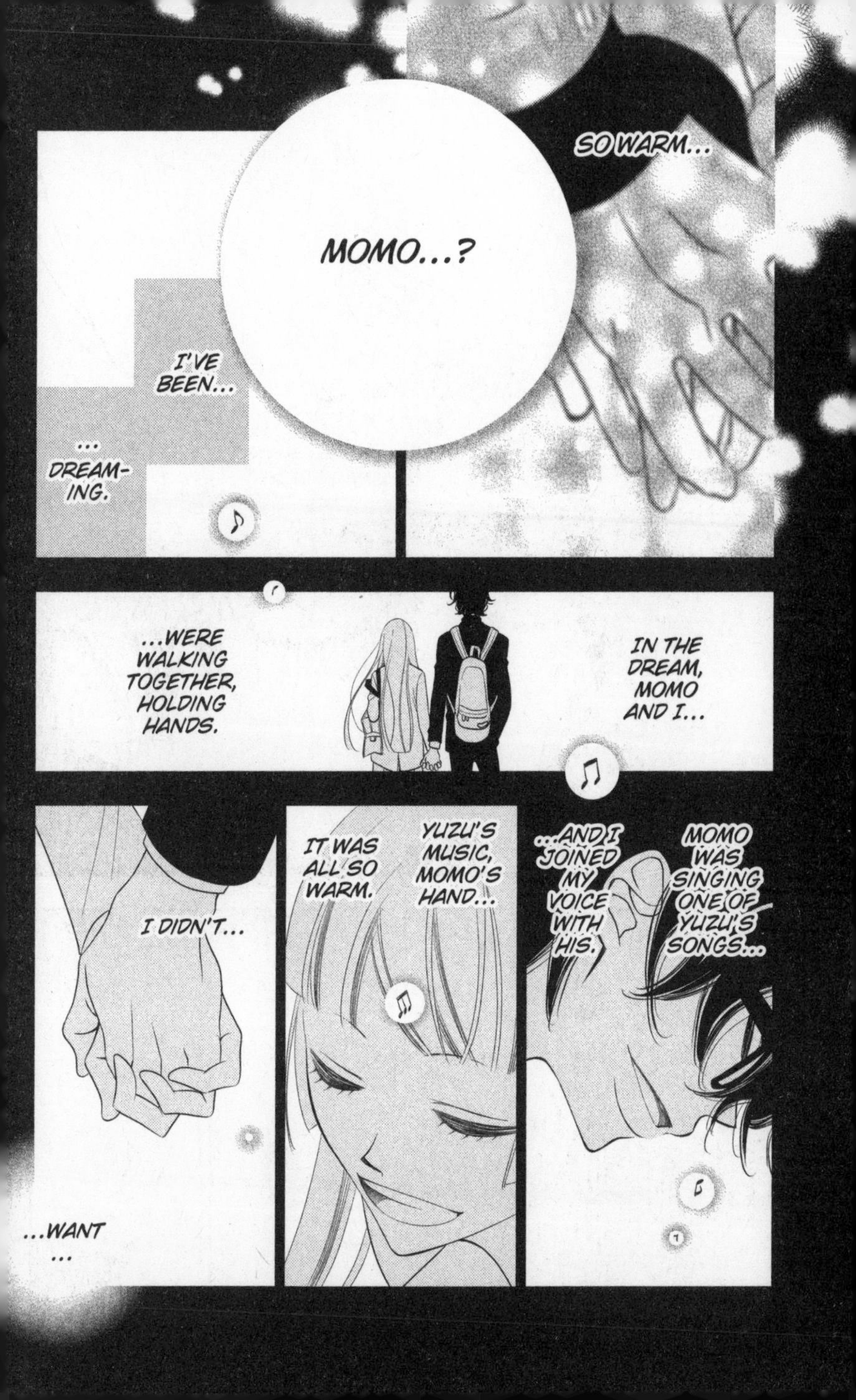
SO WARM...
MOMO...?
I'VE BEEN...
...DREAMING.
IN THE DREAM, MOMO AND I...
...WERE WALKING TOGETHER, HOLDING HANDS.
MOMO WAS SINGING ONE OF YUZU'S SONGS...
...AND I JOINED MY VOICE WITH HIS.
YUZU'S MUSIC, MOMO'S HAND...
IT WAS ALL SO WARM.
I DIDN'T...
...WANT ...

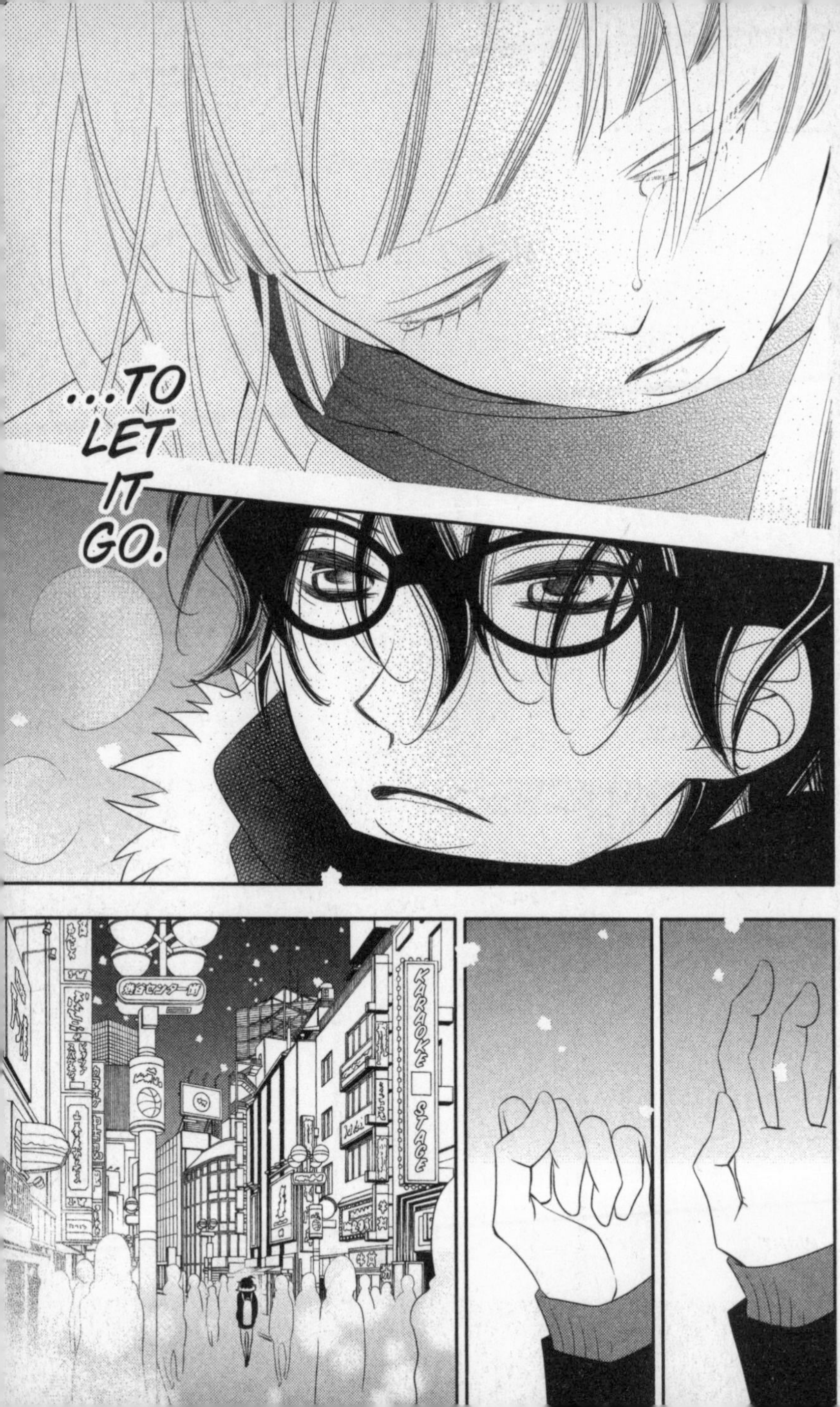
...TO LET IT GO.
KARAOKE
STAGE

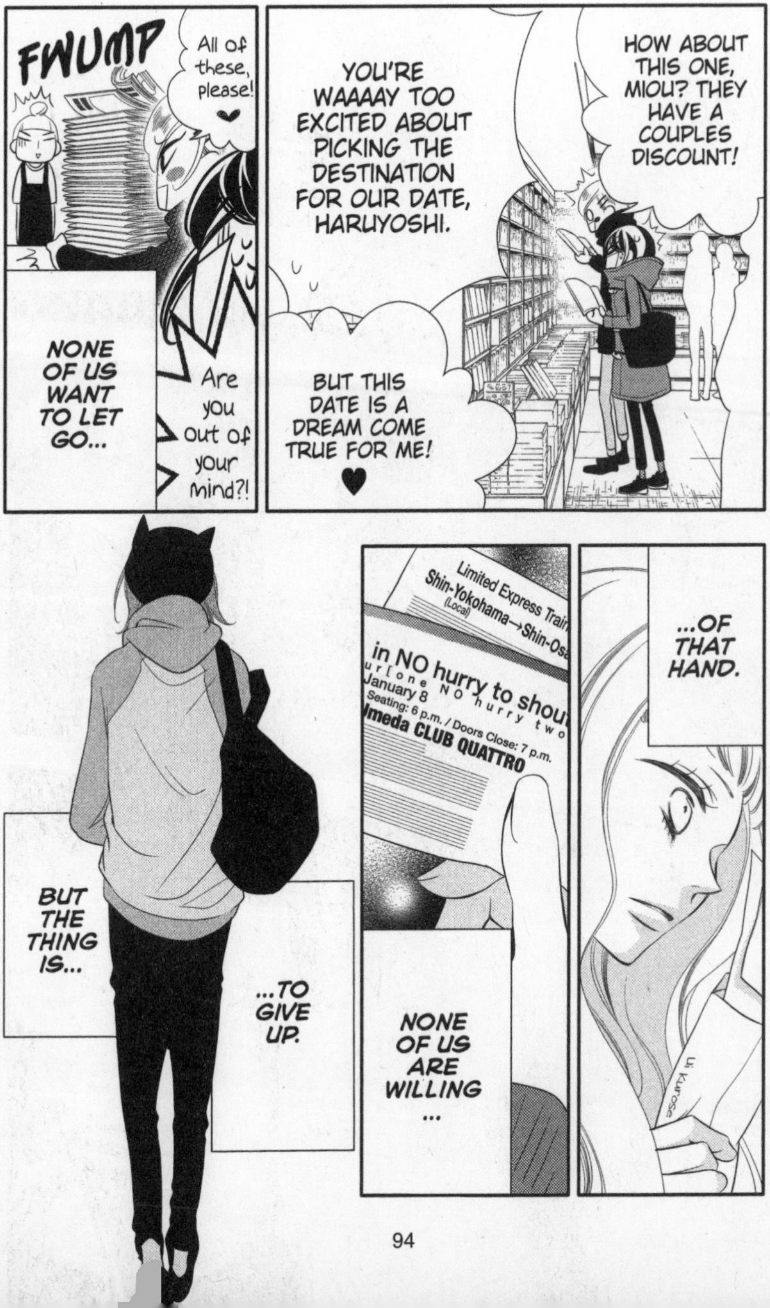
HOW ABOUT THIS ONE, MIOU? THEY HAVE A COUPLES DISCOUNT!
YOU'RE WAAAAY TOO EXCITED ABOUT PICKING THE DESTINATION FOR OUR DATE, HARUYOSHI.
BUT THIS DATE IS A DREAM COME TRUE FOR ME! ♥
All of these, please! ♥
FWUMP
Are you out of your mind?!
NONE OF US WANT TO LET GO...
...OF THAT HAND.
Li Kurose
Limited Express Train
Shin-Yokohama→Shin-Osa
(Local)
in NO hurry to shout
ur[one NO hurry two
January 8
Seating: 6 p.m. / Doors Close: 7 p.m.
Umeda CLUB QUATTRO
NONE OF US ARE WILLING ...
BUT THE THING IS...
...TO GIVE UP.

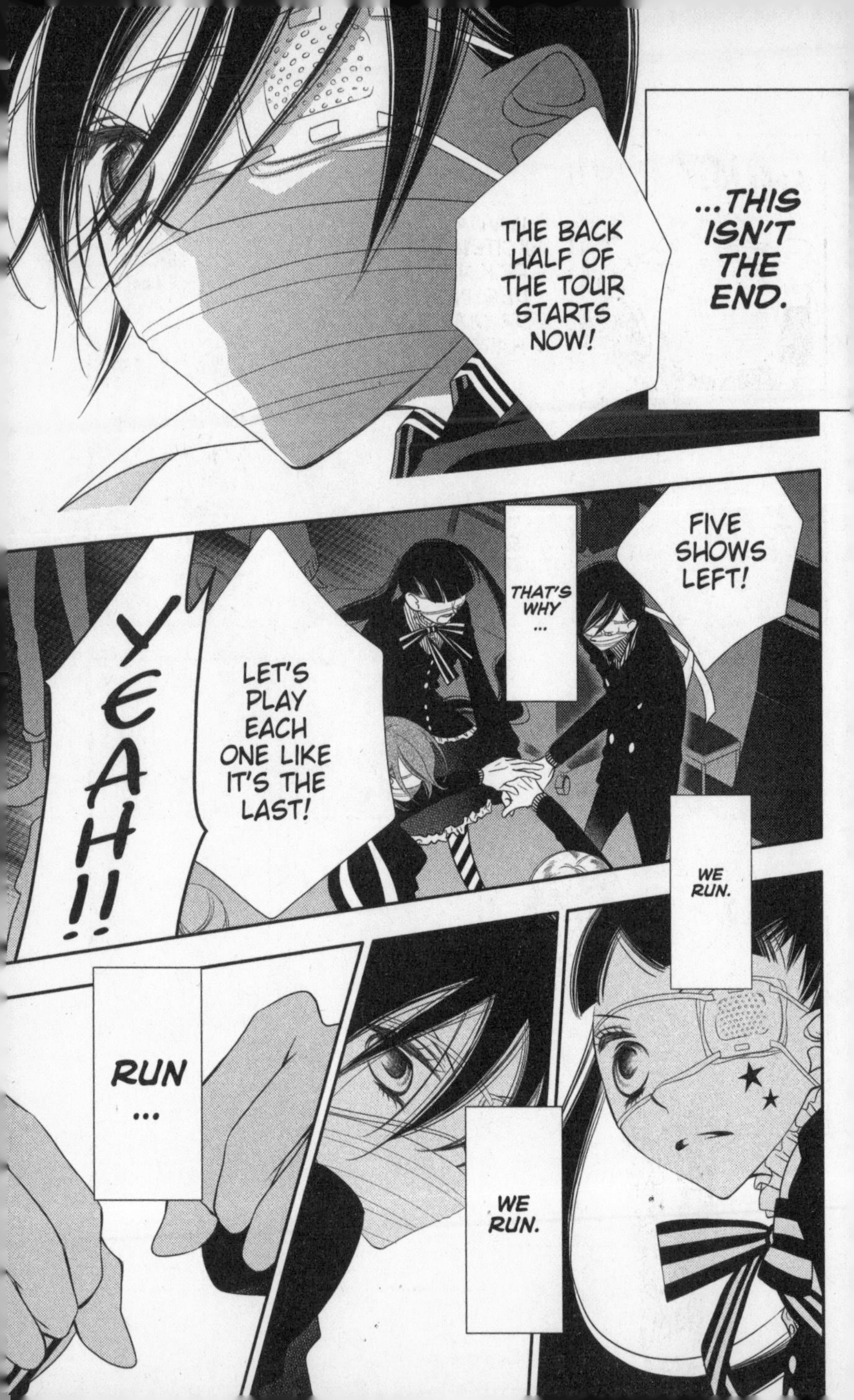
...THIS ISN'T THE END.
THE BACK HALF OF THE TOUR STARTS NOW!
FIVE SHOWS LEFT!
THAT'S WHY ...
LET'S PLAY EACH ONE LIKE IT'S THE LAST!
YEAH!!
WE RUN.
WE RUN.
RUN ...

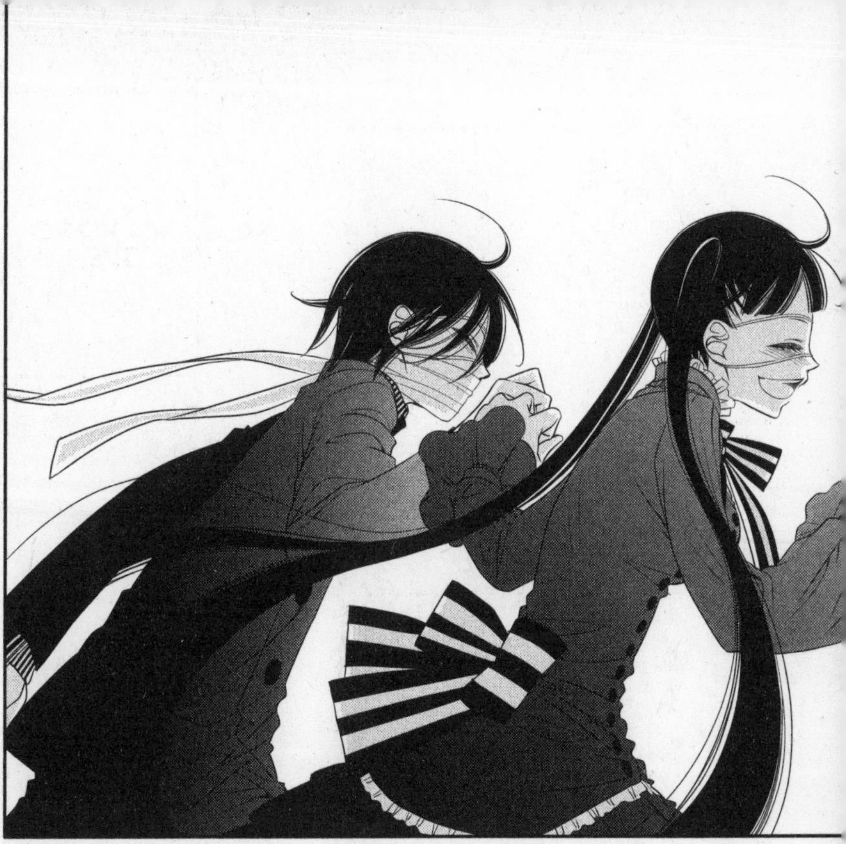

RUN...

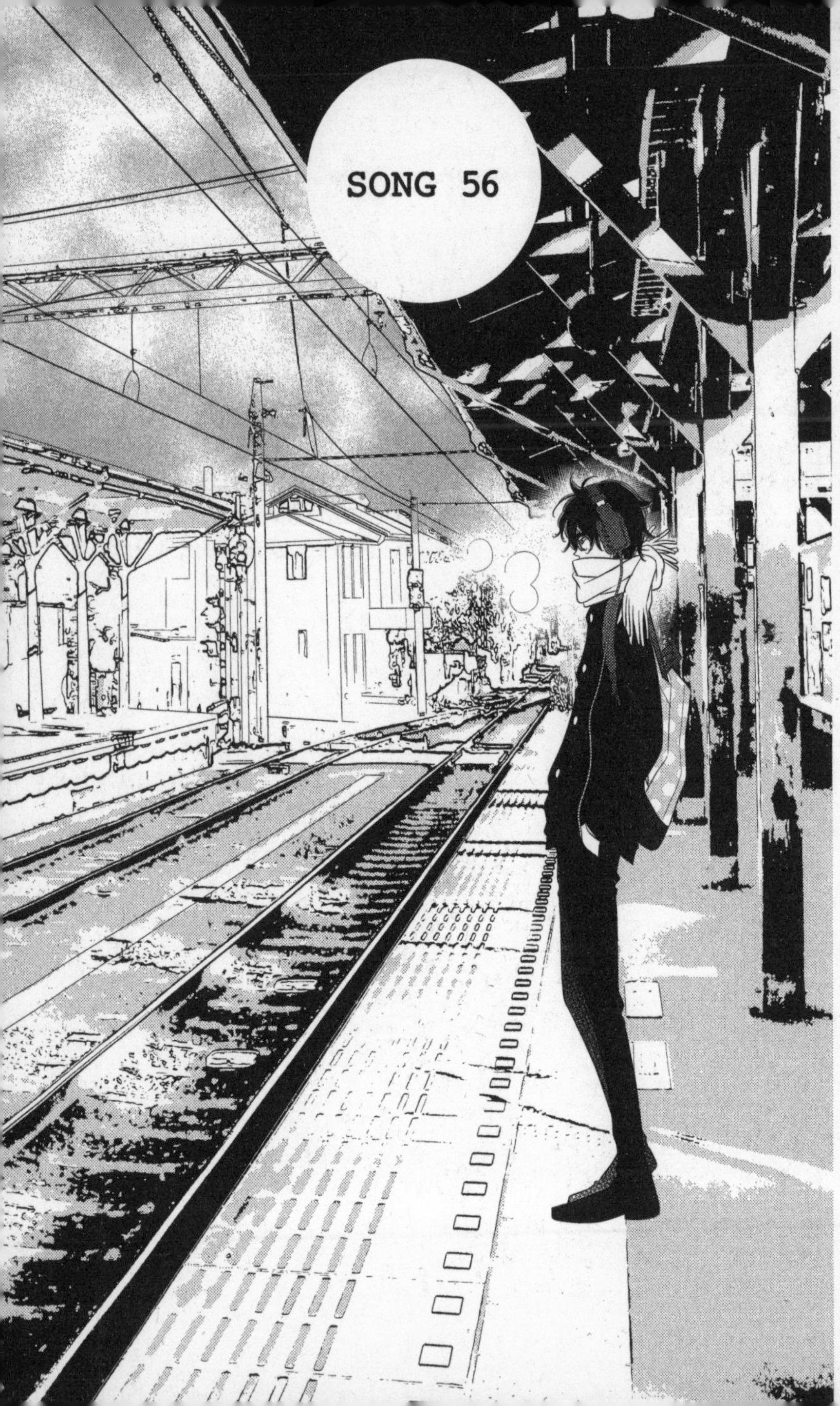
SONG 56

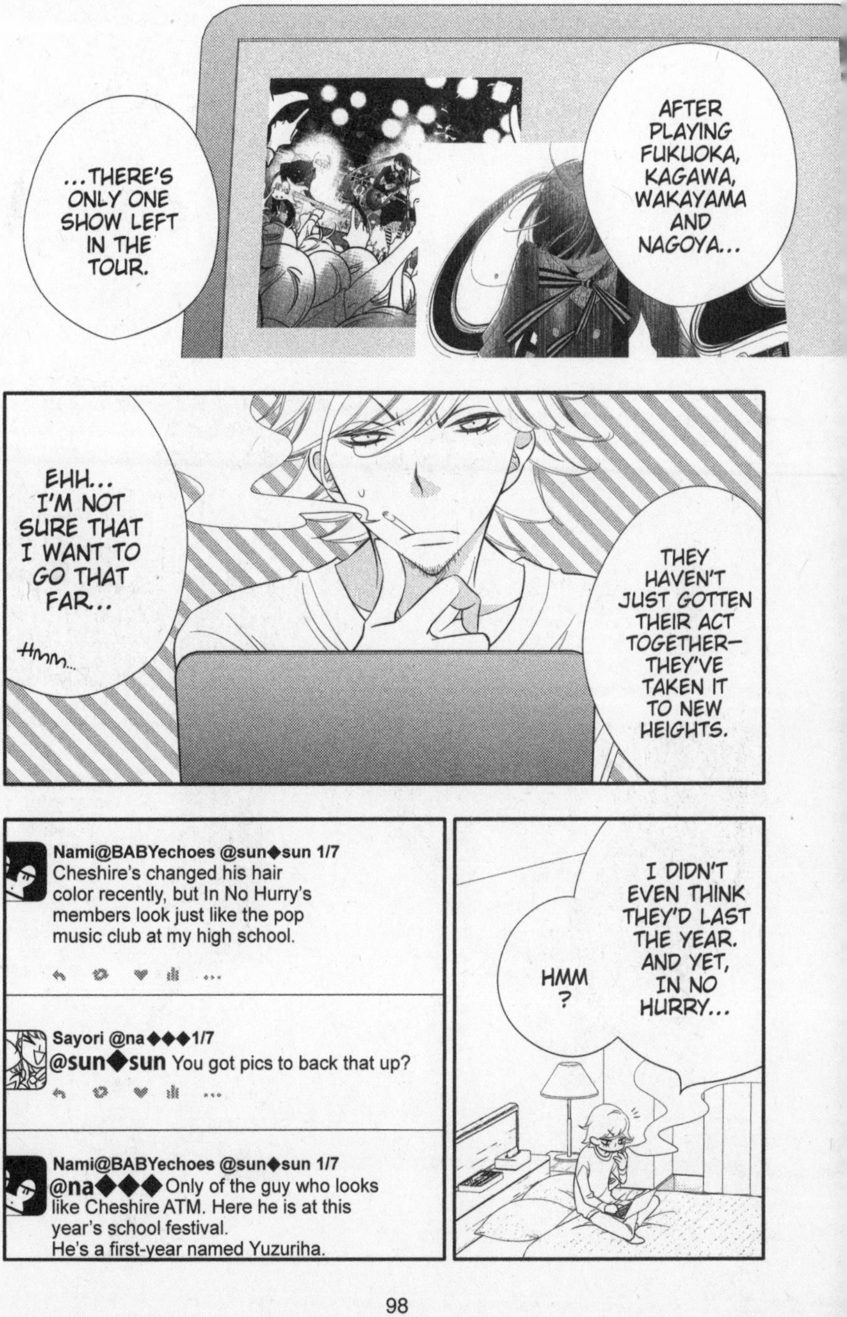
AFTER PLAYING FUKUOKA, KAGAWA, WAKAYAMA AND NAGOYA...
...THERE'S ONLY ONE SHOW LEFT IN THE TOUR.
THEY HAVEN'T JUST GOTTEN THEIR ACT TOGETHER—THEY'VE TAKEN IT TO NEW HEIGHTS.
EHH... I'M NOT SURE THAT I WANT TO GO THAT FAR...
Hmm...
I DIDN'T EVEN THINK THEY'D LAST THE YEAR. AND YET, IN NO HURRY...
HMM ?
Nami@BABYechoes @sun◆sun 1/7
Cheshire's changed his hair color recently, but In No Hurry's members look just like the pop music club at my high school.
Sayori @na◆◆◆1/7
@sun◆sun You got pics to back that up?
Nami@BABYechoes @sun◆sun 1/7
@na◆◆◆ Only of the guy who looks like Cheshire ATM. Here he is at this year's school festival.
He's a first-year named Yuzuriha.

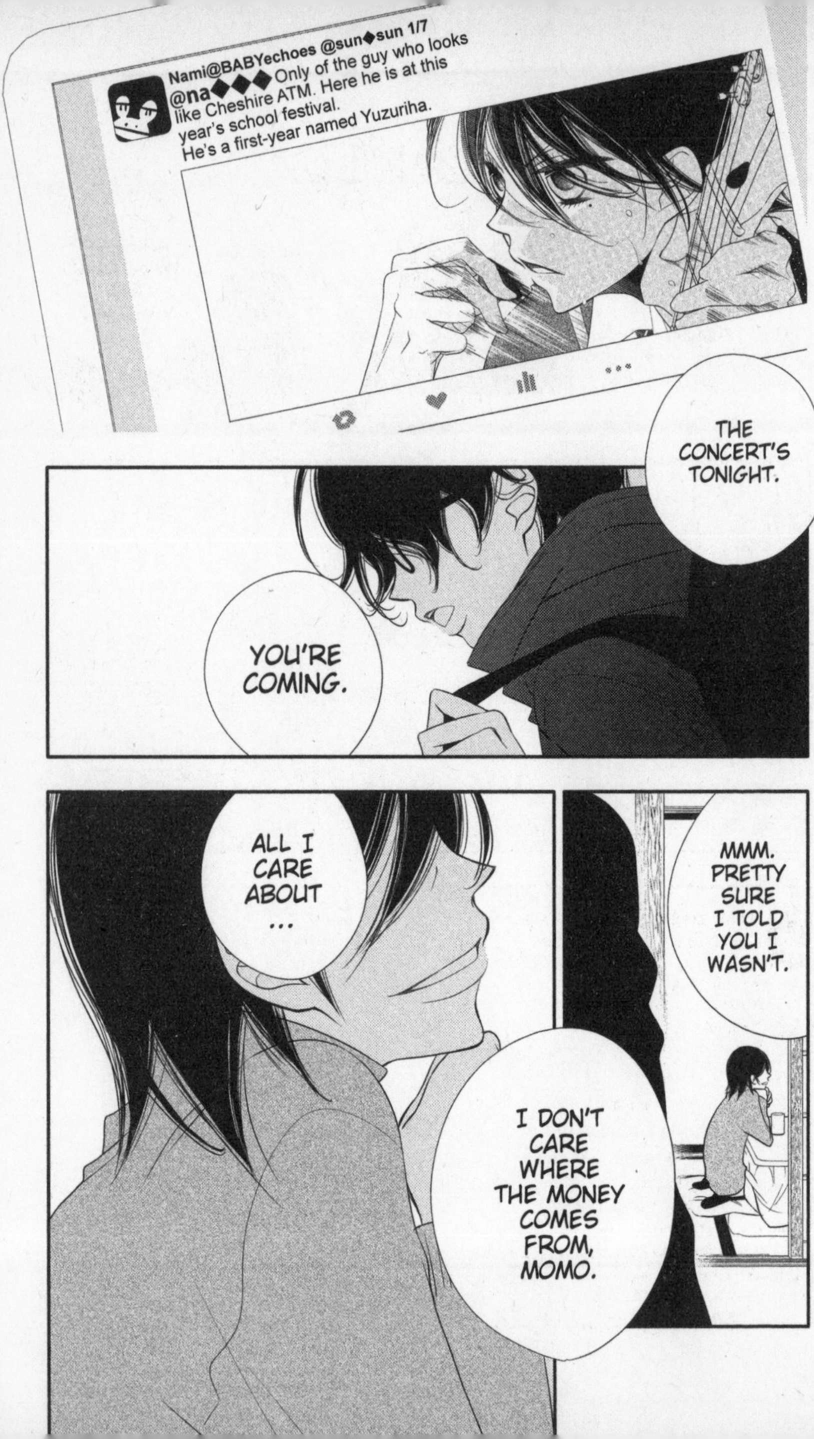
Nami@BABYechoes @sun◆sun 1/7
@na◆◆◆ Only of the guy who looks like Cheshire ATM. Here he is at this year's school festival. He's a first-year named Yuzuriha.
THE CONCERT'S TONIGHT.
YOU'RE COMING.
MMM. PRETTY SURE I TOLD YOU I WASN'T.
ALL I CARE ABOUT...
I DON'T CARE WHERE THE MONEY COMES FROM, MOMO.

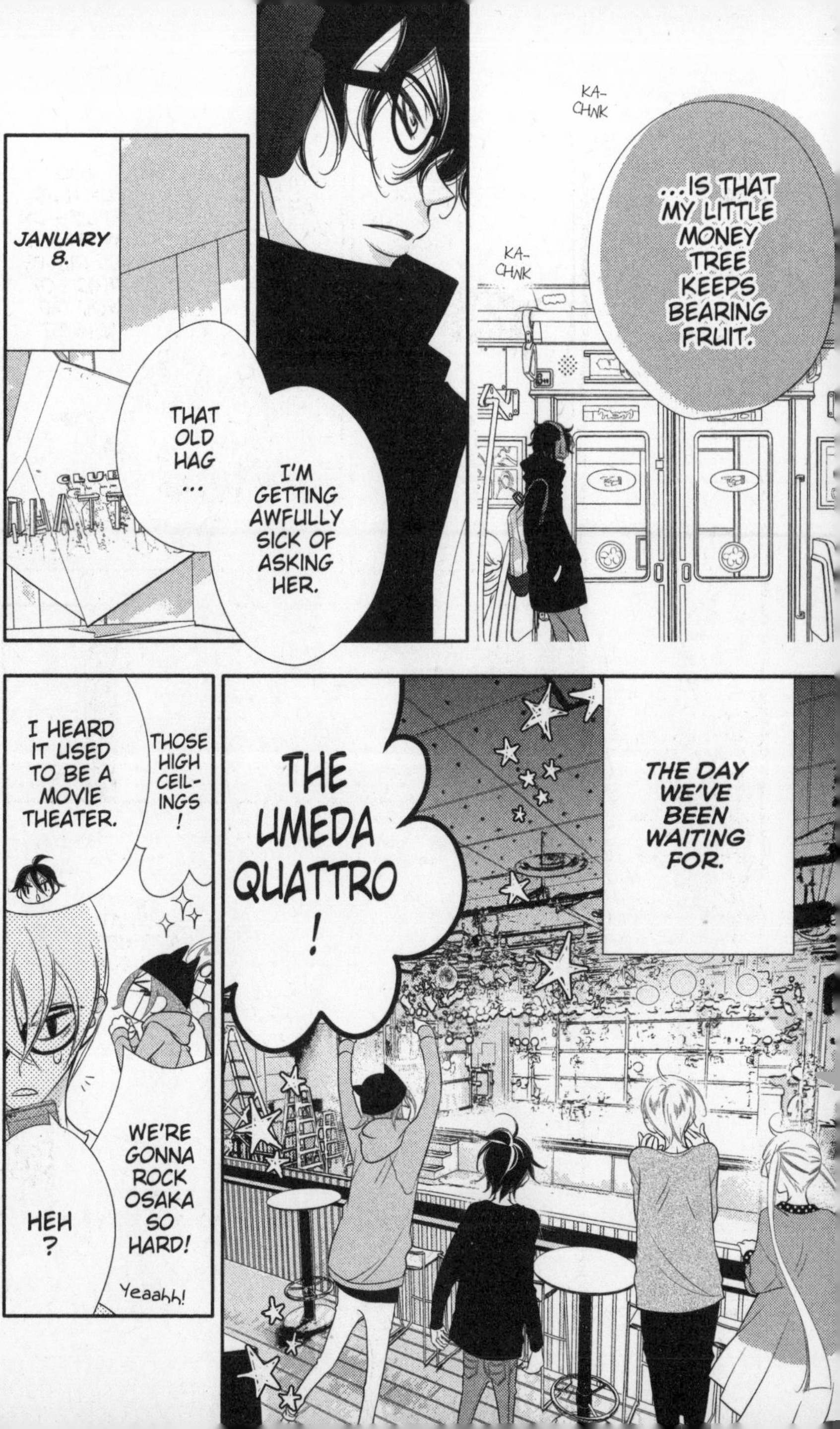
KA-CHNK
...IS THAT MY LITTLE MONEY TREE KEEPS BEARING FRUIT.
KA-CHNK
I'M GETTING AWFULLY SICK OF ASKING HER.
THAT OLD HAG ...
JANUARY 8.
THE DAY WE'VE BEEN WAITING FOR.
THE UMEDA QUATTRO!
THOSE HIGH CEILINGS!
I HEARD IT USED TO BE A MOVIE THEATER.
WE'RE GONNA ROCK OSAKA SO HARD!
HEH?
Yeaahh!

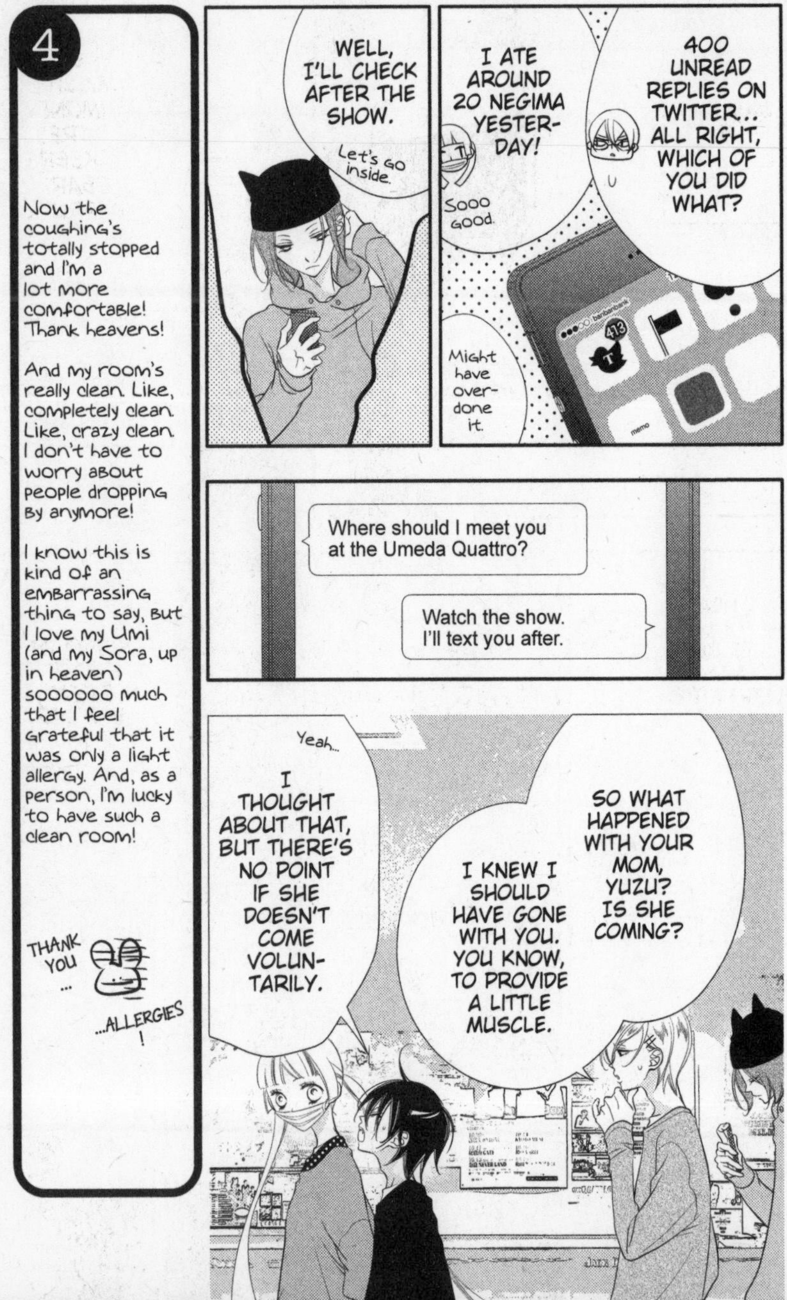
400 UNREAD REPLIES ON TWITTER... ALL RIGHT, WHICH OF YOU DID WHAT?
I ATE AROUND 20 NEGIMA YESTERDAY!
Sooo good.
Might have overdone it.
memo
WELL, I'LL CHECK AFTER THE SHOW.
Let's go inside.
Where should I meet you at the Umeda Quattro?
Watch the show. I'll text you after.
SO WHAT HAPPENED WITH YOUR MOM, YUZU? IS SHE COMING?
I KNEW I SHOULD HAVE GONE WITH YOU. YOU KNOW, TO PROVIDE A LITTLE MUSCLE.
Yeah...
I THOUGHT ABOUT THAT, BUT THERE'S NO POINT IF SHE DOESN'T COME VOLUNTARILY.

4

Now the coughing's totally stopped and I'm a lot more comfortable! Thank heavens!

And my room's really clean. Like, completely clean. Like, crazy clean. I don't have to worry about people dropping by anymore!

I know this is kind of an embarrassing thing to say, but I love my Umi (and my Sora, up in heaven) soooooo much that I feel grateful that it was only a light allergy. And, as a person, I'm lucky to have such a clean room!

THANK YOU ... ...ALLERGIES!

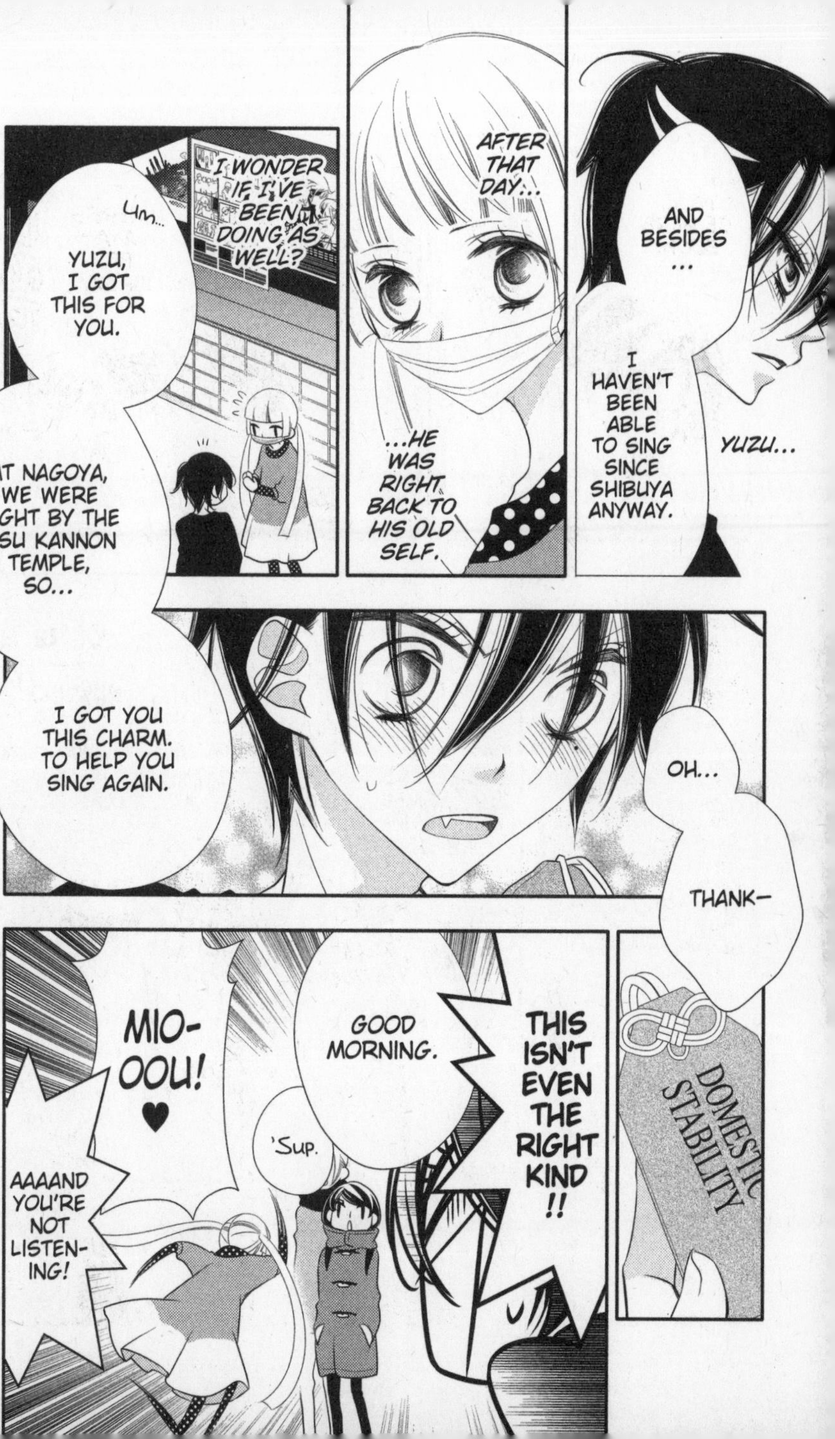
AND BESIDES ...
I HAVEN'T BEEN ABLE TO SING SINCE SHIBUYA ANYWAY.
YUZU...
AFTER THAT DAY...
...HE WAS RIGHT BACK TO HIS OLD SELF.
I WONDER IF I'VE BEEN DOING AS WELL?
Um...
YUZU, I GOT THIS FOR YOU.
AT NAGOYA, WE WERE RIGHT BY THE OSU KANNON TEMPLE, SO...
I GOT YOU THIS CHARM. TO HELP YOU SING AGAIN.
OH...
THANK-
DOMESTIC STABILITY
THIS ISN'T EVEN THE RIGHT KIND !!
GOOD MORNING.
MIO-OOU! ♥
'Sup.
AAAAND YOU'RE NOT LISTEN-ING!

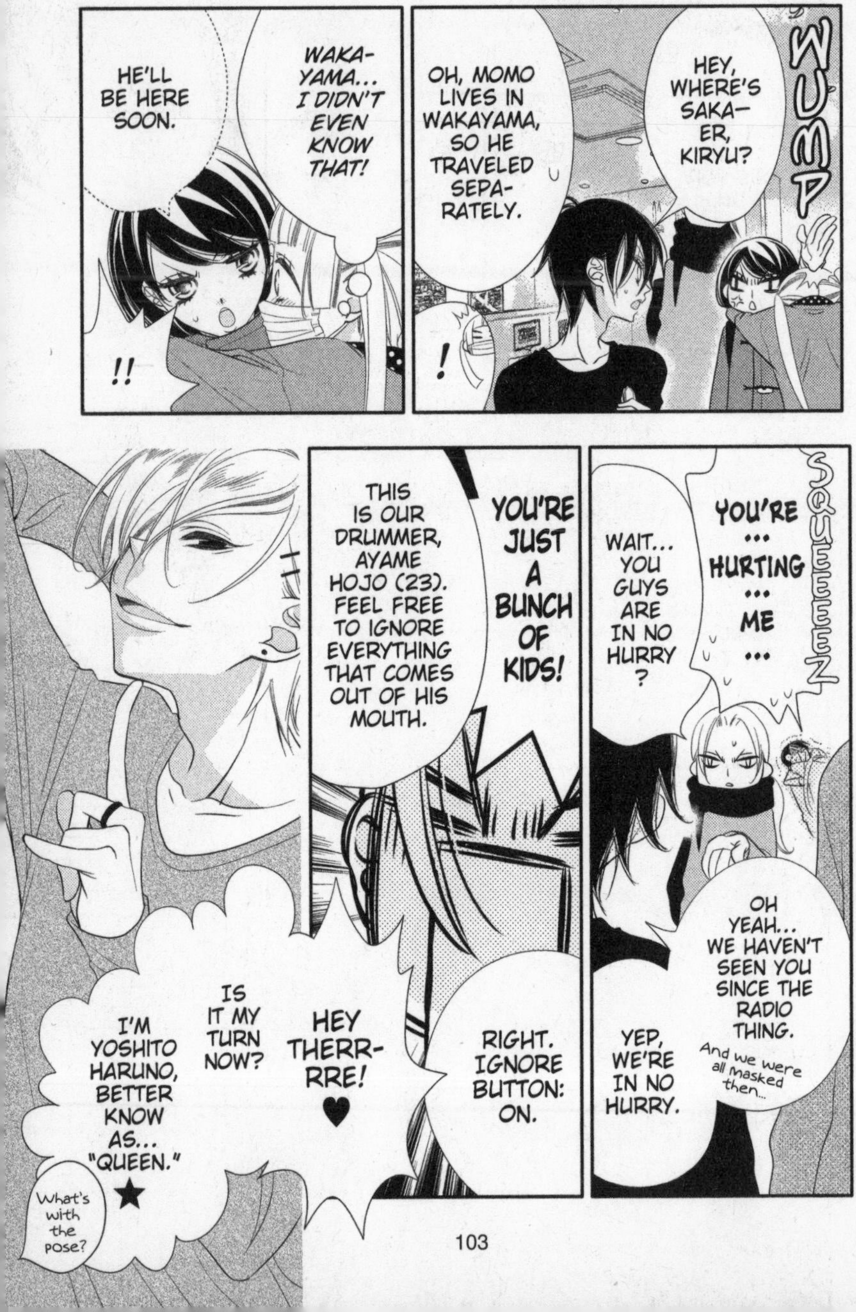
WUMP
HEY, WHERE'S SAKA-ER, KIRYU?
OH, MOMO LIVES IN WAKAYAMA, SO HE TRAVELED SEPA-RATELY.
!
WAKA-YAMA... I DIDN'T EVEN KNOW THAT!
HE'LL BE HERE SOON.
!!
SQUEEEZ
YOU'RE ... HURTING ... ME ...
WAIT... YOU GUYS ARE IN NO HURRY?
OH YEAH... WE HAVEN'T SEEN YOU SINCE THE RADIO THING.
And we were all masked then...
YEP, WE'RE IN NO HURRY.
YOU'RE JUST A BUNCH OF KIDS!
THIS IS OUR DRUMMER, AYAME HOJO (23). FEEL FREE TO IGNORE EVERYTHING THAT COMES OUT OF HIS MOUTH.
RIGHT. IGNORE BUTTON: ON.
HEY THERRR-RRE! ♥
IS IT MY TURN NOW?
I'M YOSHITO HARUNO, BETTER KNOW AS... "QUEEN." ★
What's with the pose?

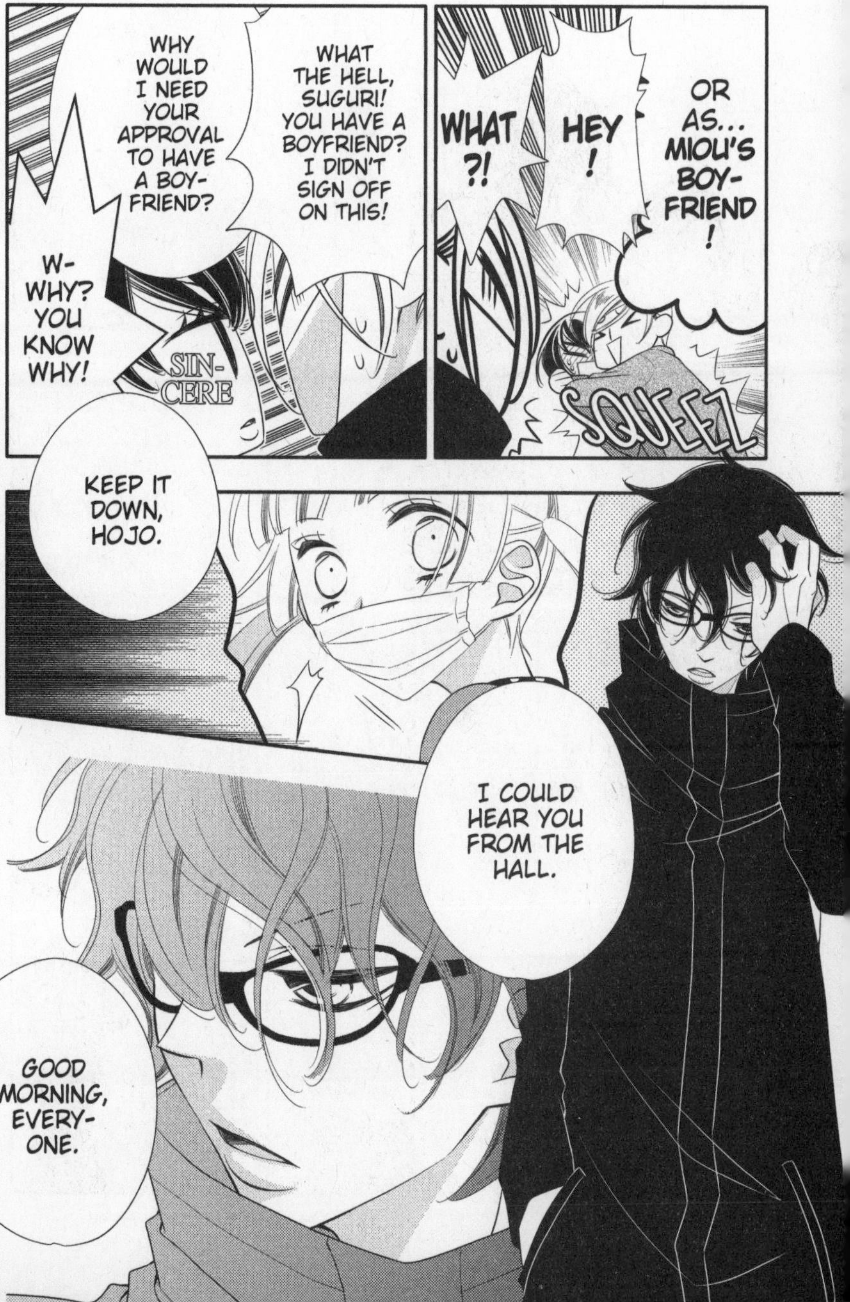
OR AS... MIOU'S BOY-FRIEND!
HEY!
WHAT?!
SQUEEZ
WHAT THE HELL, SUGURI! YOU HAVE A BOYFRIEND? I DIDN'T SIGN OFF ON THIS!
WHY WOULD I NEED YOUR APPROVAL TO HAVE A BOY-FRIEND?
SIN-CERE
W-WHY? YOU KNOW WHY!
KEEP IT DOWN, HOJO.
I COULD HEAR YOU FROM THE HALL.
GOOD MORNING, EVERY-ONE.

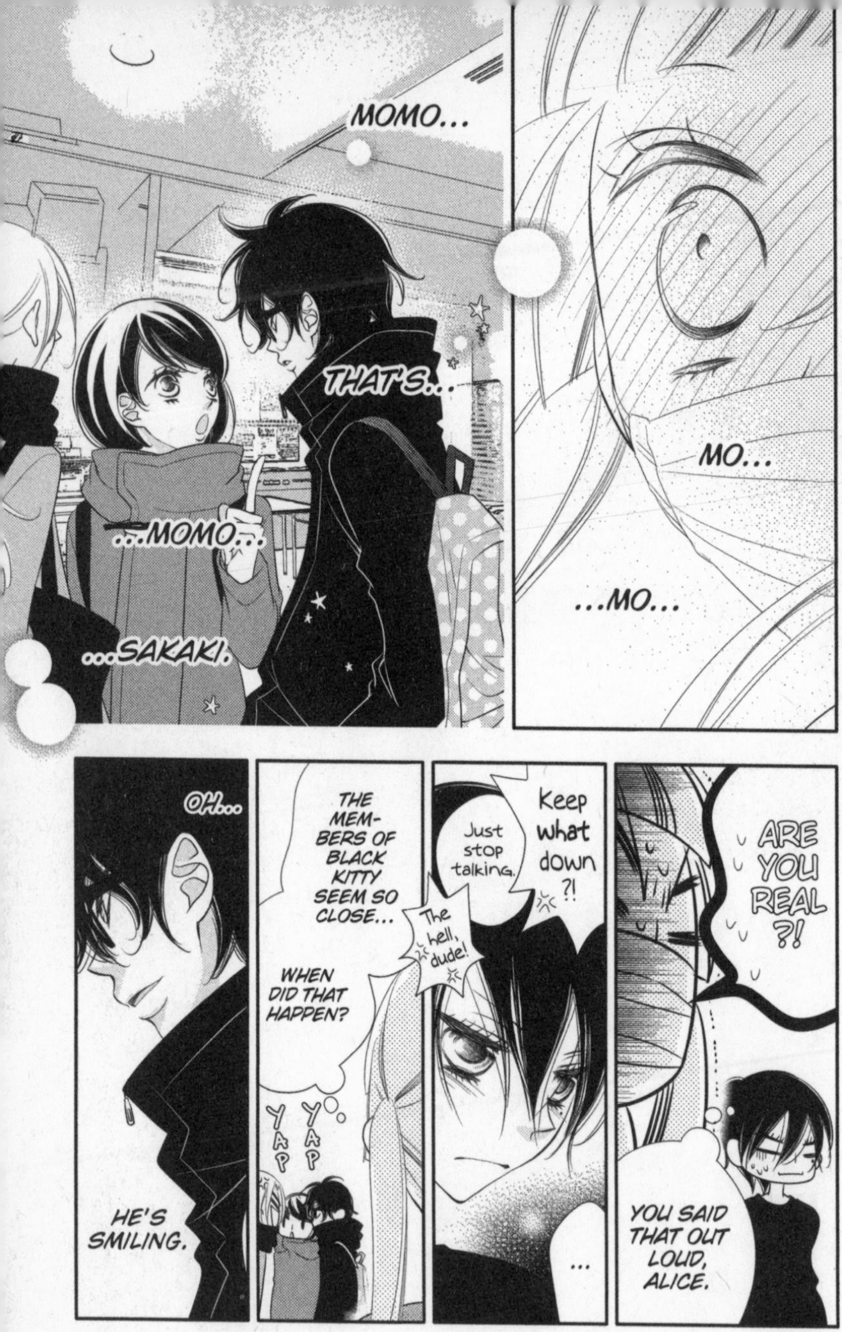
MO...
...MO...
MOMO...
THAT'S...
...MOMO...
...SAKAKI.
ARE YOU REAL?!
YOU SAID THAT OUT LOUD, ALICE.
Keep what down?!
Just stop talking.
The hell, dude!
...
THE MEMBERS OF BLACK KITTY SEEM SO CLOSE...
WHEN DID THAT HAPPEN?
YAP YAP
OH...
HE'S SMILING.

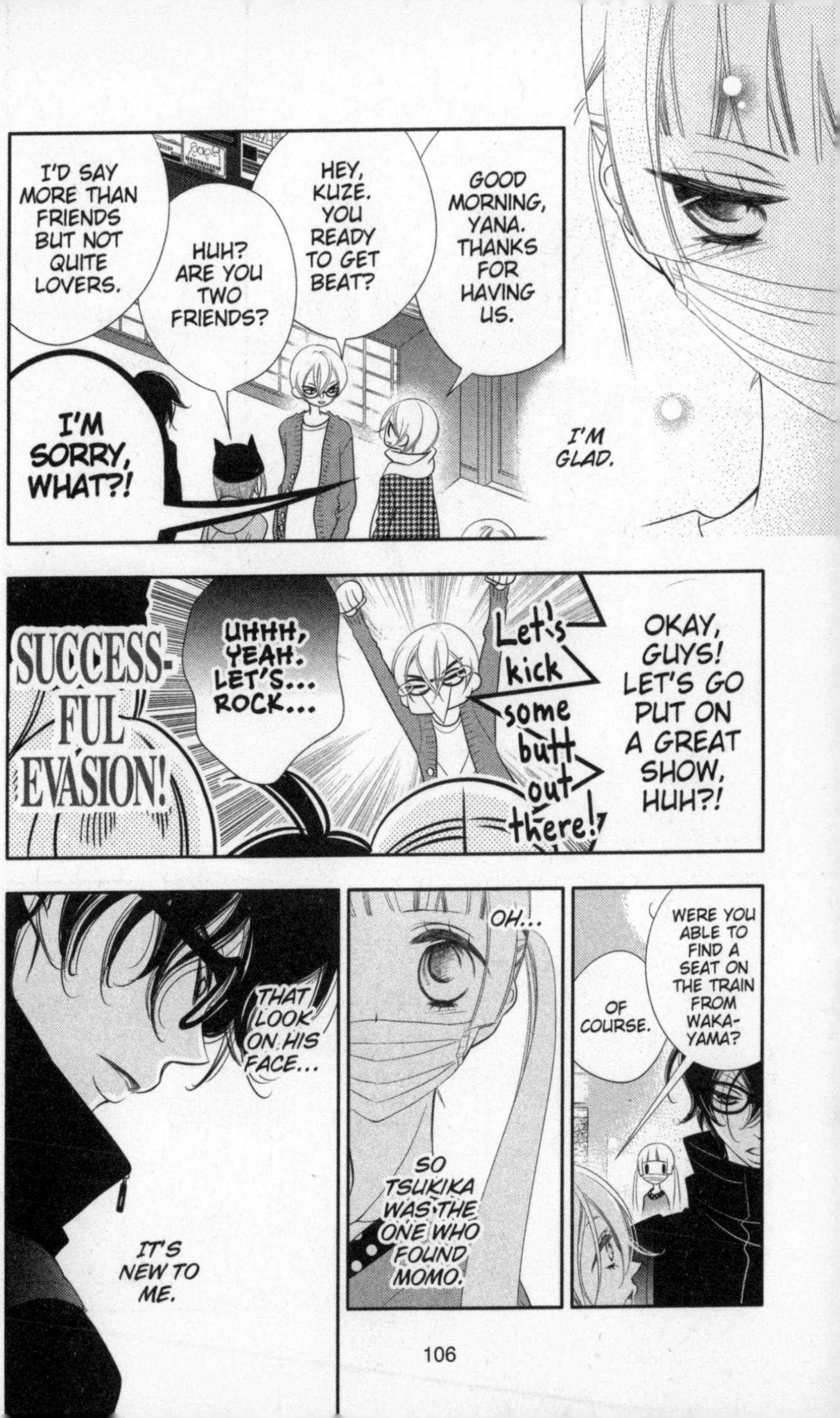
I'M GLAD.
GOOD MORNING, YANA. THANKS FOR HAVING US.
HEY, KUZE. YOU READY TO GET BEAT?
HUH? ARE YOU TWO FRIENDS?
I'D SAY MORE THAN FRIENDS BUT NOT QUITE LOVERS.
I'M SORRY, WHAT?!
OKAY, GUYS! LET'S GO PUT ON A GREAT SHOW, HUH?!
Let's kick some butt out there!
UHHH, YEAH. LET'S... ROCK...
SUCCESS-FUL EVASION!
WERE YOU ABLE TO FIND A SEAT ON THE TRAIN FROM WAKA-YAMA?
OF COURSE.
OH...
SO TSUKIKA WAS THE ONE WHO FOUND MOMO.
THAT LOOK ON HIS FACE...
IT'S NEW TO ME.

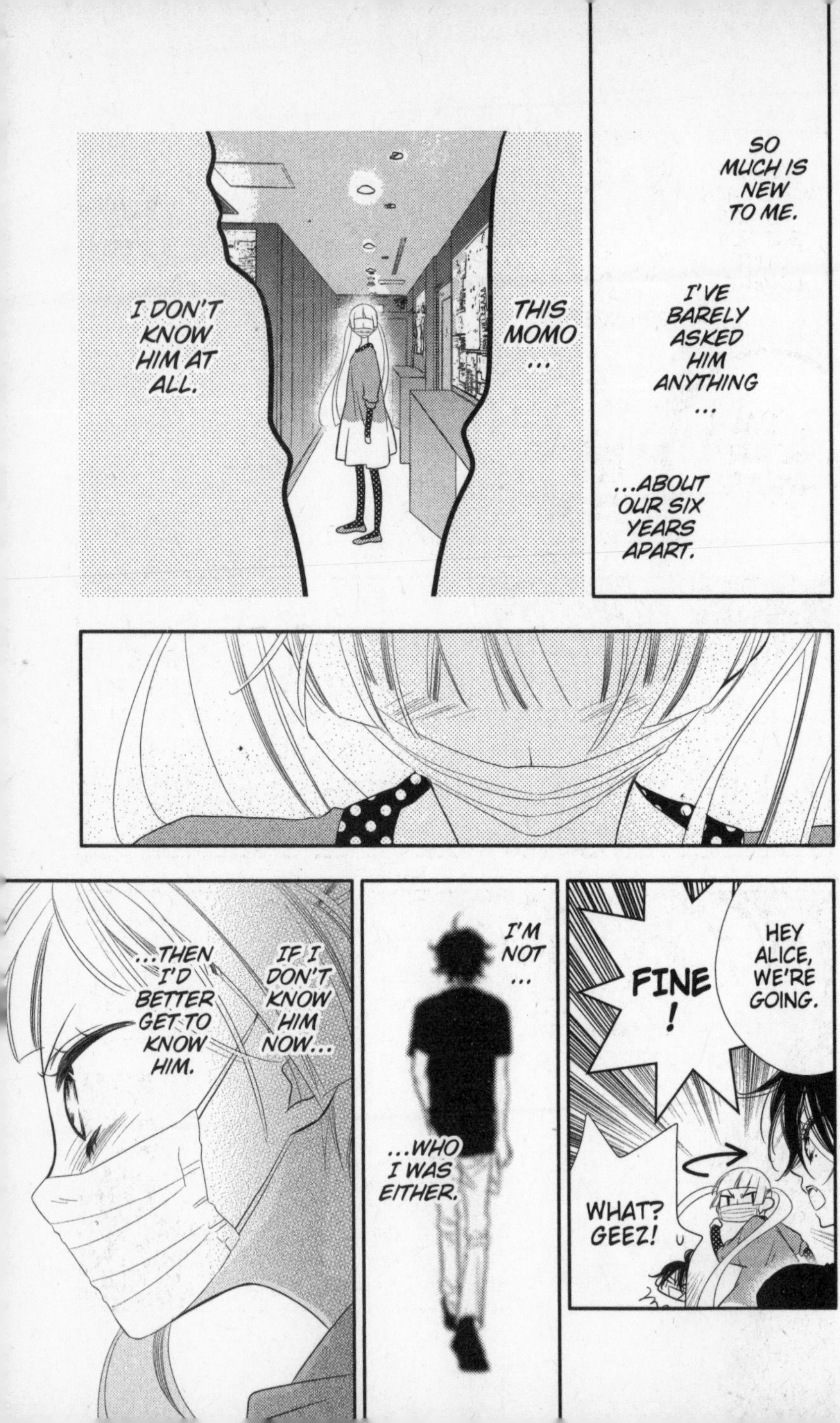
SO MUCH IS NEW TO ME.
I'VE BARELY ASKED HIM ANYTHING...
...ABOUT OUR SIX YEARS APART.
THIS MOMO...
I DON'T KNOW HIM AT ALL.
HEY ALICE, WE'RE GOING.
FINE!
WHAT? GEEZ!
I'M NOT...
...WHO I WAS EITHER.
IF I DON'T KNOW HIM NOW...
...THEN I'D BETTER GET TO KNOW HIM.

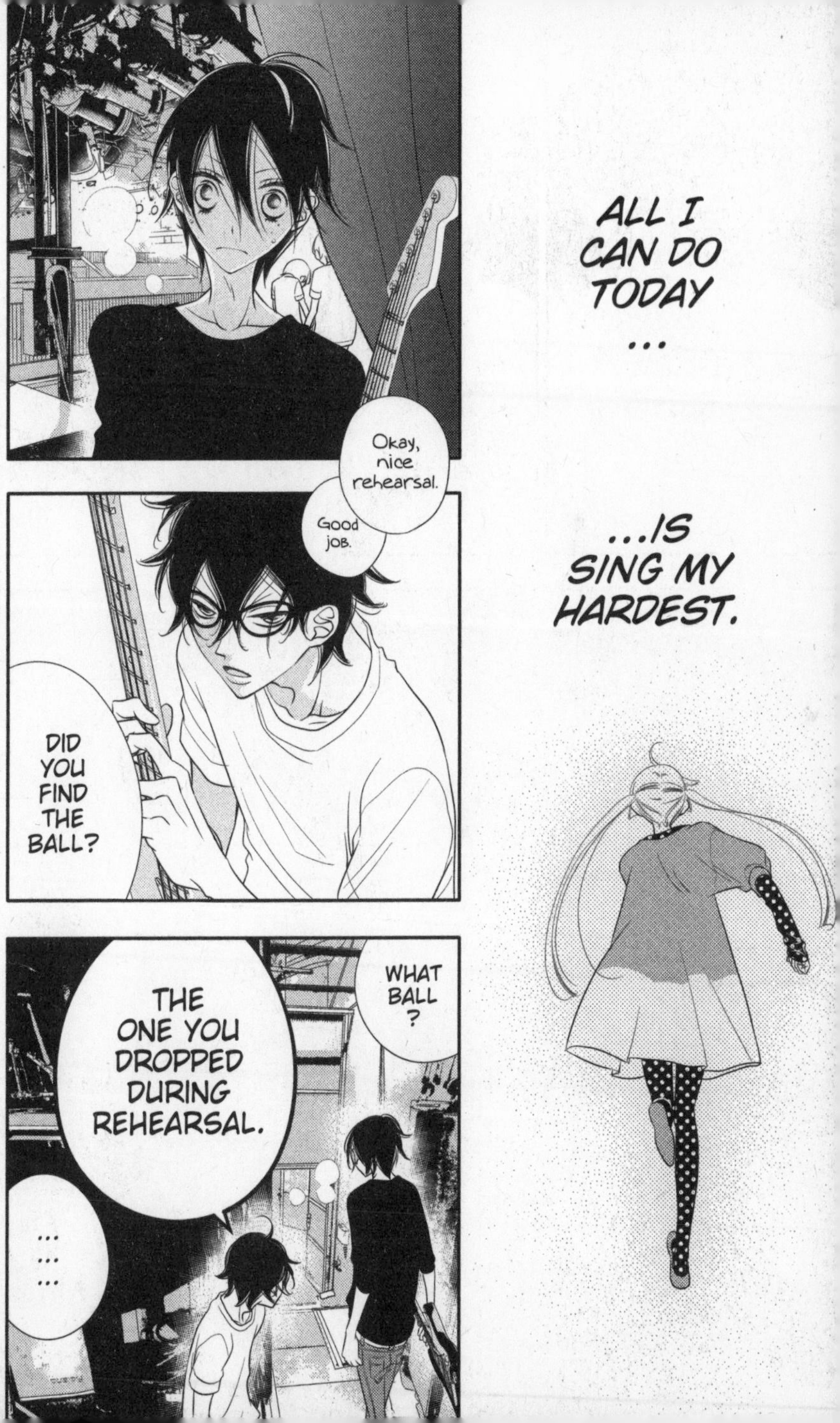
ALL I CAN DO TODAY ...
...IS SING MY HARDEST.
Okay, nice rehearsal.
Good job.
DID YOU FIND THE BALL?
WHAT BALL ?
THE ONE YOU DROPPED DURING REHEARSAL.
... ...

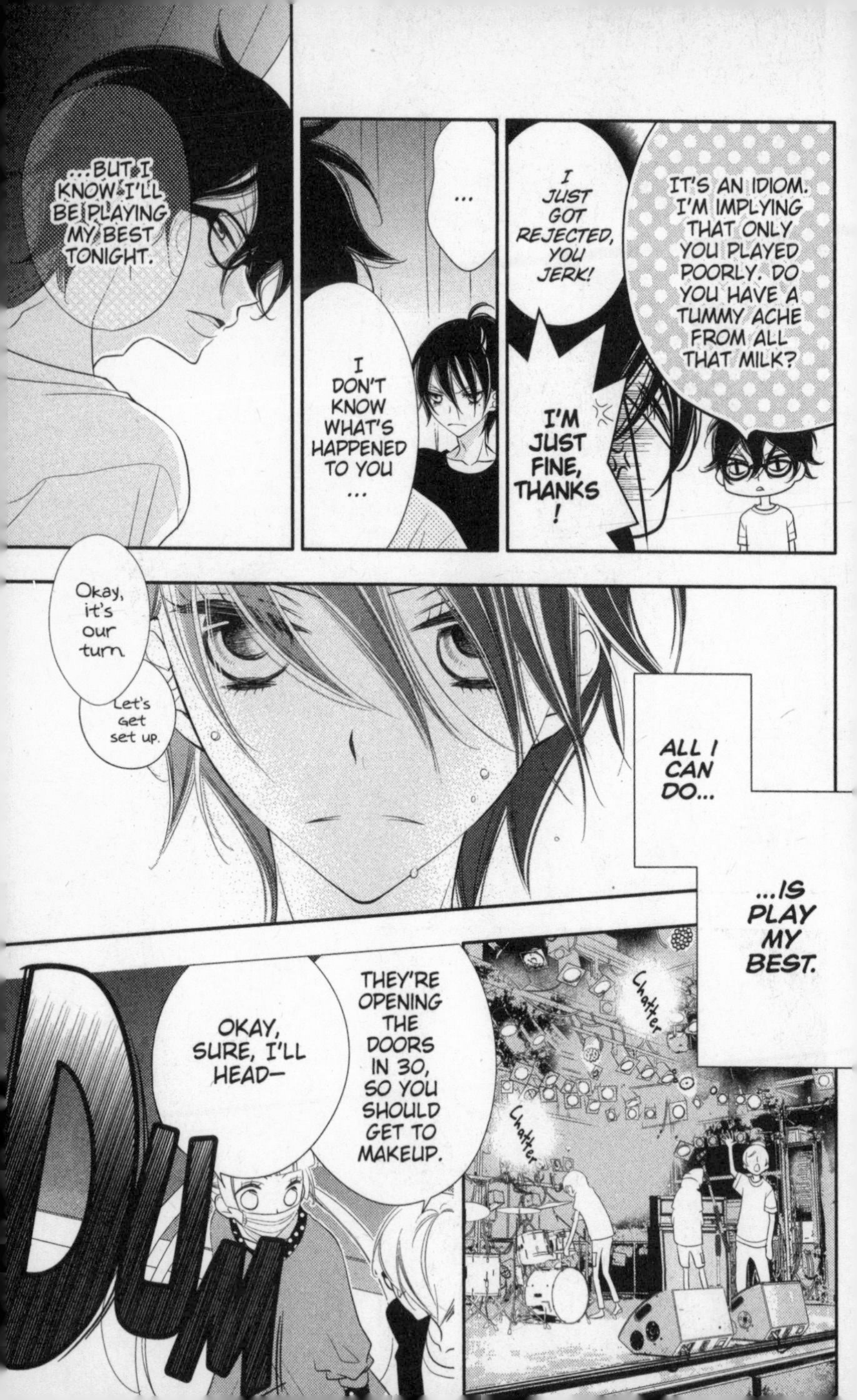
IT'S AN IDIOM. I'M IMPLYING THAT ONLY YOU PLAYED POORLY. DO YOU HAVE A TUMMY ACHE FROM ALL THAT MILK?
I JUST GOT REJECTED, YOU JERK!
I'M JUST FINE, THANKS!
...
I DON'T KNOW WHAT'S HAPPENED TO YOU ...
...BUT I KNOW I'LL BE PLAYING MY BEST TONIGHT.
ALL I CAN DO...
...IS PLAY MY BEST.
Okay, it's our turn.
Let's get set up.
Chatter
Chatter
THEY'RE OPENING THE DOORS IN 30, SO YOU SHOULD GET TO MAKEUP.
OKAY, SURE, I'LL HEAD—
DUM

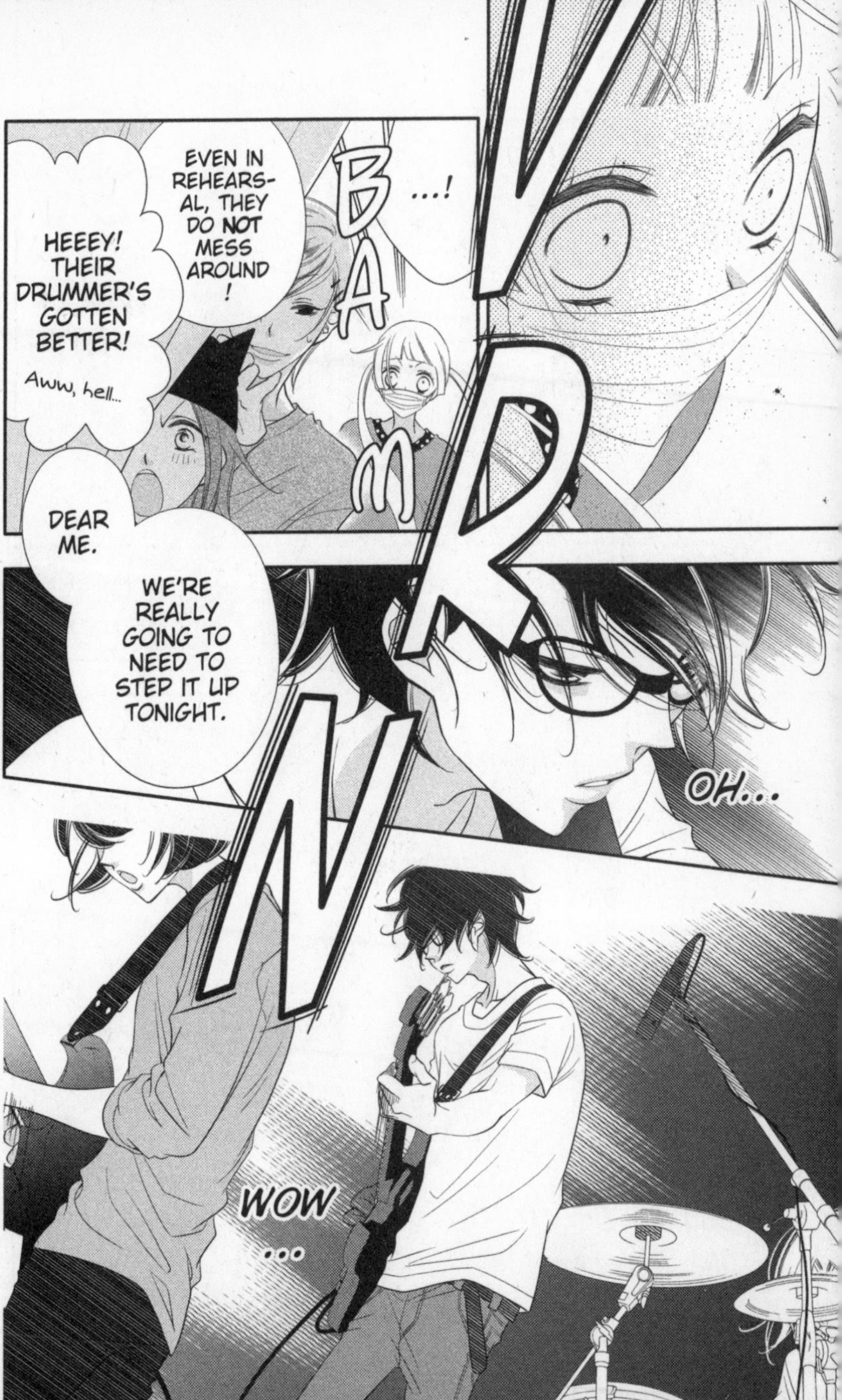
...!
BAMRN
EVEN IN REHEARS-AL, THEY DO NOT MESS AROUND!
HEEEY! THEIR DRUMMER'S GOTTEN BETTER!
Aww, hell...
DEAR ME.
WE'RE REALLY GOING TO NEED TO STEP IT UP TONIGHT.
OH...
WOW...

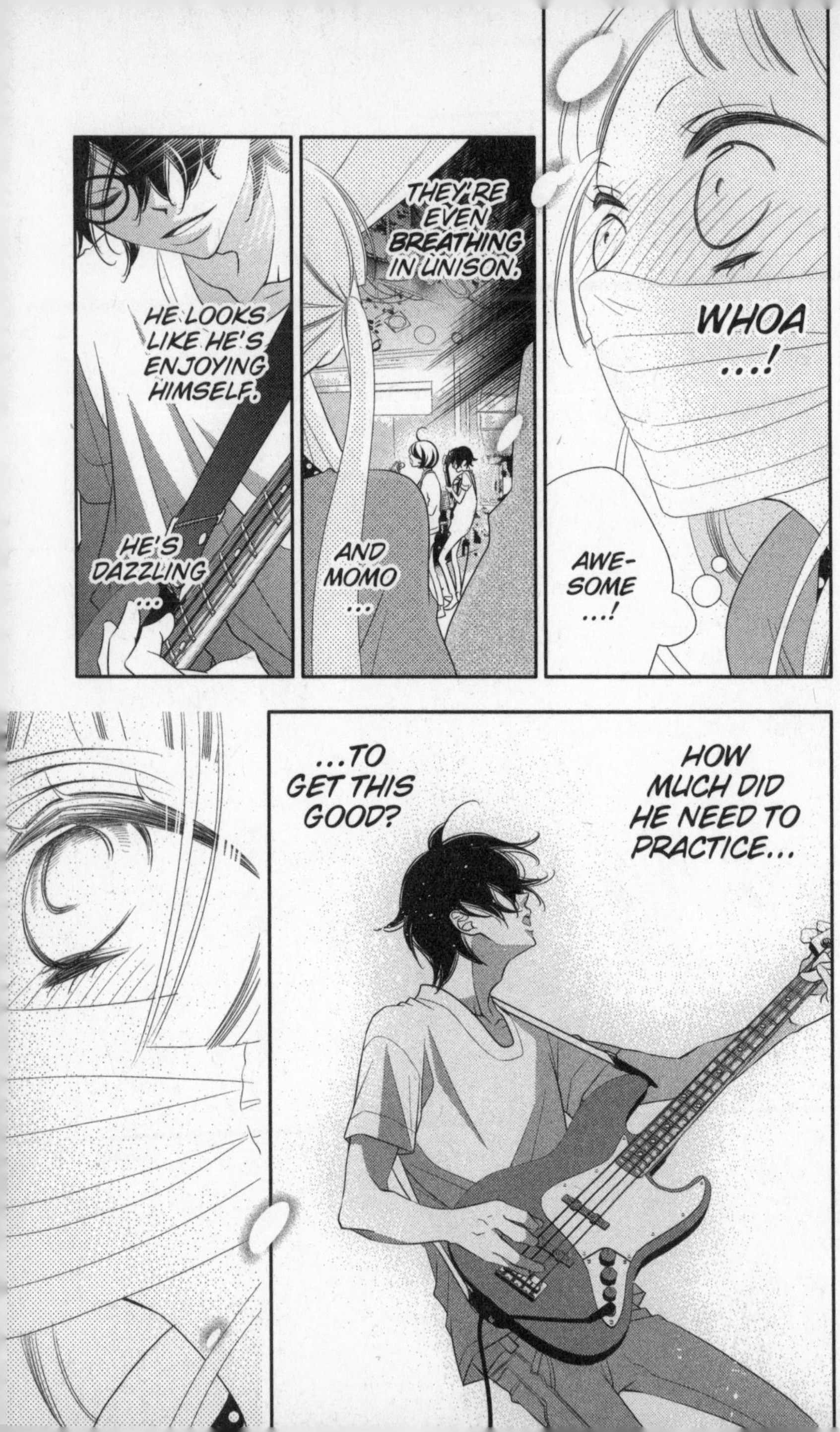
WHOA ...!
AWE-SOME ...!
THEY'RE EVEN BREATHING IN UNISON.
AND MOMO ...
HE LOOKS LIKE HE'S ENJOYING HIMSELF.
HE'S DAZZLING ...
HOW MUCH DID HE NEED TO PRACTICE...
...TO GET THIS GOOD?

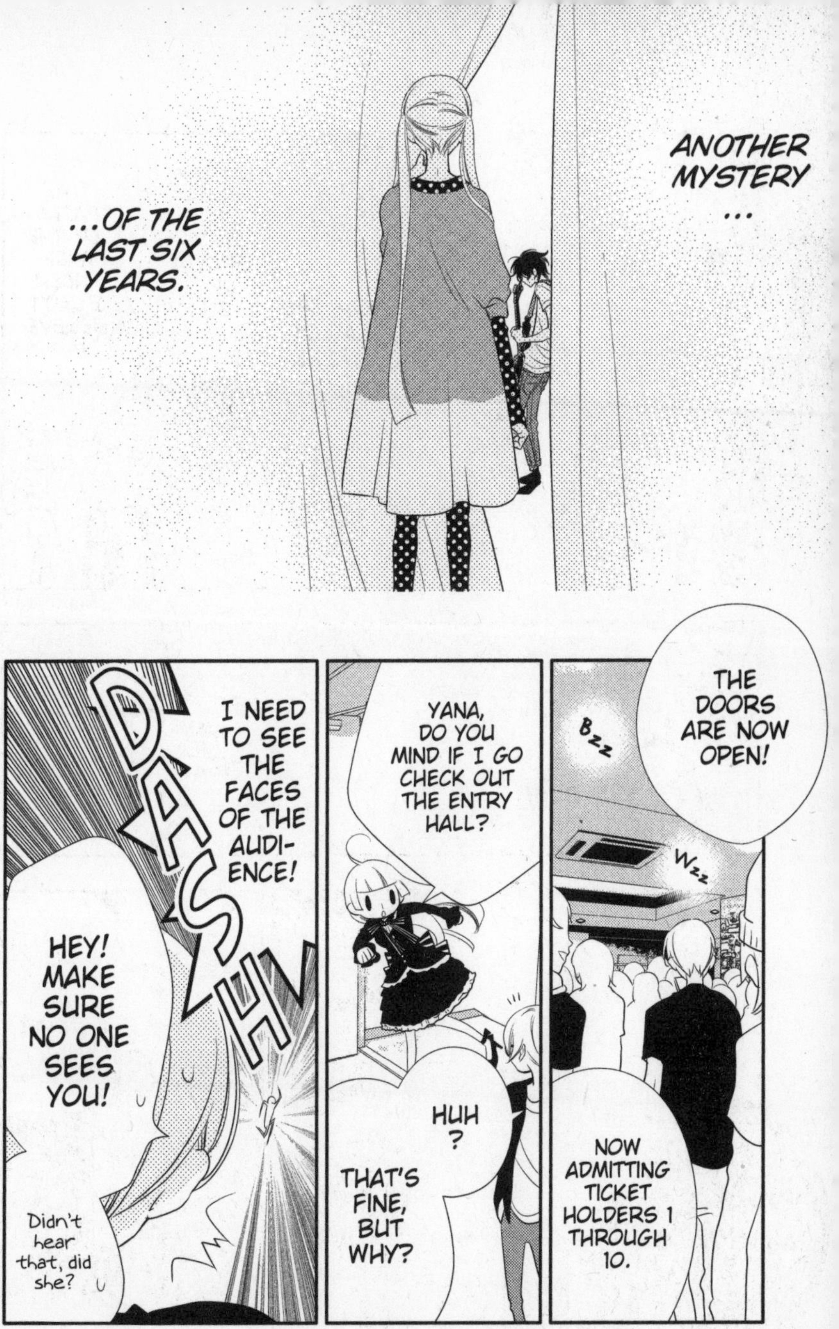
ANOTHER MYSTERY ...
...OF THE LAST SIX YEARS.
THE DOORS ARE NOW OPEN!
Bzz
Wzz
NOW ADMITTING TICKET HOLDERS 1 THROUGH 10.
YANA, DO YOU MIND IF I GO CHECK OUT THE ENTRY HALL?
HUH?
THAT'S FINE, BUT WHY?
I NEED TO SEE THE FACES OF THE AUDIENCE!
DASH
HEY! MAKE SURE NO ONE SEES YOU!
Didn't hear that, did she?

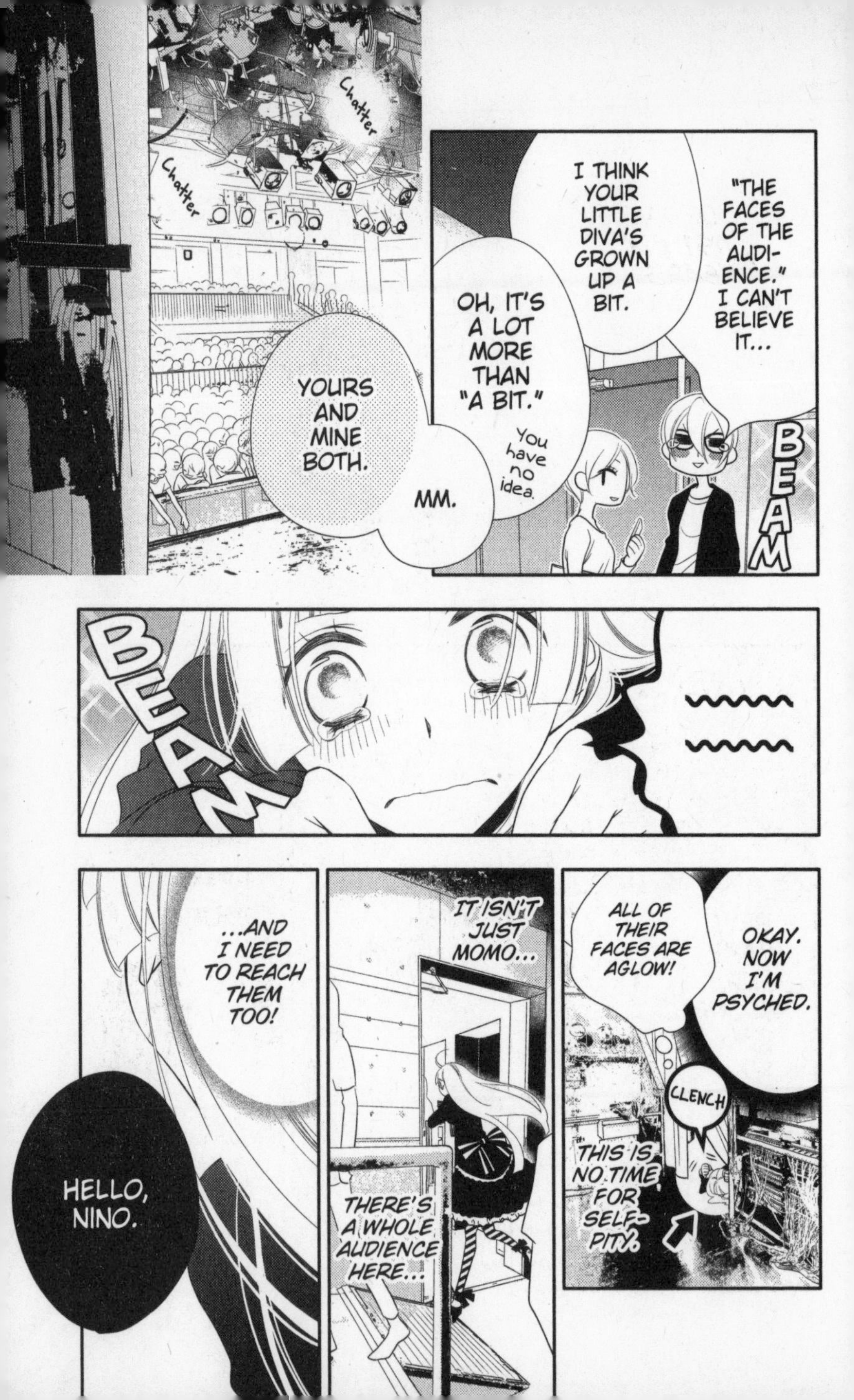
"THE FACES OF THE AUDI- ENCE." I CAN'T BELIEVE IT...
I THINK YOUR LITTLE DIVA'S GROWN UP A BIT.
OH, IT'S A LOT MORE THAN "A BIT."
You have no idea.
BEAM
MM.
YOURS AND MINE BOTH.
Chatter
Chatter
BEAM
OKAY. NOW I'M PSYCHED.
ALL OF THEIR FACES ARE AGLOW!
CLENCH
THIS IS NO TIME FOR SELF- PITY.
IT ISN'T JUST MOMO...
THERE'S A WHOLE AUDIENCE HERE...
...AND I NEED TO REACH THEM TOO!
HELLO, NINO.

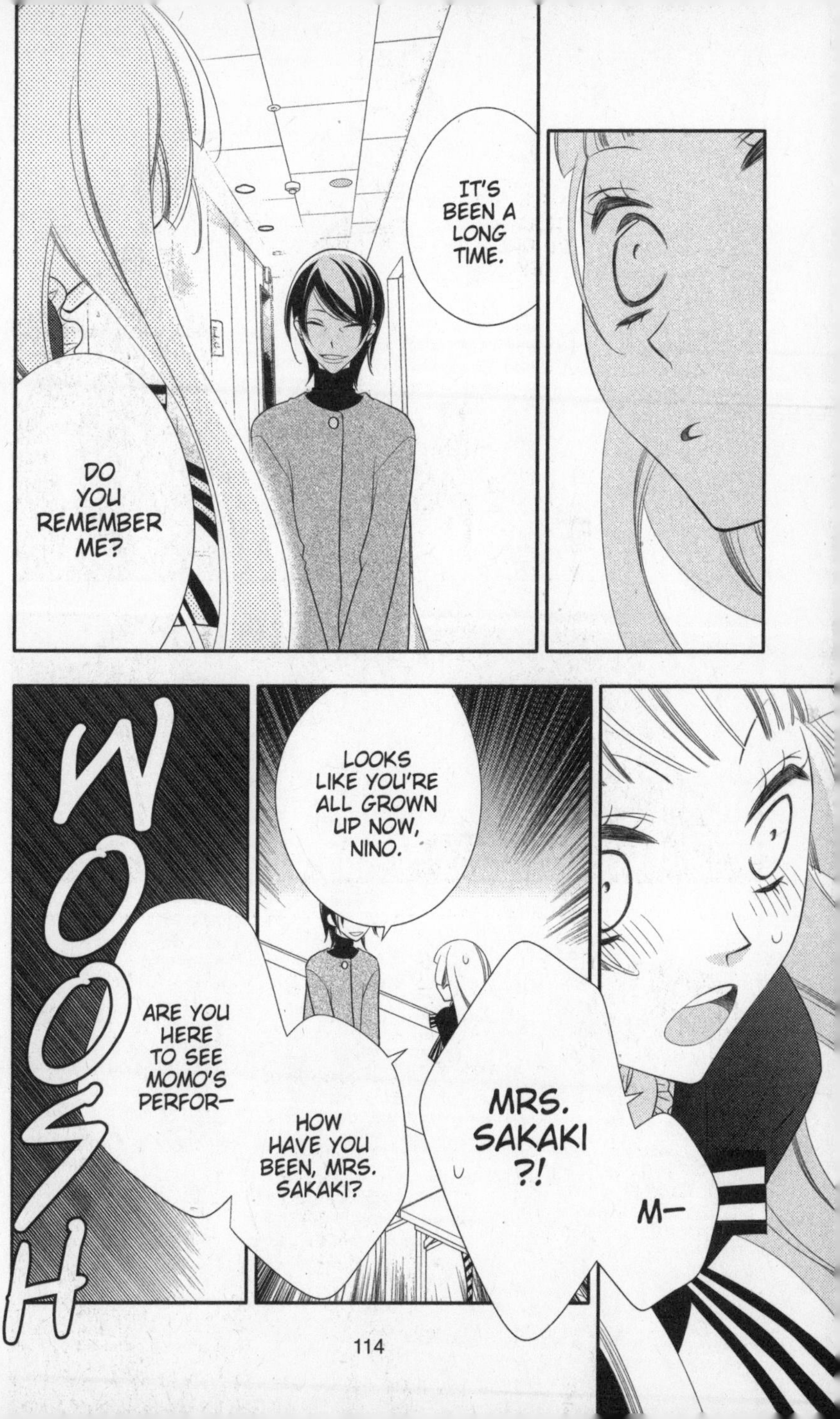
IT'S BEEN A LONG TIME.
DO YOU REMEMBER ME?
M—
MRS. SAKAKI ?!
LOOKS LIKE YOU'RE ALL GROWN UP NOW, NINO.
HOW HAVE YOU BEEN, MRS. SAKAKI?
ARE YOU HERE TO SEE MOMO'S PERFOR—
WOOSH

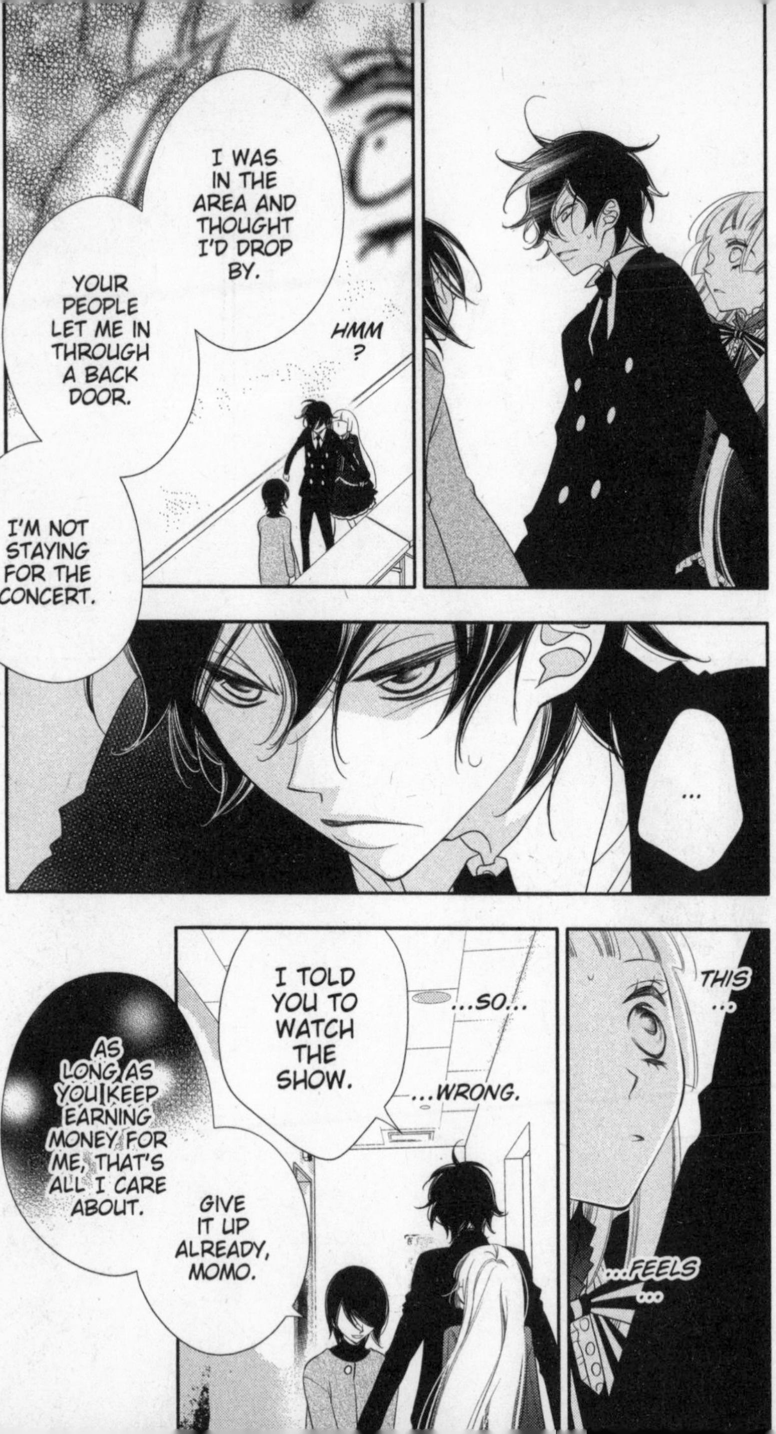
I WAS IN THE AREA AND THOUGHT I'D DROP BY.
HMM?
YOUR PEOPLE LET ME IN THROUGH A BACK DOOR.
I'M NOT STAYING FOR THE CONCERT.
...
THIS...
...FEELS...
...SO...
...WRONG.
I TOLD YOU TO WATCH THE SHOW.
AS LONG AS YOU KEEP EARNING MONEY FOR ME, THAT'S ALL I CARE ABOUT.
GIVE IT UP ALREADY, MOMO.

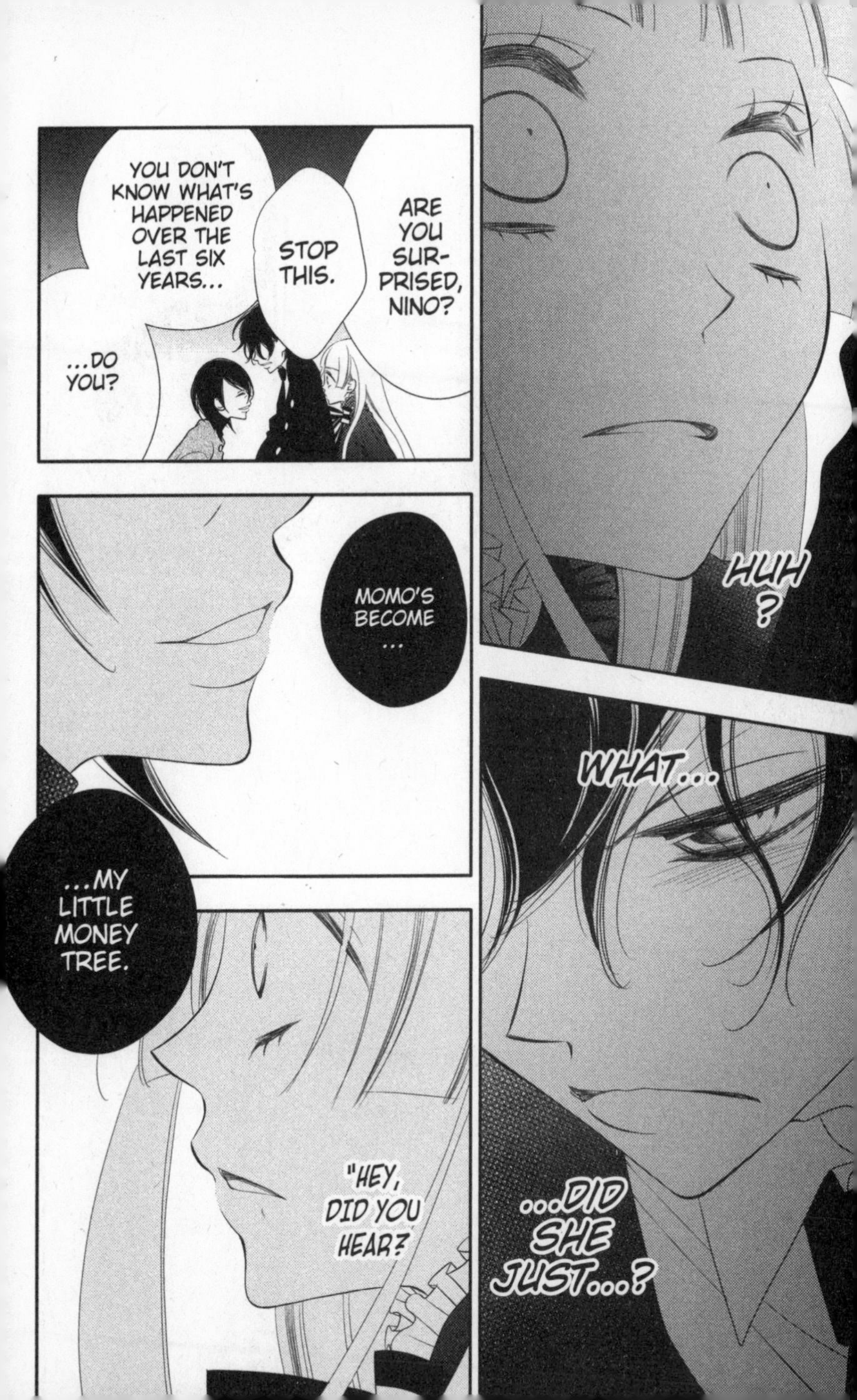
HUH?
WHAT...
...DID SHE JUST...?
ARE YOU SUR-PRISED, NINO?
STOP THIS.
YOU DON'T KNOW WHAT'S HAPPENED OVER THE LAST SIX YEARS...
...DO YOU?
MOMO'S BECOME...
...MY LITTLE MONEY TREE.
"HEY, DID YOU HEAR?

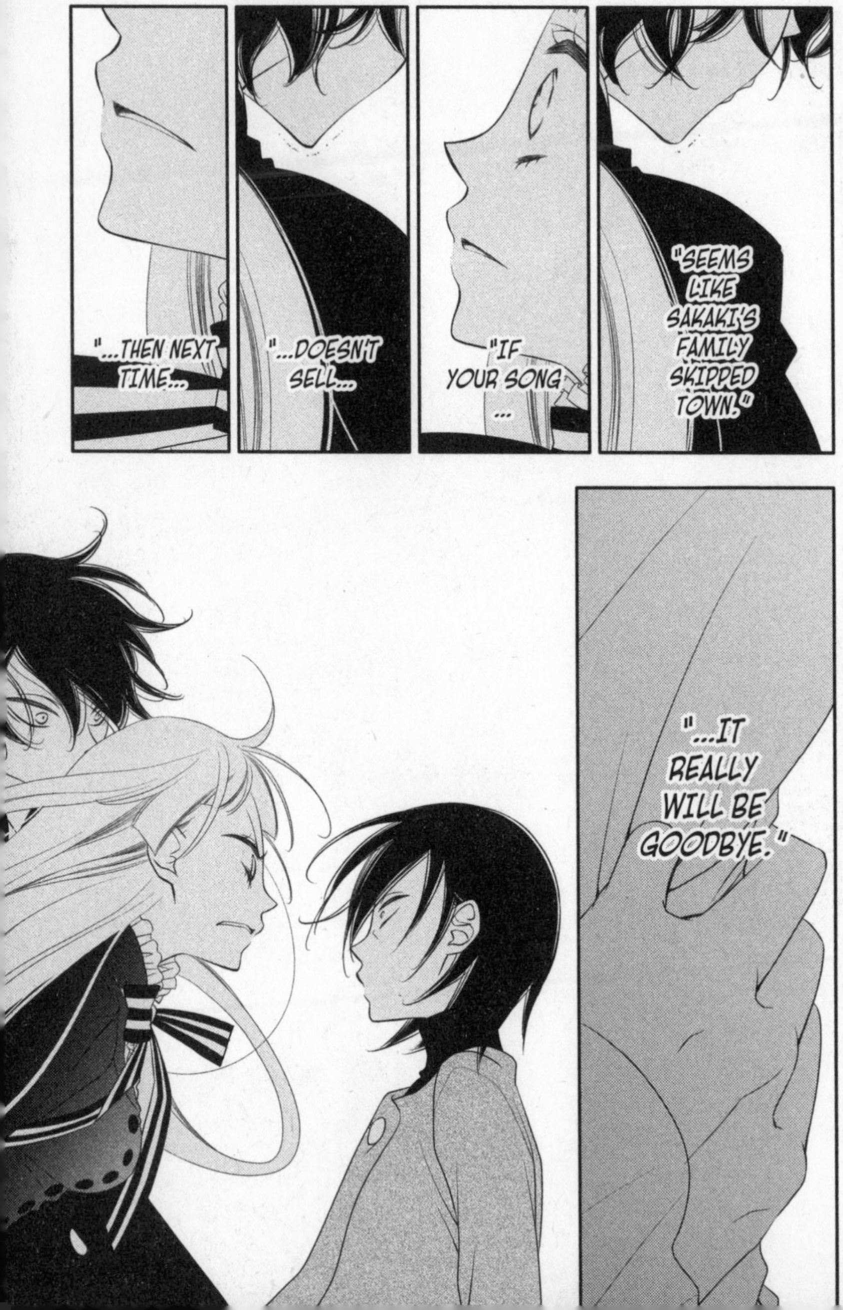
"SEEMS LIKE SAKAKI'S FAMILY SKIPPED TOWN."
"IF YOUR SONG ...
"...DOESN'T SELL...
"...THEN NEXT TIME...
"...IT REALLY WILL BE GOODBYE."

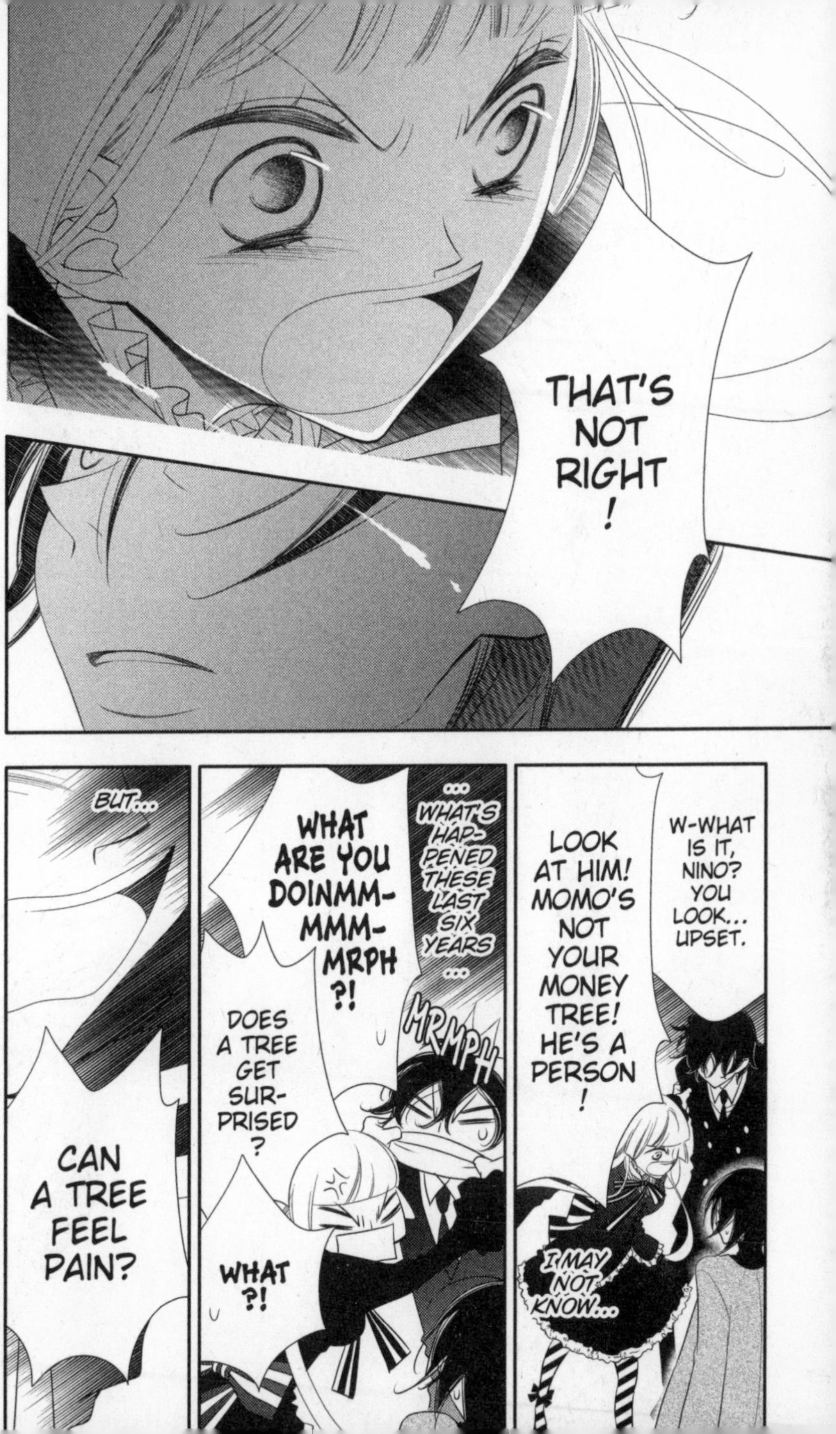
THAT'S NOT RIGHT!
W-WHAT IS IT, NINO? YOU LOOK... UPSET.
LOOK AT HIM! MOMO'S NOT YOUR MONEY TREE! HE'S A PERSON!
I MAY NOT KNOW...
...WHAT'S HAPPENED THESE LAST SIX YEARS...
WHAT ARE YOU DOINMM-MMM-MRPH?!
MRMPH
DOES A TREE GET SURPRISED?
WHAT?!
BUT...
CAN A TREE FEEL PAIN?

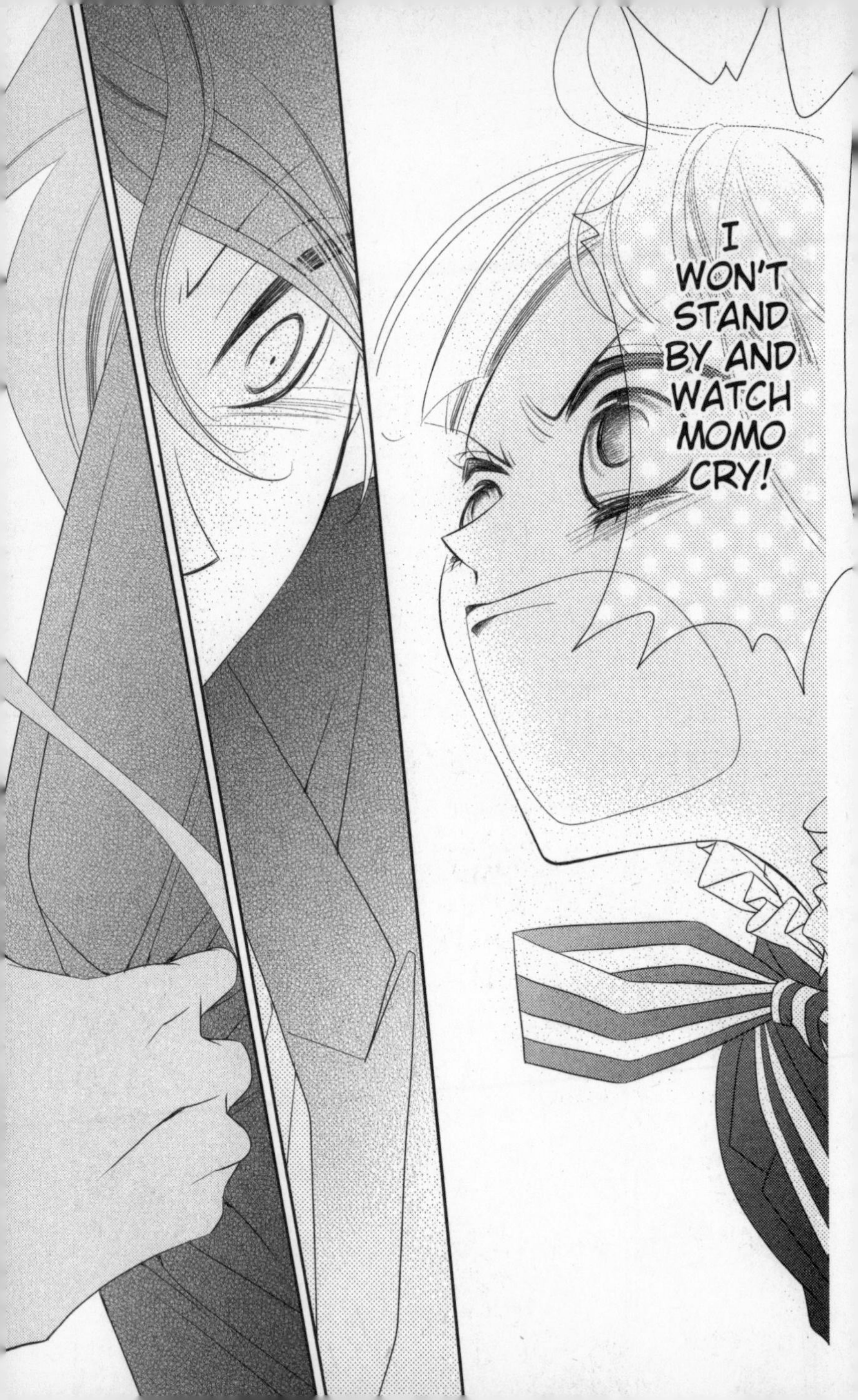
I WON'T STAND BY AND WATCH MOMO CRY!

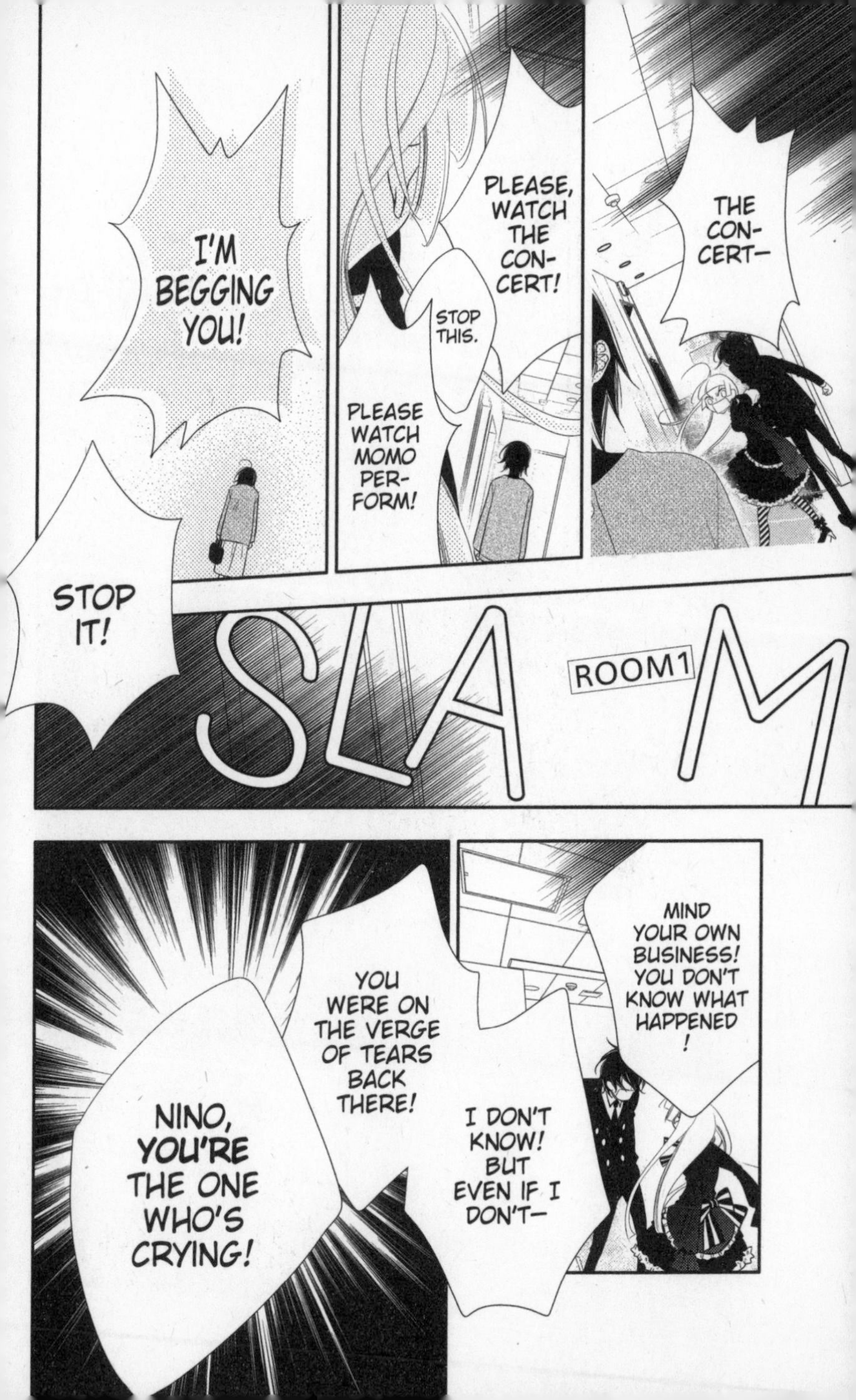
THE CON-CERT—
PLEASE, WATCH THE CON-CERT!
STOP THIS.
PLEASE WATCH MOMO PER-FORM!
I'M BEGGING YOU!
STOP IT!
SLAM
ROOM1
MIND YOUR OWN BUSINESS! YOU DON'T KNOW WHAT HAPPENED!
I DON'T KNOW! BUT EVEN IF I DON'T—
YOU WERE ON THE VERGE OF TEARS BACK THERE!
NINO, YOU'RE THE ONE WHO'S CRYING!

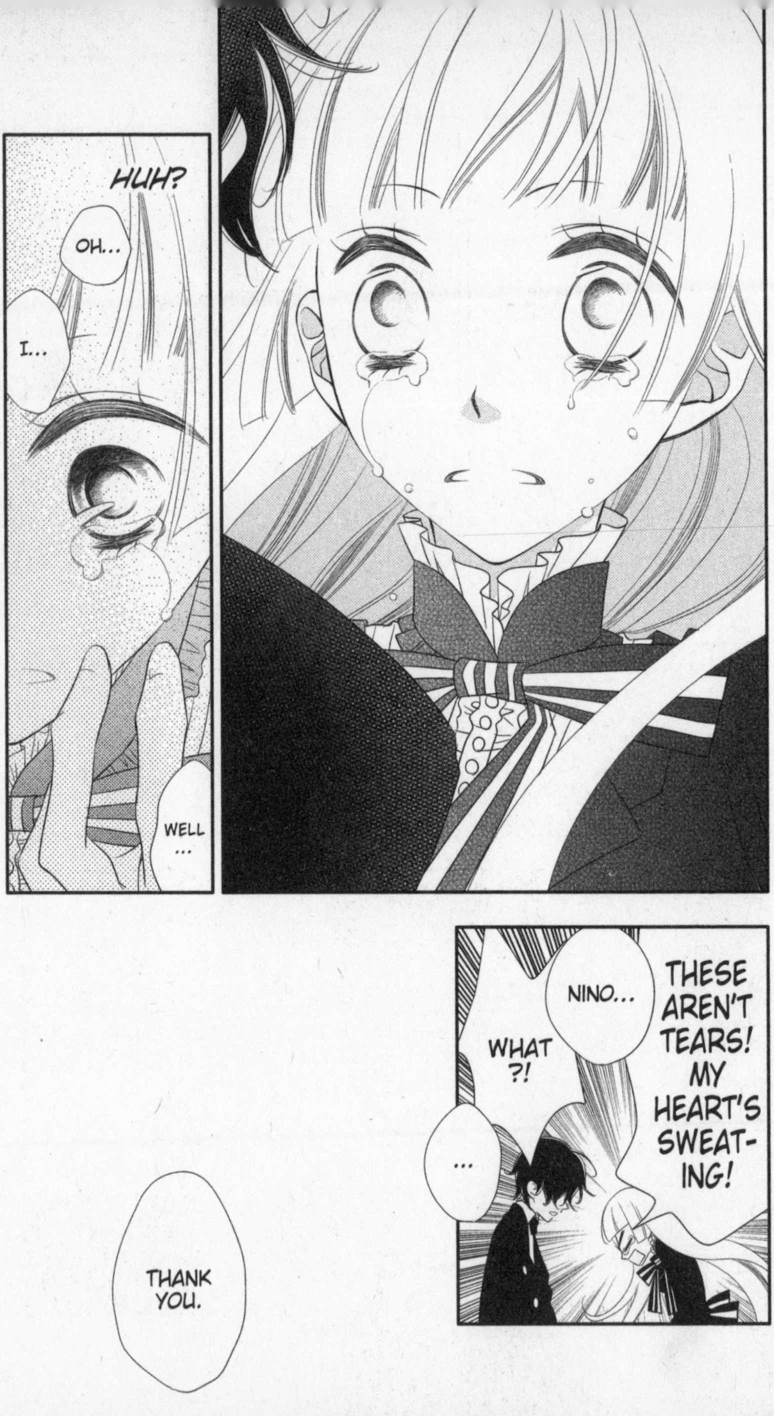
HUH?
OH...
I...
WELL...
THESE AREN'T TEARS! MY HEART'S SWEAT-ING!
NINO...
WHAT?!
...
THANK YOU.

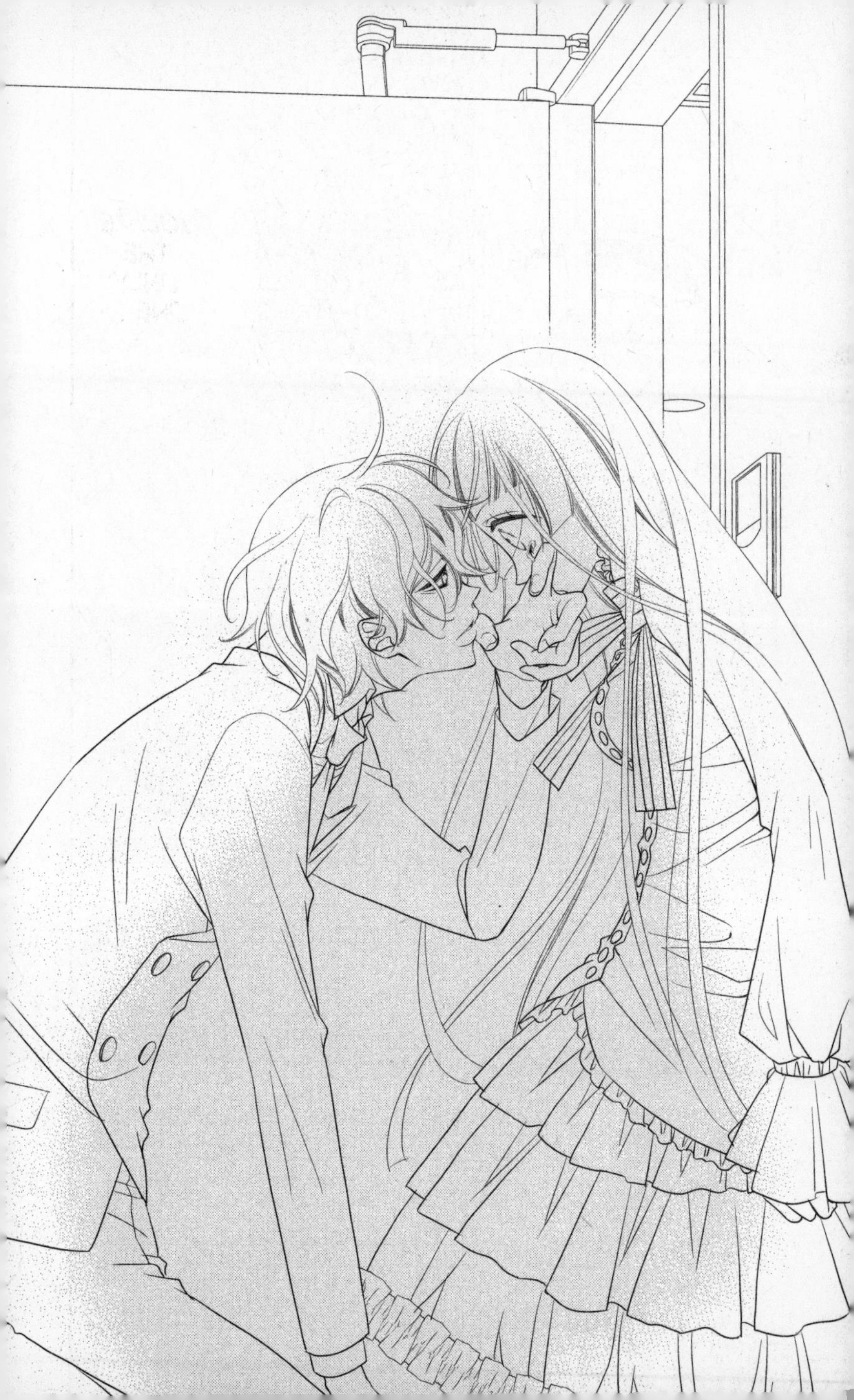

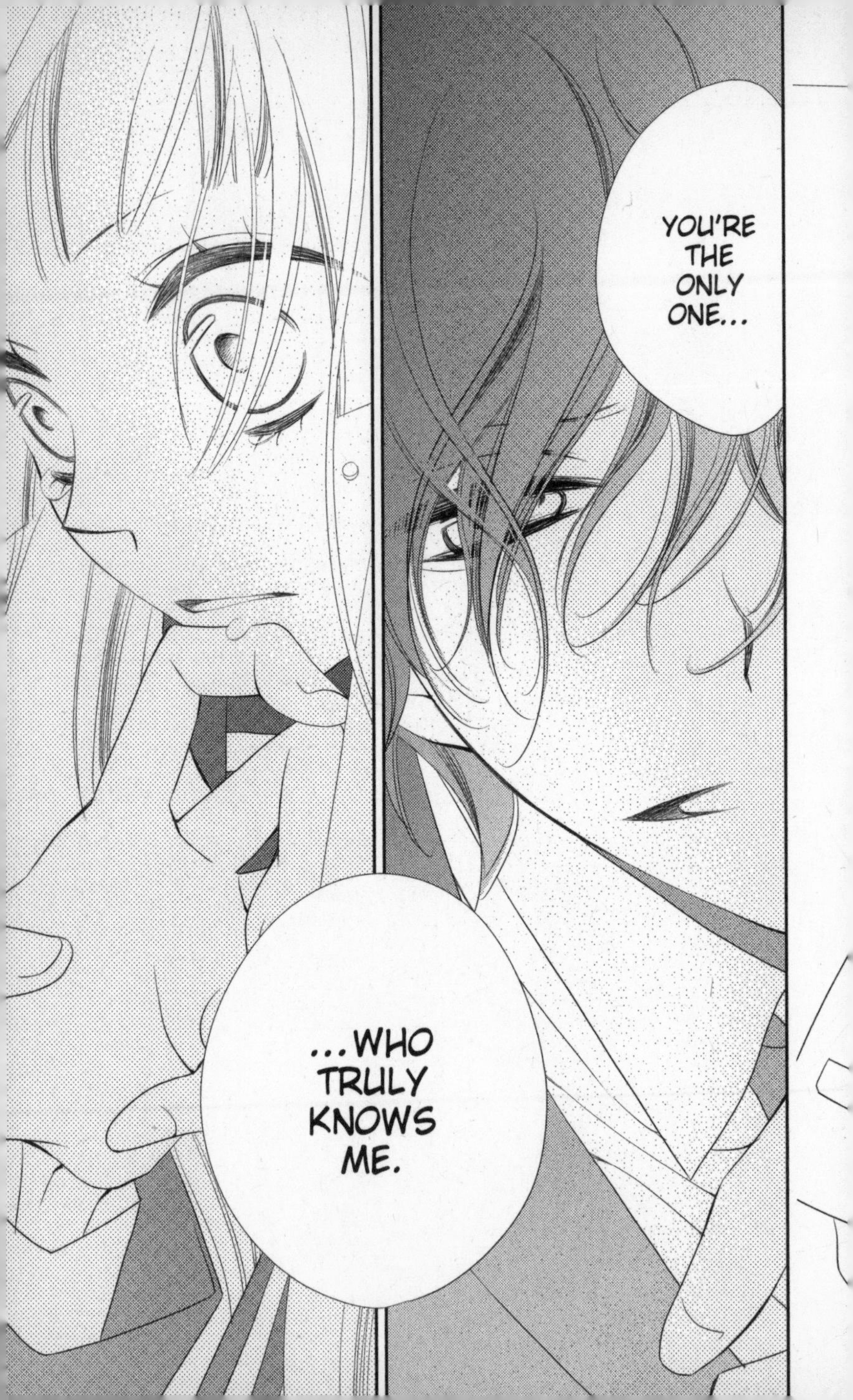
YOU'RE THE ONLY ONE...
...WHO TRULY KNOWS ME.

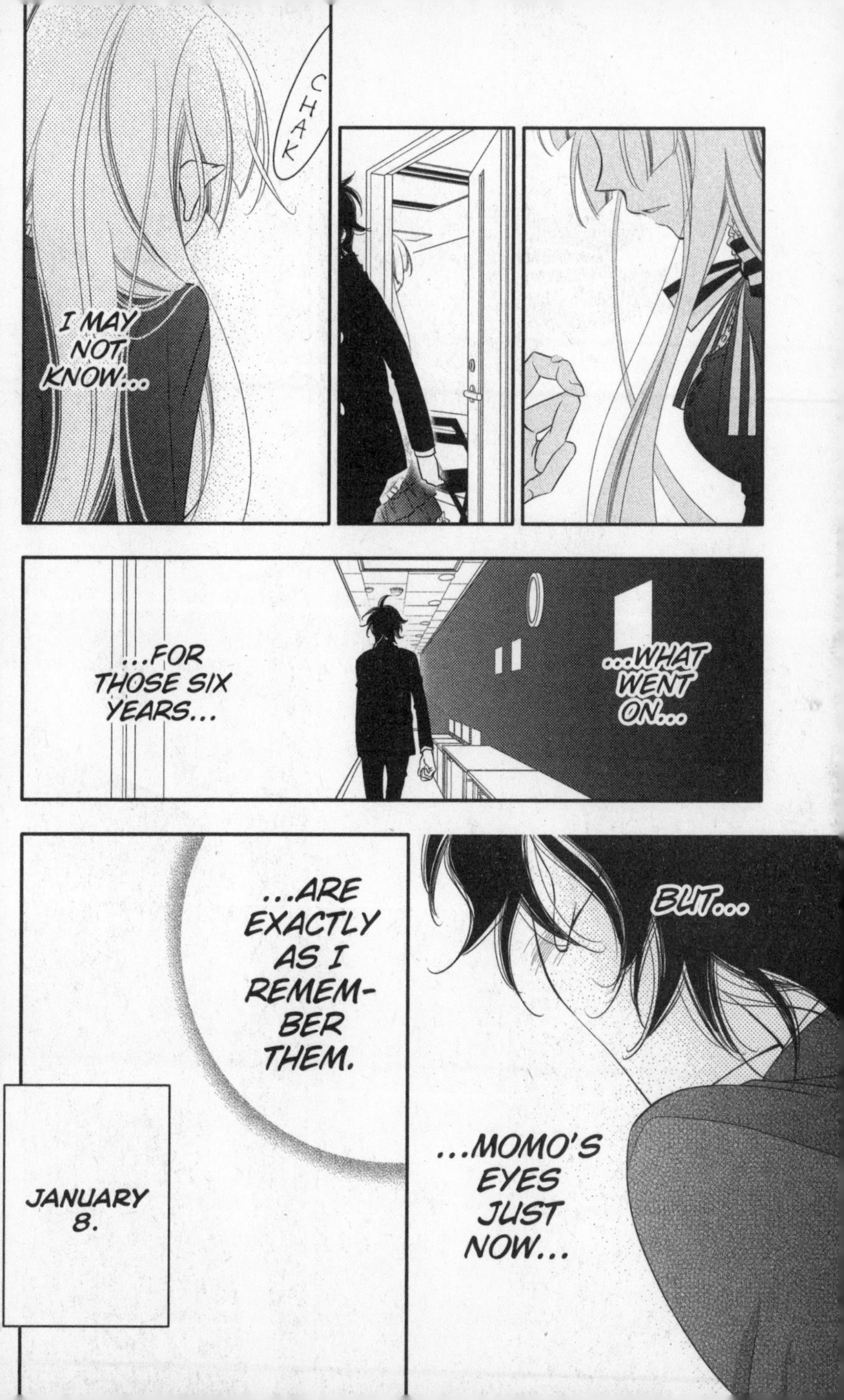
CHAK
I MAY NOT KNOW...
...WHAT WENT ON...
...FOR THOSE SIX YEARS...
BUT...
...MOMO'S EYES JUST NOW...
...ARE EXACTLY AS I REMEM-BER THEM.
JANUARY 8.

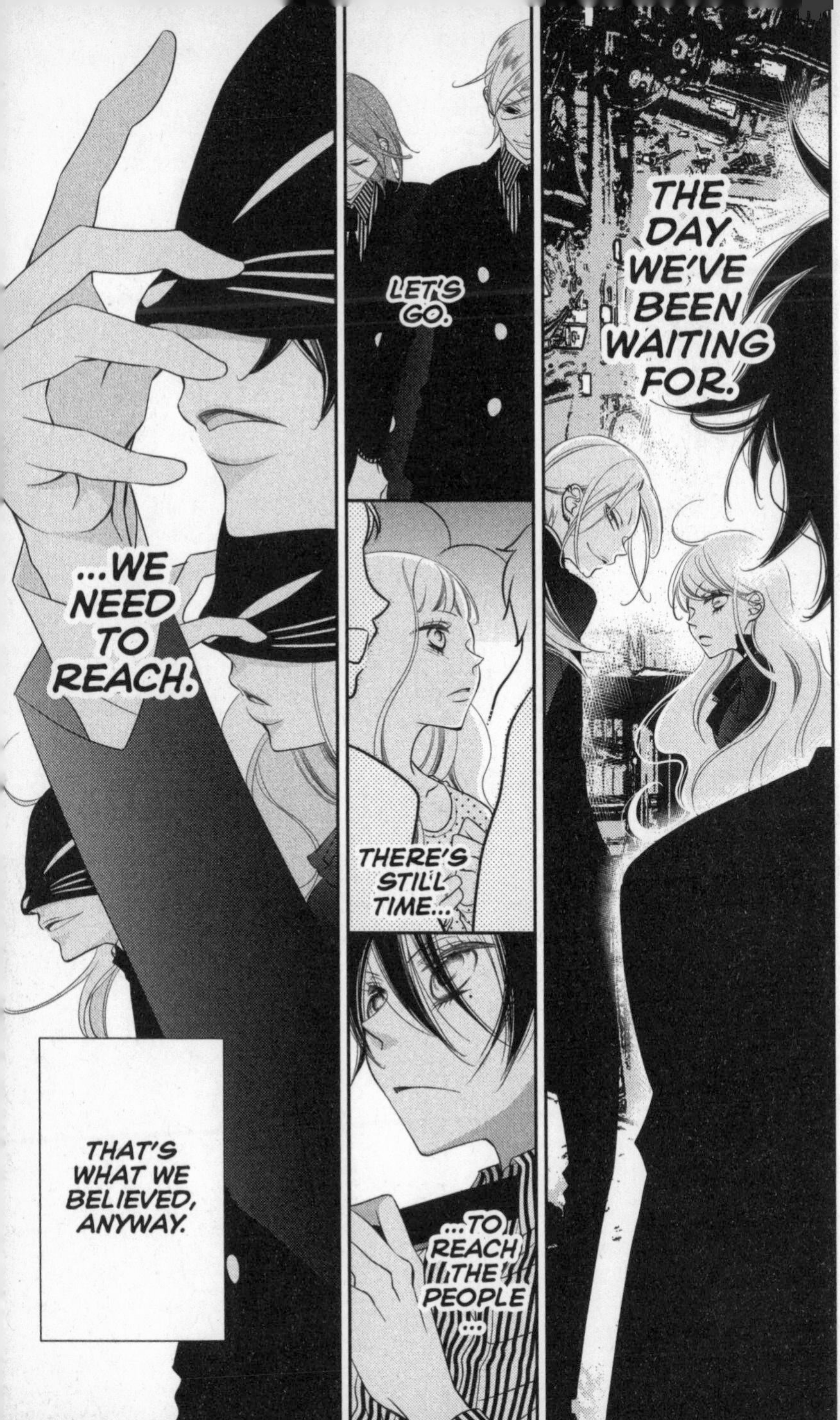
THE DAY WE'VE BEEN WAITING FOR.
LET'S GO.
THERE'S STILL TIME...
...TO REACH THE PEOPLE...
...WE NEED TO REACH.
THAT'S WHAT WE BELIEVED, ANYWAY.

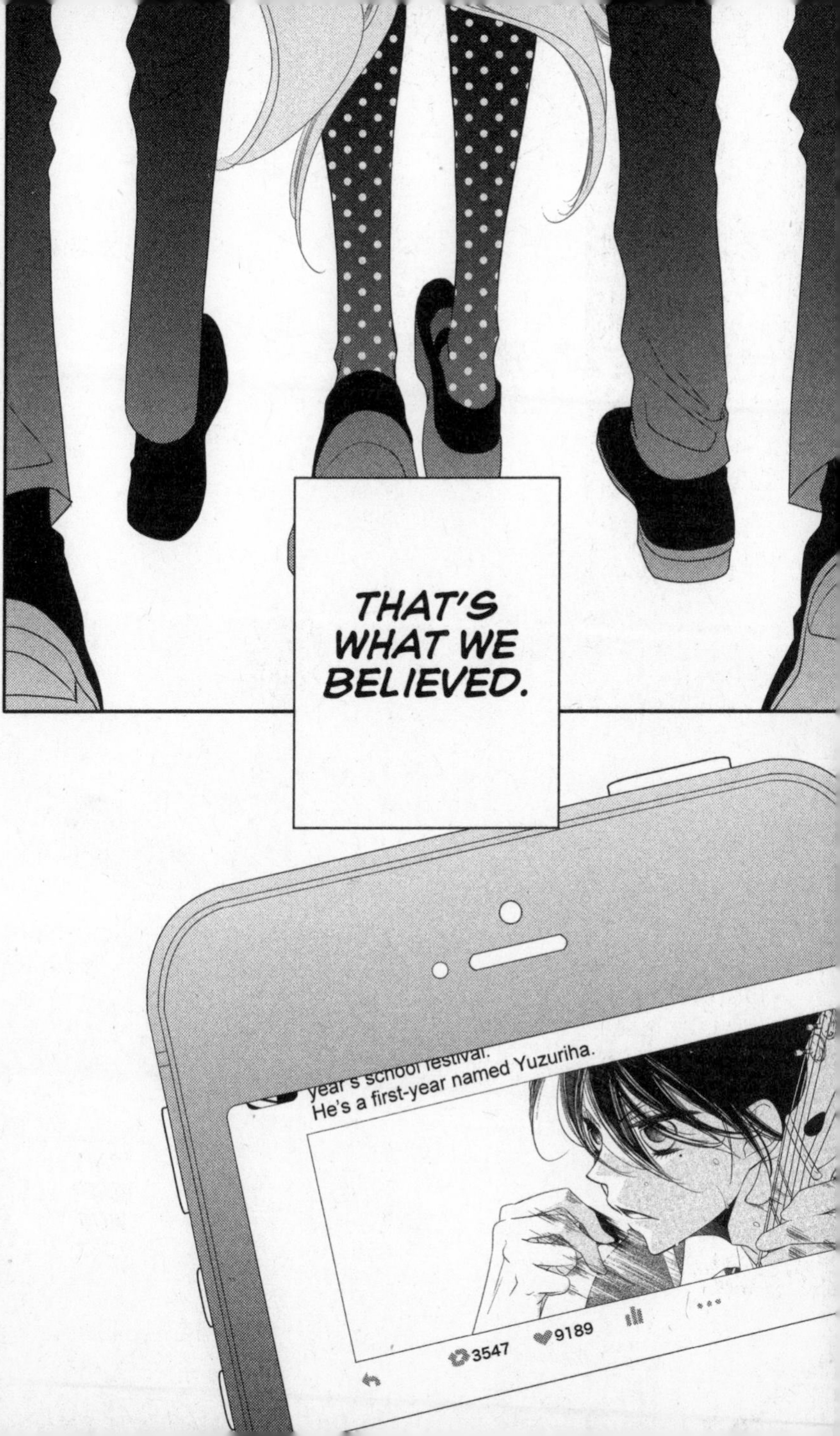
THAT'S WHAT WE BELIEVED.
year's school festival.
He's a first-year named Yuzuriha.
3547
9189

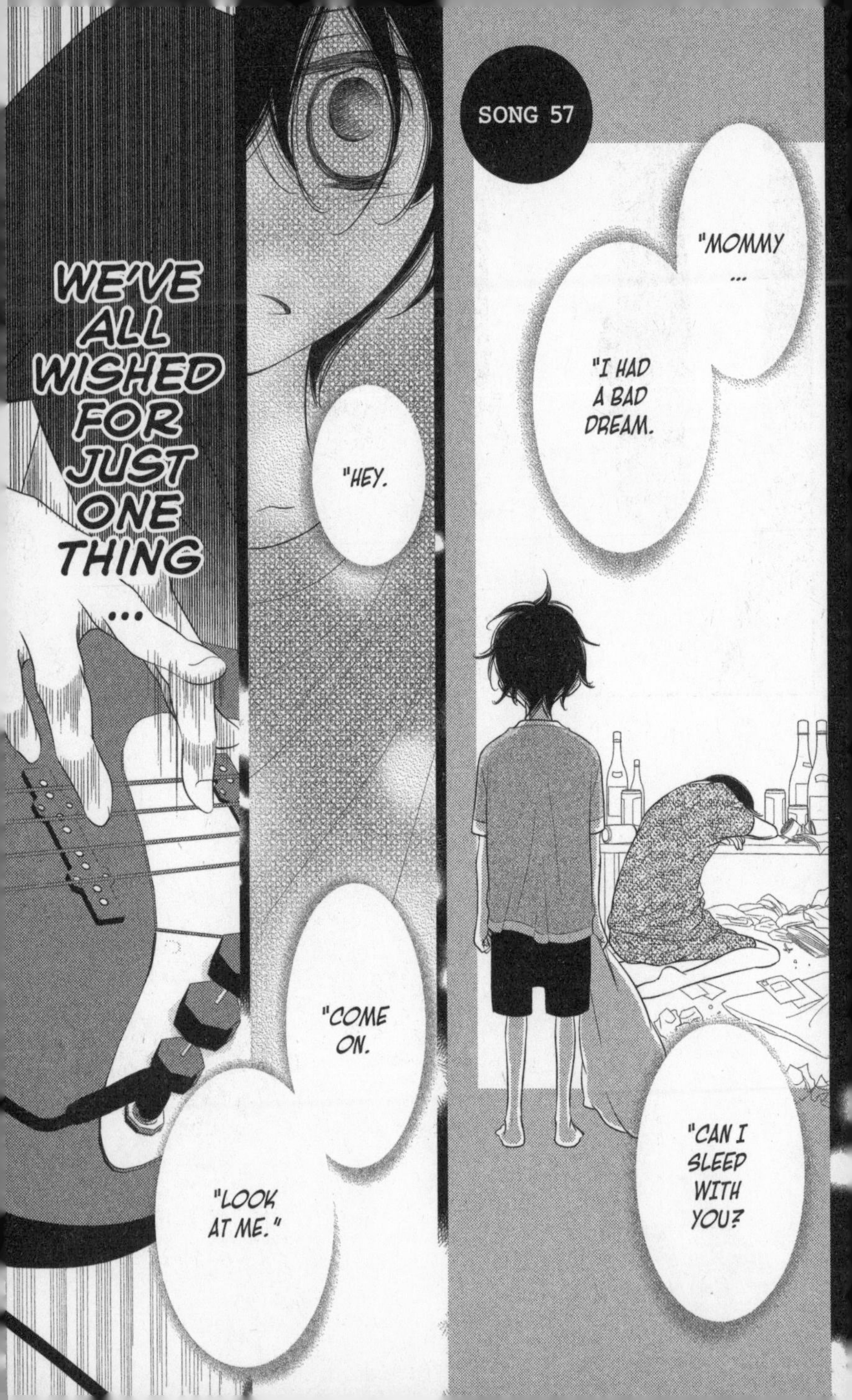
SONG 57
"MOMMY ...
"I HAD A BAD DREAM.
"CAN I SLEEP WITH YOU?
"HEY.
"COME ON.
"LOOK AT ME."
WE'VE ALL WISHED FOR JUST ONE THING ...

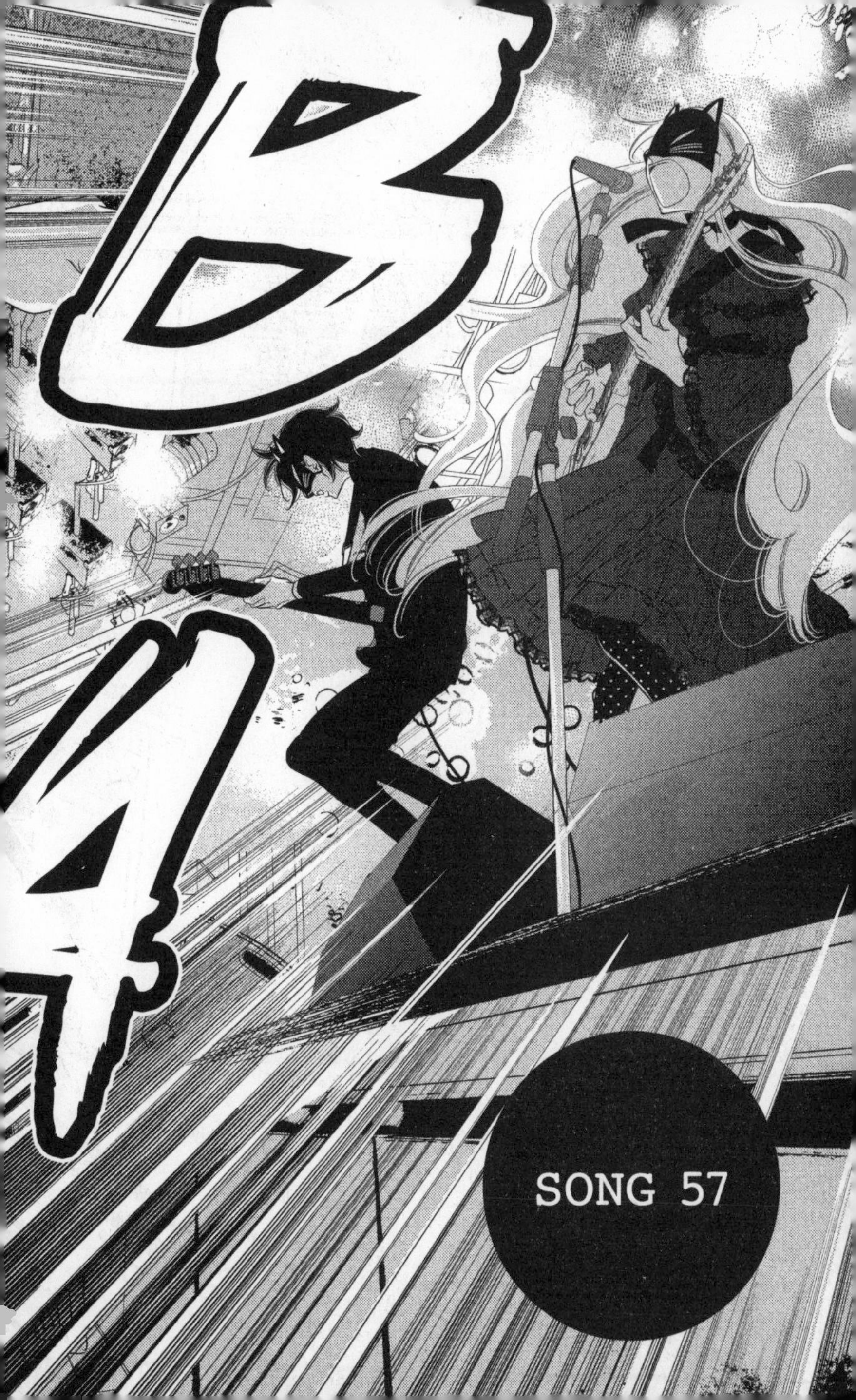
SONG 57

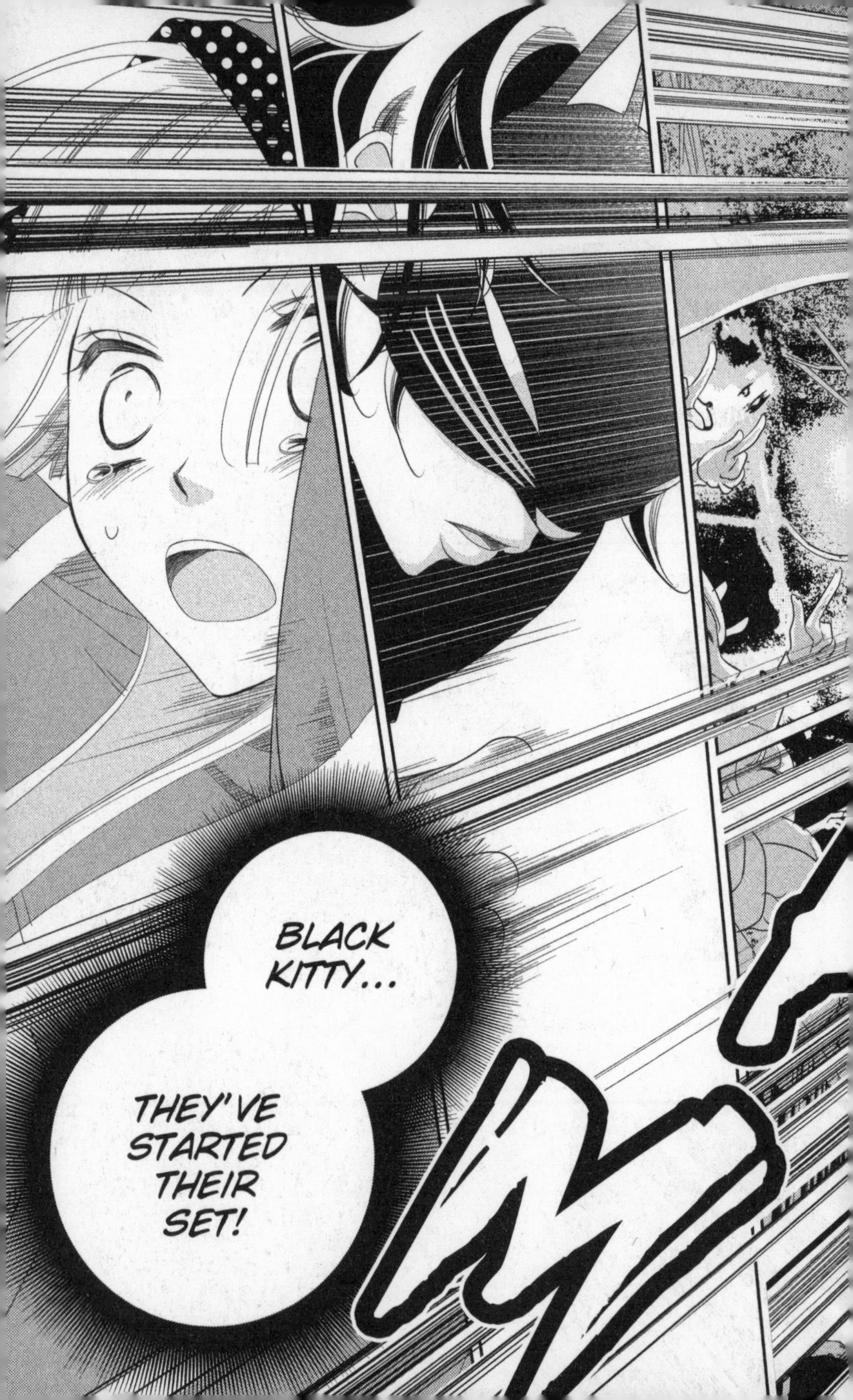
BLACK KITTY...
THEY'VE STARTED THEIR SET!

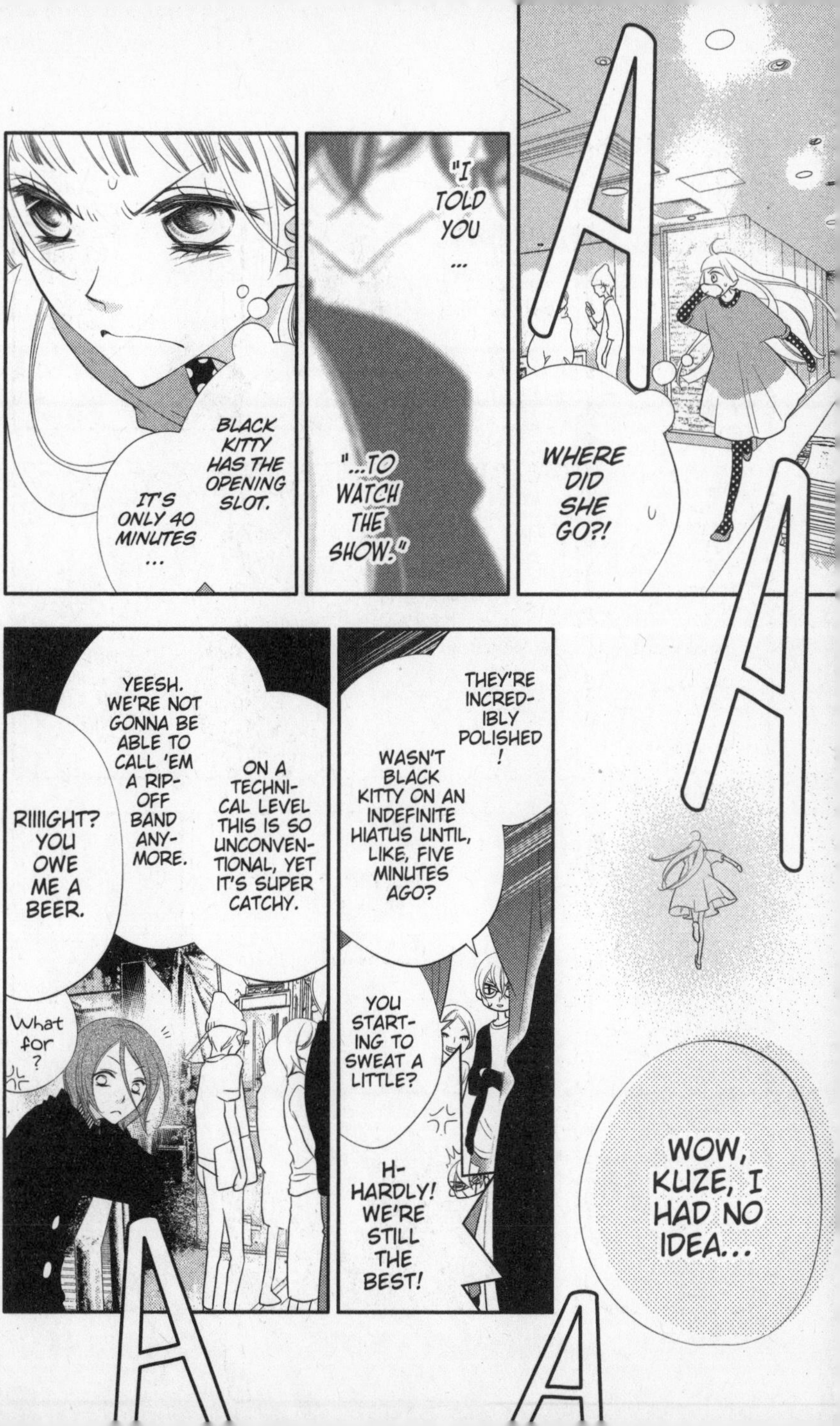
WHERE DID SHE GO?!
AAAAA
"I TOLD YOU ...
"...TO WATCH THE SHOW."
BLACK KITTY HAS THE OPENING SLOT.
IT'S ONLY 40 MINUTES ...
WOW, KUZE, I HAD NO IDEA...
THEY'RE INCRED-IBLY POLISHED!
WASN'T BLACK KITTY ON AN INDEFINITE HIATUS UNTIL, LIKE, FIVE MINUTES AGO?
YOU START-ING TO SWEAT A LITTLE?
H-HARDLY! WE'RE STILL THE BEST!
ON A TECHNI-CAL LEVEL THIS IS SO UNCONVEN-TIONAL, YET IT'S SUPER CATCHY.
YEESH. WE'RE NOT GONNA BE ABLE TO CALL 'EM A RIP-OFF BAND ANY-MORE.
RIIIGHT? YOU OWE ME A BEER.
What for?

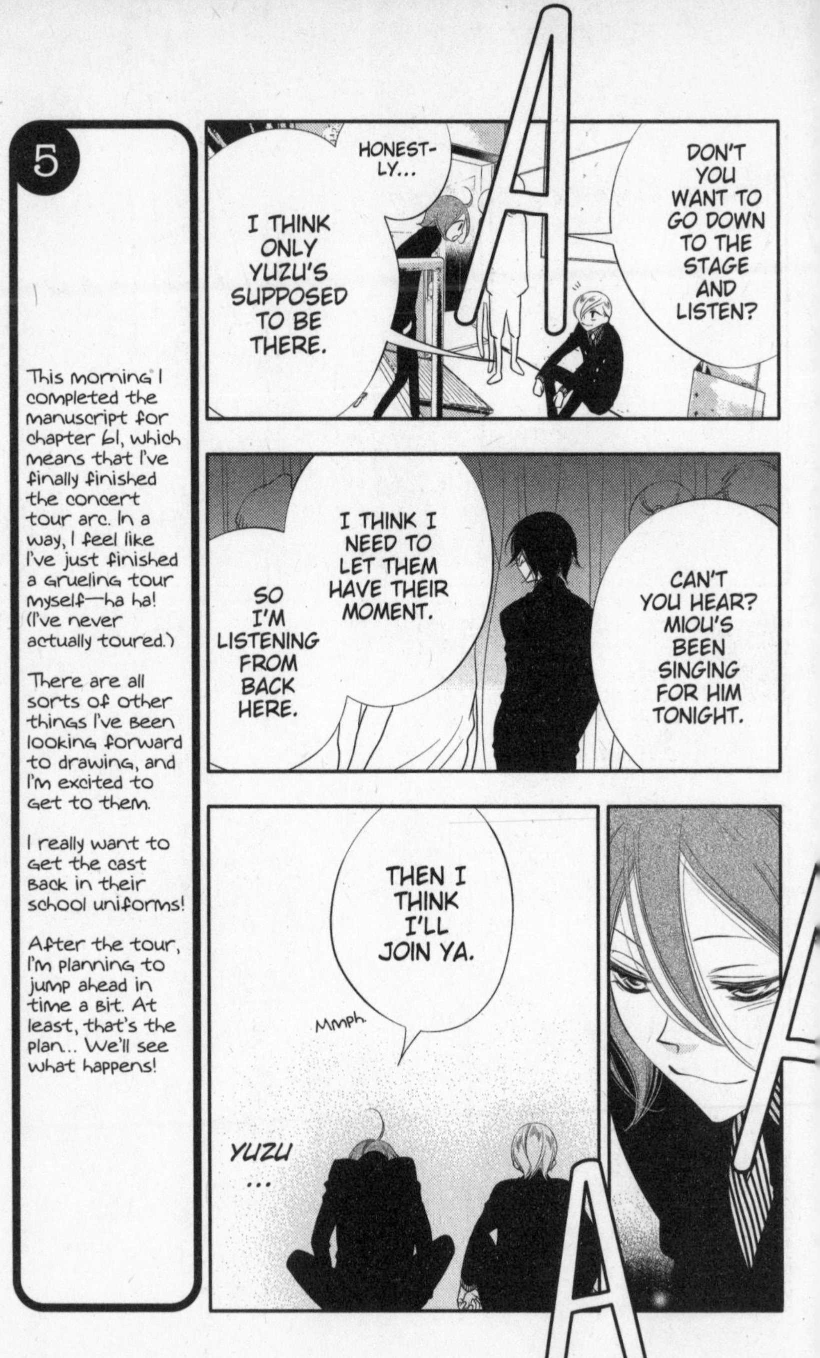
A
DON'T YOU WANT TO GO DOWN TO THE STAGE AND LISTEN?
HONEST-LY...
I THINK ONLY YUZU'S SUPPOSED TO BE THERE.
CAN'T YOU HEAR? MIOU'S BEEN SINGING FOR HIM TONIGHT.
I THINK I NEED TO LET THEM HAVE THEIR MOMENT.
SO I'M LISTENING FROM BACK HERE.
A
A
THEN I THINK I'LL JOIN YA.
Mmph.
YUZU...

5

This morning I completed the manuscript for chapter 61, which means that I've finally finished the concert tour arc. In a way, I feel like I've just finished a grueling tour myself—ha ha! (I've never actually toured.)

There are all sorts of other things I've been looking forward to drawing, and I'm excited to get to them.

I really want to get the cast back in their school uniforms!

After the tour, I'm planning to jump ahead in time a bit. At least, that's the plan... We'll see what happens!

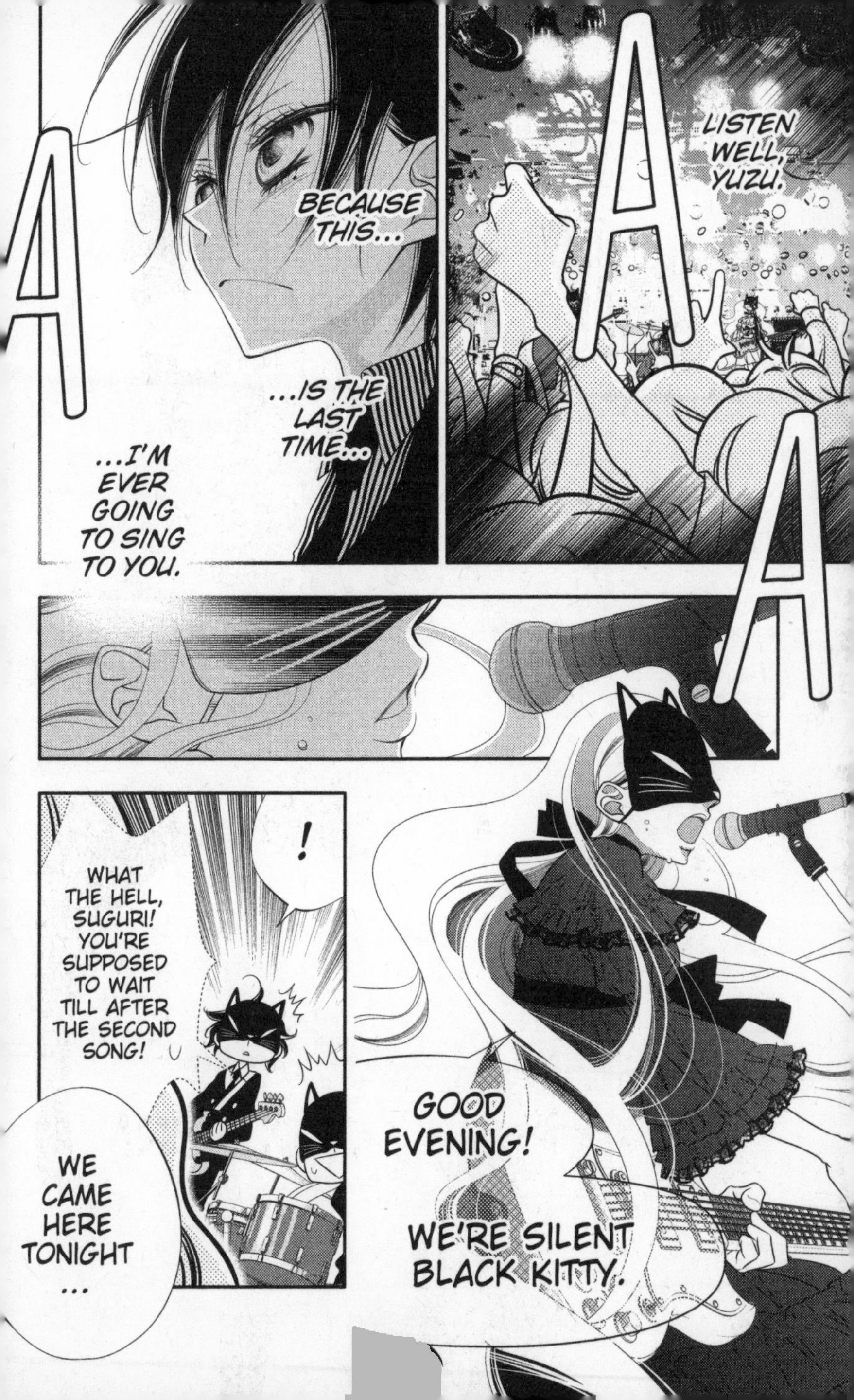
LISTEN WELL, YUZU.
A
A
A
BECAUSE THIS...
...IS THE LAST TIME...
...I'M EVER GOING TO SING TO YOU.
A
GOOD EVENING!
WE'RE SILENT BLACK KITTY.
!
WHAT THE HELL, SUGURI! YOU'RE SUPPOSED TO WAIT TILL AFTER THE SECOND SONG!
WE CAME HERE TONIGHT ...

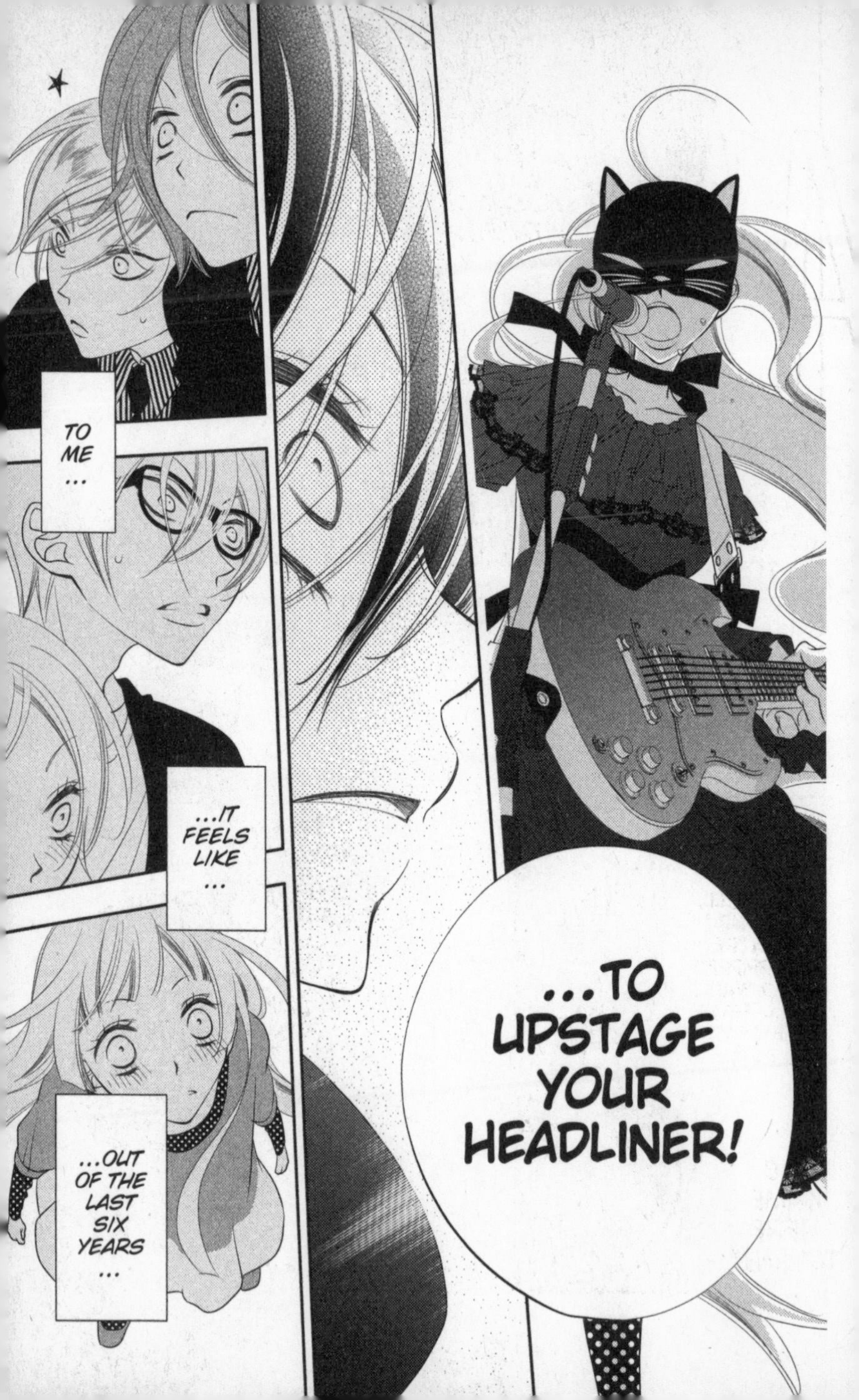
...TO UPSTAGE YOUR HEADLINER!
TO ME ...
...IT FEELS LIKE ...
...OUT OF THE LAST SIX YEARS ...

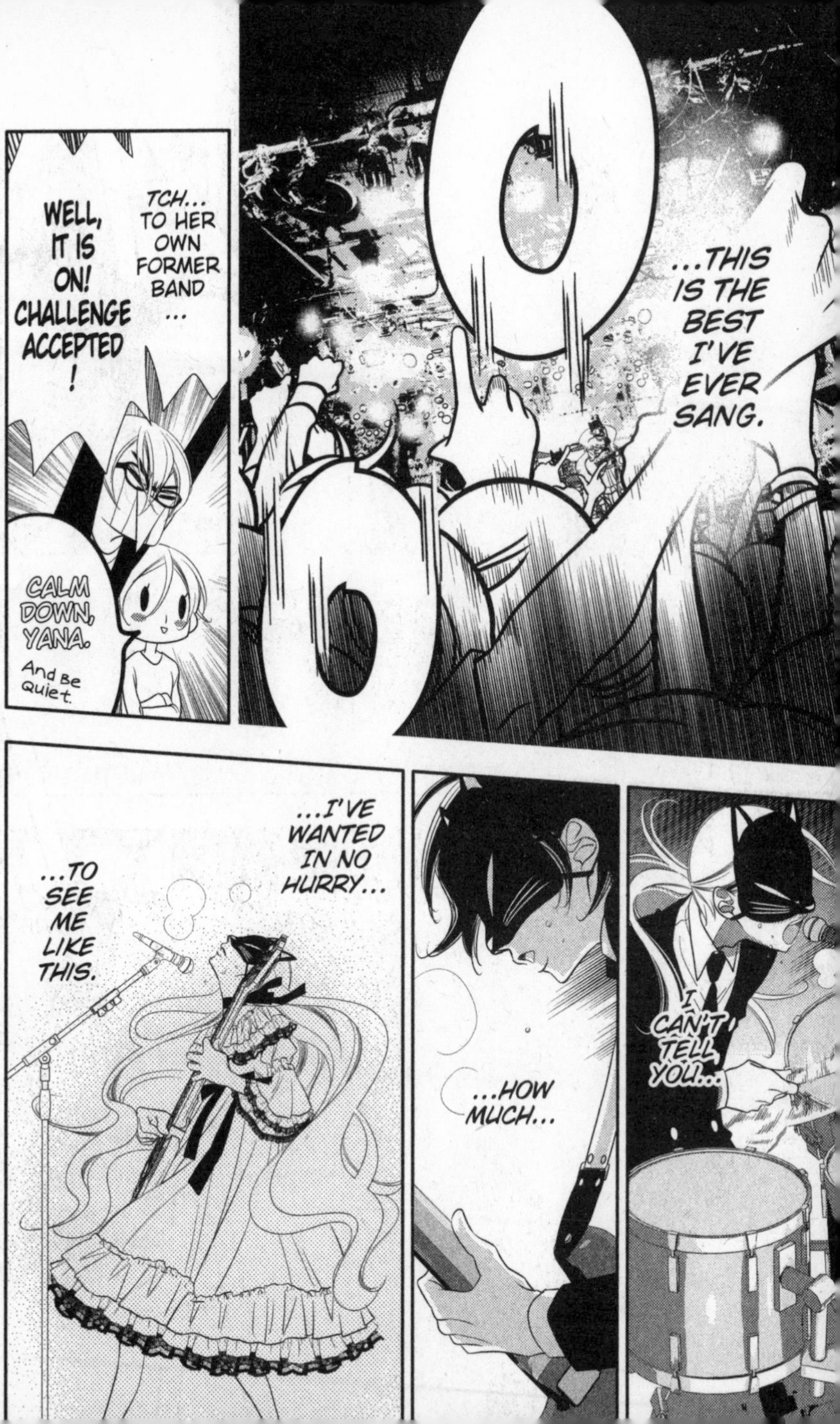
...THIS IS THE BEST I'VE EVER SANG.
TCH... TO HER OWN FORMER BAND...
WELL, IT IS ON! CHALLENGE ACCEPTED!
CALM DOWN, YANA.
And Be Quiet.
I CAN'T TELL YOU...
...HOW MUCH...
...I'VE WANTED IN NO HURRY...
...TO SEE ME LIKE THIS.

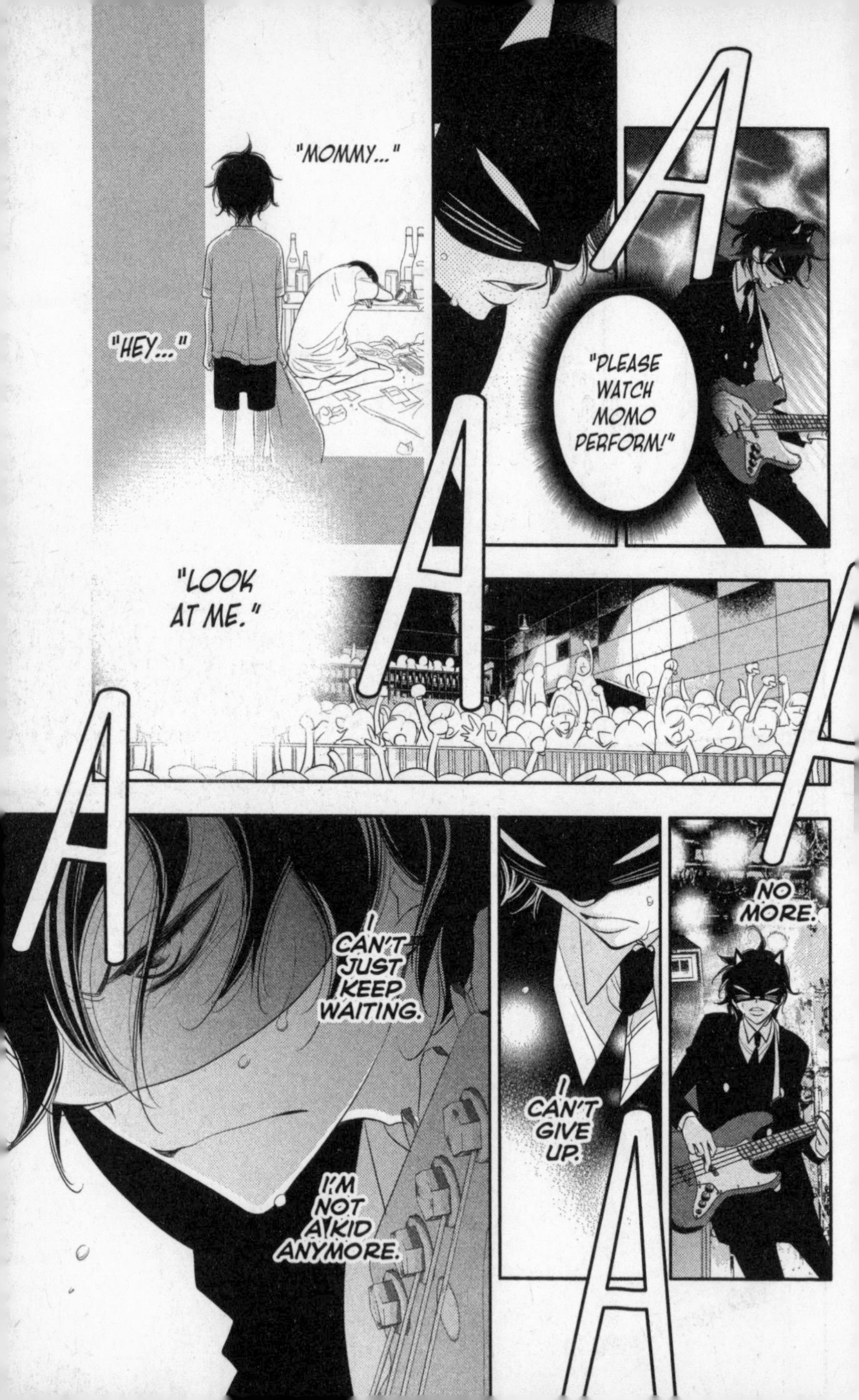
"PLEASE WATCH MOMO PERFORM!"
"MOMMY..."
"HEY..."
"LOOK AT ME."
AAAAA
NO MORE.
I CAN'T GIVE UP.
I CAN'T JUST KEEP WAITING.
I'M NOT A KID ANYMORE.

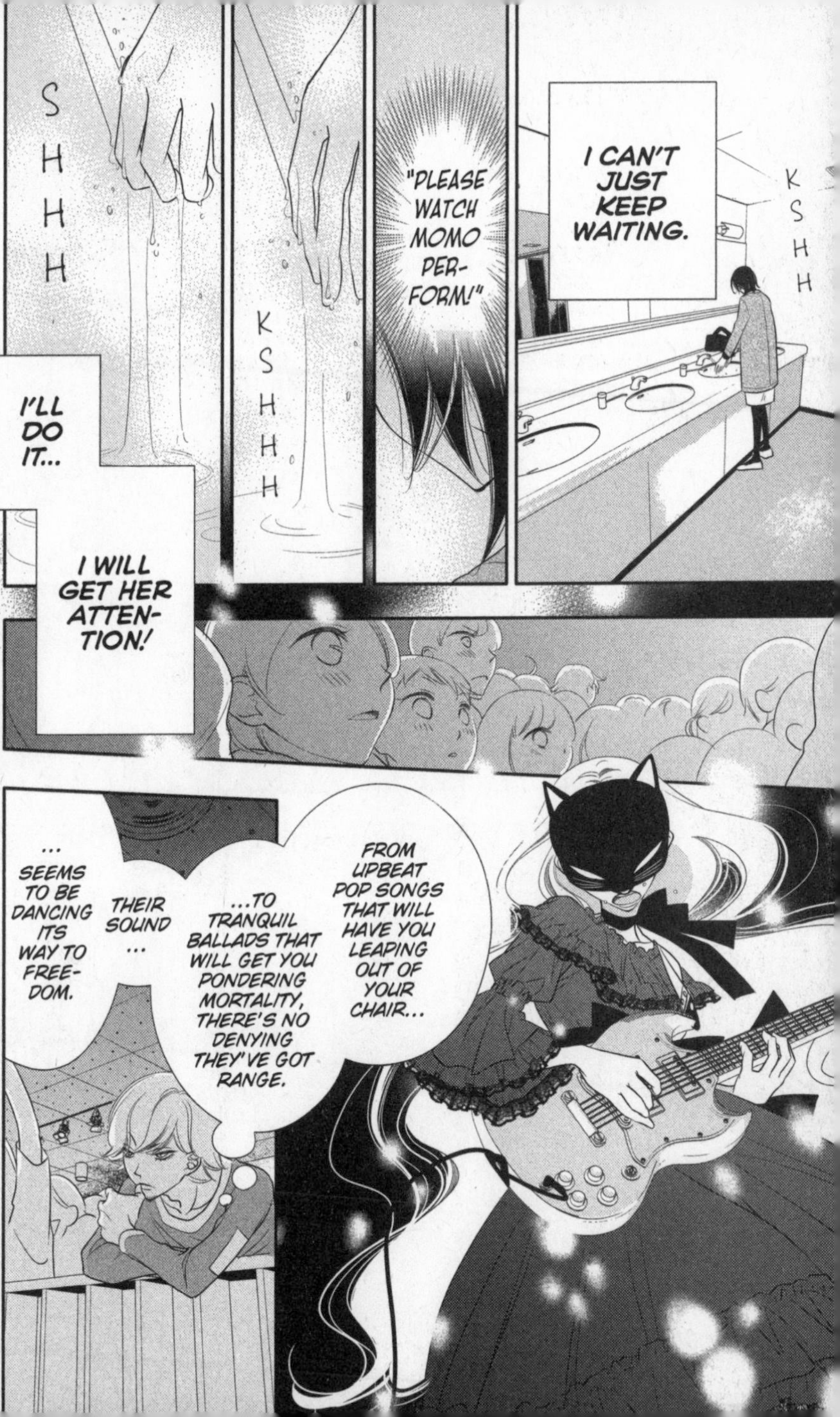
I CAN'T JUST KEEP WAITING.
KSHH
"PLEASE WATCH MOMO PER-FORM!"
KSHHH
SHHH
I'LL DO IT...
I WILL GET HER ATTEN-TION!
FROM UPBEAT POP SONGS THAT WILL HAVE YOU LEAPING OUT OF YOUR CHAIR...
...TO TRANQUIL BALLADS THAT WILL GET YOU PONDERING MORTALITY, THERE'S NO DENYING THEY'VE GOT RANGE.
THEIR SOUND...
...SEEMS TO BE DANCING ITS WAY TO FREE-DOM.

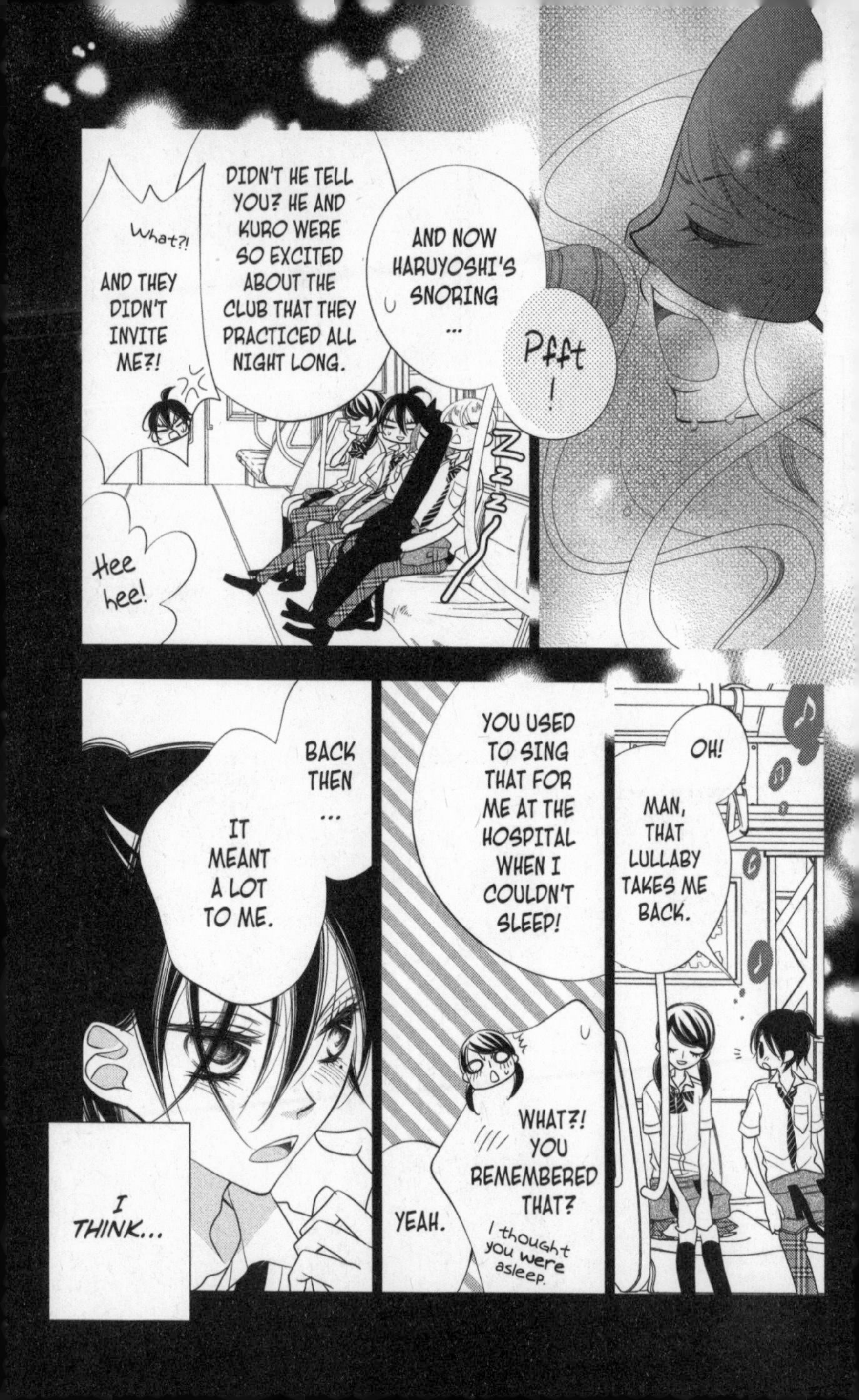
Pfft!
AND NOW HARUYOSHI'S SNORING...
DIDN'T HE TELL YOU? HE AND KURO WERE SO EXCITED ABOUT THE CLUB THAT THEY PRACTICED ALL NIGHT LONG.
What?!
AND THEY DIDN'T INVITE ME?!
Hee hee!
OH!
MAN, THAT LULLABY TAKES ME BACK.
YOU USED TO SING THAT FOR ME AT THE HOSPITAL WHEN I COULDN'T SLEEP!
WHAT?! YOU REMEMBERED THAT?
I thought you were asleep.
YEAH.
BACK THEN...
IT MEANT A LOT TO ME.
I THINK...

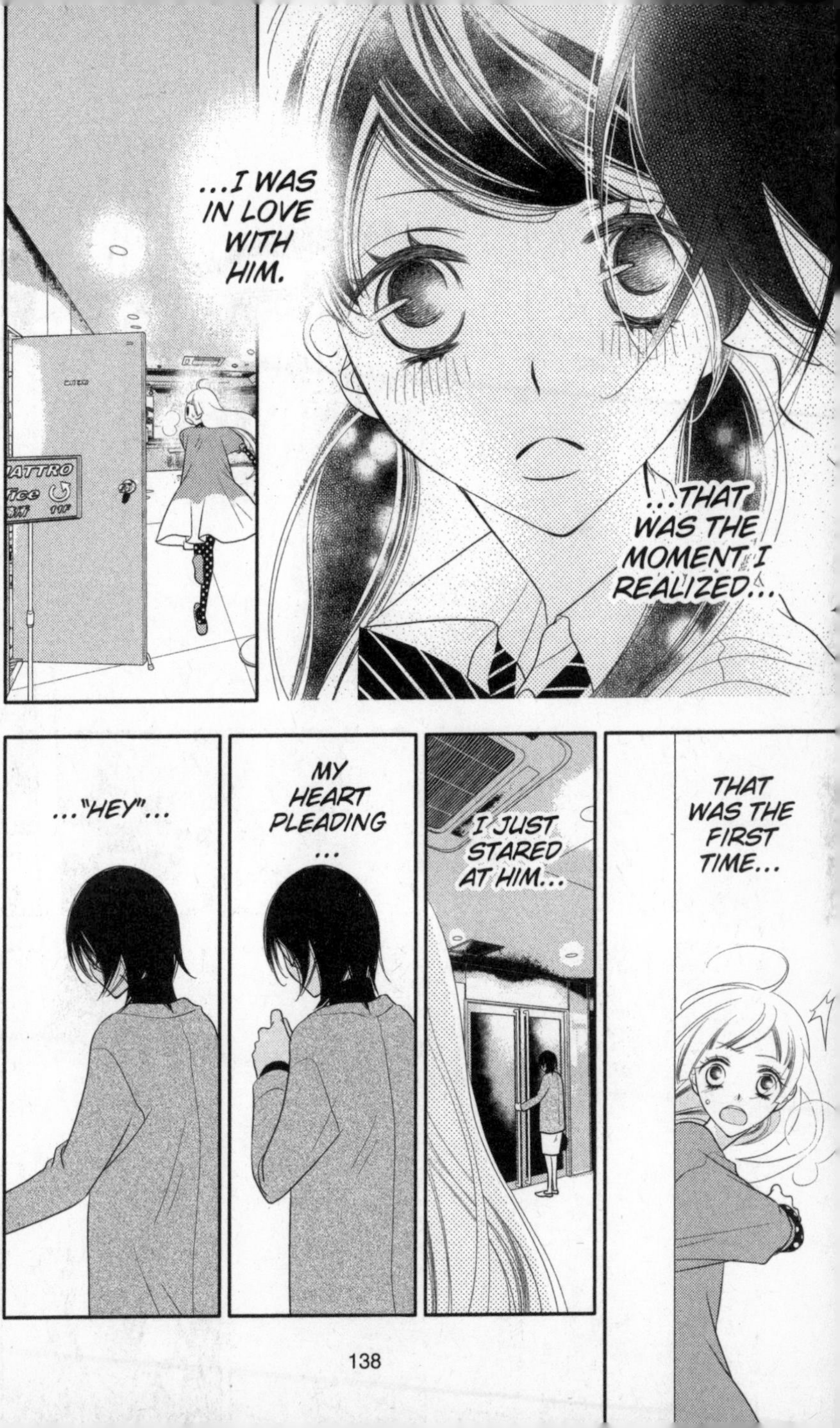
...THAT WAS THE MOMENT I REALIZED...
...I WAS IN LOVE WITH HIM.
THAT WAS THE FIRST TIME...
I JUST STARED AT HIM...
MY HEART PLEADING ...
..."HEY"...

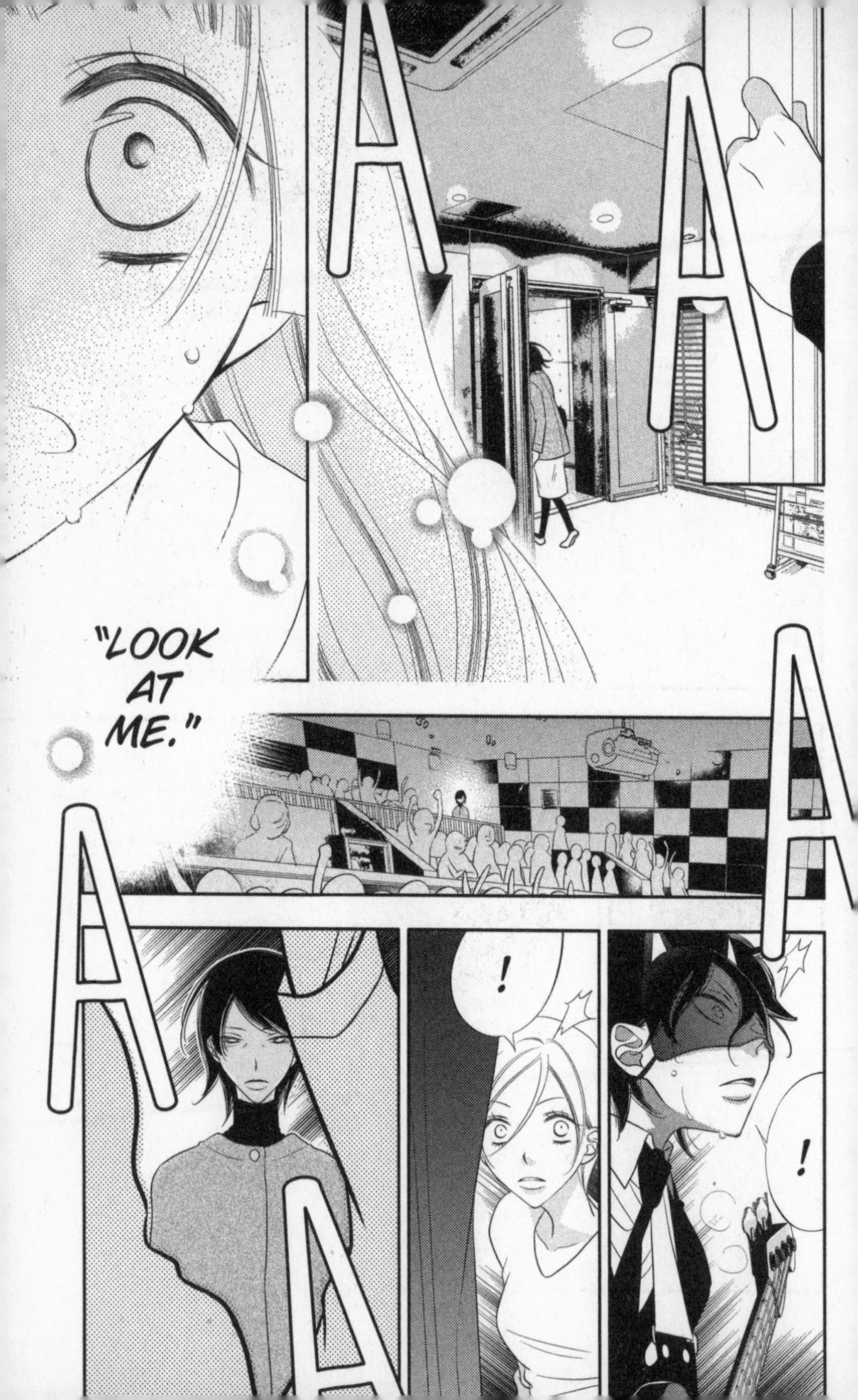

AAAAA
"LOOK AT ME."
!
!

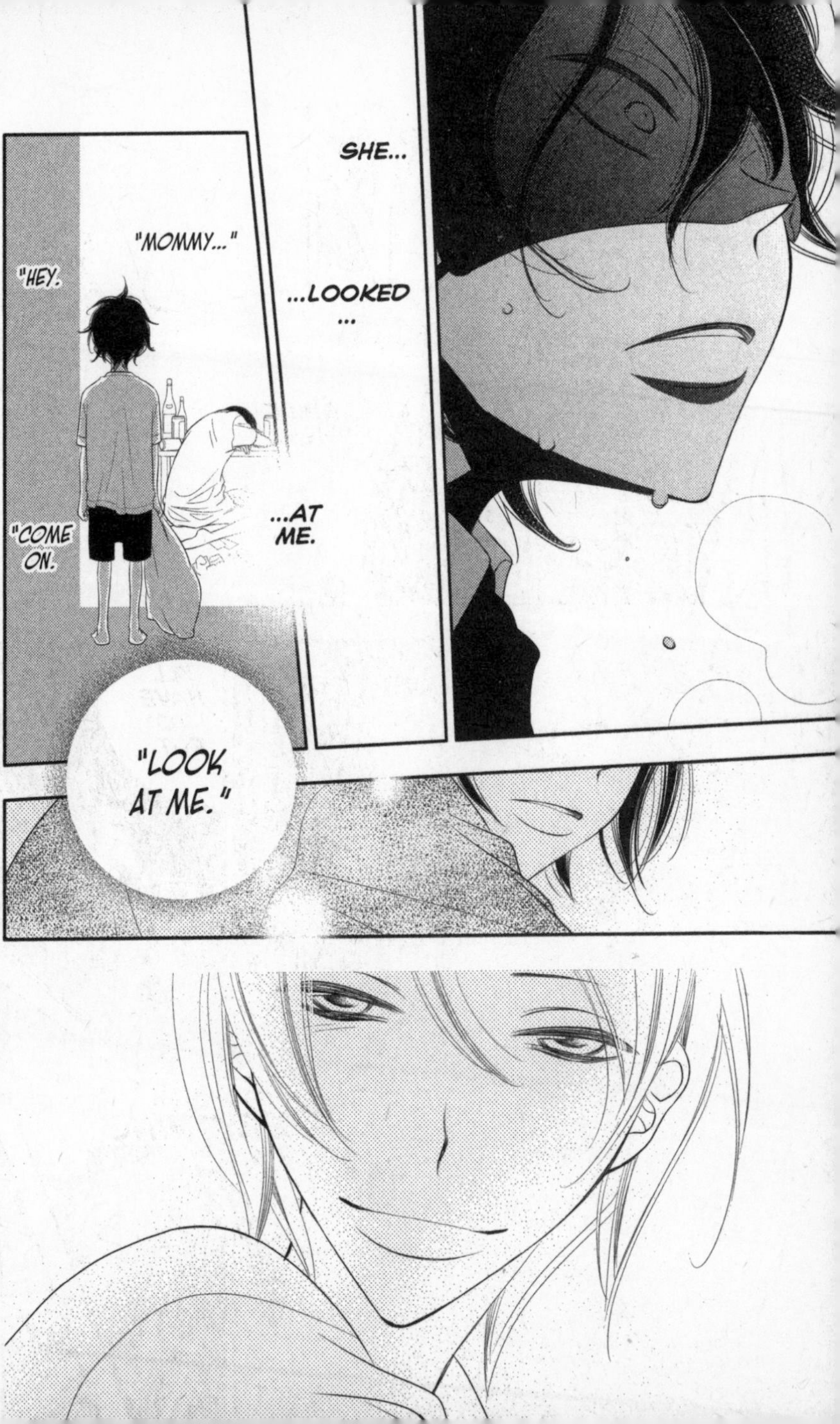
SHE...
...LOOKED ...
...AT ME.
"MOMMY..."
"HEY.
"COME ON.
"LOOK AT ME."

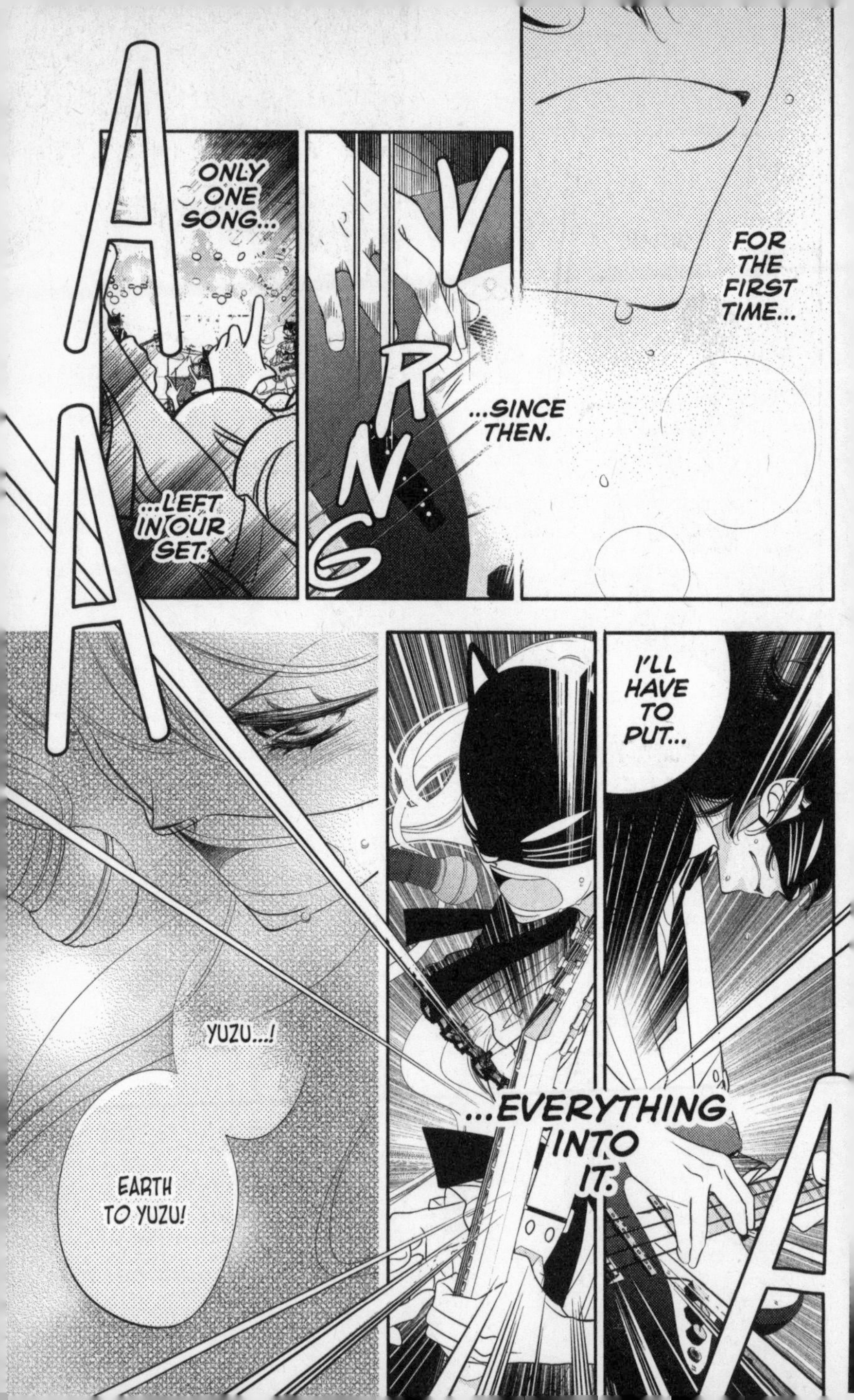
FOR THE FIRST TIME...
...SINCE THEN.
VRNG
ONLY ONE SONG...
...LEFT IN OUR SET.
AAA
I'LL HAVE TO PUT...
...EVERYTHING INTO IT.
A
YUZU...!
EARTH TO YUZU!

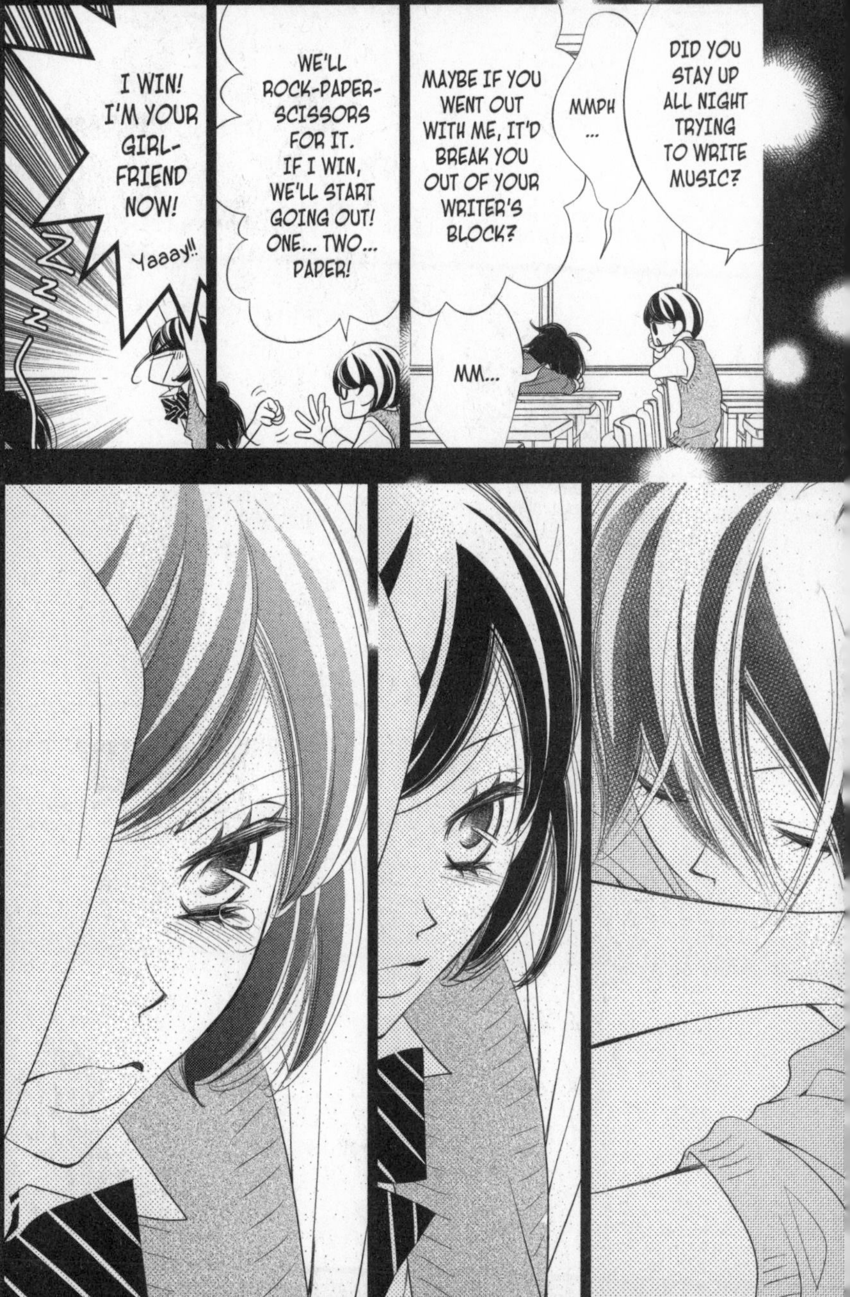
DID YOU STAY UP ALL NIGHT TRYING TO WRITE MUSIC?
MMPH...
MAYBE IF YOU WENT OUT WITH ME, IT'D BREAK YOU OUT OF YOUR WRITER'S BLOCK?
MM...
WE'LL ROCK-PAPER-SCISSORS FOR IT. IF I WIN, WE'LL START GOING OUT! ONE... TWO... PAPER!
I WIN! I'M YOUR GIRL-FRIEND NOW!
Yaaay!!
ZZZ

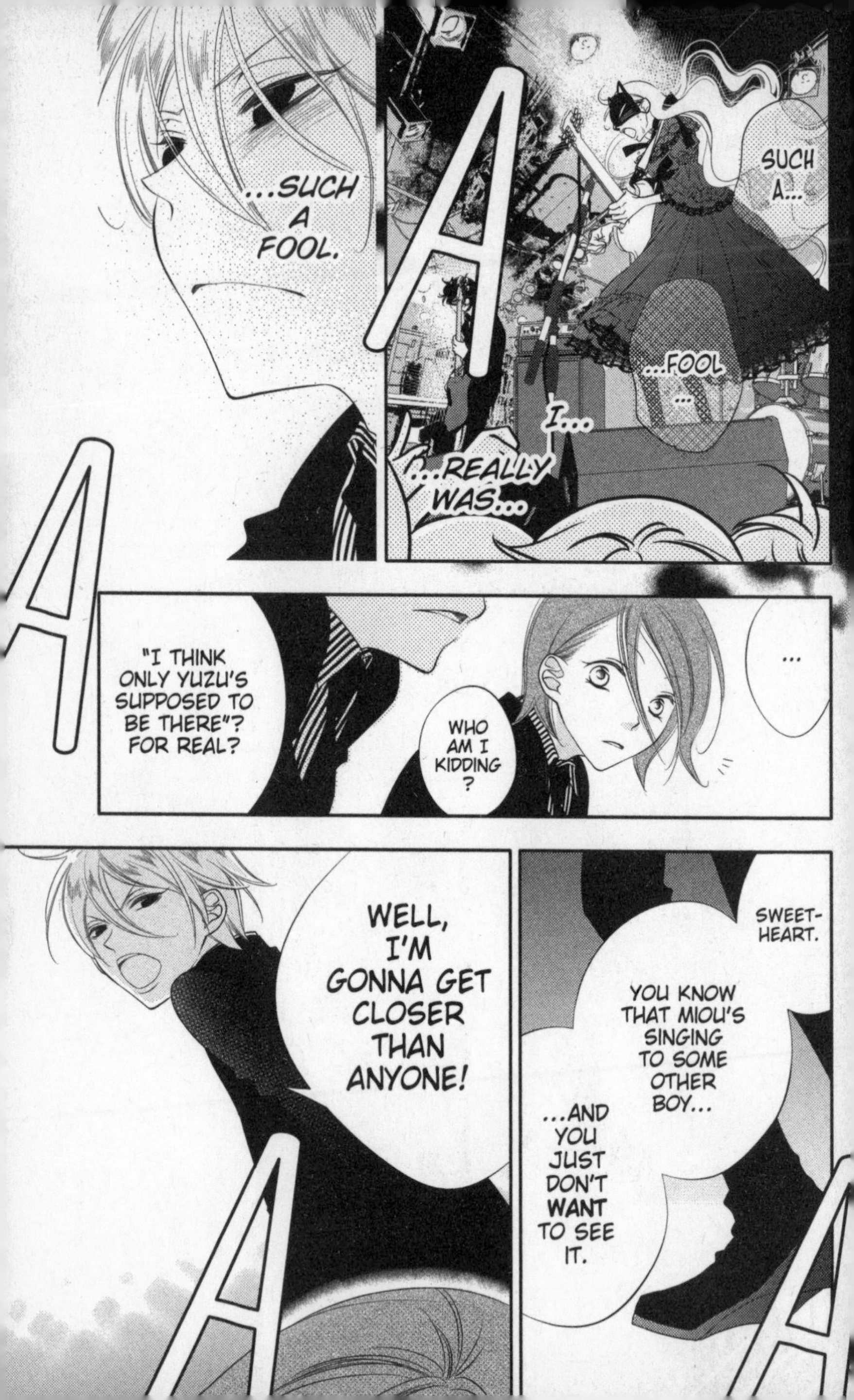
SUCH A...
...FOOL ...
I...
...REALLY WAS...
...SUCH A FOOL.
...
WHO AM I KIDDING ?
"I THINK ONLY YUZU'S SUPPOSED TO BE THERE"? FOR REAL?
SWEET-HEART.
YOU KNOW THAT MIOU'S SINGING TO SOME OTHER BOY...
...AND YOU JUST DON'T WANT TO SEE IT.
WELL, I'M GONNA GET CLOSER THAN ANYONE!

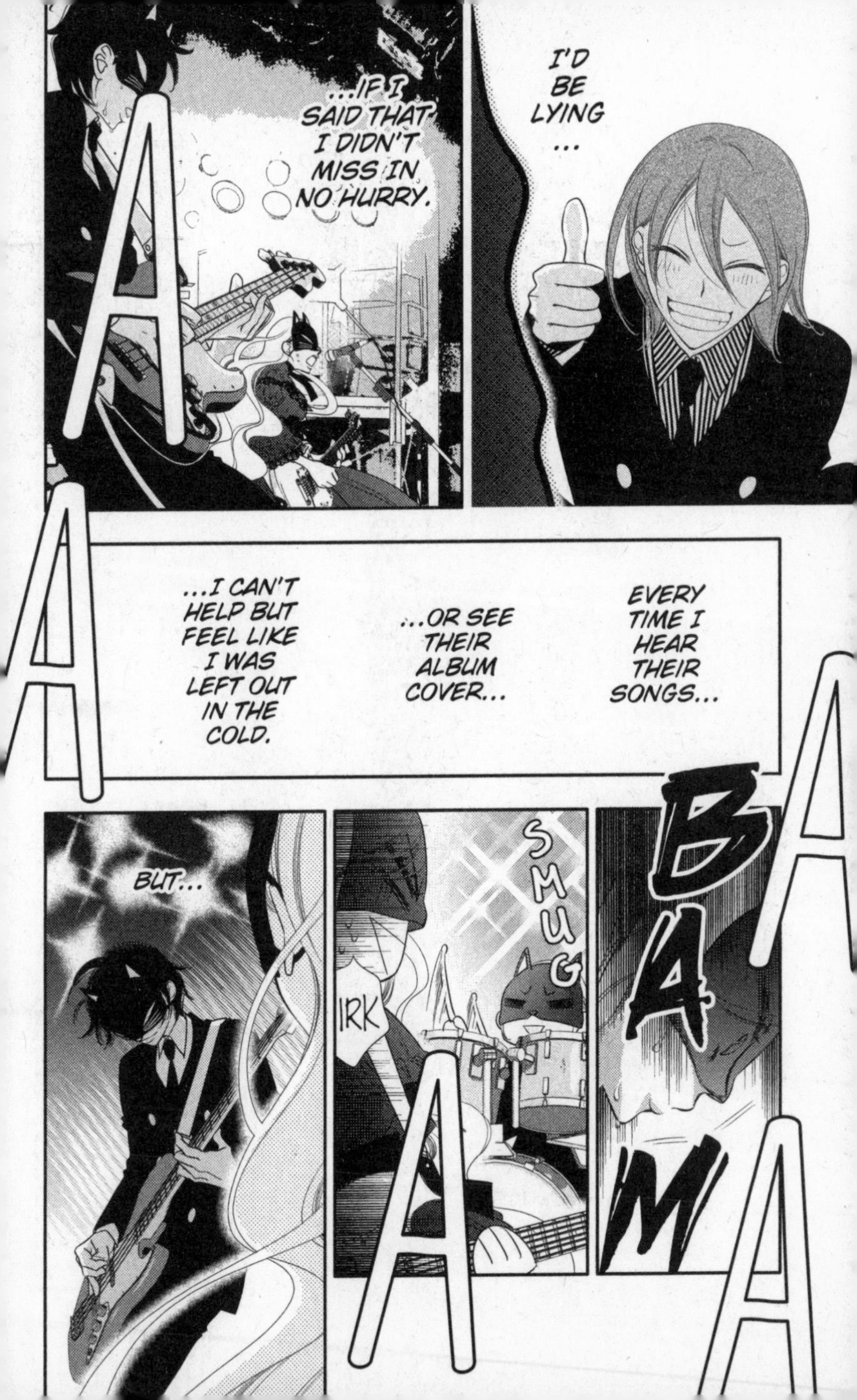
I'D BE LYING...
...IF I SAID THAT I DIDN'T MISS IN NO HURRY.
EVERY TIME I HEAR THEIR SONGS...
...OR SEE THEIR ALBUM COVER...
...I CAN'T HELP BUT FEEL LIKE I WAS LEFT OUT IN THE COLD.
BAM
SMUG
IRK
BUT...

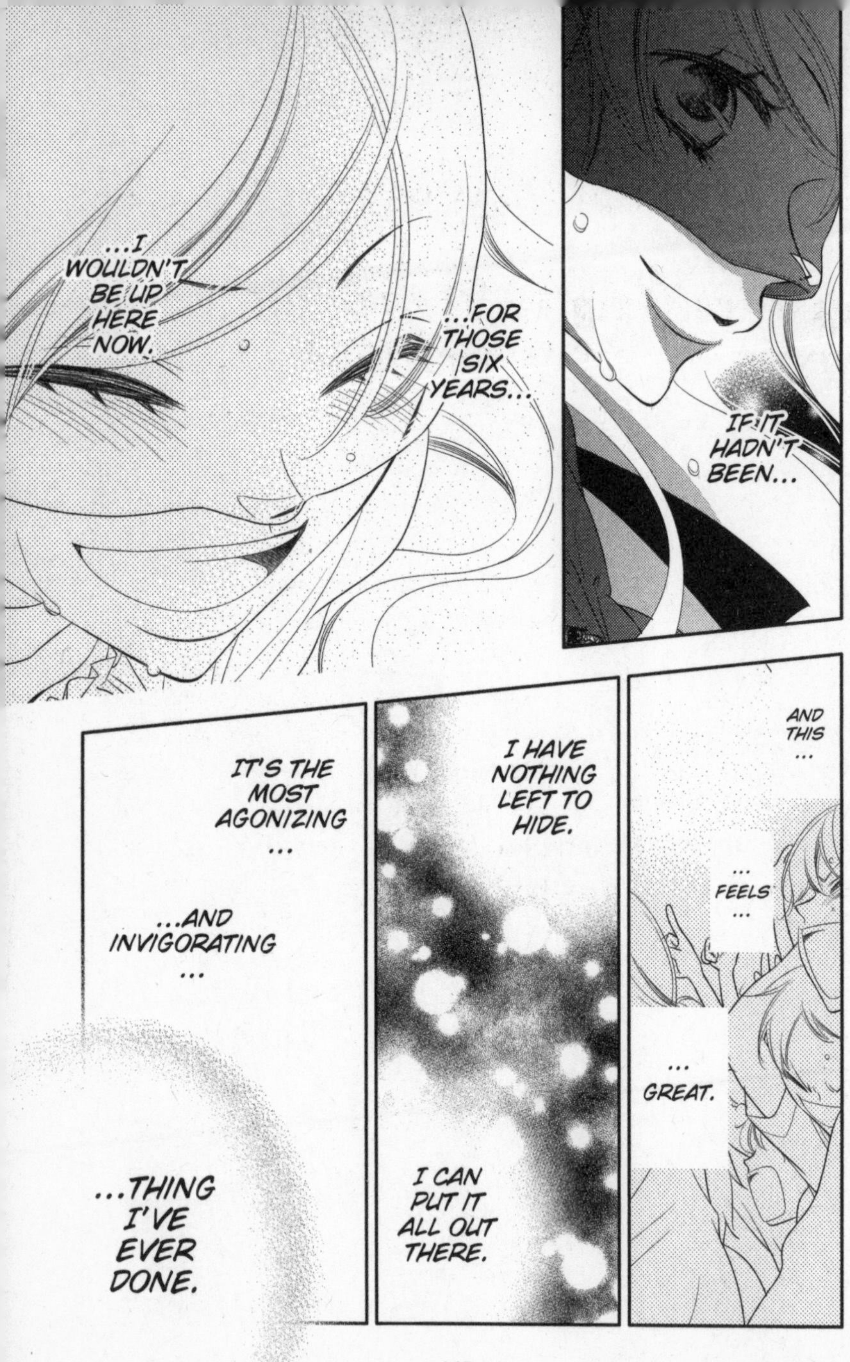
IF IT HADN'T BEEN...
...FOR THOSE SIX YEARS...
...I WOULDN'T BE UP HERE NOW.
AND THIS...
...FEELS...
...GREAT.
I HAVE NOTHING LEFT TO HIDE.
I CAN PUT IT ALL OUT THERE.
IT'S THE MOST AGONIZING...
...AND INVIGORATING...
...THING I'VE EVER DONE.

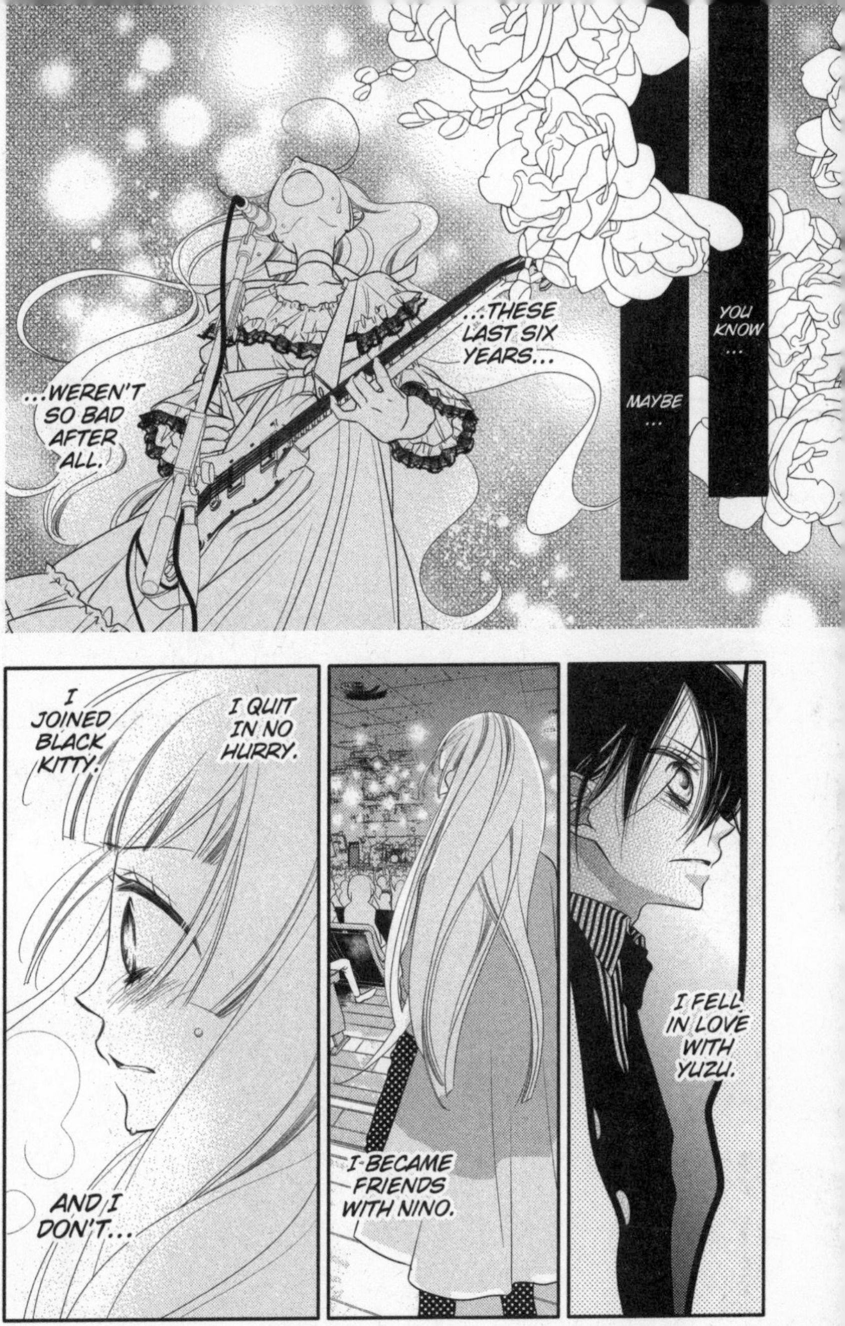
YOU KNOW...
MAYBE...
...THESE LAST SIX YEARS...
...WEREN'T SO BAD AFTER ALL.
I FELL IN LOVE WITH YUZU.
I BECAME FRIENDS WITH NINO.
I QUIT IN NO HURRY.
I JOINED BLACK KITTY.
AND I DON'T...

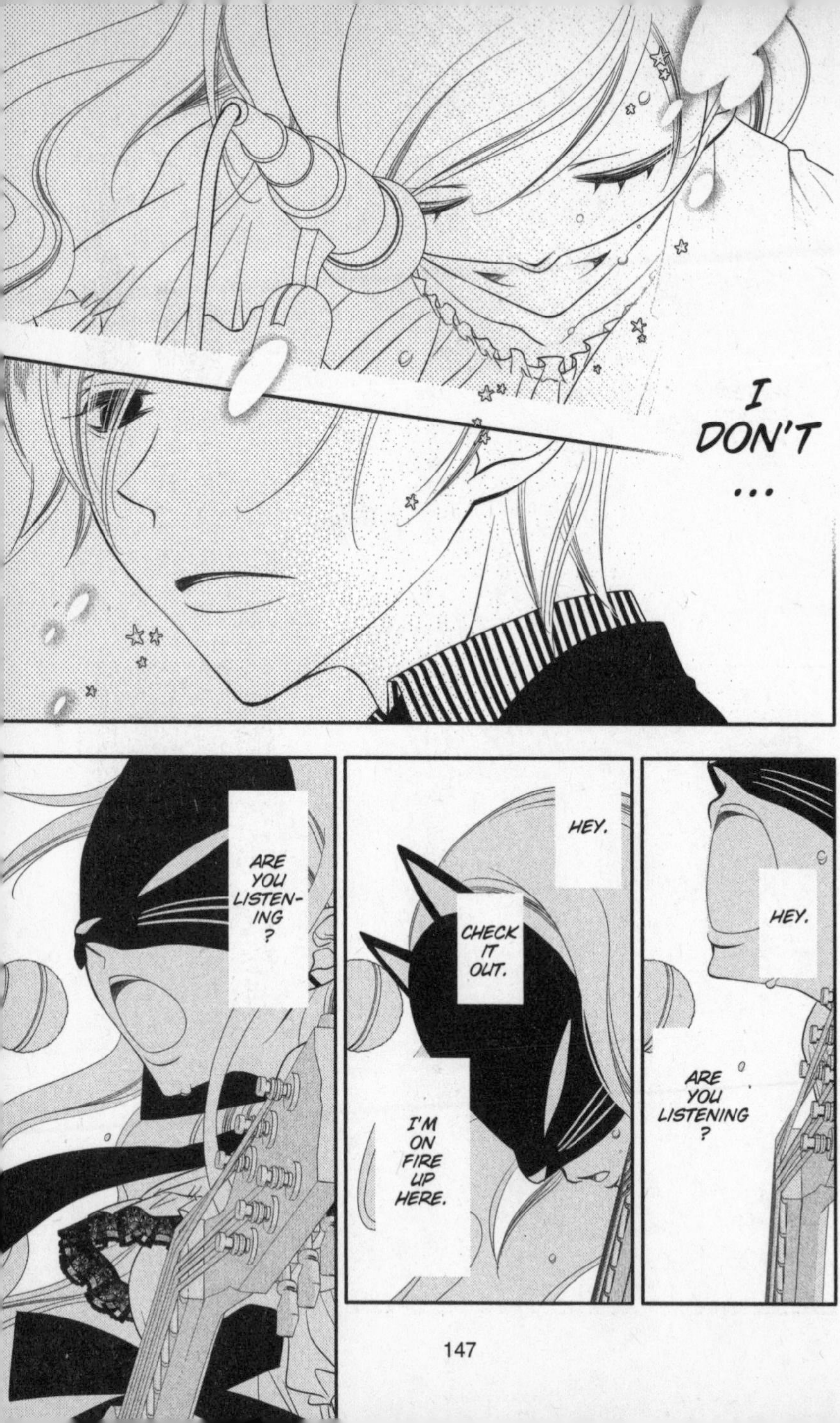
I DON'T ...
HEY.
ARE YOU LISTENING?
HEY.
CHECK IT OUT.
I'M ON FIRE UP HERE.
ARE YOU LISTEN-ING?

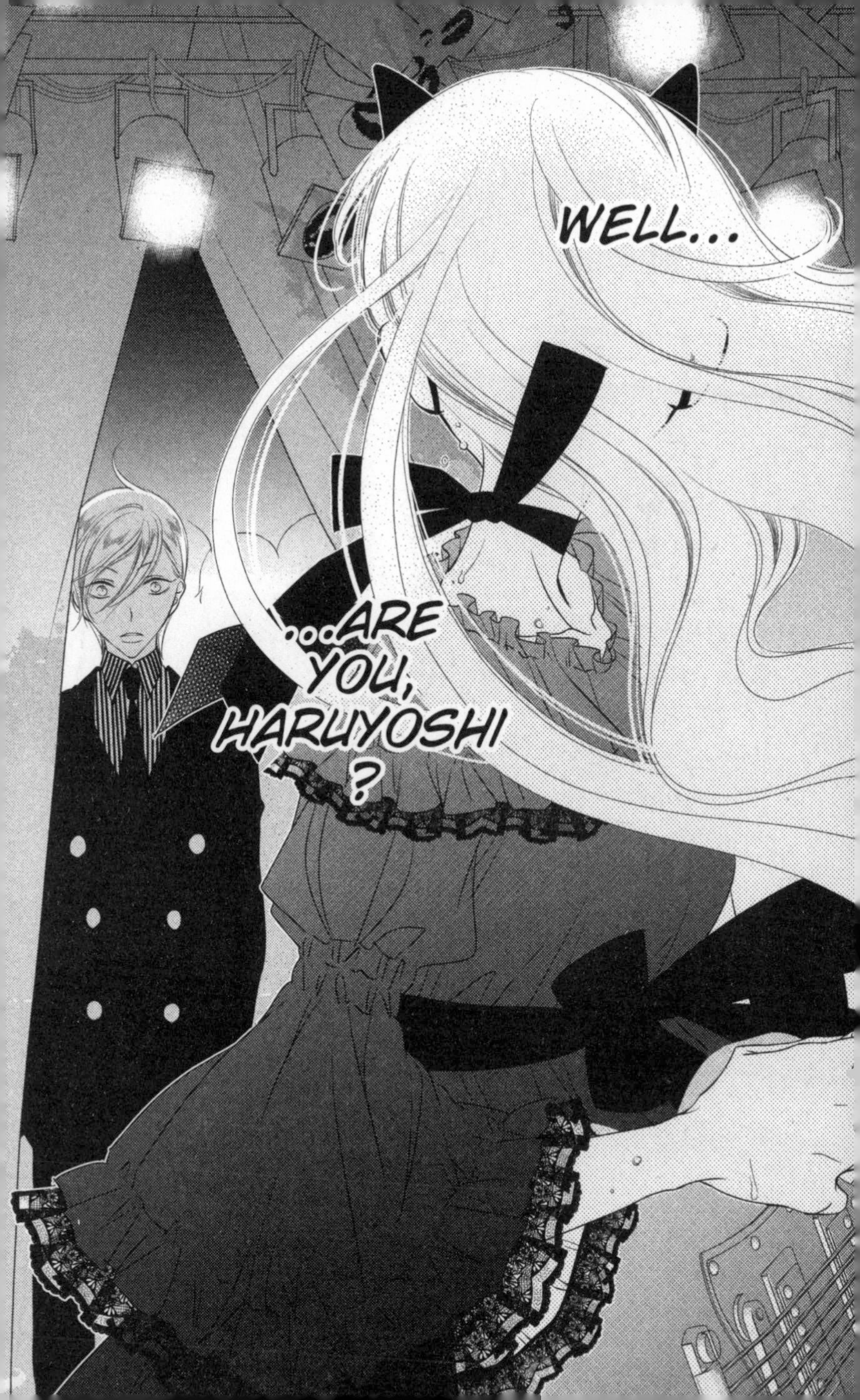
WELL...
...ARE YOU, HARUYOSHI?

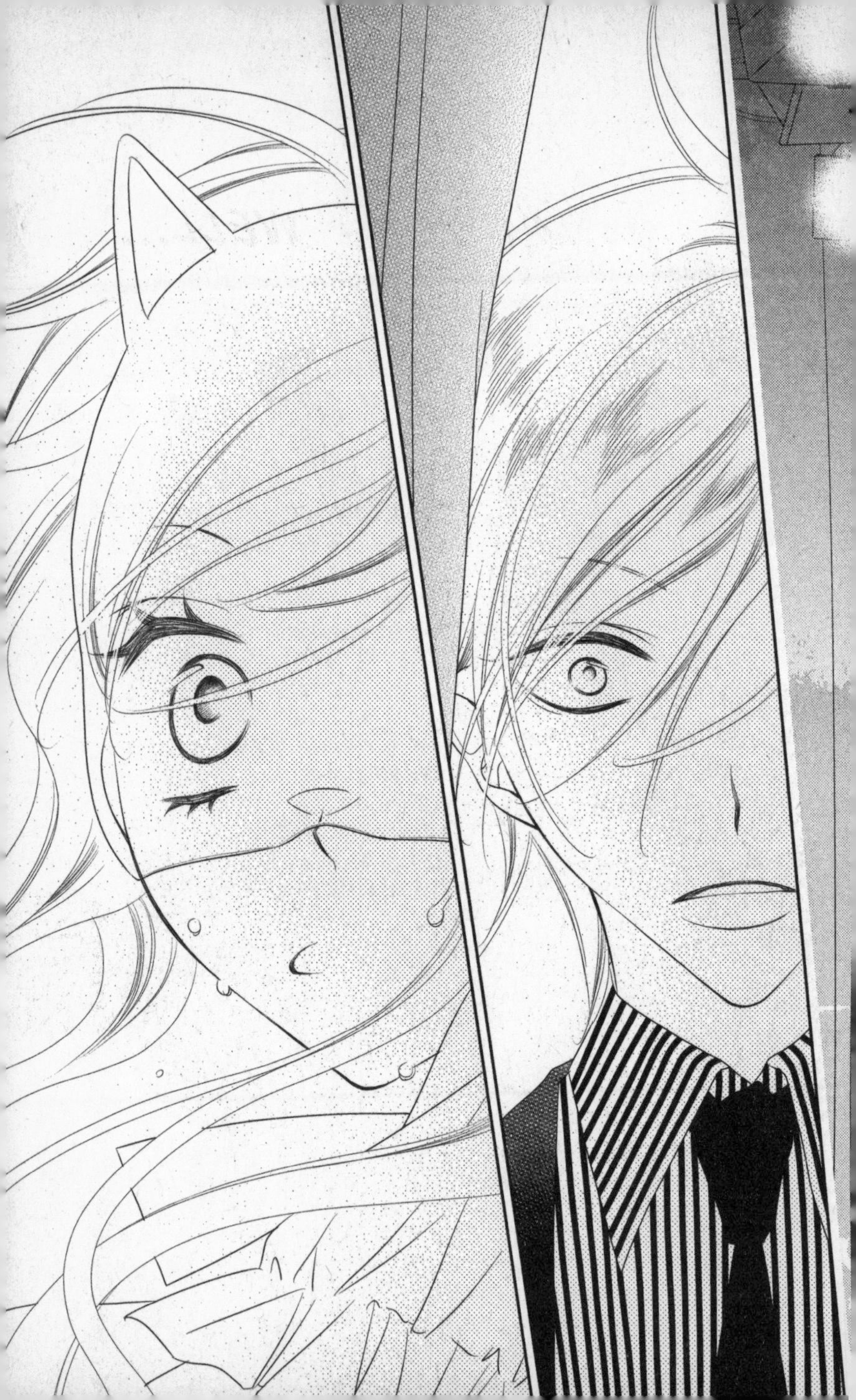

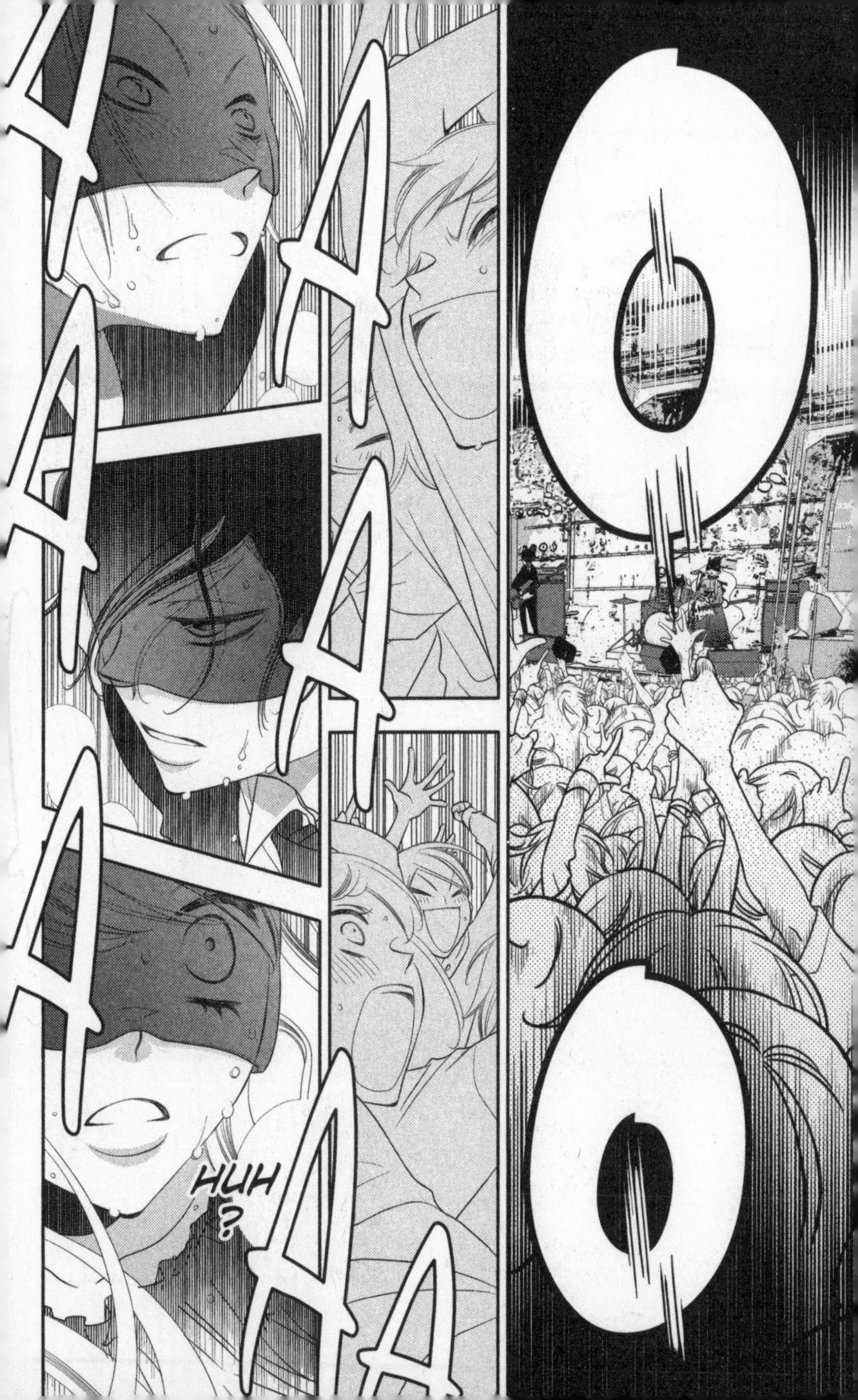
OO
AAAAAAAAAAAA
HUH?

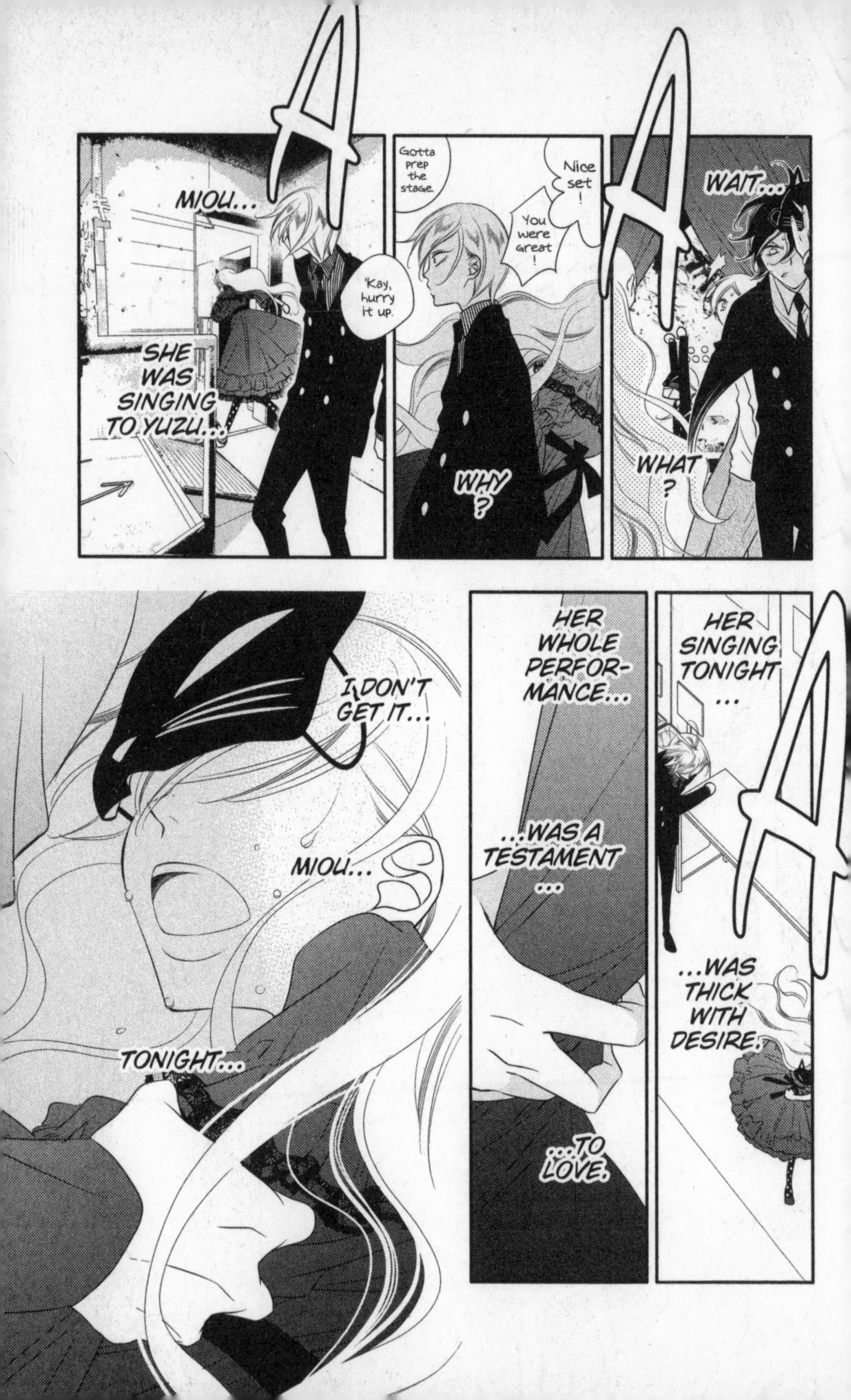
A
WAIT...
WHAT?
A
Nice set!
You were great!
Gotta prep the stage.
'Kay, hurry it up.
WHY?
A
MIOU...
SHE WAS SINGING TO YUZU...
A
HER SINGING TONIGHT...
...WAS THICK WITH DESIRE.
HER WHOLE PERFORMANCE...
...WAS A TESTAMENT...
...TO LOVE.
I DON'T GET IT...
MIOU...
TONIGHT...

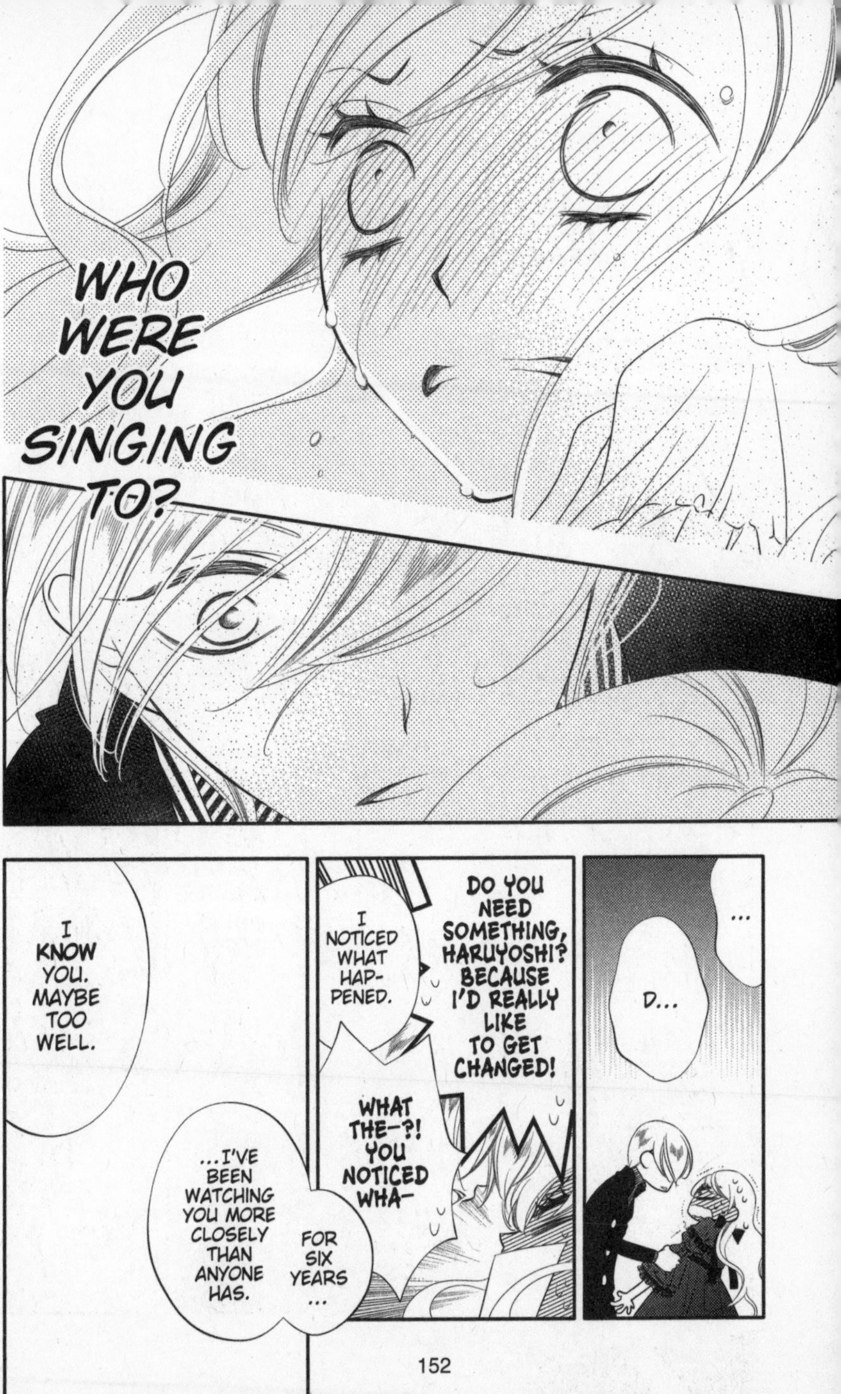
WHO WERE YOU SINGING TO?
...
D...
DO YOU NEED SOMETHING, HARUYOSHI? BECAUSE I'D REALLY LIKE TO GET CHANGED!
I NOTICED WHAT HAPPENED.
WHAT THE-?! YOU NOTICED WHA-
I KNOW YOU. MAYBE TOO WELL.
FOR SIX YEARS...
...I'VE BEEN WATCHING YOU MORE CLOSELY THAN ANYONE HAS.

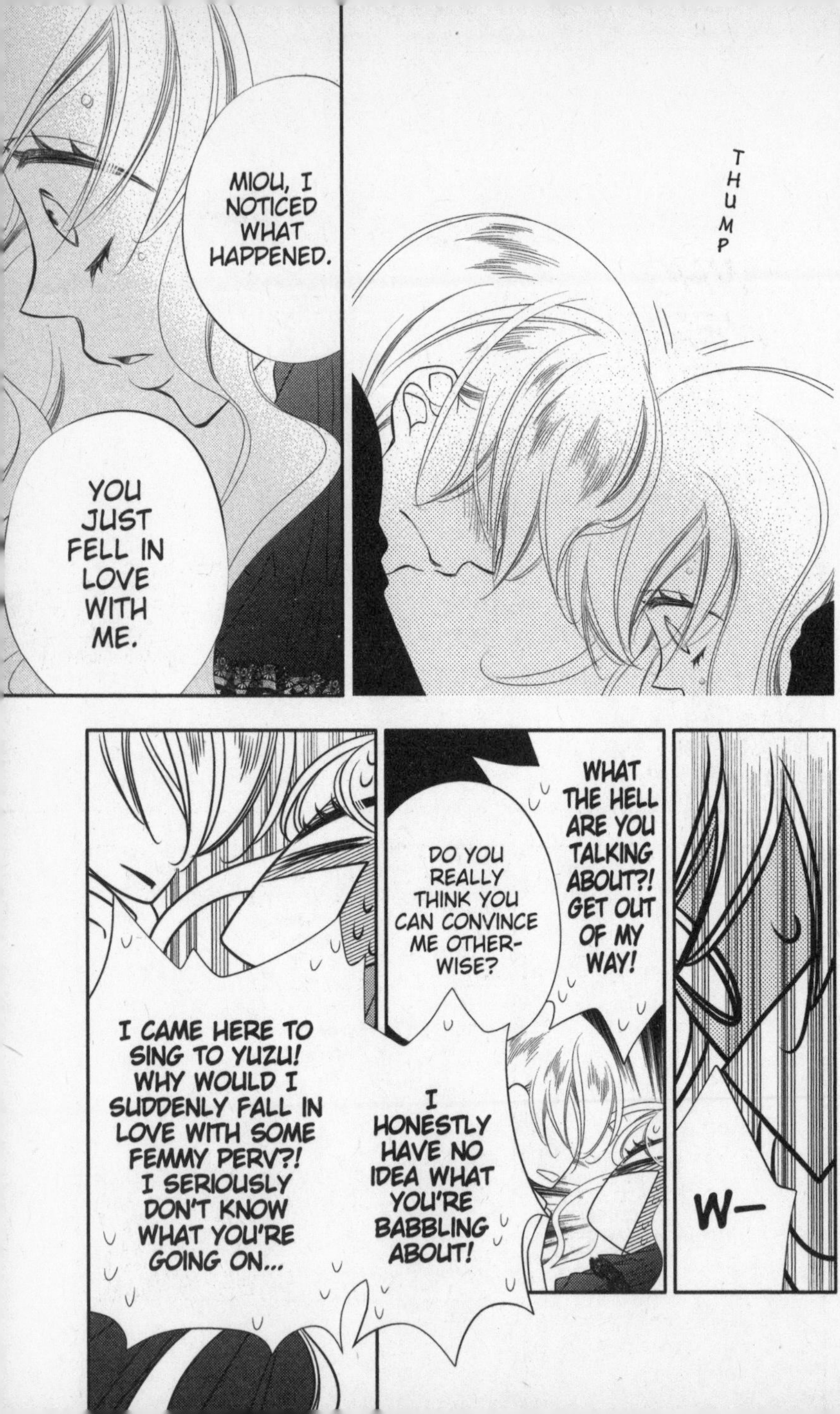
THUMP
MIOU, I NOTICED WHAT HAPPENED.
YOU JUST FELL IN LOVE WITH ME.
W—
WHAT THE HELL ARE YOU TALKING ABOUT?! GET OUT OF MY WAY!
DO YOU REALLY THINK YOU CAN CONVINCE ME OTHER-WISE?
I HONESTLY HAVE NO IDEA WHAT YOU'RE BABBLING ABOUT!
I CAME HERE TO SING TO YUZU! WHY WOULD I SUDDENLY FALL IN LOVE WITH SOME FEMMY PERV?! I SERIOUSLY DON'T KNOW WHAT YOU'RE GOING ON...

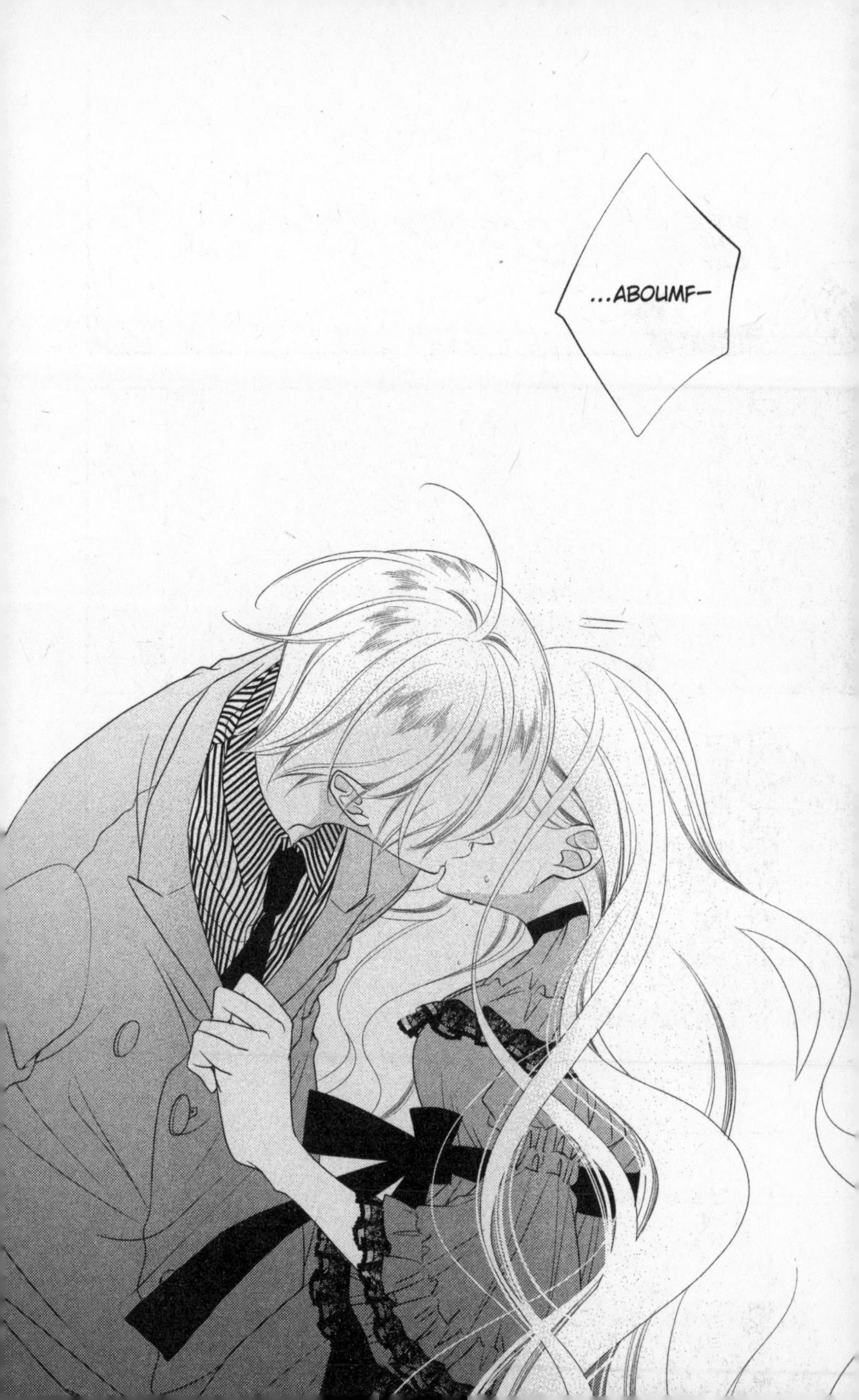
...ABOUMF—

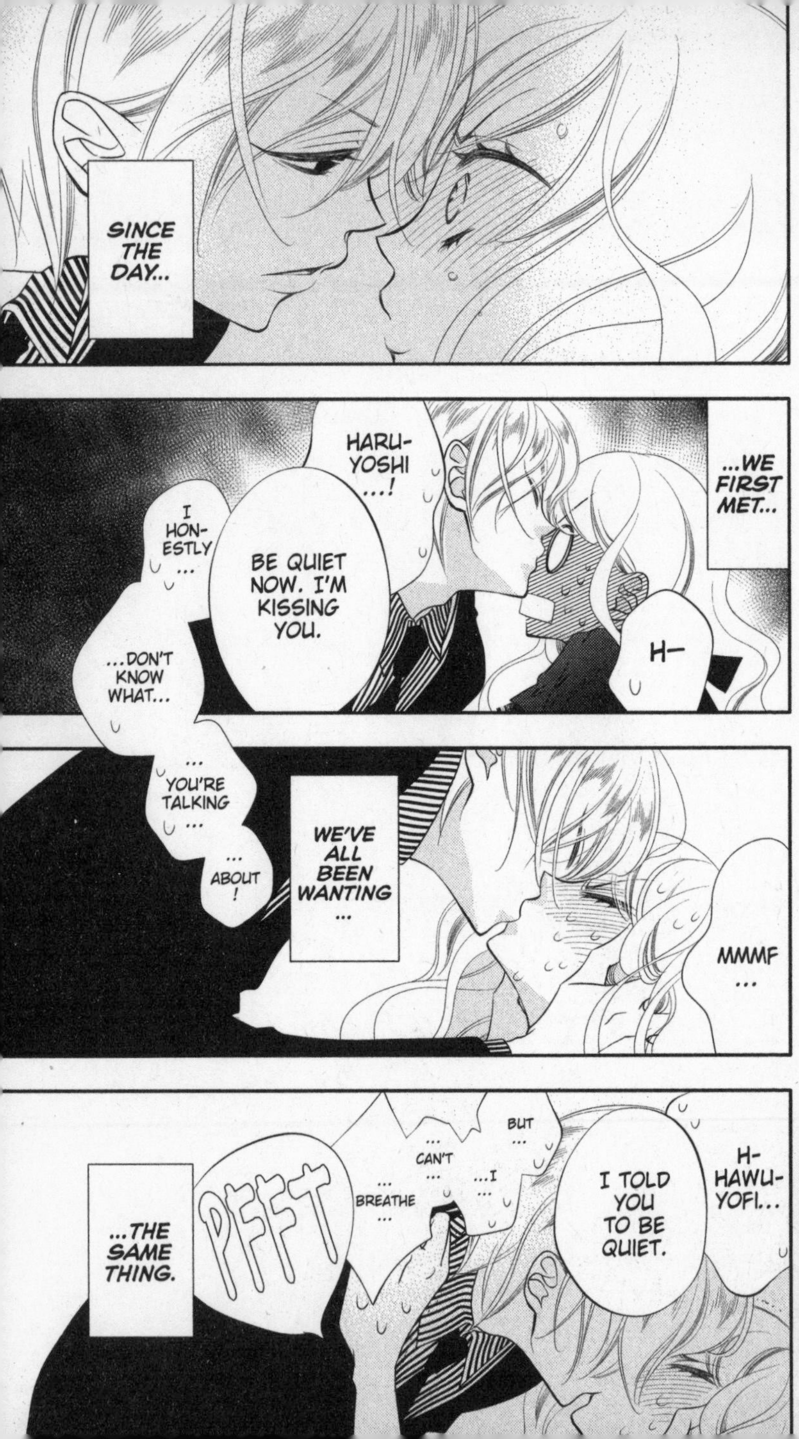
SINCE THE DAY...
...WE FIRST MET...
H—
HARU-YOSHI ...!
BE QUIET NOW. I'M KISSING YOU.
I HON-ESTLY ...
...DON'T KNOW WHAT...
... YOU'RE TALKING ...
... ABOUT !
MMMF ...
WE'VE ALL BEEN WANTING ...
H-HAWU-YOFI...
I TOLD YOU TO BE QUIET.
BUT ...
...I ...
... CAN'T ...
... BREATHE ...
PFFT
...THE SAME THING.

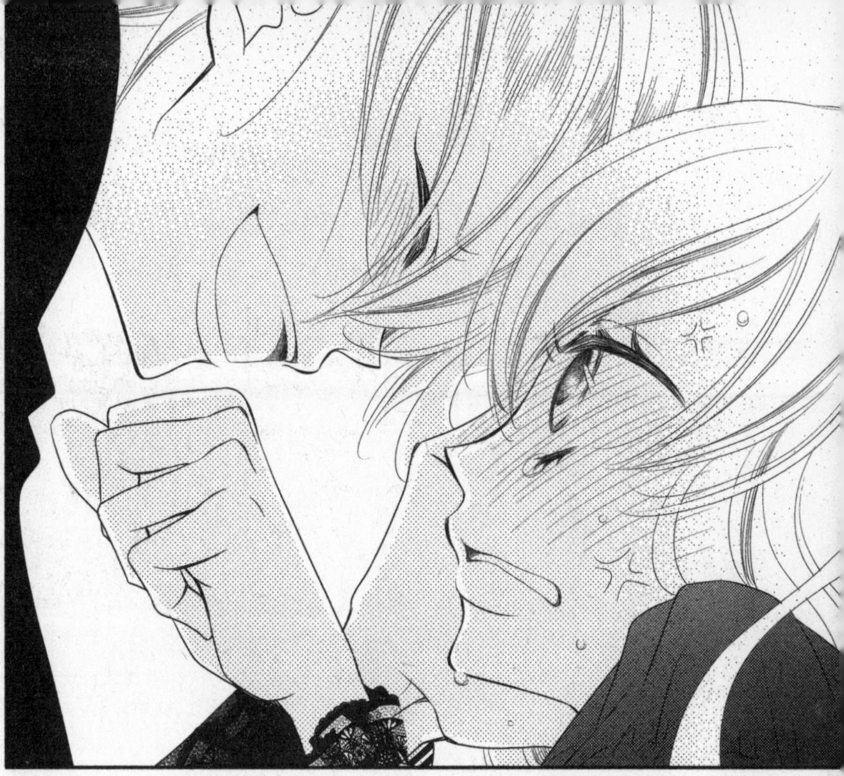

"LOOK AT ME."

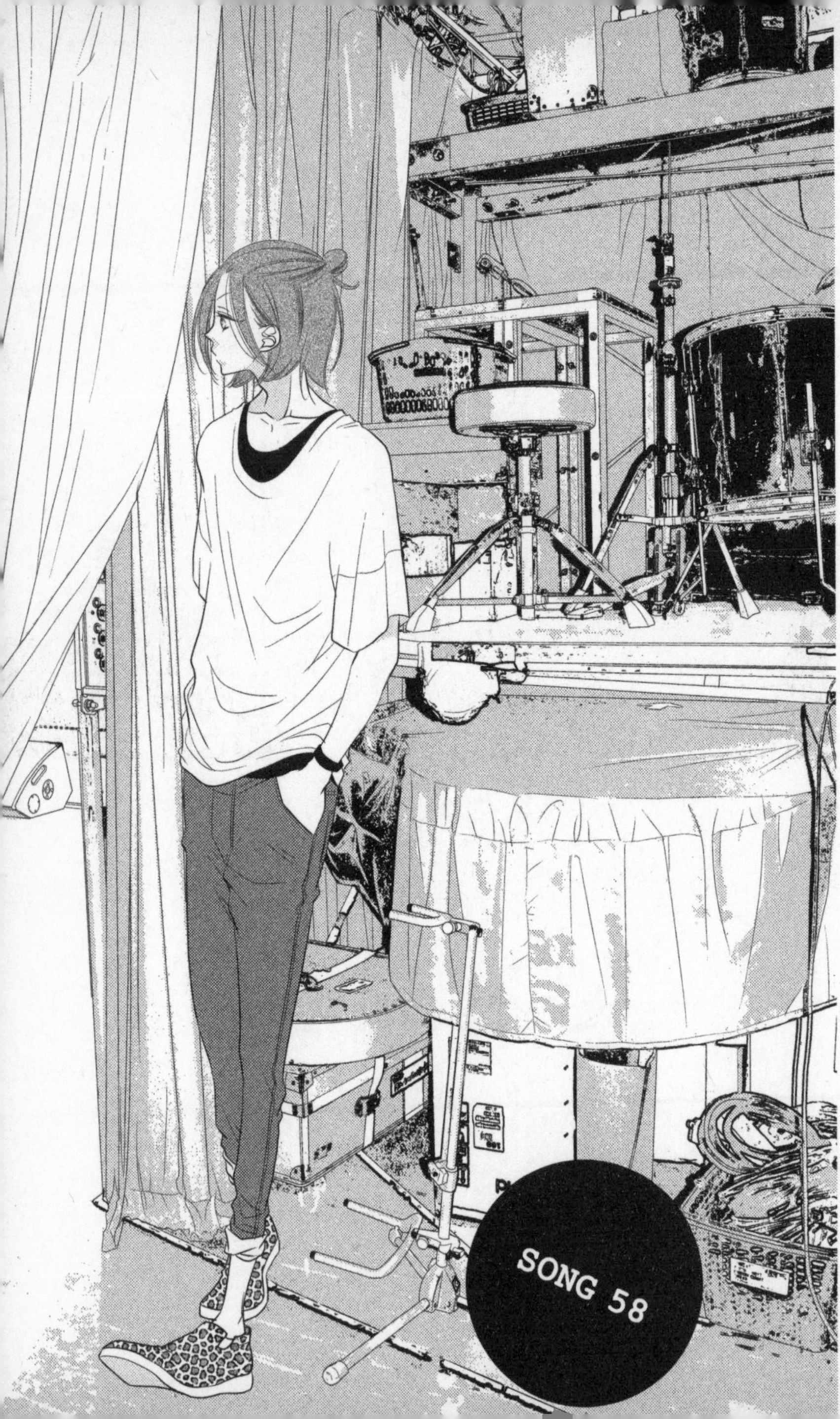
SONG 58

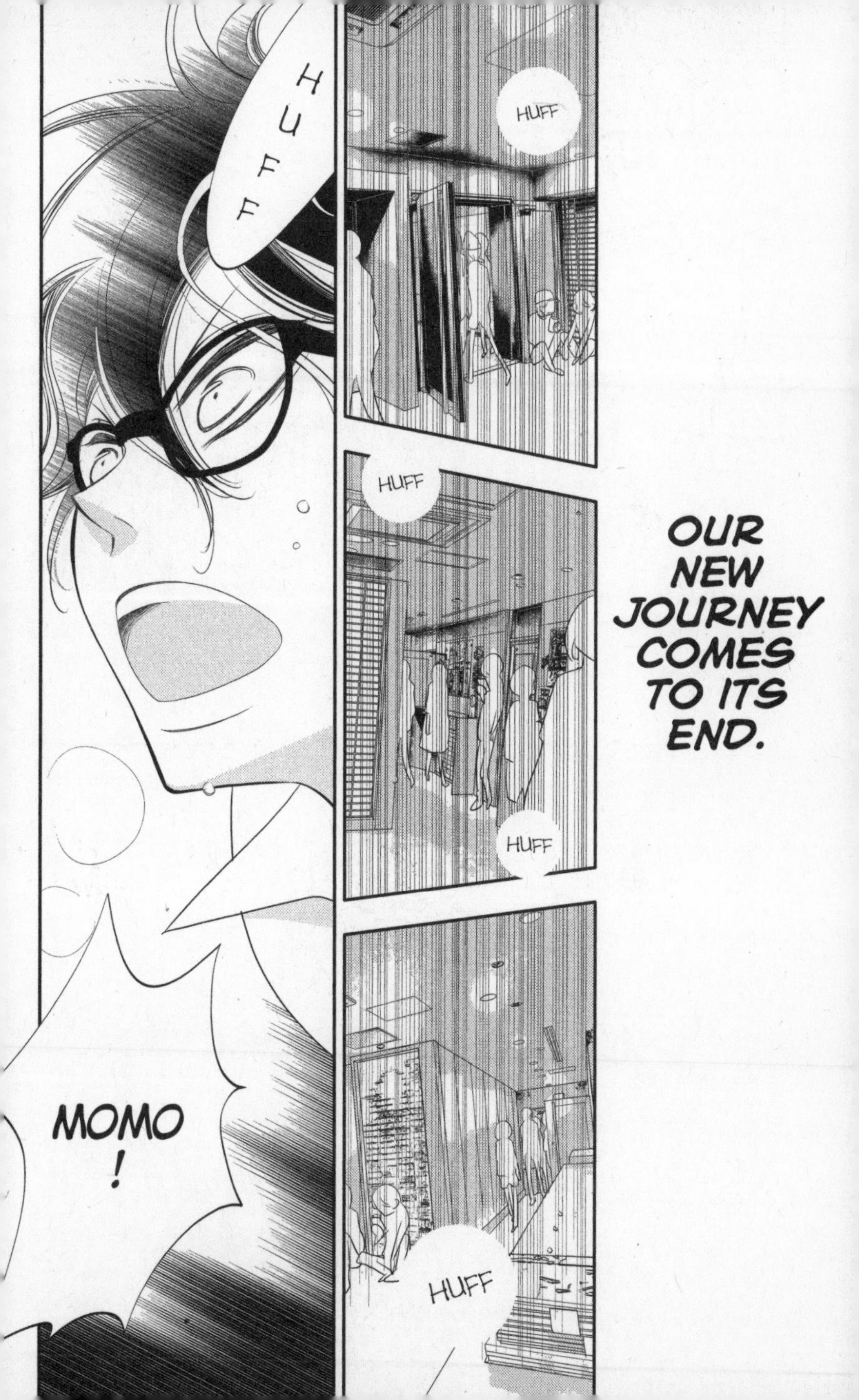
OUR NEW JOURNEY COMES TO ITS END.
HUFF
HUFF
HUFF
HUFF
HUFF
HUFF
MOMO!

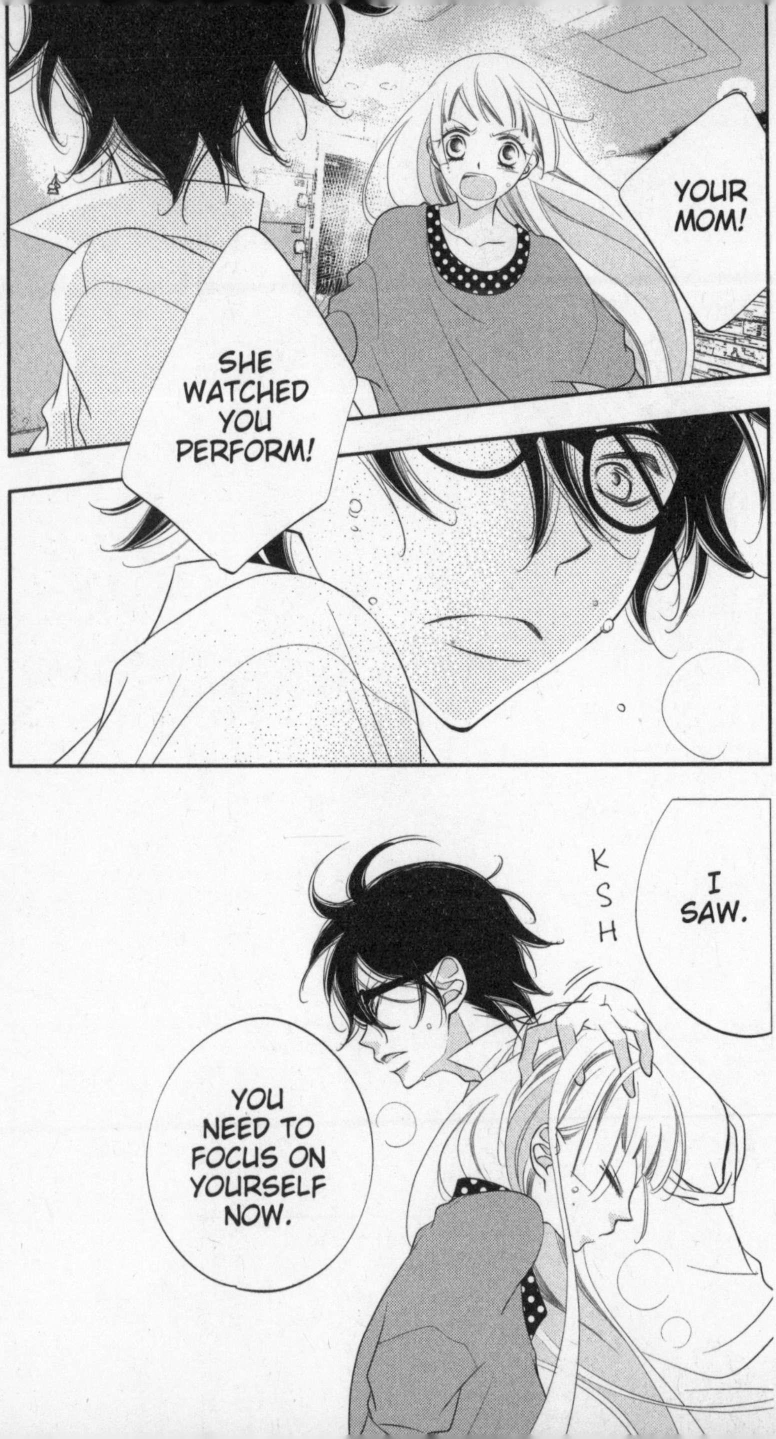
YOUR MOM!
SHE WATCHED YOU PERFORM!
I SAW.
KSH
YOU NEED TO FOCUS ON YOURSELF NOW.

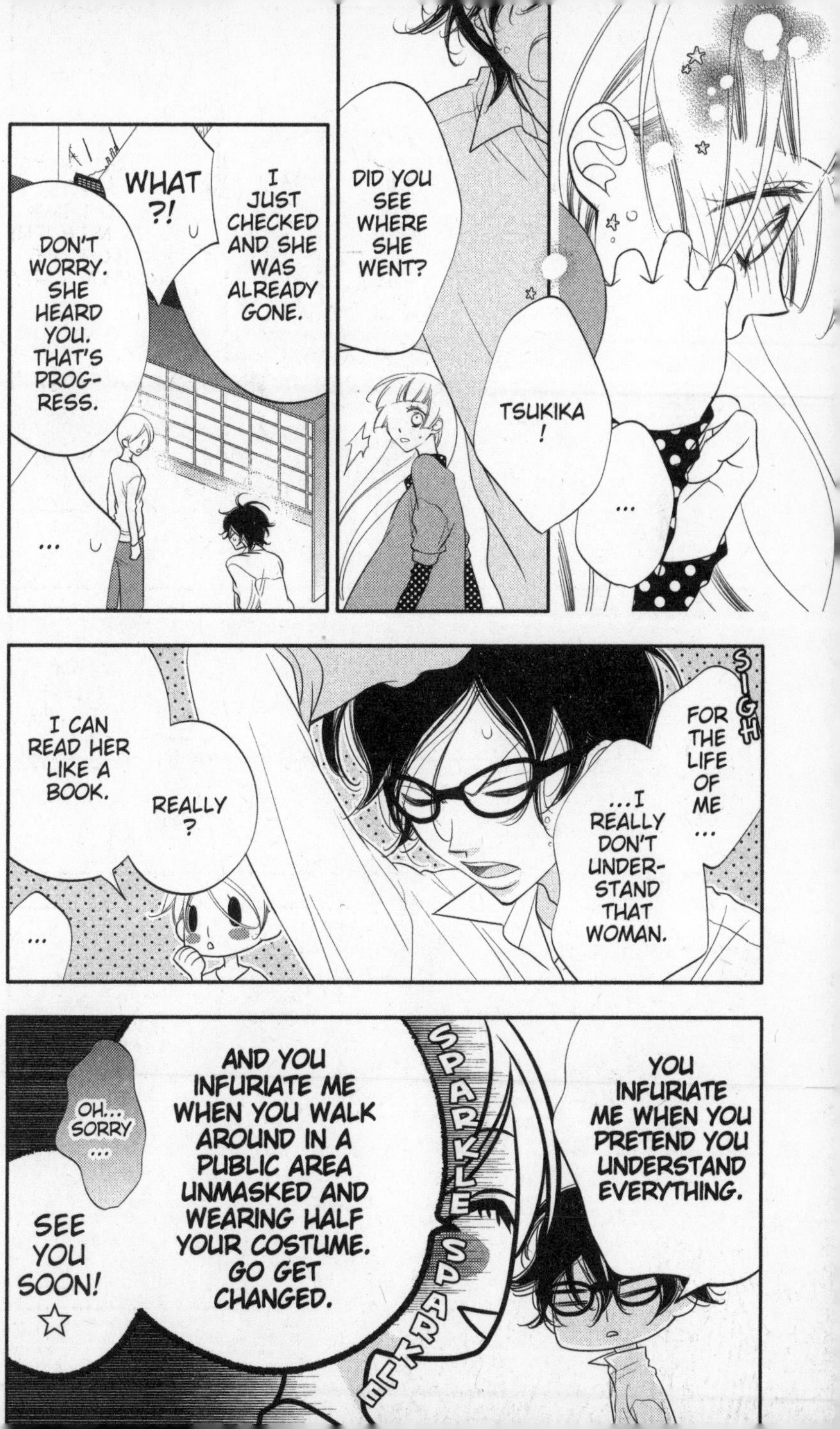
TSUKIKA!
...
DID YOU SEE WHERE SHE WENT?
I JUST CHECKED AND SHE WAS ALREADY GONE.
WHAT?!
DON'T WORRY. SHE HEARD YOU. THAT'S PROG-RESS.
...
SIGH
FOR THE LIFE OF ME...
...I REALLY DON'T UNDER-STAND THAT WOMAN.
REALLY?
I CAN READ HER LIKE A BOOK.
...
YOU INFURIATE ME WHEN YOU PRETEND YOU UNDERSTAND EVERYTHING.
SPARKLE SPARKLE SPARKLE
AND YOU INFURIATE ME WHEN YOU WALK AROUND IN A PUBLIC AREA UNMASKED AND WEARING HALF YOUR COSTUME. GO GET CHANGED.
OH... SORRY...
SEE YOU SOON! ☆

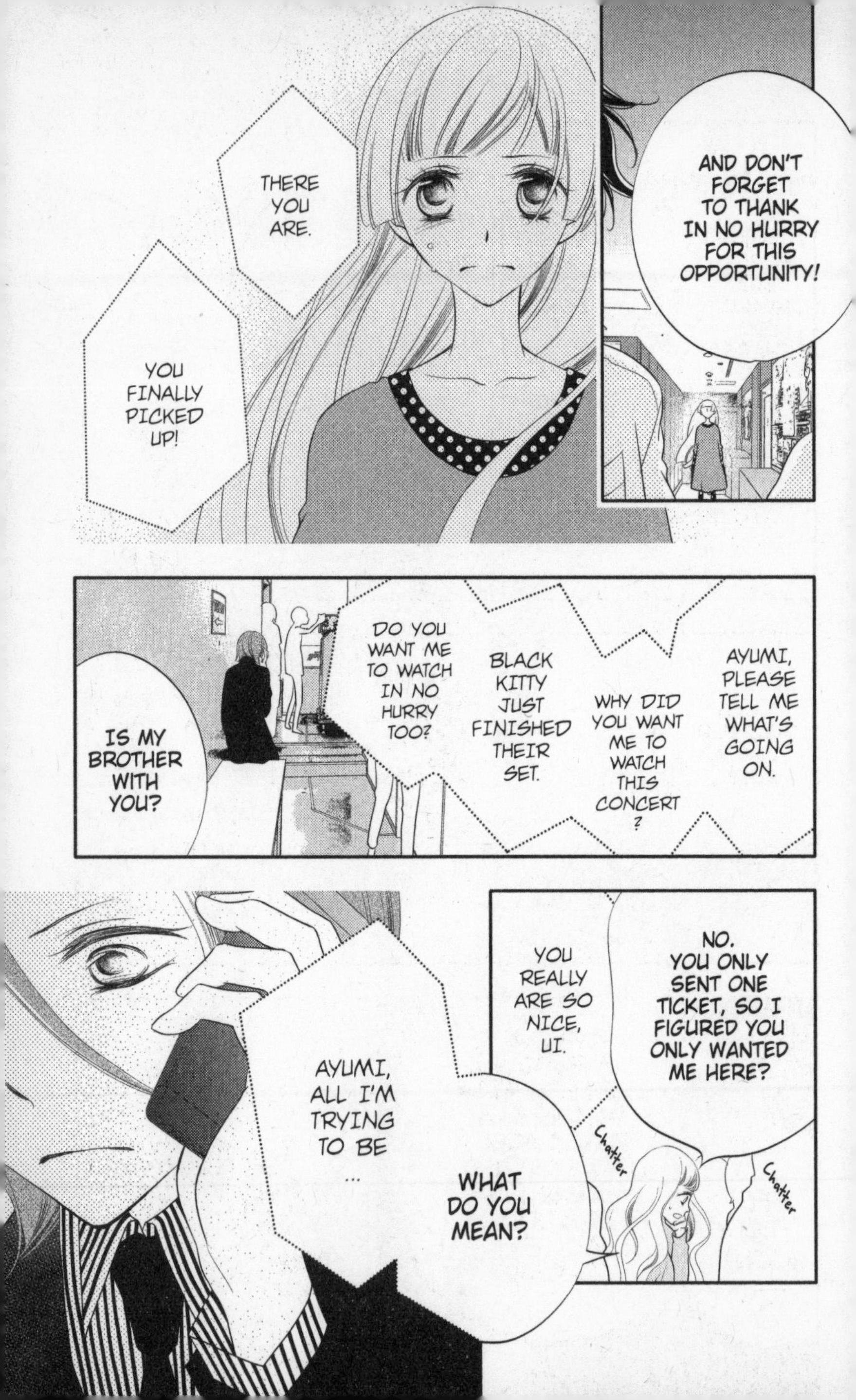
AND DON'T FORGET TO THANK IN NO HURRY FOR THIS OPPORTUNITY!
THERE YOU ARE.
YOU FINALLY PICKED UP!
AYUMI, PLEASE TELL ME WHAT'S GOING ON.
WHY DID YOU WANT ME TO WATCH THIS CONCERT?
BLACK KITTY JUST FINISHED THEIR SET.
DO YOU WANT ME TO WATCH IN NO HURRY TOO?
IS MY BROTHER WITH YOU?
NO. YOU ONLY SENT ONE TICKET, SO I FIGURED YOU ONLY WANTED ME HERE?
YOU REALLY ARE SO NICE, UI.
Chatter
Chatter
WHAT DO YOU MEAN?
AYUMI, ALL I'M TRYING TO BE ...

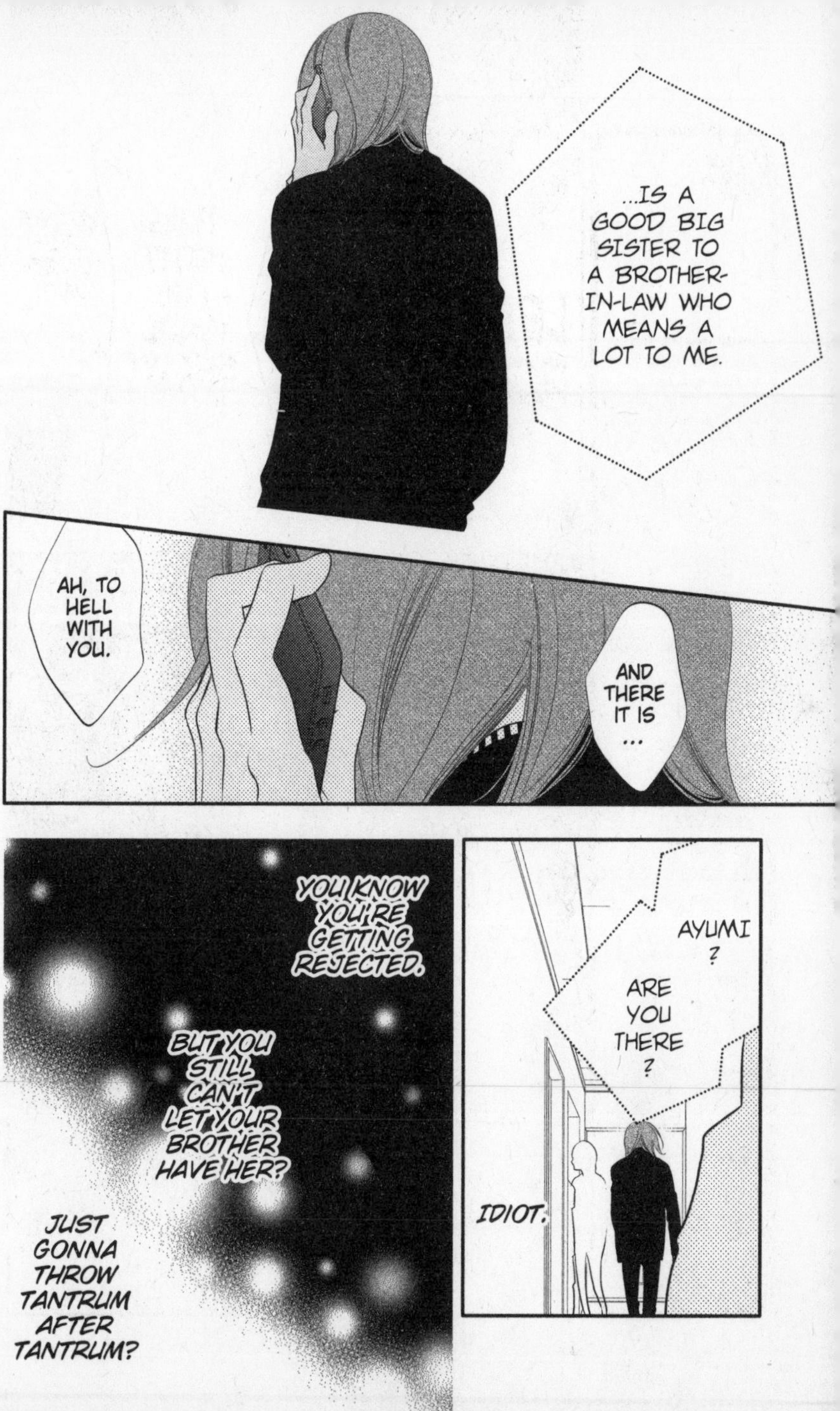
...IS A GOOD BIG SISTER TO A BROTHER-IN-LAW WHO MEANS A LOT TO ME.
AND THERE IT IS ...
AH, TO HELL WITH YOU.
AYUMI?
ARE YOU THERE?
IDIOT.
YOU KNOW YOU'RE GETTING REJECTED.
BUT YOU STILL CAN'T LET YOUR BROTHER HAVE HER?
JUST GONNA THROW TANTRUM AFTER TANTRUM?

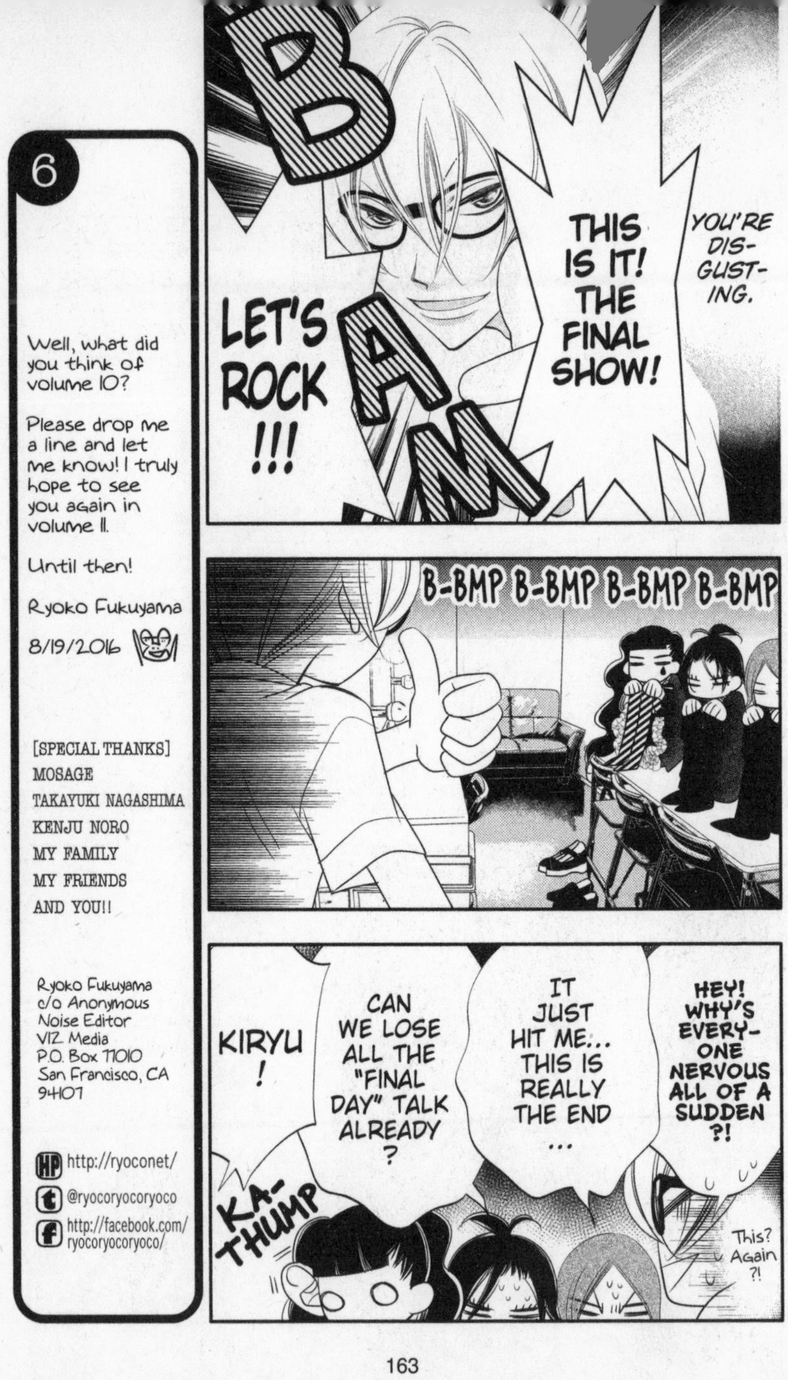
YOU'RE DIS-GUST-ING.
THIS IS IT! THE FINAL SHOW!
BAM
LET'S ROCK!!!
B-BMP B-BMP B-BMP B-BMP
HEY! WHY'S EVERYONE NERVOUS ALL OF A SUDDEN?!
IT JUST HIT ME... THIS IS REALLY THE END...
CAN WE LOSE ALL THE "FINAL DAY" TALK ALREADY?
KIRYU!
This? Again?!
KA-THUMP

6

Well, what did you think of volume 10?

Please drop me a line and let me know! I truly hope to see you again in volume 11.

Until then!

Ryoko Fukuyama

8/19/2016

[SPECIAL THANKS]
MOSAGE
TAKAYUKI NAGASHIMA
KENJU NORO
MY FAMILY
MY FRIENDS
AND YOU!!

Ryoko Fukuyama
c/o Anonymous Noise Editor
VIZ Media
P.O. Box 77010
San Francisco, CA 94107

HP http://ryoconet/
@ryocoryocoryoco
http://facebook.com/ryocoryocoryoco/

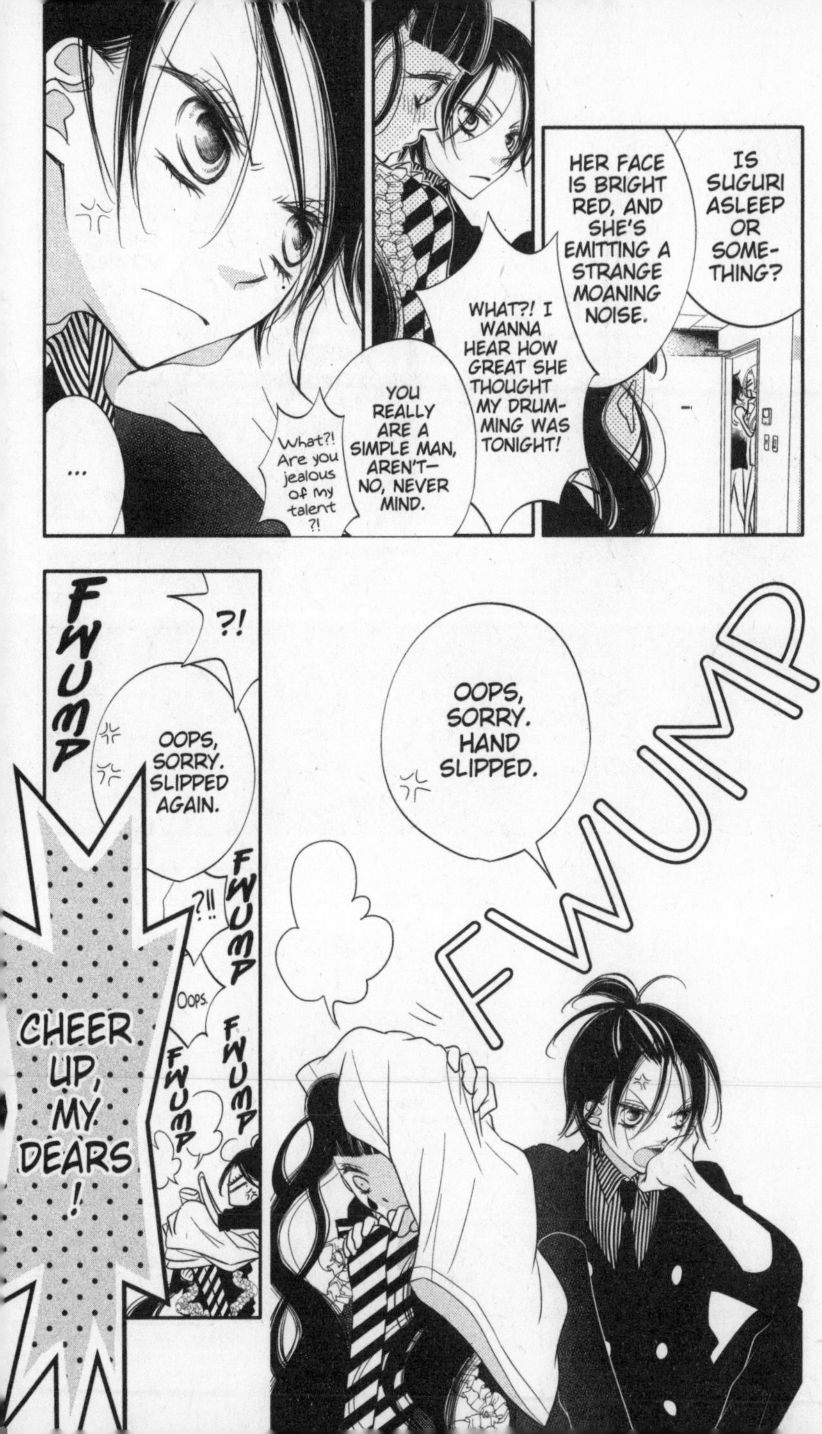
IS SUGURI ASLEEP OR SOME-THING?
HER FACE IS BRIGHT RED, AND SHE'S EMITTING A STRANGE MOANING NOISE.
WHAT?! I WANNA HEAR HOW GREAT SHE THOUGHT MY DRUM-MING WAS TONIGHT!
YOU REALLY ARE A SIMPLE MAN, AREN'T— NO, NEVER MIND.
What?! Are you jealous of my talent ?!
...
FWUMP
OOPS, SORRY. HAND SLIPPED.
FWUMP
?!
OOPS, SORRY. SLIPPED AGAIN.
FWUMP
?!!
Oops.
FWUMP
FWUMP
CHEER UP, MY DEARS!

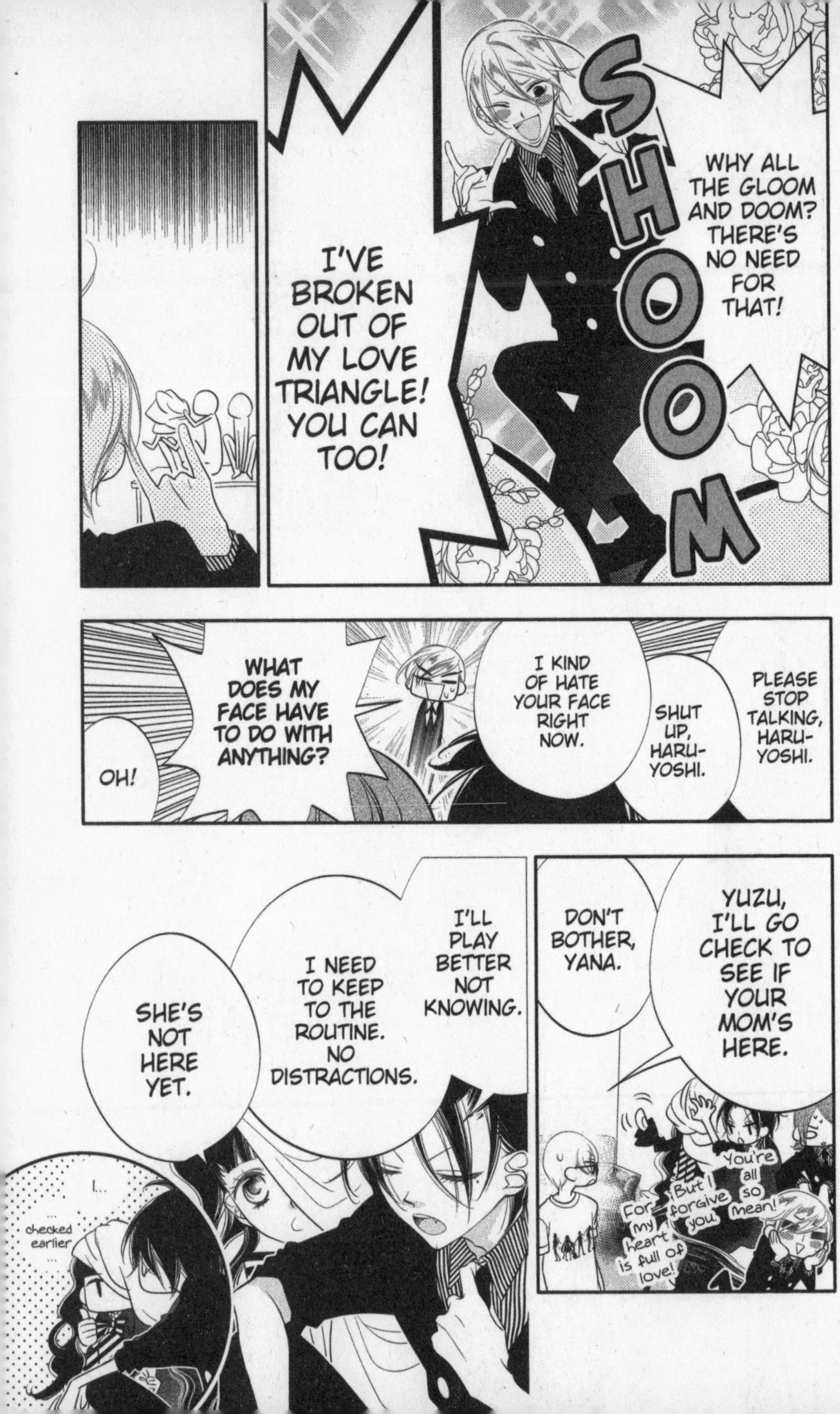
WHY ALL THE GLOOM AND DOOM? THERE'S NO NEED FOR THAT!
SHOOM
I'VE BROKEN OUT OF MY LOVE TRIANGLE! YOU CAN TOO!
PLEASE STOP TALKING, HARU-YOSHI.
SHUT UP, HARU-YOSHI.
I KIND OF HATE YOUR FACE RIGHT NOW.
WHAT DOES MY FACE HAVE TO DO WITH ANYTHING?
OH!
YUZU, I'LL GO CHECK TO SEE IF YOUR MOM'S HERE.
DON'T BOTHER, YANA.
You're all so mean!
But I forgive you.
For my heart is full of love!
I'LL PLAY BETTER NOT KNOWING.
I NEED TO KEEP TO THE ROUTINE. NO DISTRACTIONS.
SHE'S NOT HERE YET.
I...
...checked earlier...

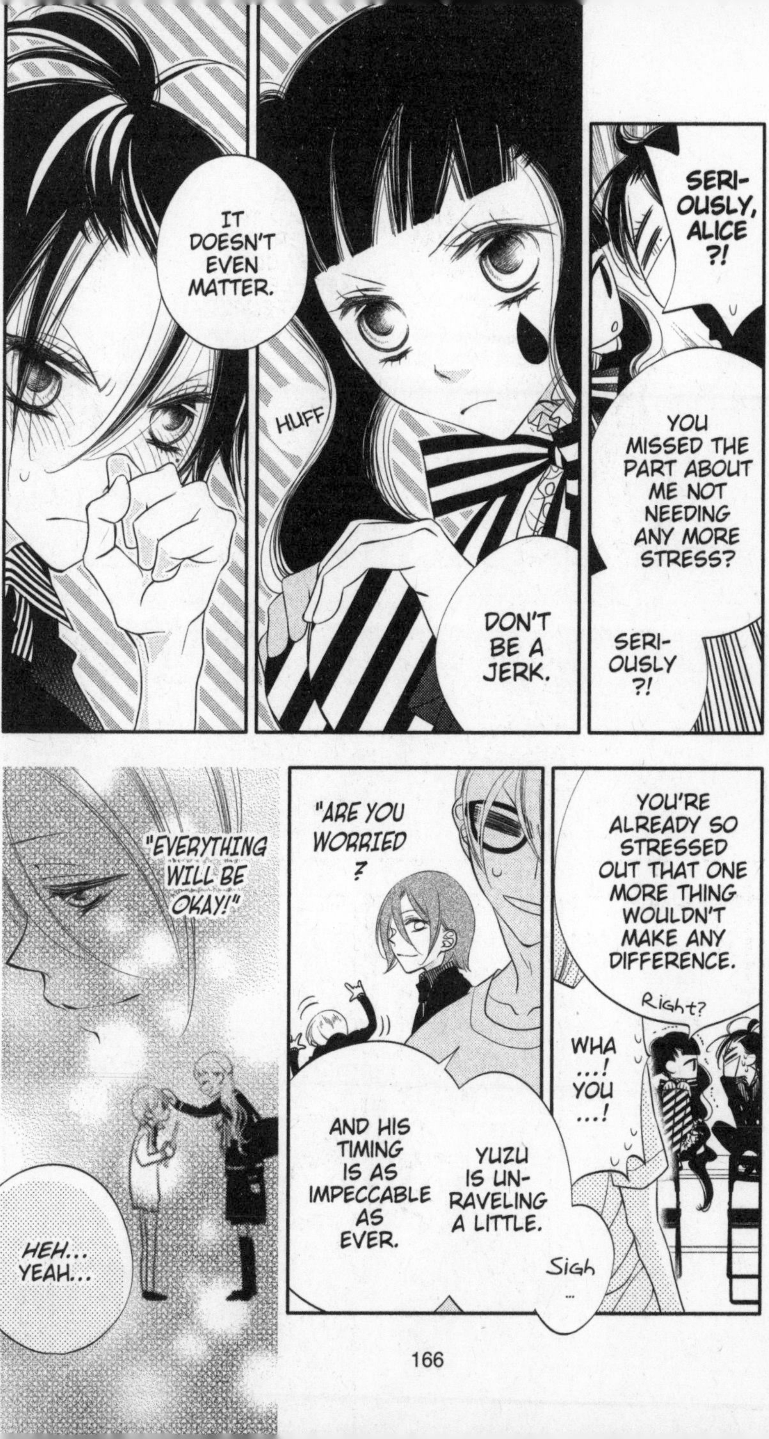
SERI-OUSLY, ALICE?!
YOU MISSED THE PART ABOUT ME NOT NEEDING ANY MORE STRESS?
SERI-OUSLY?!
HUFF
DON'T BE A JERK.
IT DOESN'T EVEN MATTER.
YOU'RE ALREADY SO STRESSED OUT THAT ONE MORE THING WOULDN'T MAKE ANY DIFFERENCE.
Right?
WHA...! YOU...!
"ARE YOU WORRIED?
YUZU IS UN-RAVELING A LITTLE.
AND HIS TIMING IS AS IMPECCABLE AS EVER.
Sigh...
"EVERYTHING WILL BE OKAY!"
HEH... YEAH...

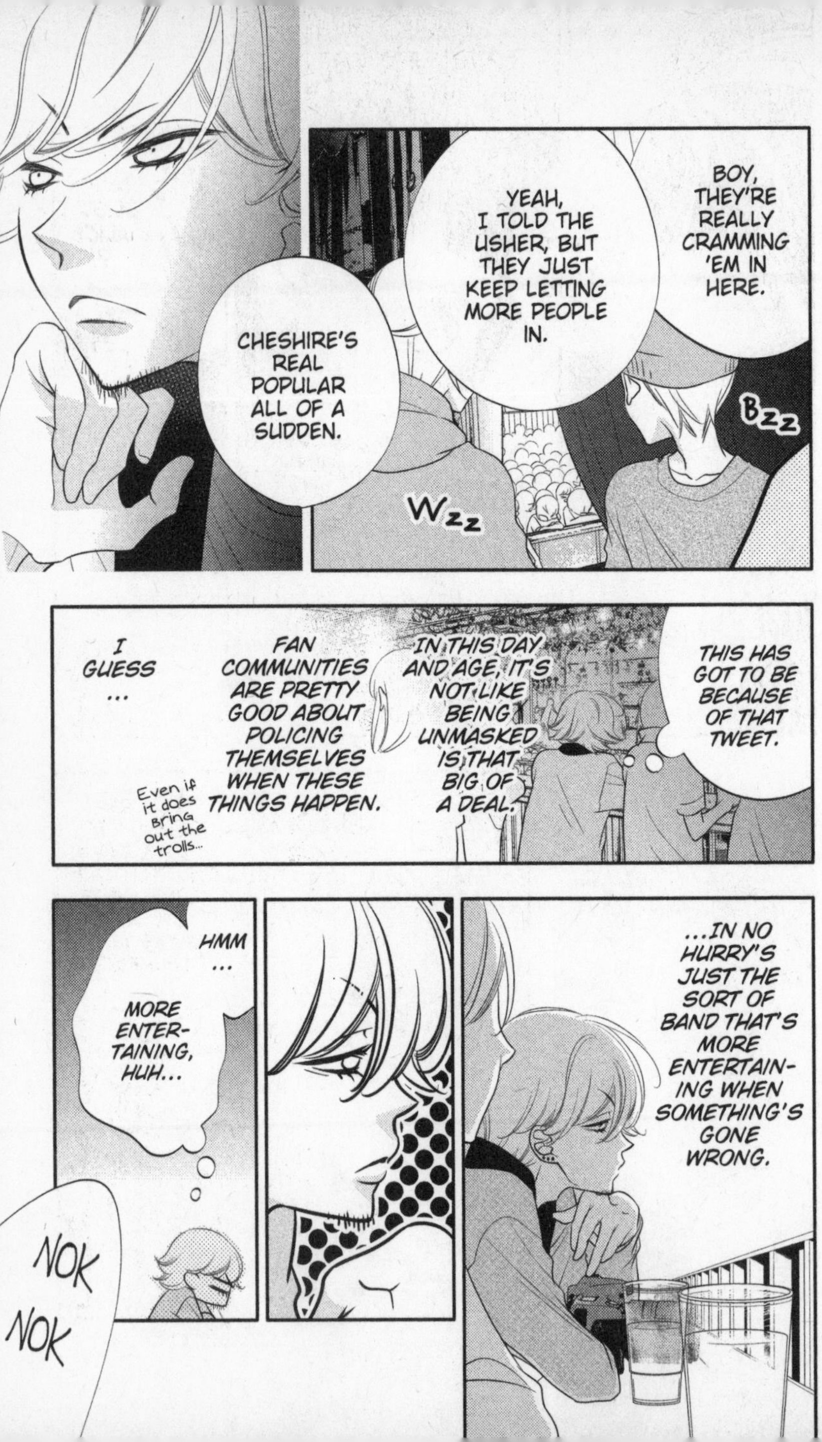
BOY, THEY'RE REALLY CRAMMING 'EM IN HERE.
YEAH, I TOLD THE USHER, BUT THEY JUST KEEP LETTING MORE PEOPLE IN.
CHESHIRE'S REAL POPULAR ALL OF A SUDDEN.
Bzz
Wzz
THIS HAS GOT TO BE BECAUSE OF THAT TWEET.
IN THIS DAY AND AGE, IT'S NOT LIKE BEING UNMASKED IS THAT BIG OF A DEAL.
FAN COMMUNITIES ARE PRETTY GOOD ABOUT POLICING THEMSELVES WHEN THESE THINGS HAPPEN.
I GUESS ...
Even if it does bring out the trolls...
...IN NO HURRY'S JUST THE SORT OF BAND THAT'S MORE ENTERTAIN-ING WHEN SOMETHING'S GONE WRONG.
HMM ...
MORE ENTER-TAINING, HUH...
NOK
NOK

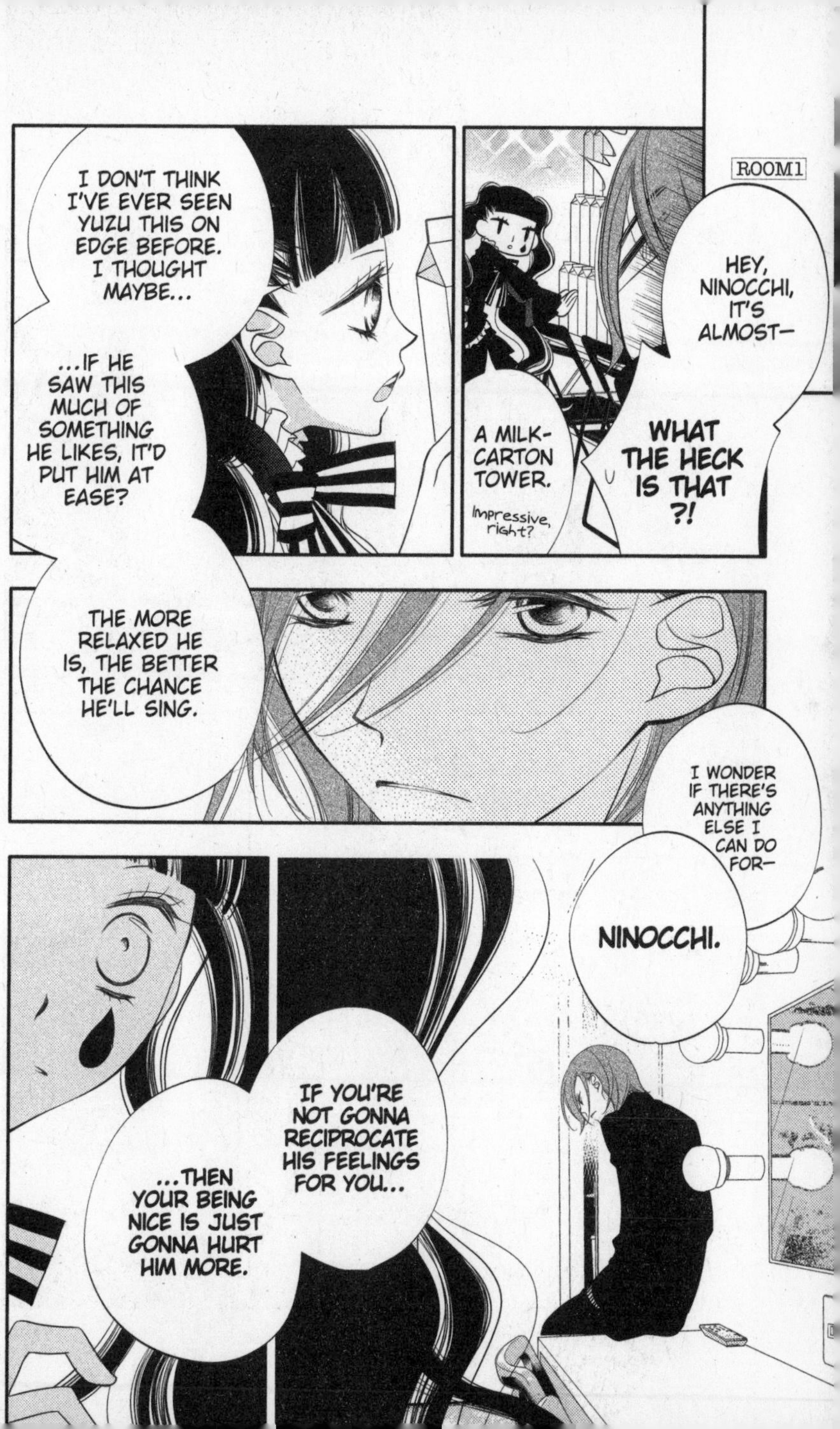
HEY, NINOCCHI, IT'S ALMOST—
WHAT THE HECK IS THAT ?!
A MILK-CARTON TOWER.
Impressive, right?
I DON'T THINK I'VE EVER SEEN YUZU THIS ON EDGE BEFORE. I THOUGHT MAYBE...
...IF HE SAW THIS MUCH OF SOMETHING HE LIKES, IT'D PUT HIM AT EASE?
THE MORE RELAXED HE IS, THE BETTER THE CHANCE HE'LL SING.
I WONDER IF THERE'S ANYTHING ELSE I CAN DO FOR—
NINOCCHI.
IF YOU'RE NOT GONNA RECIPROCATE HIS FEELINGS FOR YOU...
...THEN YOUR BEING NICE IS JUST GONNA HURT HIM MORE.

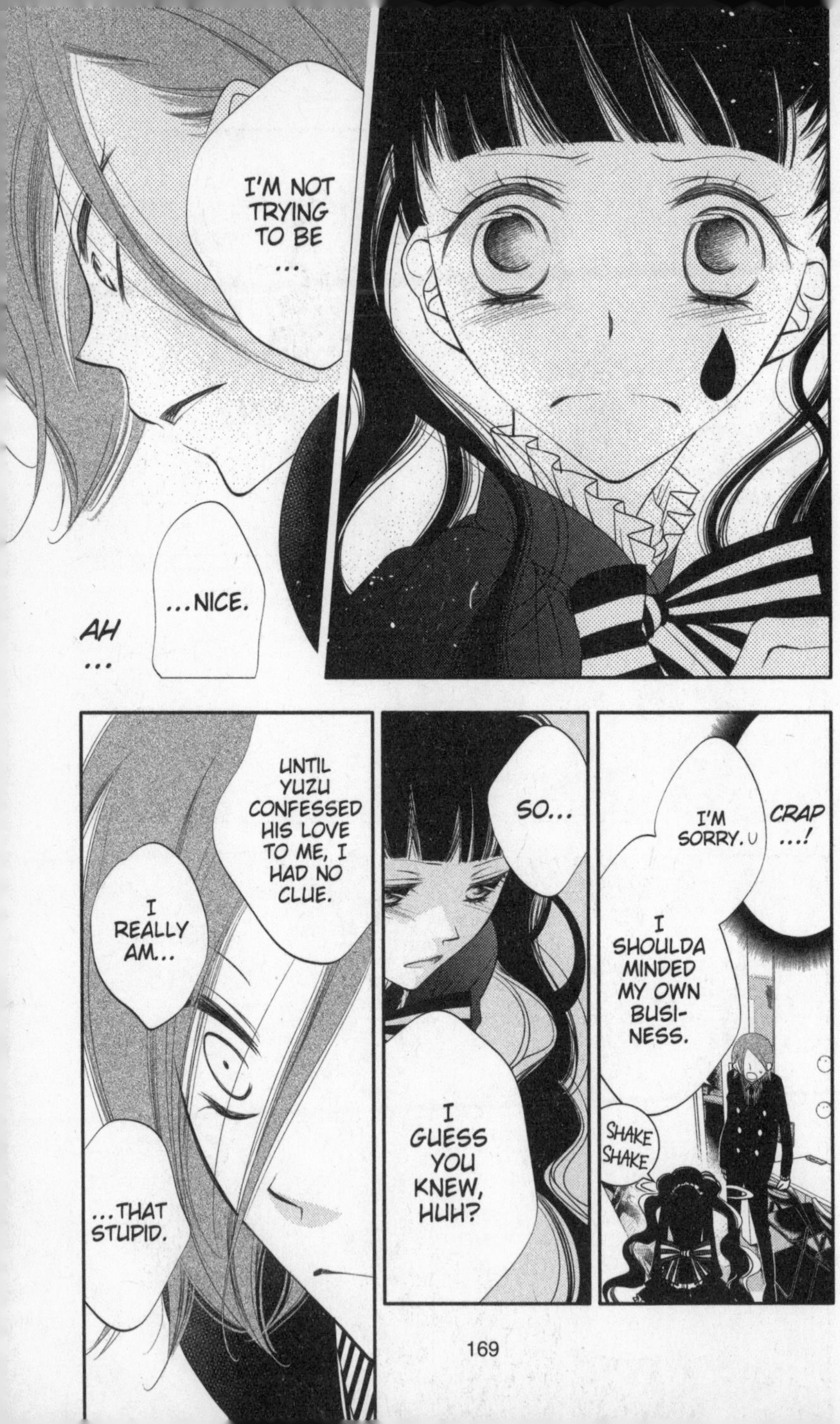
I'M NOT TRYING TO BE ...
...NICE.
AH ...
CRAP ...!
I'M SORRY.
I SHOULDA MINDED MY OWN BUSI-NESS.
SHAKE SHAKE
SO...
I GUESS YOU KNEW, HUH?
UNTIL YUZU CONFESSED HIS LOVE TO ME, I HAD NO CLUE.
I REALLY AM...
...THAT STUPID.

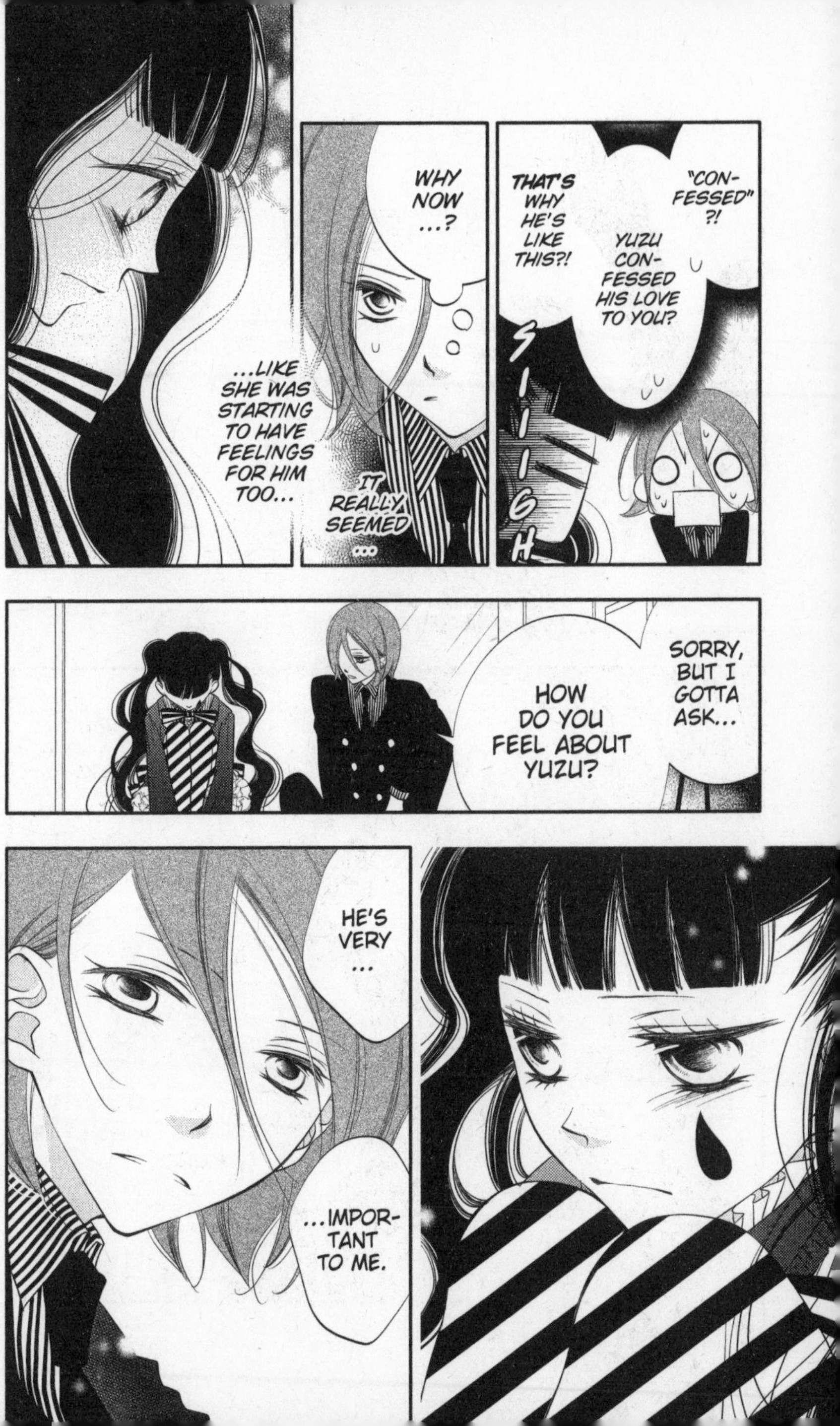
"CON-FESSED"?!
YUZU CON-FESSED HIS LOVE TO YOU?
THAT'S WHY HE'S LIKE THIS?!
SIIIGH
WHY NOW ...?
IT REALLY SEEMED ...
...LIKE SHE WAS STARTING TO HAVE FEELINGS FOR HIM TOO...
SORRY, BUT I GOTTA ASK...
HOW DO YOU FEEL ABOUT YUZU?
HE'S VERY ...
...IMPOR-TANT TO ME.

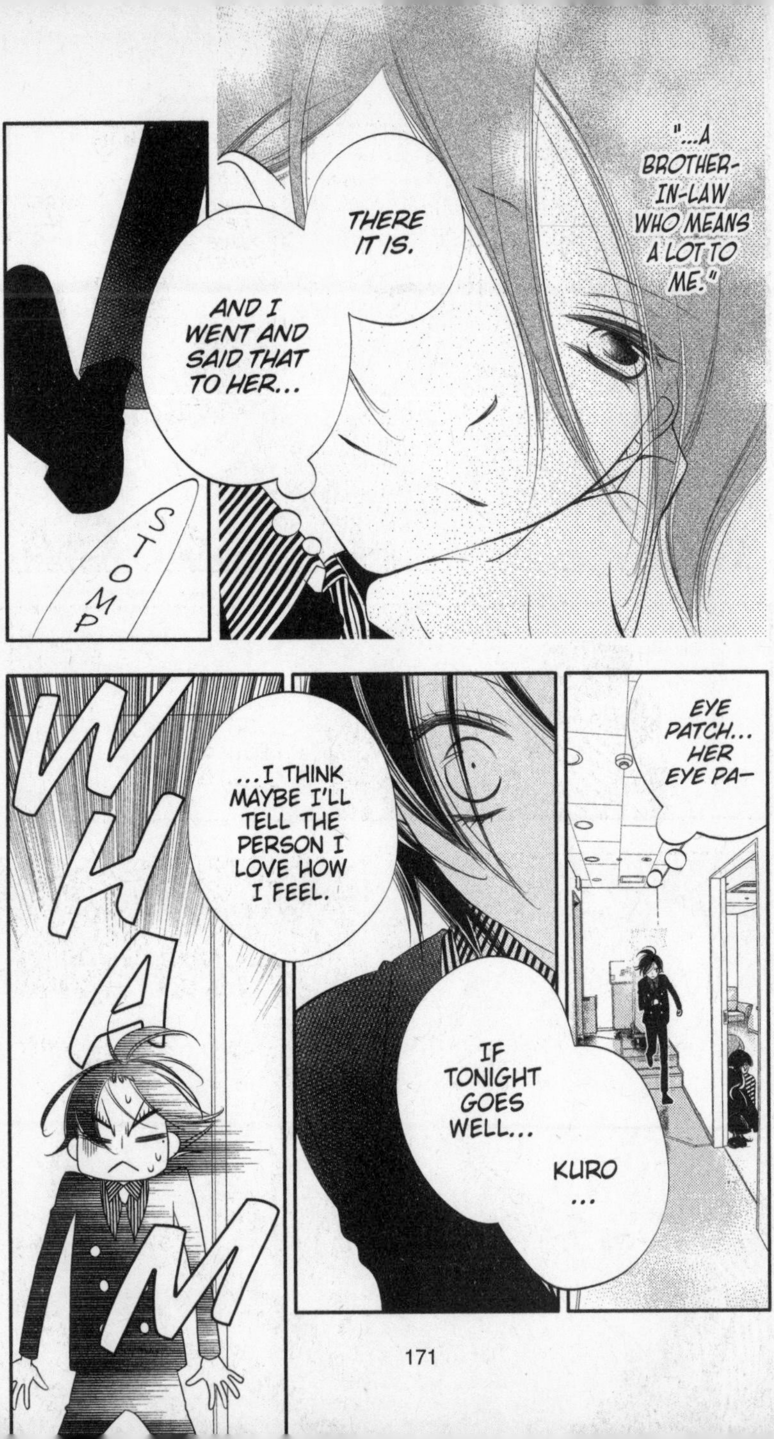
"...A BROTHER-IN-LAW WHO MEANS A LOT TO ME."
THERE IT IS.
AND I WENT AND SAID THAT TO HER...
STOMP
EYE PATCH... HER EYE PA—
...I THINK MAYBE I'LL TELL THE PERSON I LOVE HOW I FEEL.
IF TONIGHT GOES WELL...
KURO...
WHAM

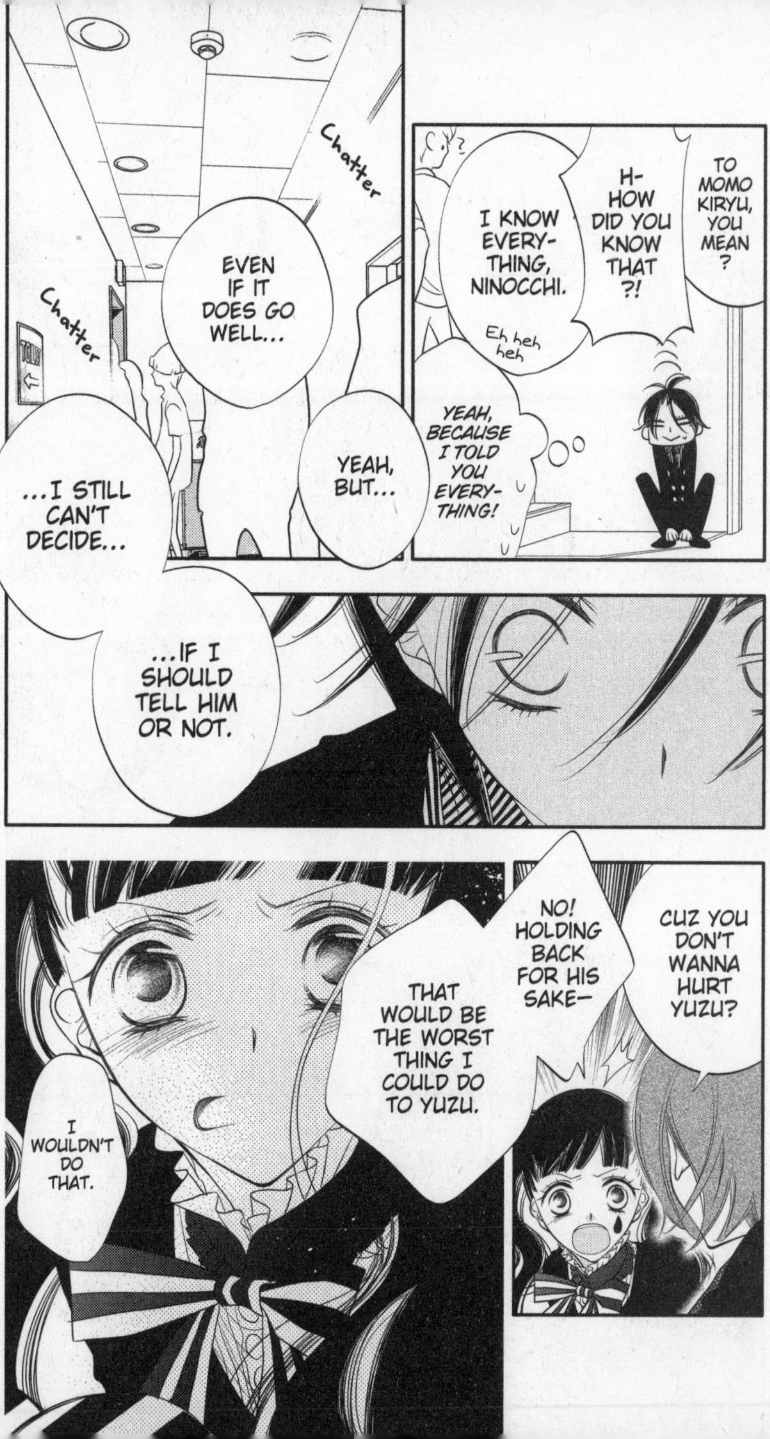
TO MOMO KIRYU, YOU MEAN?
H-HOW DID YOU KNOW THAT?!
I KNOW EVERYTHING, NINOCCHI.
Eh heh heh
YEAH, BECAUSE I TOLD YOU EVERYTHING!
Chatter
EVEN IF IT DOES GO WELL...
Chatter
YEAH, BUT...
...I STILL CAN'T DECIDE...
...IF I SHOULD TELL HIM OR NOT.
CUZ YOU DON'T WANNA HURT YUZU?
NO! HOLDING BACK FOR HIS SAKE—
THAT WOULD BE THE WORST THING I COULD DO TO YUZU.
I WOULDN'T DO THAT.

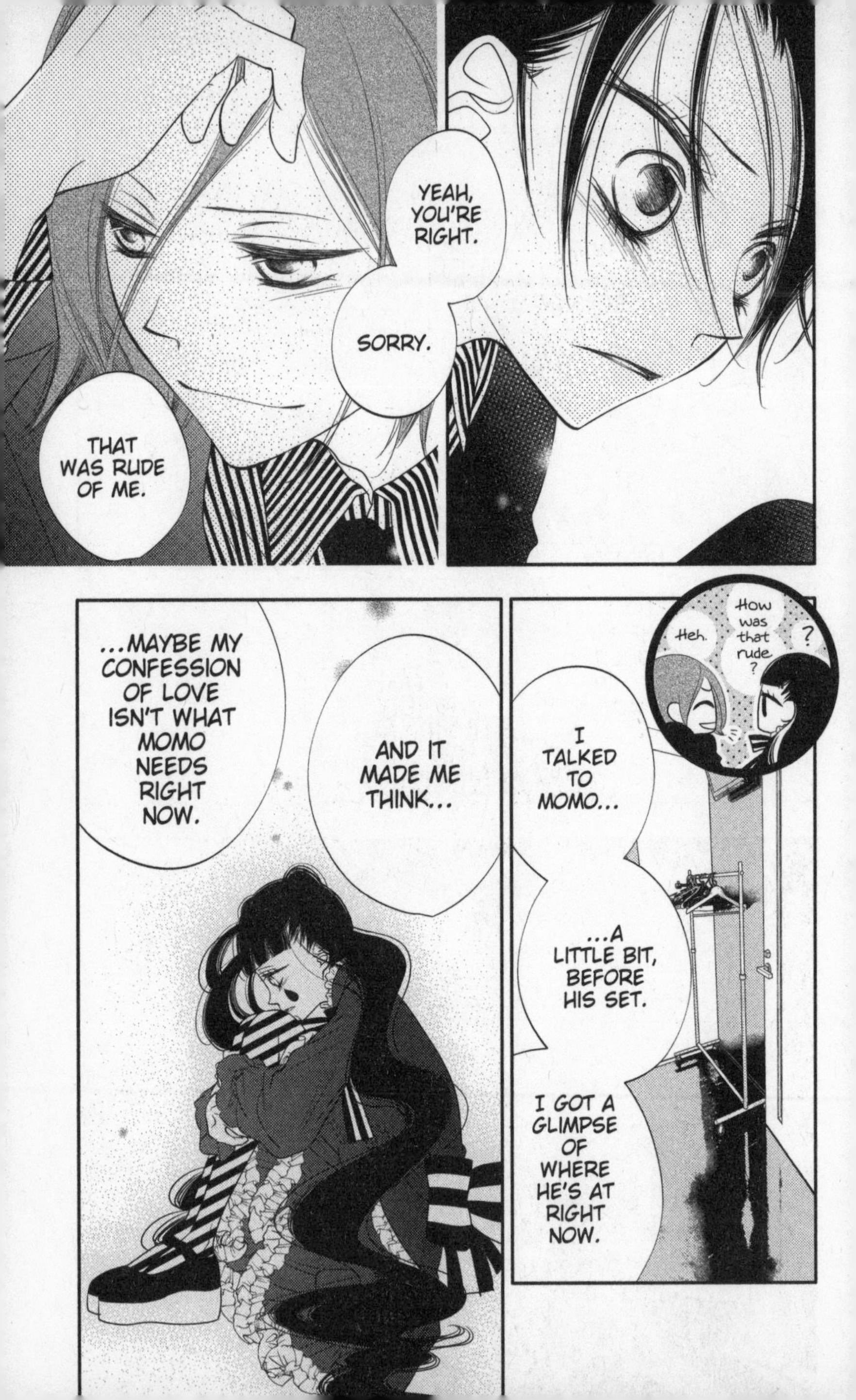
YEAH, YOU'RE RIGHT.
SORRY.
THAT WAS RUDE OF ME.
?
How was that rude ?
Heh.
I TALKED TO MOMO...
...A LITTLE BIT, BEFORE HIS SET.
I GOT A GLIMPSE OF WHERE HE'S AT RIGHT NOW.
AND IT MADE ME THINK...
...MAYBE MY CONFESSION OF LOVE ISN'T WHAT MOMO NEEDS RIGHT NOW.

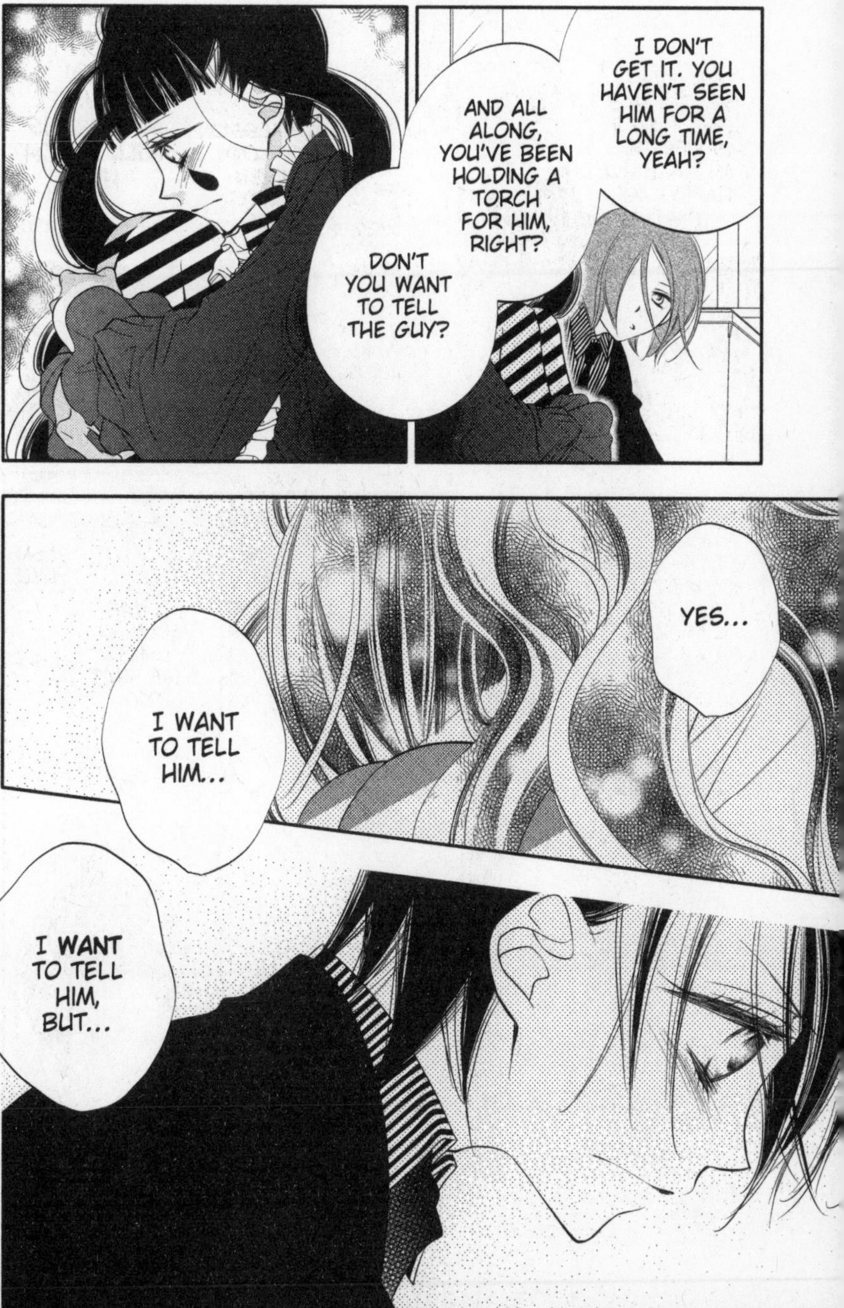
I DON'T GET IT. YOU HAVEN'T SEEN HIM FOR A LONG TIME, YEAH?
AND ALL ALONG, YOU'VE BEEN HOLDING A TORCH FOR HIM, RIGHT?
DON'T YOU WANT TO TELL THE GUY?
YES...
I WANT TO TELL HIM...
I WANT TO TELL HIM, BUT...

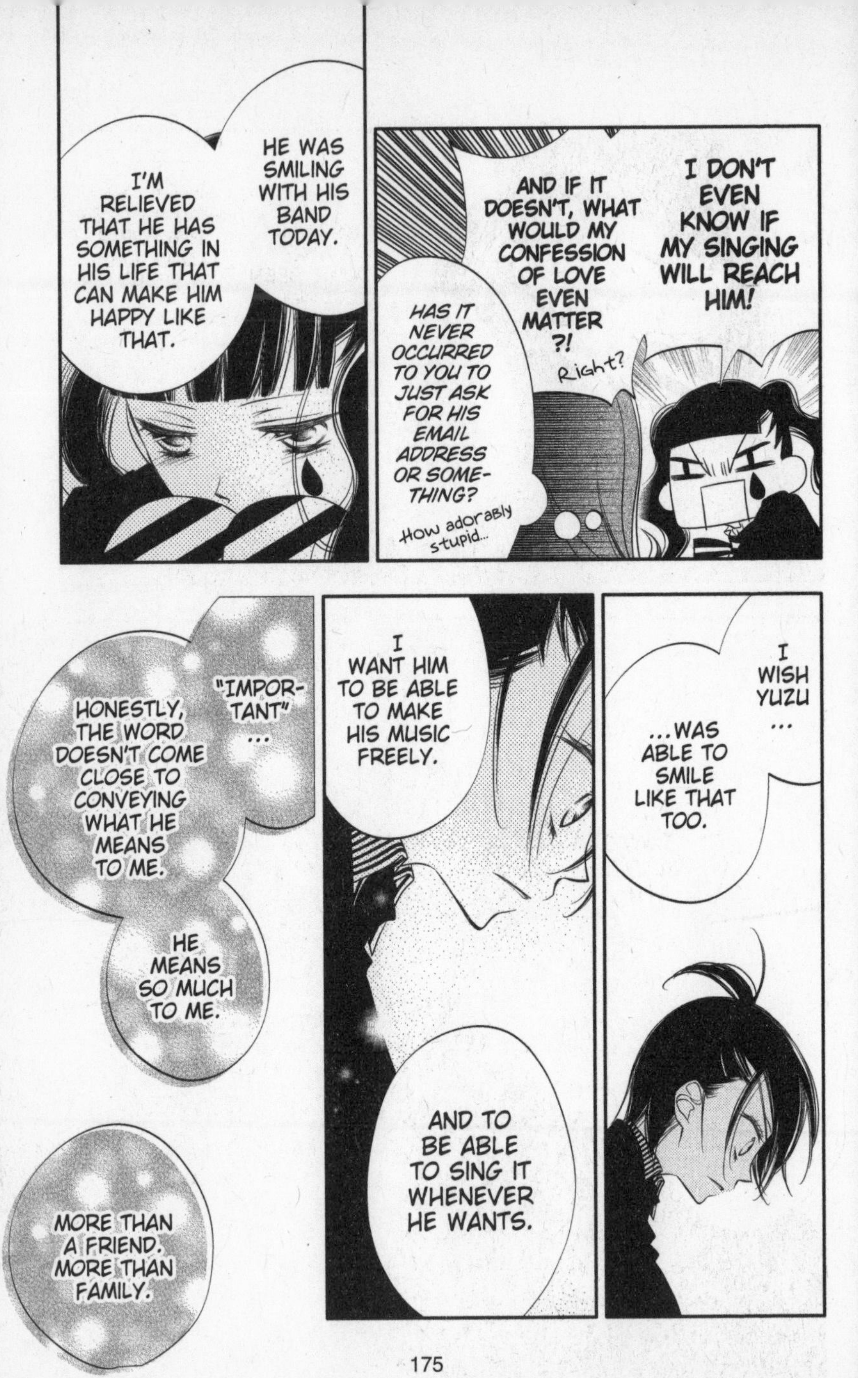
I DON'T EVEN KNOW IF MY SINGING WILL REACH HIM!
AND IF IT DOESN'T, WHAT WOULD MY CONFESSION OF LOVE EVEN MATTER ?!
Right?
HAS IT NEVER OCCURRED TO YOU TO JUST ASK FOR HIS EMAIL ADDRESS OR SOME-THING?
How adorably stupid...
HE WAS SMILING WITH HIS BAND TODAY.
I'M RELIEVED THAT HE HAS SOMETHING IN HIS LIFE THAT CAN MAKE HIM HAPPY LIKE THAT.
I WISH YUZU ...
...WAS ABLE TO SMILE LIKE THAT TOO.
I WANT HIM TO BE ABLE TO MAKE HIS MUSIC FREELY.
AND TO BE ABLE TO SING IT WHENEVER HE WANTS.
"IMPOR-TANT" ...
HONESTLY, THE WORD DOESN'T COME CLOSE TO CONVEYING WHAT HE MEANS TO ME.
HE MEANS SO MUCH TO ME.
MORE THAN A FRIEND. MORE THAN FAMILY.

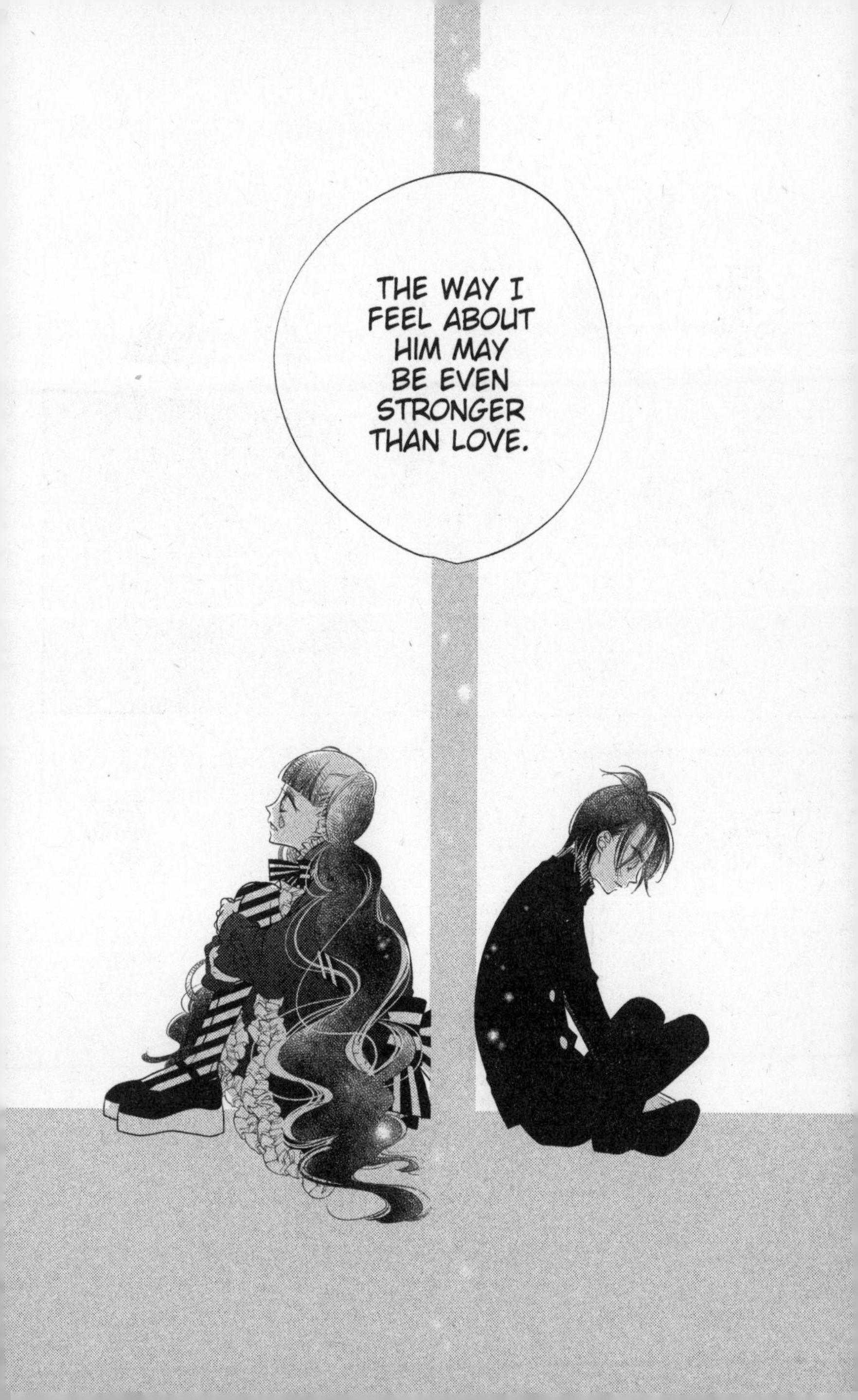
THE WAY I FEEL ABOUT HIM MAY BE EVEN STRONGER THAN LOVE.

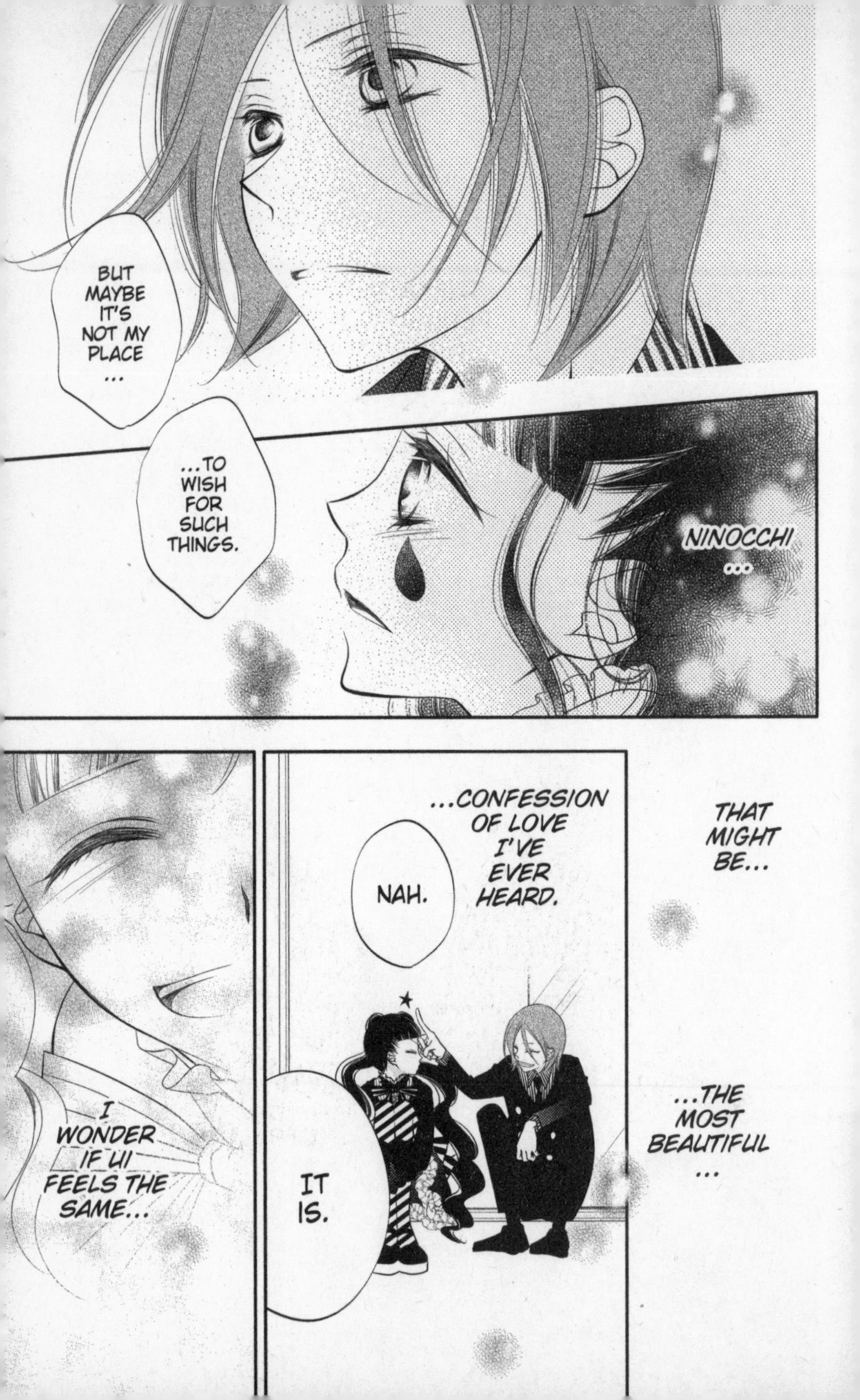
BUT MAYBE IT'S NOT MY PLACE...
...TO WISH FOR SUCH THINGS.
NINOCCHI...
THAT MIGHT BE...
...THE MOST BEAUTIFUL...
...CONFESSION OF LOVE I'VE EVER HEARD.
NAH.
IT IS.
I WONDER IF UI FEELS THE SAME...

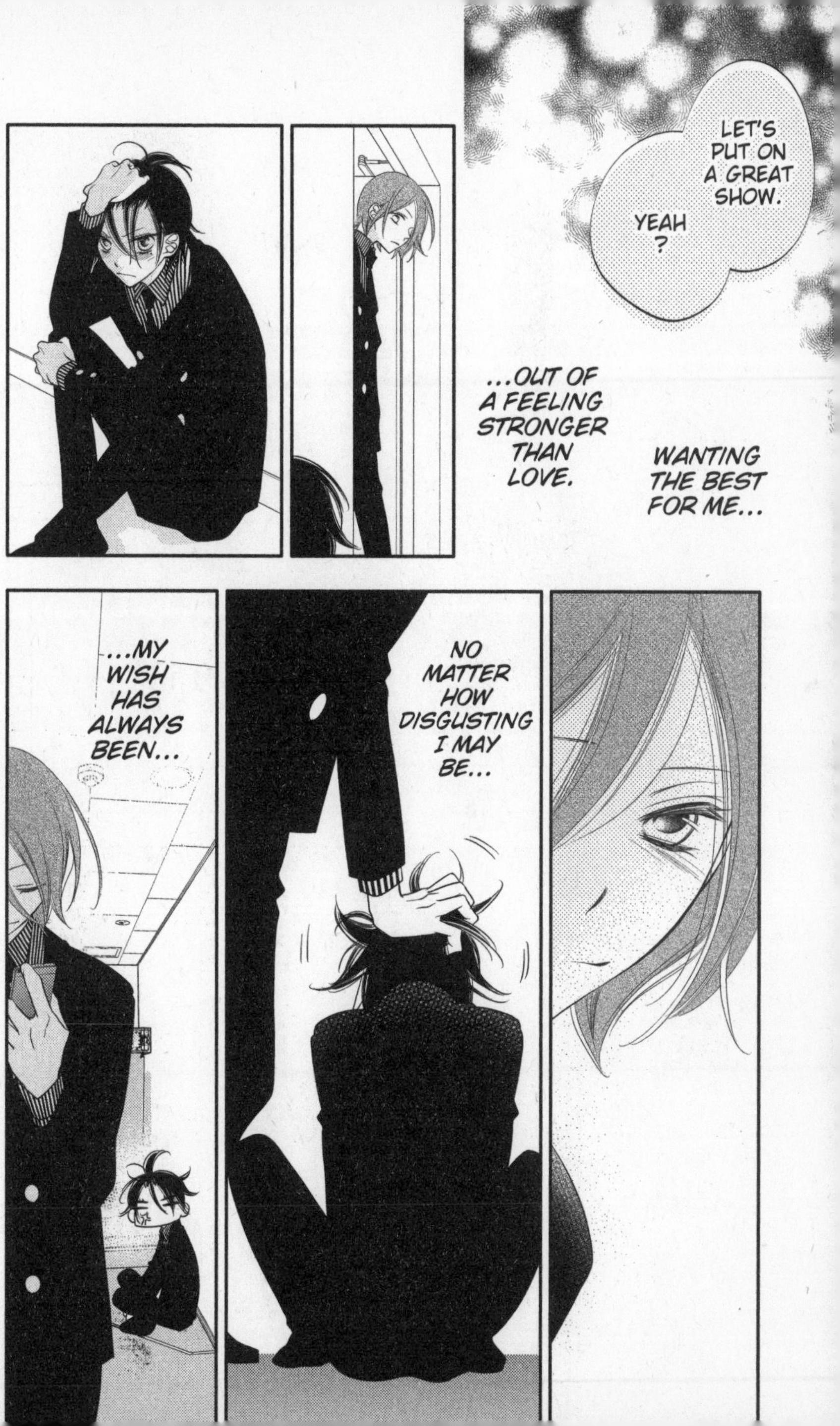
LET'S PUT ON A GREAT SHOW. YEAH?
WANTING THE BEST FOR ME...
...OUT OF A FEELING STRONGER THAN LOVE.
NO MATTER HOW DISGUSTING I MAY BE...
...MY WISH HAS ALWAYS BEEN...

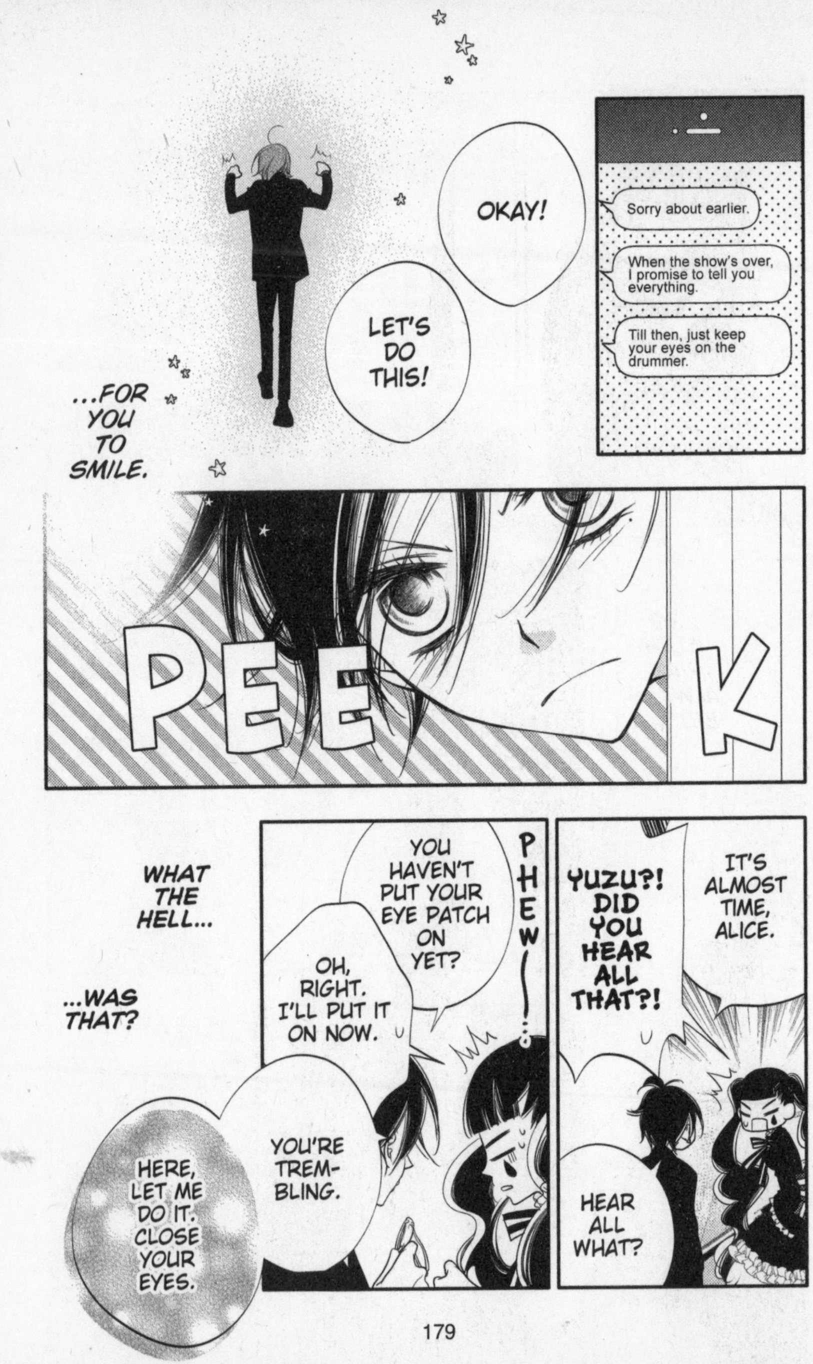
Sorry about earlier.
When the show's over, I promise to tell you everything.
Till then, just keep your eyes on the drummer.
OKAY!
LET'S DO THIS!
...FOR YOU TO SMILE.
PEEK
IT'S ALMOST TIME, ALICE.
YUZU?! DID YOU HEAR ALL THAT?!
HEAR ALL WHAT?
PHEW—!
YOU HAVEN'T PUT YOUR EYE PATCH ON YET?
OH, RIGHT. I'LL PUT IT ON NOW.
YOU'RE TREM-BLING.
HERE, LET ME DO IT. CLOSE YOUR EYES.
WHAT THE HELL...
...WAS THAT?

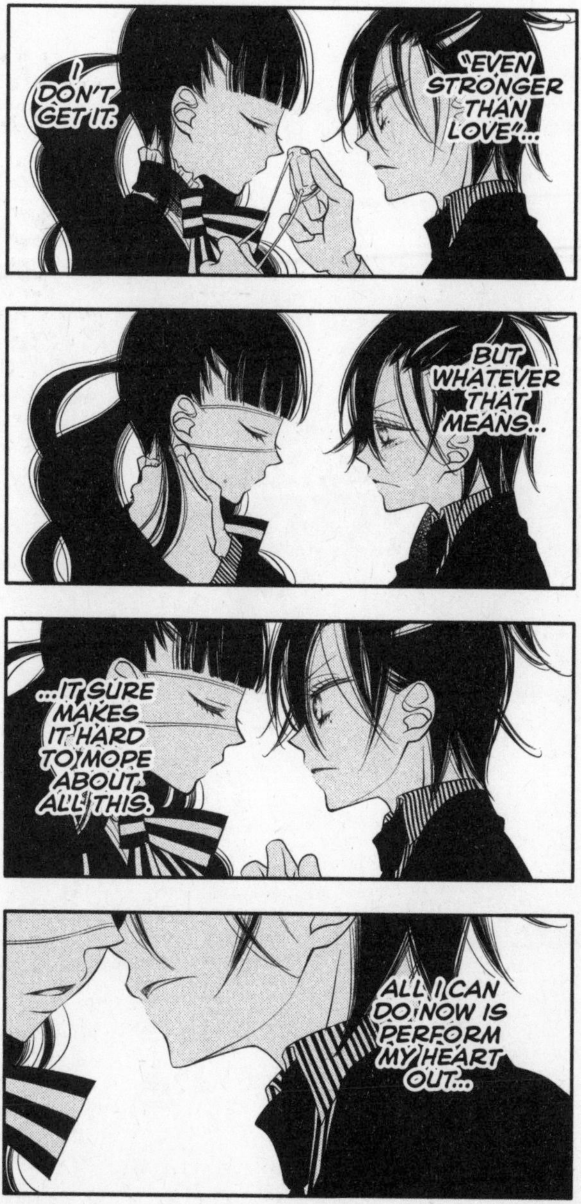
"EVEN STRONGER THAN LOVE"...
I DON'T GET IT.
BUT WHATEVER THAT MEANS...
...IT SURE MAKES IT HARD TO MOPE ABOUT ALL THIS.
ALL I CAN DO NOW IS PERFORM MY HEART OUT...

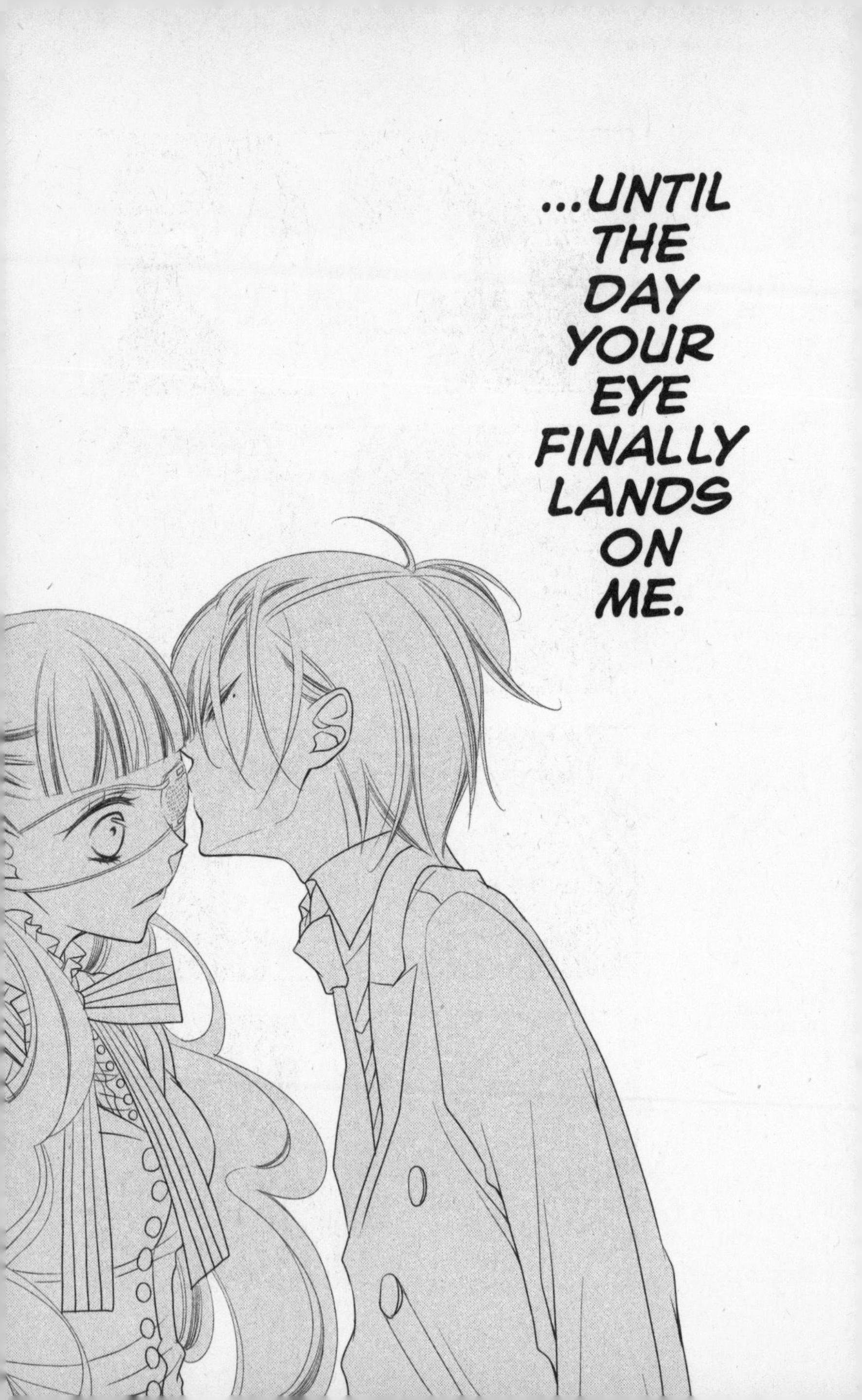
...UNTIL THE DAY YOUR EYE FINALLY LANDS ON ME.

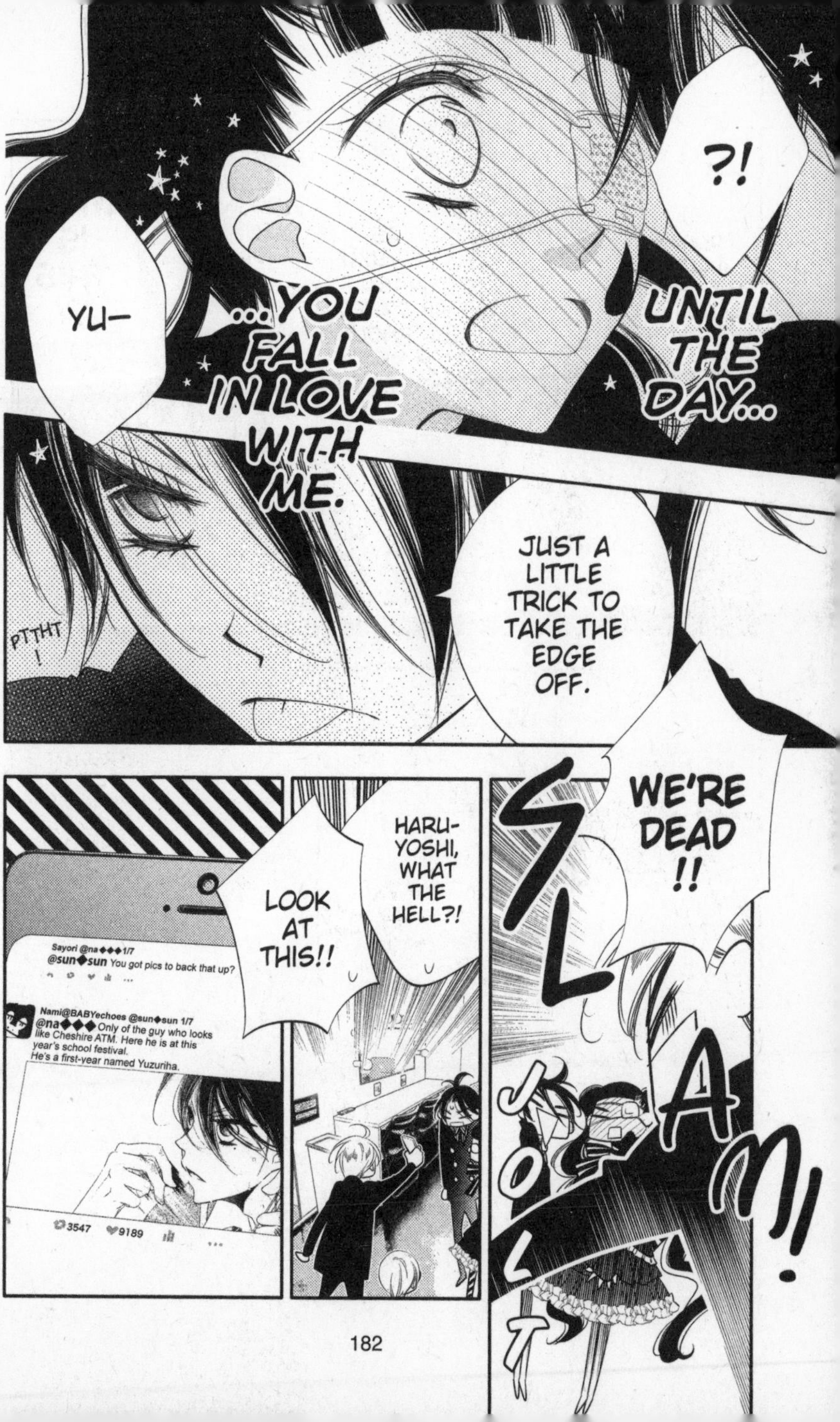
?!
UNTIL THE DAY...
...YOU FALL IN LOVE WITH ME.
YU—
JUST A LITTLE TRICK TO TAKE THE EDGE OFF.
PTTHT!
WE'RE DEAD!!
SLAM!!
JOLT
HARU-YOSHI, WHAT THE HELL?!
LOOK AT THIS!!
Sayori @na◆◆◆ 1/7
@sun◆sun You got pics to back that up?
Nami@BABYechoes @sun◆sun 1/7
@na◆◆◆ Only of the guy who looks like Cheshire ATM. Here he is at this year's school festival.
He's a first-year named Yuzuriha.
3547 9189

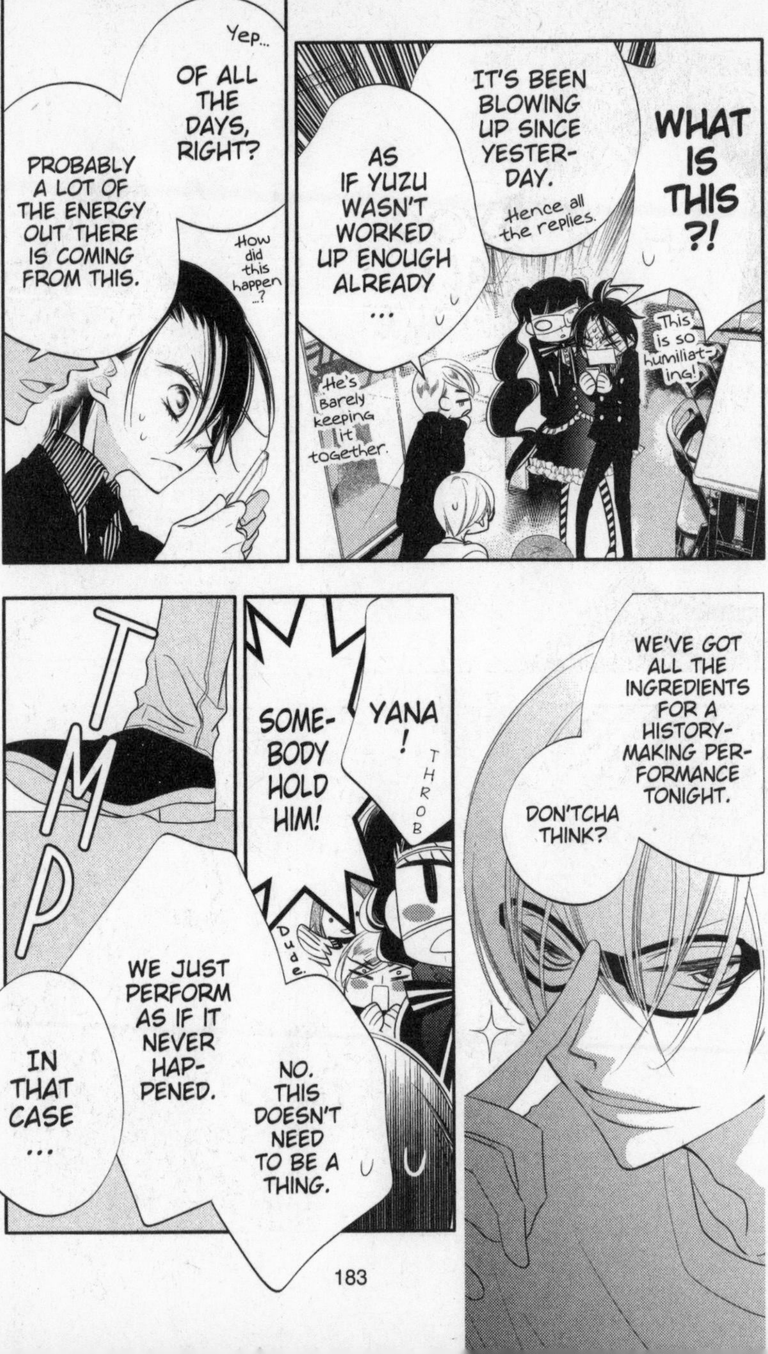
WHAT IS THIS?!
IT'S BEEN BLOWING UP SINCE YESTER-DAY.
Hence all the replies.
AS IF YUZU WASN'T WORKED UP ENOUGH ALREADY...
This is so humiliat-ing!
He's barely keeping it together.
Yep...
OF ALL THE DAYS, RIGHT?
PROBABLY A LOT OF THE ENERGY OUT THERE IS COMING FROM THIS.
How did this happen...?
WE'VE GOT ALL THE INGREDIENTS FOR A HISTORY-MAKING PER-FORMANCE TONIGHT.
DON'TCHA THINK?
YANA!
THROB
SOME-BODY HOLD HIM!
Dude.
NO. THIS DOESN'T NEED TO BE A THING.
TMP
WE JUST PERFORM AS IF IT NEVER HAP-PENED.
IN THAT CASE...

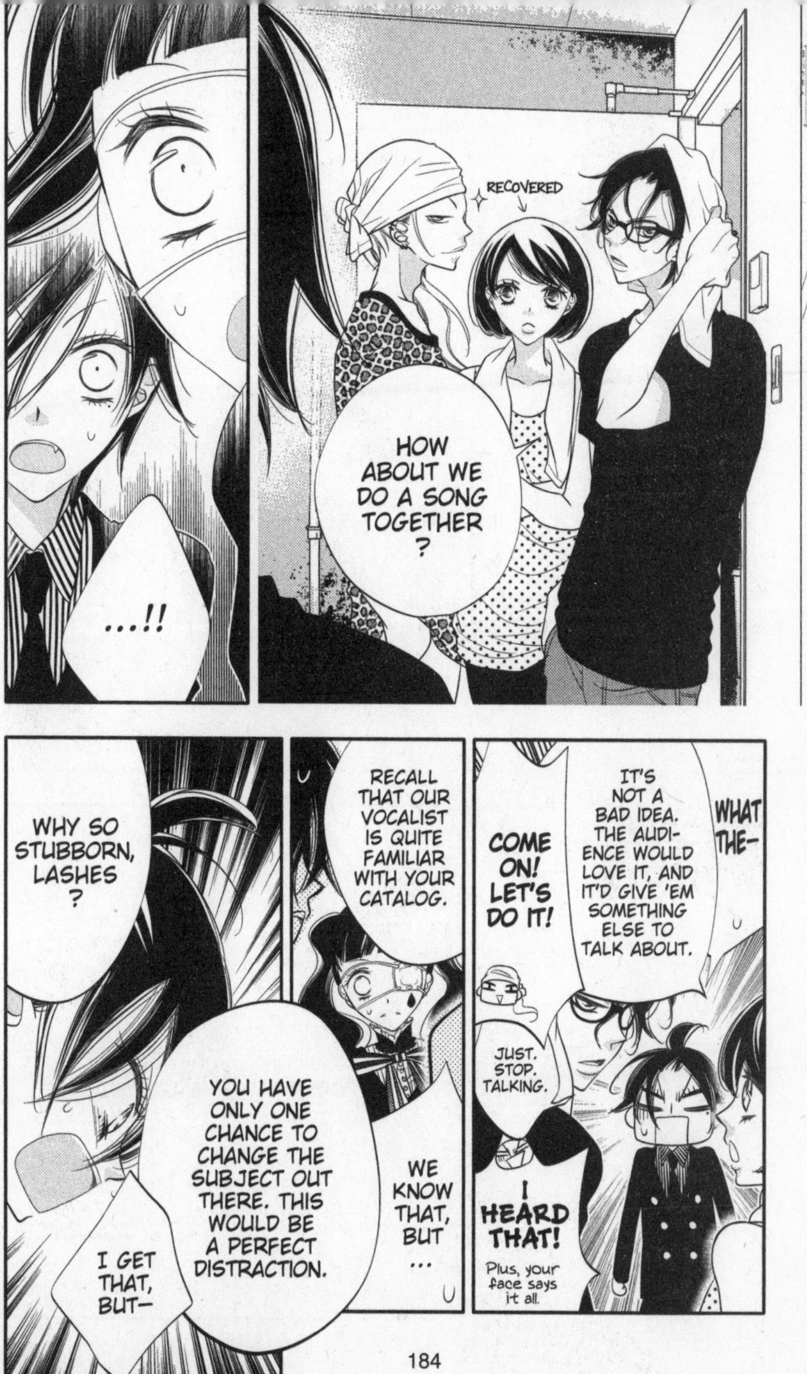
RECOVERED
HOW ABOUT WE DO A SONG TOGETHER?
...!!
WHAT THE—
IT'S NOT A BAD IDEA. THE AUDIENCE WOULD LOVE IT, AND IT'D GIVE 'EM SOMETHING ELSE TO TALK ABOUT.
COME ON! LET'S DO IT!
JUST. STOP. TALKING.
I HEARD THAT!
Plus, your face says it all.
RECALL THAT OUR VOCALIST IS QUITE FAMILIAR WITH YOUR CATALOG.
WE KNOW THAT, BUT...
WHY SO STUBBORN, LASHES?
YOU HAVE ONLY ONE CHANCE TO CHANGE THE SUBJECT OUT THERE. THIS WOULD BE A PERFECT DISTRACTION.
I GET THAT, BUT—

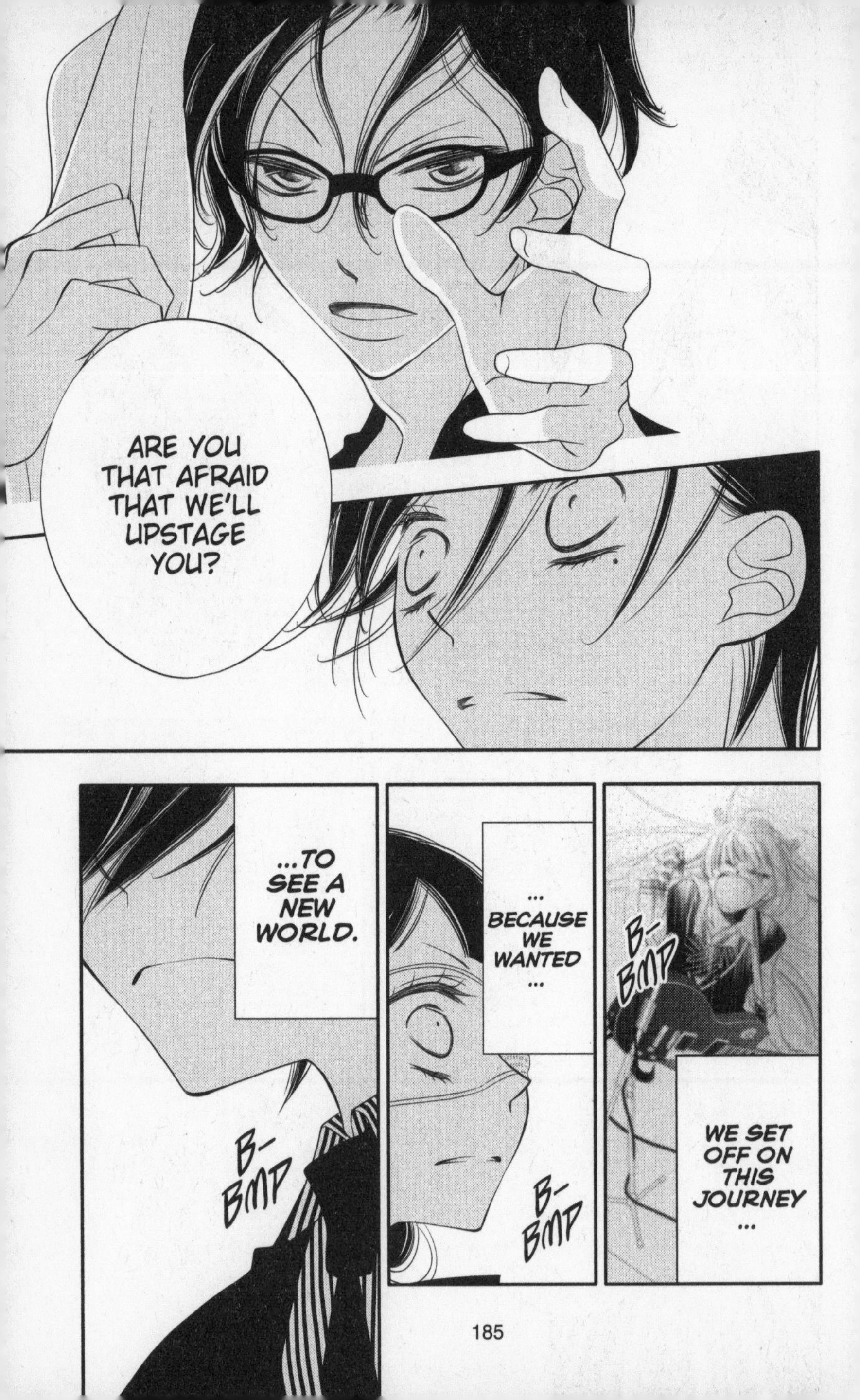
ARE YOU THAT AFRAID THAT WE'LL UPSTAGE YOU?
B-BMP
WE SET OFF ON THIS JOURNEY ...
... BECAUSE WE WANTED ...
B-BMP
...TO SEE A NEW WORLD.
B-BMP

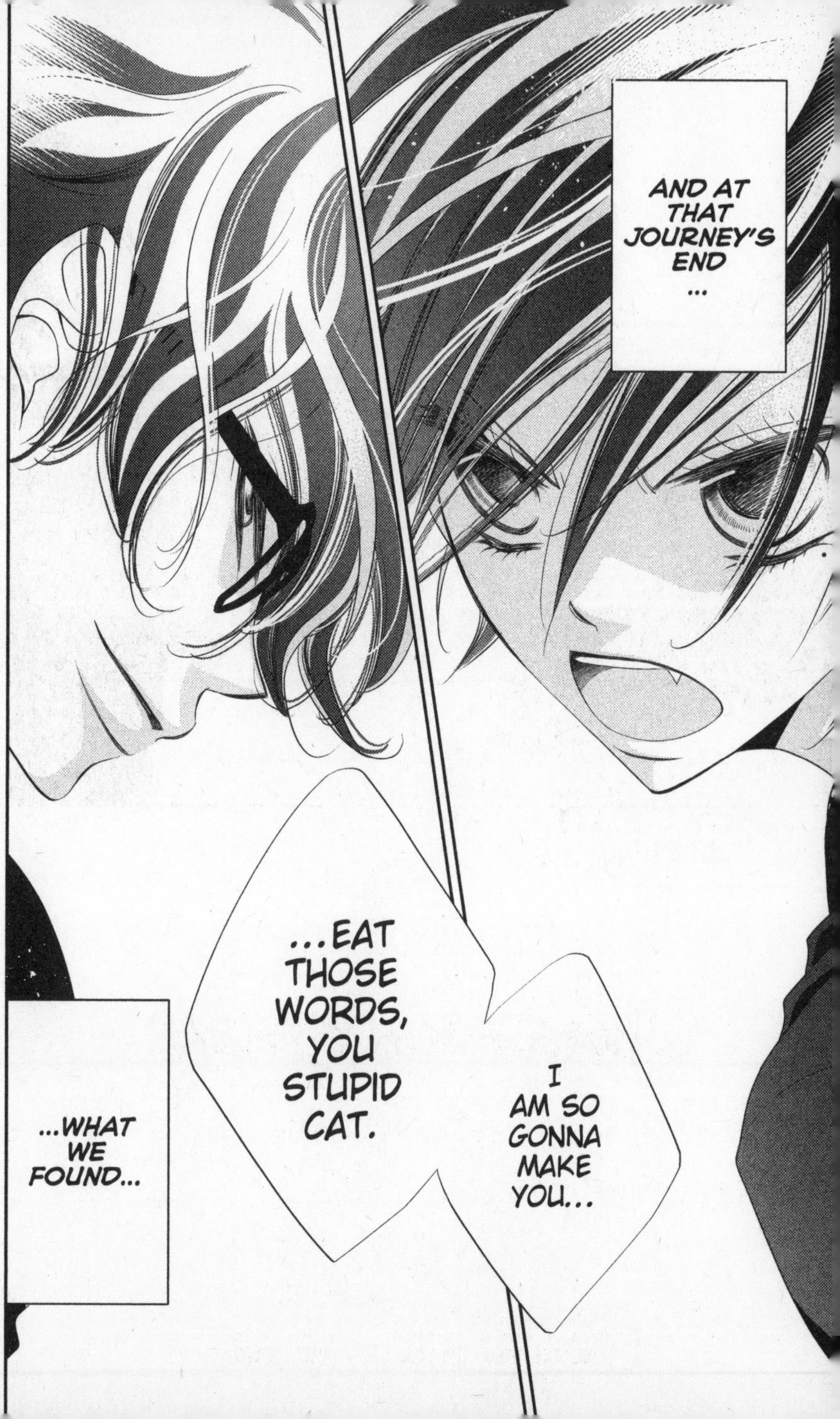
AND AT THAT JOURNEY'S END ...
I AM SO GONNA MAKE YOU...
...EAT THOSE WORDS, YOU STUPID CAT.
...WHAT WE FOUND...

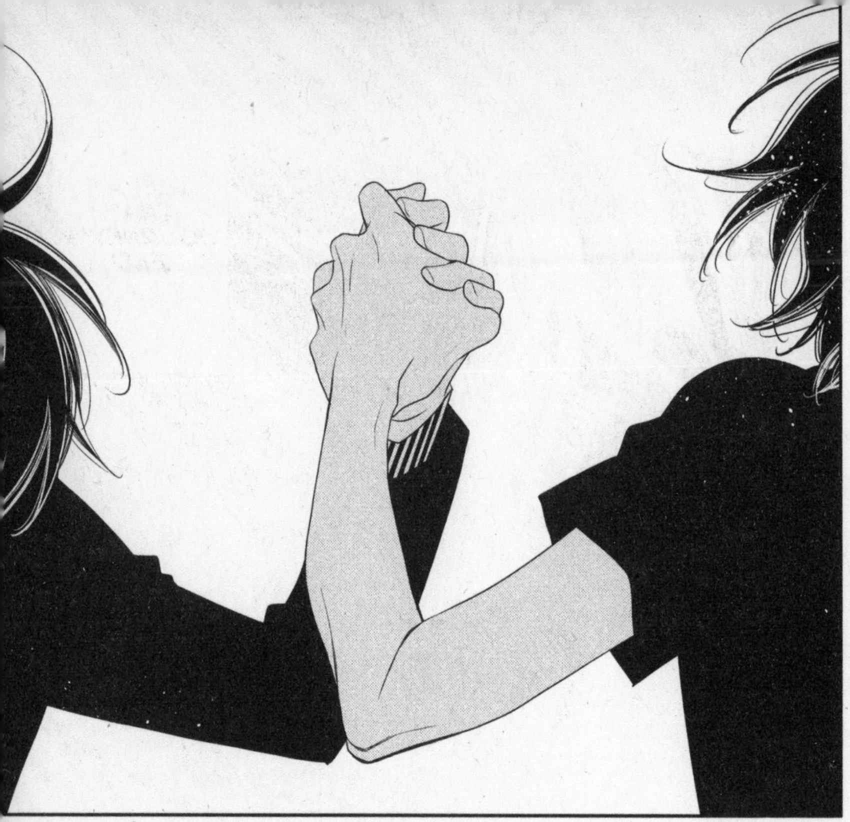

...WAS EACH OTHER.

ANONYMOUS NOISE ⑩ / THE END

A'S COSTUME→
DESIGN

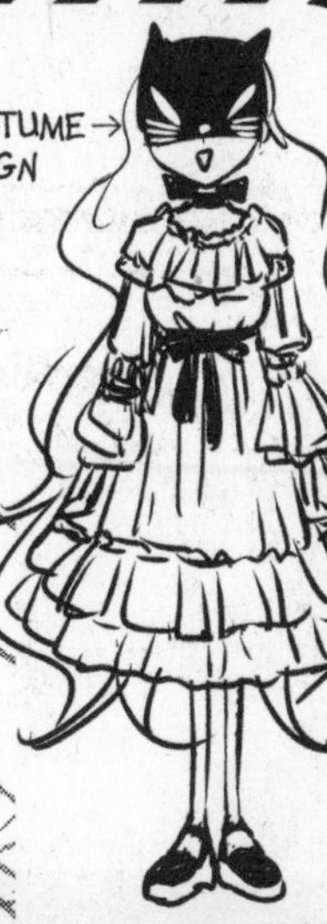

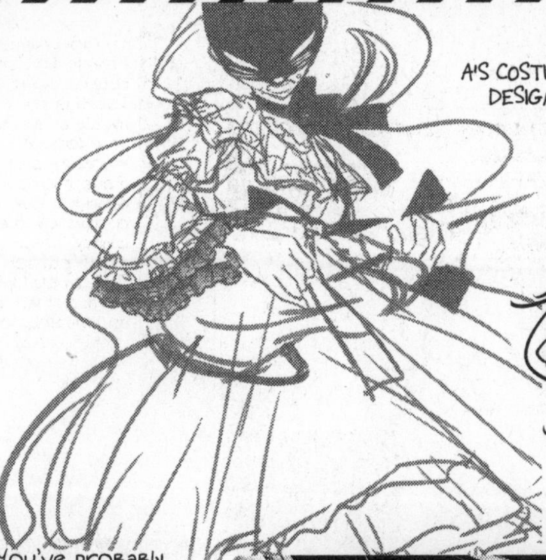

↑You've probably already forgotten, but Black Kitty's vocalist is called "A." A's current costume is the most time-consuming design I've ever come up with, and every time I draw her I ask myself what possessed me to choose it. (LOL.) I wonder what sort of costume I should give her next?

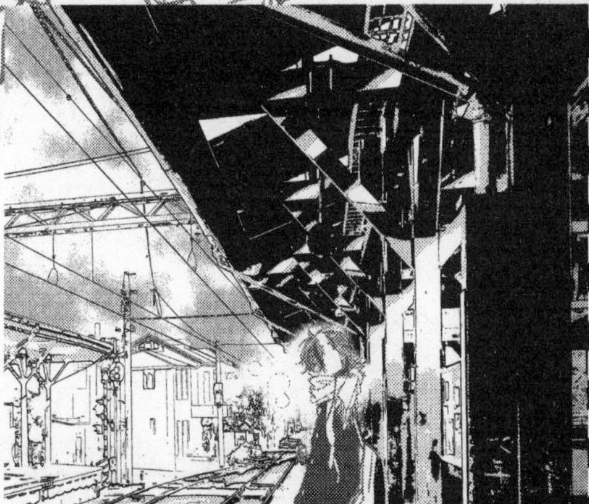

→I drew Hase Station for the title page of chapter 56. I was curious to see what it would look like to have Momo standing there in this uniform. I love Hase Station—it has a real unique vibe.

← I ran down to Gokurakuji Temple just so I could draw it for this scene. I'm sure I must have looked incredibly suspicious, photographing every corner of the empty Gokurakuji station. But I'm glad I did. My assistant did an amazing job putting the finishing touches on this.

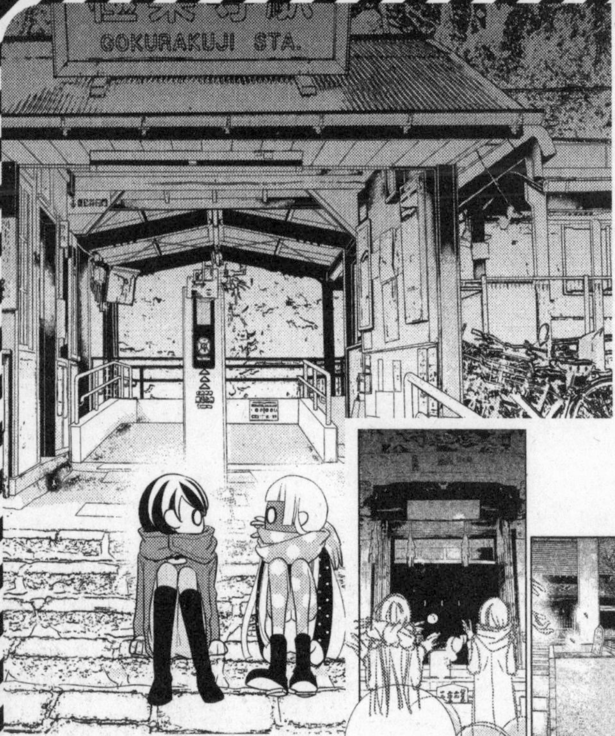
GOKURAKUJI STA.

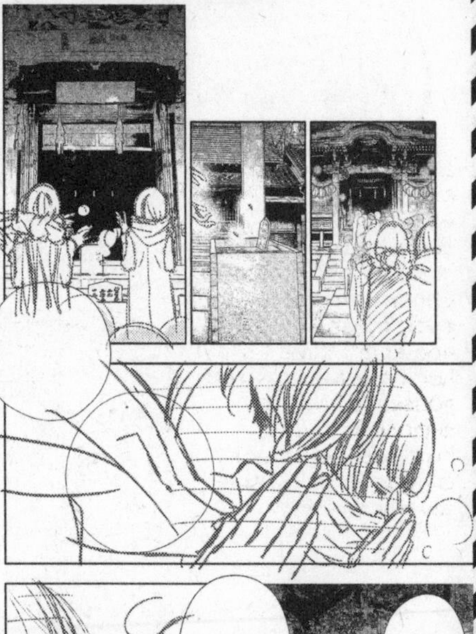

→ The Goryo Shrine near Hase Station is one of my favorite places. I really need to go there for New Year's one of these years! The lanterns look so beautiful in the pictures I've seen. If you ever have a chance, you should pay it a visit!

That's enough for now. See you in volume 11!

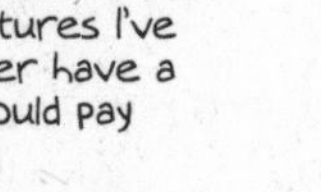
BYE-BYE!

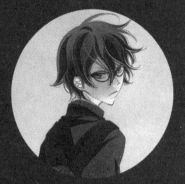

The next volume concludes the tour
arc that began in volume 9. After
that, it's finally time for a new arc
and some new characters.
(That's the plan, anyway.)
I hope to see you there!

- Ryoko Fukuyama

Born on January 5 in Wakayama Prefecture in
Japan, Ryoko Fukuyama debuted as a manga
artist after winning the Hakusensha Athena
Shinjin Taisho Prize from Hakusensha's *Hana to
Yume* magazine. She is also the author
of *Nosatsu Junkie*. *Anonymous Noise* was
adapted into an anime in 2017.

ANONYMOUS NOISE
Vol. 10
Shojo Beat Edition

STORY AND ART BY
RYOKO FUKUYAMA

English Translation & Adaptation/Casey Loe
Touch-Up Art & Lettering/Joanna Estep
Design/Yukiko Whitley
Editor/Amy Yu

Fukumenkei Noise by Ryoko Fukuyama
© Ryoko Fukuyama 2016
All rights reserved.
First published in Japan in 2016 by HAKUSENSHA, Inc., Tokyo.
English language translation rights arranged with HAKUSENSHA, Inc., Tokyo.

Printed in Canada

Published by VIZ Media, LLC
P.O. Box 77010
San Francisco, CA 94107

10 9 8 7 6 5 4 3 2 1
First printing, September 2018

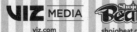
VIZ MEDIA
viz.com

Shojo **Beat**
shojobeat.com

Surpri

You may be reading the wrong way!

D0546400

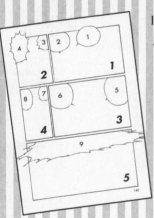

It's true: In keeping with the original Japanese comic format, this book reads from right to left—so action, sound effects and word balloons are completely reversed. This preserves the orientation of the original artwork—plus, it's fun! Check out the diagram shown here to get the hang of things, and then turn to the other side of the book to get started!

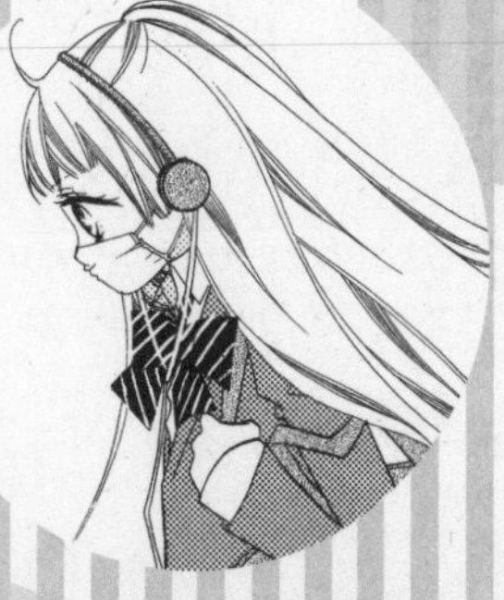